Lecture Notes in Computer Science 3966

Commenced Publication in 1973
Founding and Former Series Editors:
Gerhard Goos, Juris Hartmanis, and Jan van Leeuwen

Qing Wang   Dietmar Pfahl
David M. Raffo   Paul Wernick (Eds.)

Software Process Change

International Software Process Workshop and
International Workshop on Software Process
Simulation and Modeling, SPW/ProSim 2006
Shanghai, China, May 20-21, 2006
Proceedings

 Springer

Volume Editors

Qing Wang
Chinese Academy of Sciences
Institute of Software
No. 4 South Fourth Street, Zhong Guan Cun, Beijing 10 00 80, China
E-mail: wq@itechs.iscas.ac.cn

Dietmar Pfahl
University of Calgary
Schulich School of Engineering
2500 University Drive N.W., Calgary, Alberta T2N 1N4, Canada
E-mail: dpfahl@ucalgary.ca

David M. Raffo
Portland State University
School of Business Administration
P.O. Box 8491, Portland, OR 97207, USA
E-mail: raffod@pdx.edu

Paul Wernick
University of Hertfordshire
Department of Computer Science
College Lane, Hatfield, Herts, AL10 9AB, UK
E-mail: p.d.wernick@herts.ac.uk

Library of Congress Control Number: 2006925301

CR Subject Classification (1998): D.2, K.6.3, K.6, K.4.2, J.1

LNCS Sublibrary: SL 2 – Programming and Software Engineering

ISSN   0302-9743
ISBN-10   3-540-34199-4 Springer Berlin Heidelberg New York
ISBN-13   978-3-540-34199-4 Springer Berlin Heidelberg New York

Springer is a part of Springer Science+Business Media

springer.com

© Springer-Verlag Berlin Heidelberg 2006
Printed in Germany

Typesetting: Camera-ready by author, data conversion by Scientific Publishing Services, Chennai, India
Printed on acid-free paper   SPIN: 11754305   06/3142   5 4 3 2 1 0

Preface

This volume contains papers presented at the first joint conference of the Software Process Workshop and the International Workshop on Software Process Simulation and Modeling (SPW/ProSim 2006) held in Shanghai, P.R. China, on May 20-21, 2006.

The theme of SPW/ProSim 2006 was "Software Process Change – Meeting the Challenge." Software developers are under ever-increasing pressure to deliver their products more quickly and with higher levels of quality. These demands are set in a dynamic context of frequently changing technologies, limited resources and globally distributed development teams. At the same time, global competition is forcing organizations that develop software to cut costs by rationalizing processes, outsourcing part or all of their activities, reusing existing software in new or modified applications and evolving existing systems to meet new needs, while still minimizing the risk of projects failing to deliver.

To address these difficulties, new or modified processes are emerging, including agile methods and plan-based product line development. Open Source, COTS and community-developed software are becoming more popular. Outsourcing coupled with 24/7 development demands well-defined processes and interfaces to support the coordination of organizationally and geographically separated teams. All of these challenges combine to increase demands on the efficiency and effectiveness of software processes.

For the first time, in 2006 two successful series of conferences combined efforts to address these and other related questions. Previous Software Process Workshops have provided a high-quality forum for assessing current and emerging software process capabilities, and for obtaining insights into worthwhile directions in software process research. ProSim is the leading event for researchers and practitioners focusing on the simulation and modeling of software processes.

In response to the call for papers, 225 submissions were received from 17 different countries and regions: Australia, Belgium, Canada, China, France, Germany, Hong Kong, India, Italy, Japan, Korea, Mexico, Pakistan, Spain, Taiwan, UK, and USA. Every paper was rigorously reviewed and held to very high-quality standards, and finally 34 papers were accepted as regular papers for presentation at the workshop, representing a 15% acceptance rate for regular papers.

The papers were clustered around topics and presented in seven regular sessions, each consisting of two threads. Topics included Process Tailoring and Decision-Support, Process Tools and Metrics, Process Management, Process Representation, Analysis and Modeling, Process Simulation Modeling, Process Simulation Applications, and Experience Reports.

The SPW/ProSim2006 program was highlighted by four keynote speeches, delivered by (in alphabetical order): Barry Boehm (University of Southern California: "A Value-Based Software Process Framework"), Ross Jeffery (University of New South Wales: "Exploring the Business Process–Software Process Relationship"), Mingshu Li (Institute of Software at the Chinese Academy of Sciences: "3-D Integrated Software

Development Processes: A New Benchmark"), and Leon J. Osterweil (University of Massachusetts Amherst: "Ubiquitous Process Engineering: Applying Software Process Technology to Other Domains").

A conference such as this can only succeed as a team effort. All of this work would not have been possible without the dedication and professional work of many colleagues. We wish to express our gratitude to all contributors for submitting papers. Their work forms the basis for the success of the workshop. We also would like to thank the Program Committee members and reviewers because their work is the guarantee for the high quality of the workshop. Particular thanks also go to the keynote speakers for their excellent presentations. Finally, we also would like to thank the members of the Steering Committee for their advice, encouragement and support.

We wish to express our thanks to the organizers for their hard work. The workshop was sponsored by the Institute of Software, the Chinese Academy of Sciences (ISCAS) and the ISCAS Laboratory for Internet Software Technologies, and the Shanghai Municipal Informatization Commission (SMIC). We also wish to thank the 28th International Conference on Software Engineering (ICSE 2006) for sponsoring this meeting as an ICSE Co-Located Event. Finally, we acknowledge the editorial support from Springer for the publication of this proceeding.

For further information, please visit our website at http://www.cnsqa.com/~spwprosim2006.

March 2006

David M. Raffo
Qing Wang
Dietmar Pfahl
Paul Wernick

Software Process Workshop
Workshop on Software Process Simulation and Modeling 2006

Shanghai, China
May 20-21, 2006

General Chair

David M. Raffo, Portland State University, USA

Steering Committee

Barry Boehm, University of Southern California, USA
Mingshu Li, Institute of Software, Chinese Academy of Sciences, China
Leon J. Osterweil, University of Massachusetts, USA

Program Co-chairs

Dietmar Pfahl, University of Calgary, Canada
Qing Wang, Institute of Software, Chinese Academy of Sciences, China

Publicity Chair

Paul Wernick, University of Hertfordshire, UK

Program Committee Members

Thomas Birkhölzer	University of Applied Science, Konstanz, Germany
Keith C.C. Chan	Hong Kong Polytechnic University, Hong Kong
Sorana Cimpan	University of Savoie at Annecy, France
James Collofello	Arizona State University, USA
Bill Curtis	Borland Software Corporation, USA
Jacky Estublier	French National Research Center in Grenoble, France
Anthony Finkelstein	University College London, UK
Volker Gruhn	University of Leipzig, Germany
Paul Grünbacher	Johannes Kepler University Linz, Austria
Dan Houston	Honeywell, USA
Liguo Huang	University of Southern California, USA
Watts S. Humphrey	Carnegie Mellon University, USA

Organizing Committee Chair

External Reviewers

Silvia Acuña
Ahmed Al-Emran
Wei Chen
Yue Chen
Oscar Dieste
Liping Ding
Shuanzhu Du
Andreas Jedlitschka
Nan Jiang
Gou Lang
Juan Li
Nao Li
Marta Lopez
Li Ruan
M. Isabel Sanchez-Segura
Fengdi Shu
Martin Solari
Sira Vegas
Jizhe Wang
Shujian Wu
Zhanchun Wu
Junchao Xiao
Da Yang
Qiusong Yang
Feng Yuan
Rong Yuan

Table of Contents

Process Management

Process Representation, Analysis and Modeling

Process Simulation Modeling

Process Simulation Applications

Experience Report

A Value-Based Software Process Framework

Barry Boehm and Apurva Jain

University of Southern California,
Computer Science Department, University Park Campus, Los Angeles, CA 90089
{boehm, apurvaja}@usc.edu

Abstract. This paper presents a value-based software process framework that has been derived from the 4+1 theory of value-based software engineering (VBSE). The value-based process framework integrates the four component theories – dependency, utility, decision, and control, to the central theory W, and orients itself as a 7-step process guide to practice value-based software engineering. We also illustrate applying the process framework to a supply chain organization through a case study analysis.

1 Introduction

In this paper we present a value-based software process framework that has been derived from the 4+1 theory of value-based software engineering (VBSE) as described in [2]. The value-based process framework presented here integrates the four component theories of the 4+1 theory – dependency, utility, decision, and control theories – to the central theory W, and orients itself as a 7-step process guide to practice VBSE. We also illustrate applying the theory and process framework to a supply chain organization through a case study analysis.

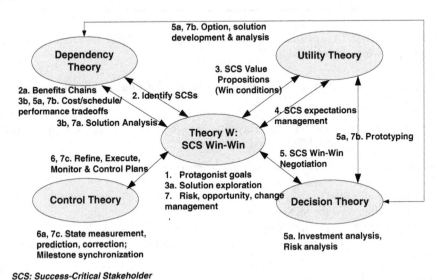

Fig. 1. The VBSE Theory and Process Framework

Q. Wang et al. (Eds.): SPW/ProSim 2006, LNCS 3966, pp. 1–10, 2006.
© Springer-Verlag Berlin Heidelberg 2006

2   The "4+1" Theory of VBSE

Figure 1 summarizes the "4+1" structure of the VBSE theory. The engine in the center is the success-critical stakeholder (SCS) win-win Theory W [5], which addresses the questions of "what values are important?" and "how is success assured?" for a given software engineering enterprise. The four additional theories that it draws upon are dependency theory (how do dependencies affect value realization? On what stakeholders does success depend), utility theory (how important are the values?), decision theory (how do stakeholders' values determine decisions?), and control theory (how to adapt to change and control value realization?).

2.1   The Central Engine: Theory W

The core of Theory W is the Enterprise Success Theorem: *"Your enterprise will succeed if and only if it makes winners of your success-critical stakeholders"*. An informal proof follows in Table 1, and further explained in [2].

Table 1. Informal proof of the Enterprise Success Theorem

Proof of "if"	Proof of "only if"
1. Everyone significant is a winner. 2. Nobody significant is left to complain.	1. Nobody wants to lose. 2. Prospective losers will refuse to participate, or will counterattack. 3. The usual result is lose-lose.

The proof of "if" is reasonably clear. The full proof of "only if" requires further explanation, which is provided in [2].

2.2   Achieving and Maintaining a Win-Win State: The Four Supporting Theories

However, the Enterprise Success Theorem does not tell us how to achieve and maintain a win-win state. This is provided by the:

WinWin Achievement Theorem: Making winners of your success-critical stake-holders requires:
1. Identifying all of the success-critical stakeholders (SCSs).
2. Understanding how the SCSs want to win.
3. Having the SCSs negotiate a win-win set of product and process plans.
4. Controlling progress toward SCS win-win realization, including adaptation to change.

Identifying all of the success-critical stakeholders involves the organizational and human aspects of dependency theory [12][7] and techniques such as the DMR Consulting Group's Results Chains [16].

Understanding how the SCSs want to win involves utility theory, in identifying the SCS's relative utility functions with respect to capability, levels of service, budget, and schedule objectives [15][11][13].

Having the SCSs negotiate win-win product and process plans primarily involves decision theory, but also involves go-backs to other aspects of dependency theory and utility theory to address conflicts among the SCS's utility functions. Users prefer products with many powerful capabilities, and processes allowing easy changing of desired capabilities. Acquirers have limited resources and prefer stable acquisitions. Developers prefer to reuse artifacts that may be incompatible with users' and acquirers' existing artifacts. Exploring options for reconciling these utility conflicts may involve other aspects of dependency theory, such as theories of product interdependencies (physics, computer science, architecture), process interdependencies (scheduling, systems dynamics), and general interdependencies (constraint theory, optimization theory, economic theories). If these theories clearly identify an over-constrained situation, this can help adjust SCS's utility functions or expectations about what levels of desired capability are affordable. This can enable arrival at a mutually satisfactory or win-win shared commitment, using such decision theory elements as statistical decision theory, game theory, or negotiation theory [1][14][17].

Controlling progress toward SCS win-win realization basically involves the feedback control theory aspects of observability, predictability, controllability, and stability. But it also involves adaptive control theory in identifying environmental changes or changes in SCS utility functions and renegotiating a new SCS win-win decision, involving go-backs to the earlier steps and theories.

In a world involving people and changing circumstances, these theorems fall short of the guarantees accompanying physical or mathematics theorems. For example, an inexperienced team can violate all four of the WinWin Achievement conditions and be on a clear path to failure, but can be turned into a SCS win-win success by the timely appearance of a new COTS product that provides the desired solution.

More details on the component theories discussed above are in [2]. The rest of this paper shows how the theories and process contribute to realizing and maintaining a successful win-win outcome in a case study. The case study is a synthesis of two similar projects that did not apply the component theories well and ended up as failures.

3   The VBSE Software Process Framework

As shown in Figure 1, step 1 of the process starts with a protagonist or change agent who provides the motivating force to get a new project, initiative, or enterprise started. As examples, protagonists can be organization leaders with goals, authority, and resources, entrepreneurs with goals and resources, inventors with goals and ideas, or consortia with shared goals and distributed leadership and resources.

Each class of protagonist will take a somewhat different approach in visiting the seven main steps in Figure 3 to create and sustain a win-win combination of SCSs to achieve their goals. In this Section, we will trace the approach taken by a leader whose goals involve a combination of opportunities and problems, who has the authority and resources to address the goals, and who is open to different ideas for addressing them. She is Susan Swanson, an experienced MBA-holding executive, former bicycling champion, and newly-hired CEO of Sierra Mountainbikes, Inc. (a fictitious company representative of two similar companies with less successful projects).

Sierra Mountainbikes Opportunities and Problems

Susan began by convening her management and technology leaders, along with a couple of external consultants, to develop a constructive shared vision of Sierra Mountainbikes' primary opportunities and problems. The results determined a significant opportunity for growth, as Sierra's bicycles were considered top quality and competitively priced. The major problem area was in Sierra's old manual order processing system. Distributors, retailers, and customers were very frustrated with the high rates of late or wrong deliveries; poor synchronization between order entry, confirmation, and fulfillment; and disorganized responses to problem situations. As sales volumes increased, the problems and overhead expenses continued to escalate.

In considering solution options, Susan and her Sierra team concluded that since their primary core competence was in bicycles rather than software, their best strategy would be to outsource the development of a new order processing system, but to do it in a way that gave the external developers a share in the system's success. As a result, to address these problems, Sierra entered into a strategic partnership with eServices Inc. for joint development of a new order processing and fulfillment system. eServices was a growing innovator in the development of supply chain management systems (an inventor with ideas looking for protagonist leaders with compatible goals and resources to apply their ideas).

Step 2. Identifying the Success-Critical Stakeholders (SCSs)

Step 2 in the VBSE process shown in Figure 1 involves identifying all of the success-critical stakeholders involved in achieving a project's goals. As seen in Figure 2, the Step 2a Benefits Chain jointly determined by Sierra and eServices, this includes not only the sales personnel, distributors, retailers, and customers involved in order processing, but also the suppliers involved in timely delivery of Sierra's bicycle components (our Benefits Chain extension to the Thorp/DMR Results Chain includes identifying SCSs in parallelograms and unifying Assumptions into a table).

The Benefits Chain includes initiatives to integrate the new system with an upgrade of Sierra's supplier, financial, production, and human resource management information systems. The Sierra-eServices strategic partnership is organized around rewards reflecting both the system's benefits chain and business case, so that both parties share in the responsibilities and rewards of realizing the system's benefits. Thus, both parties share a motivation to understand and accommodate each other's value propositions or win conditions and to use value-based feedback control to manage the program of initiatives.

This illustrates the "only if" part of the Fundamental System Success Theorem. For the "if" part, if Susan had been a traditional cost-cutting, short-horizon executive, Sierra would have aggressively contracted for a lowest-bidder, fixed-price order processing system, and would have ended up with a buggy, unmaintainable stovepipe order processing system and many downstream order-fulfillment and supplier problems to plague its future. In terms of the framework in Figure 1, however, Sierra and eServices used the Benefits Chain form of Dependency Theory to identify additional SCSs (sales personnel, distributors, retailers, customers, suppliers) who also need to be brought into the SCS WinWin equilibrium state.

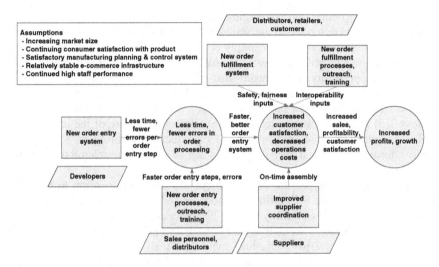

Fig. 2. Benefits Chain for Sierra Supply Chain Management

Steps 3 and 4. Understanding SCS Value Propositions; Managing Expectations

Step 3 (understanding all of the SCSs' value propositions or win conditions) primarily involves utility theory. But it also involves Theory W in reconciling SCS win conditions with achievable solutions (Step 3a), and various forms of dependency theory in conducting cost/schedule/performance solution tradeoff and sensitivity analyses (Step 3b).

For example, the suppliers and distributors may identify some complex exception reporting, trend analysis, and customer relations management features they would like to have in the system's Initial Operational Capability (IOC) in early 2005. However, the use of forms of dependency theory such as software cost and schedule estimation models may show that there is too much proposed IOC software to try to develop by the IOC date. In such a case, Sierra and eServices will have to revisit the SCSs' utility functions in Step 4 (expectations management) by showing them the cost and schedule model credentials and results, and asking them to recalibrate their utility functions, prioritize their desired features, and participate in further solution exploration (a go-back to Step 3a) to achieve a win-win consensus on the top-priority subset of features to include in the IOC.

It may be in some cases that the SCSs' IOC needs are irreconcilable with the IOC schedule. If so, the SCSs may need to live with a later IOC, or to declare that a SCS win-win state is unachievable and to abort the project. Again, it is better to do this earlier rather than later.

Step 5. SCSs Negotiate a WinWin Decision

Actually, the previous paragraph anticipates the content of Step 5, in which the SCSs negotiate a win-win decision to commit themselves to go forward. Once the SCSs have identified and calibrated their Win Conditions in Steps 3 and 4, the process of identifying conflicts or Issues among Win Conditions; inventing and exploring Options to resolve Issues; and converging on Agreements to adopt Win Conditions or Options proceeds as described in the WinWin Negotiation Model above.

In a situation such as the Sierra supply chain project, the number of SCSs and the variety of their win conditions (cost, schedule, personnel, functionality, performance, usability, interoperability, etc.) means that multi-attribute decision theory will be involved as well as negotiation theory. Susan will also be concerned with investment theory or business case analysis to assure her stakeholders that the supply chain initiative will generate a strong return on investment. As many of the decisions will involve uncertainties (market trends, COTS product compatibilities, user interface choices), forms of statistical decision theory such as buying information to reduce risk will be involved as well.

User interface prototypes are actually ways of buying information to reduce the risk of misunderstanding SCS utility functions, as indicated in Figure 1 by the arrow between decision theory and utility theory. The other components of Step 5a in Figure 1 involve other aspects of dependency theory, such as performance analysis, business case analysis, or critical-path schedule analysis. As also shown in Figure 1, these analyses will often proceed at increasing levels of detail in supporting steps 3a, 5a, and 7a as the project proceeds into detailed design, development, integration, and test.

Figure 3 summarizes the business case analysis for the Sierra project. Dollar values are all in millions of 2004 dollars ($M) for simplicity. The analysis compares the expected sales and profits for the current system (columns 4, 5) and the new system

| Date | Current System | | | New System | | | | | | | | | | Customers | | |
| | | | | Financial | | | | | | | | | | | | |
	Market Size ($M)	Market Share %	Sales	Profits	Market Share %	Sales	Profits	Cost Savings	Change in Profits	Cum. Change in Profits	Cum. Cost	ROI	Late Delivery %	Customer Satisfaction (0-5)	In-Transit Visibility (0-5)	Ease of Use (0-5)
12/31/03	360	20	72	7	20	72	7	0	0	0	0	**0**	12.4	**1.7**	1.0	1.8
12/31/04	400	20	80	8	20	80	8	0	0	0	4	**-1**	11.4	**3.0**	2.5	3.0
12/31/05	440	20	88	9	22	97	10	2.2	3.2	3.2	6	**-.47**	7.0	**4.0**	3.5	4.0
12/31/06	480	20	96	10	25	120	13	3.2	6.2	9.4	6.5	**.45**	4.0	**4.3**	4.0	4.3
12/31/07	520	20	104	11	28	146	16	4.0	9.0	18.4	7	**1.63**	3.0	**4.5**	4.3	4.5
12/31/08	560	20	112	12	30	168	19	4.4	11.4	29.8	7.5	**2.97**	2.5	**4.6**	4.6	4.6

Fig. 3. Expected Benefits and Business Case

(columns 7, 8) between 2004 and 2008, the cumulative increase in profits, investment cost, and resulting return on investment (columns 11-13), and expected improvements in other dimensions such as late delivery and customer satisfaction (columns 14-17). The bottom line is a strong 2.97 ROI, plus good expected outcomes in the customer satisfaction dimensions. More details can be found in [3].

The negotiations converge on a number of win-win agreements, such as involving the suppliers and distributors in reviews, prototype exercising, and beta-testing; having Sierra provide eServices with two of their staff members to work on the software development team; and agreeing on compatible data definitions for product and financial interchange. At one point in the negotiation, an unfortunate go-back is

Milestone	Schedule	Cost ($K)	Op. Cost Savings	Market Share %	Annual Sales ($M)	Annual Profits ($M)	Cum. Profits	ROI	Late Delivery %	Customer Satisfaction	ITV	Ease of Use	Risks/Opportunities
Life Cycle Architecture	3/31/04	400		20	72	7.0			12.4	1.7	1.0	1.8	(1)
	3/31/04	427		20	72	7.0			12.4	1.7	1.0	1.8	
Core Capability Demo (CCD)	7/31/04	1050											(2)
	7/20/04	1096								2.4*	1.0*	2.7*	
Software Init. Op. Cap. (IOC)	9/30/04	1400											
	9/30/04	1532								2.7*	1.4*	2.8*	
Hardware IOC	9/30/04	3500											(3)
	10/11/04	3432											
Deployed IOC	12/31/04	4000		20	80	8.0	0.0	-1.0	11.4	3.0	2.5	3.0	(4)
	12/20/04	4041		22	88	8.6	0.6	-.85	10.8	2.8	1.6	3.2	
Responsive IOC	3/31/05	4500	300						9.0	3.5	3.0	3.5	
	3/30/05	4604	324						7.4	3.3	1.6	3.8	
Full Op. Cap. CCD	7/31/05	5200	1000							3.5*	2.5*	3.8*	(5)
	7/28/05	5328	946										
Full Op. Cap. Beta	9/30/05	5600	1700							3.8*	3.1*	4.1*	
	9/30/05	5689	1851										
Full Op. Cap. Deployed	12/31/05	6000	2200	22	106	12.2	3.2	-.47	7.0	4.0	3.5	4.0	
	12/20/05	5977	2483	24	115	13.5	5.1	-.15	4.8	4.1	3.3	4.2	
Release 2.1	6/30/06	6250											

(1) Increased COTS ITV risk, fallback identified.
(2) Using COTS ITV fallback; new HW competitor; renegotiating HW.
(3) $200K savings from renegotiated HW.
(4) New COTS ITV source identified, being prototyped.
(5) New COTS ITV source initially integrated.
* Interim ratings based on trial use

Fig. 4. Value-Based Expected/Actual Outcome Tracking

necessary when an Agreement on a product definition standard is reversed by the management of one of the distributors, who disclose that they are now committed to an emerging international standard. After some renegotiation, the other SCSs agree to this at some additional cost.

Steps 6 and 7. Planning, Executing, Monitoring, Adapting, and Controlling

As with the dependency analyses, project planning, executing, monitoring, adapting, and controlling proceed incrementally in increasing amounts of detail, generally following a risk-driven spiral process. Questions such as "how much is enough planning, specifying, prototyping, COTS evaluation, business case analysis, architecting, documenting, verifying, validating etc.?" are best resolved by balancing the risk exposures of doing too little or too much. As Risk Exposure = Probability (Loss) * Value (Loss) is a value-based concept, risk balancing is integral to the theory.

Value-based planning and control differs most significantly from traditional project planning and control in its emphasis on monitoring progress toward value realization rather than towards project completion. Particularly in an era of increasing rates of change in market, technology, organizational, and environmental conditions, there is an increasing probability that managing to a fixed initial set of plans and specifications will produce systems that are out of step and non-competitive with projects managing adaptively toward evolving value realization.

Perhaps the most provocative example is the traditional technique of "earned value management". It assigns "value" to the completion of project tasks and helps track progress with respect to planned budgets and schedules, but has no way of telling whether completing these tasks will add to or subtract from the business value or mission value of the enterprise. Example failure modes from this approach are systems that had to be 95% redeveloped on delivery because they failed to track evolving requirements and startup companies that fail to track closure of market windows.

If an organization has used steps 1-5 to identify SCSs, determine their value propositions, and develop business cases, it has developed the framework to monitor expected value realization, adjust plans, and control progress toward real SCS value achievement. Figure 4 shows how this is done for the Sierra project, based on the initial budgets, schedules, and business case in Figure 3. The planned achievables are above the line in each cell of figure 4; the actuals are below. Value-based monitoring and control for Sierra requires additional effort in terms of technology watch and market watch, but these help Sierra to discover early that their in-transit-visibility (ITV) COTS vendor was changing direction away from Sierra's needs.

This enabled Sierra to adapt by producing a timely fallback plan, and to proactively identify and approach other likely ITV COTS vendors. The results, as shown in the ITV column and explained in the Risks/Opportunities column of Figure 4, was an initial dip in achieved ITV rating relative to plans, but a recovery to close to the originally planned value. The Risks/Opportunities column also shows a "new hardware competitor" opportunity found by market watch activities that results in a $200K hardware cost savings that mostly compensated for the added software costs of the ITV fallback. The use of prioritized requirements to drive value-based Pareto- and risk-based inspection and testing is another source of software cost savings.

The bottom-line results are a good example of multi-attribute quantitative/ qualitative balanced-scorecard methods of value-based monitoring, adaptation, and control. They are also a good example of use of the necessary conditions for value-based control based on control theory. A traditional value-neutral "earned value" management system would fail on the criteria of business-value observability, predictability, and controllability, because its plans, measurements, and controls deal only with internal-project progress and not with external business-value observables and controllables. They also show the value of adaptive control in changing plans to address new risks and opportunities, along with the associated go-backs to revisit previous analyses and revise previous plans in Steps 7a, 7b, and 7c.

4   Conclusions and Areas for Further Research

The VBSE process framework presented above has been shown to apply well to a reasonably complex supply chain case study, and to avoid the sources of failure encountered in the projects represented in the case study. In other situations, variants of the framework have been successfully applied to over 100 small e-services applications, and to some very large software-intensive systems of systems. These are identifying further needs to represent the process in situations where steps 1-7 are being applied concurrently in evolutionary or spiral development, and in ways that more explicitly identify the stakeholder commitment milestones [6].

Finally, the initial VBSE theory and process need many more tests. The easiest tests to start with are tests of their ability to explain differences between success and failure on completed projects. Other tests that can be done right away are tests of its ability to generate good software engineering practices; an early example is in [5].

Further analyses can be performed on their consistency with other theories and processes such as the chaos-type theories underlying agile and adaptive software development processes [9] or the theories underlying formal software development [10] and generative programming approaches [8].

Tests of utility, generality, practicality, preciseness, and parsimony basically involve trying to apply the theory and process in different situations, observing its successes and shortfalls, and generating improvements in the theory and process that improve their capability in different situations or uncover unstated assumptions that should be made more explicit to limit their domain of dependable applicability. We hope that this initial presentation of the theory and process will be sufficiently attractive for people to give this option a try.

Acknowledgments

The research on this paper has been supported by a National Science Foundation grant, "Value Based Science of Design", and by the Affiliates of the USC Center for Software Engineering.

References

[1] D. Blackwell and M. Girshick, Theory of Games and Statistical Decisions, Wiley, 1954.

[2] B. Boehm and A. Jain, An Initial Theory of Value-Based Software Engineering, in S. Biffl, A. Aurum, B. Boehm, H. Erdogmus, P. Gruenbacher (eds.), Value-Based Software Engineering, Springer Verlag, 2005, pp 15-37.

[3] B. Boehm and L. Huang, Value-Based Software Engineering: A Case Study, IEEE Computer, March 2003, pp. 21-29.

[4] B. Boehm and R. Turner, Balancing Agility and Discipline, Addison Wesley, 2004.

[5] B. Boehm, and R. Ross, Theory-W Software Project Management: Principles and Examples, IEEE Trans. SW Engineering., July 1989, pp. 902-916.

[6] B. Boehm, Some Future Trends and Implications for Systems and Software Engineering Processes, Systems Engineering, vol. 9, no. 1, 2006, pp. 1-19.

[7] H. Booher, (ed.), Handbook of Human Systems Integration, Wiley, 2003.

[8] K. Czarnecki and U. Eisenecker, Generative Programming: Methods, Tools, and Applications, Addison-Wesley, 2000

[9] J. Highsmith, Adaptive Software Development, Dorset House, 2000.

[10] C. B. Jones, Software Development: A Rigorous Approach, Prentice Hall, 1980.

[11] R. L. Keeney and H. Raiffa, Decisions with Multiple Objectives: Preferences and Value Tradeoffs, Cambridge University Press, 1976.

[12] J. March and H. Simon, Organizations, Wiley, 1958.

[13] A. Maslow, Motivation and Personality, Harper, 1954

[14] H. Raiffa, The Art and Science of Negotiation, Belknap/Harvard U. Press, 1982.

[15] H. Simon, Models of Man, Wiley, 1957.

[16] J. Thorp and DMR's Center for Strategic Leadership, The Information Paradox: Realizing the Benefits of Information Technology, McGraw-Hill, 1998.

[17] J. von Neumann and O. Morgenstern, Theory of Games and Economic Behavior, Princeton University Press, 1944.

Exploring the Business Process-Software Process Relationship

Ross Jeffery

National ICT Australia Ltd. and The University of New South Wales,
Locked Bag 9013, Alexandria,
N.S.W., 1435, Australia

Abstract. This paper argues for the need for mechanisms to support the analysis and tracing of relationships between the business process and the software process used to instantiate elements of that business process in software. Evidence is presented to support this argument from research in software process and industry actions and needs as stated in reports to government.

1 Introduction

Software process modeling research has been pursued with varying goals over a number of years. We classify this work into four categories:

1. Understanding and communication
2. Process improvement
3. Process management, and
4. Process execution and automation.

The category that has focused on the facilitation of human understanding of the process or on the communication of that process to humans includes work such as making the process knowledge and context explicit, or graphical mechanisms to make high-level language expressions user friendly. Work in comparing process enactments with the pre-specified model is included under the category of process improvement. Research into process modeling for error detection or managing relationships between process elements falls into category three, while work on language translation and execution falls into category four.

In this paper, we explore process modeling research to date, including the links between business process modeling and software process modeling. After constructing this view of the process modeling landscape we then compare the landscape with two different perspectives. The first of these is an industry perspective. In this perspective we use the report (February 2005) of the Australian Government's SQAWP committee (Software Quality Accreditation Working Party) which provided the Federal Minister for Communications, Information Technology and the Arts (see http://www.dcita.gov.au/) an industry view on software process improvement and software sector competitiveness. This report [1] provides background in which to position future research needs.

Q. Wang et al. (Eds.): SPW/ProSim 2006, LNCS 3966, pp. 11–14, 2006.

We then look at some of the research carried out within NICTA since preparing this report for the Minister. This includes research on CMMI adoption decisions, process simulation modeling, software process lines, and software process enactment mining.

An argument is then made that there is an important relationship between the business process and the software process that needs to be addressed. An approach is proposed called problem-centered process definition.

2 The SQAWP Report and Process Modeling

In February 2005 a report was presented to the Australian Federal Minister. In this report it was noted that software process improvement is a part of business improvement. For those organizations that develop software, the software development process is their business. For those that purchase and use third party software developed by others, the business requirement is that the software meets their business needs. In the SQAWP report the committee focused on the software developing organizations that may, or may not, have software development as their core competence. The report characterized this as shown in Figure 1. In this figure the "left side of the spectrum is very much driven by cost. This has led the global community to turn to lower-cost offshore software services.... The middle of the spectrum is very much driven by process....The right side of the spectrum is very much driven by innovation."

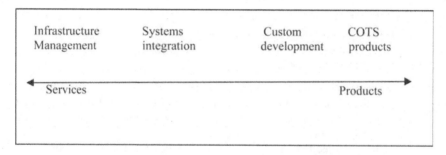

Fig. 1. The Software development spectrum (SQAWP Report p.7)

For those organizations at the innovation end of this spectrum, the process modeling research is likely to have less relevance since these organizations are more likely to be small and informal. In this setting I believe that the goals outlined above from the process modeling research landscape become less important. But for the vast majority of organizations who belong in the other three categories of figure 1, the modeling of process is one of the means to business improvement, improved capability, and improved competitiveness.

3 The Process Modeling Context

If we simplify the place of process modeling in software development we might represent it something like figure 2. In this figure we imagine a world in which the business process is satisfied in some way by the software process delivering software products. It makes little difference for our purpose whether the development organization is within the business organization or not. The point that the figure makes explicit is that the software process interacts with the business process. Therefore the nature of the business process is likely to determine the required nature of the software process. For example, in some contractual arrangements, the system requirements are documented in detail and fixed. The appropriate software process for this context will be one where the software process can deliver the requirements according to the contract at maximum profit. If however, the business processes, constraints and goals are ill defined, dynamic or dependent on the software functionality, then a quite different process model may be appropriate.

In this context, the appropriate software process is dependent on the business context. This relationship might occur at a very high level such as a choice between a waterfall methodology or an agile methodology, or it might occur at a lower level such as a choice of requirements definition method, testing methods, architecture evaluation methods and so on.

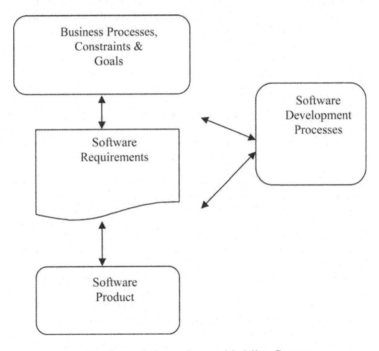

Fig. 2. The Software Process Modeling Context

The implication of this argument is that we need mechanisms to analyze the business process, constraints and goals and to relate these to software process selection decisions. One piece of empirical evidence that supports this argument is the work on Ming Huo [2]. In her paper she investigates an organization that has a well-defined software process model, implemented in an electronic process guide, and in regular use in the corporation. In her work she extracts process enactment models form the time recording system of the organization and compares the enacted model with the defined model. The evidence shows that the process followed deviates from the defined model significantly, thus supporting the argument that in certain circumstances the software process model and the client business model need to interact in a dynamic fashion. The adoption of agile methods provides a relatively informal approach to this adoption process at lower levels of the software process. In another way, the proposal from the economic-driven software development community (see for example publications in the EDSER series of workshops) is reflecting a need to consider software process as a set of activities that will be tailored to the business needs.

References

1. Jeffery, R. (Working Party Chair): Software Quality Accreditation in the Australian Context. Report of the working party to the Australian Minister for Communications, Information Technology and the Arts, February, (2005) 39 pp.
2. Huo, M., Zhang, H., Jeffery, R.:An exploratory study of process enactment as input to software process improvement, to be published in Proceedings of the 4th Workshop on Software Quality, Shanghai, May, (2006).

Assessing 3-D Integrated Software Development Processes: A New Benchmark[*]

Mingshu Li

State Key Lab of Computer Science and Lab for Internet Software Technologies,
Institute of Software at Chinese Academy of Sciences,
No. 4 South Fourth Street, Zhong Guan Cun, Beijing 100080, China
mingshu@iscas.ac.cn

Abstract. The increasing complexity and dynamic of software development
have become the most critical challenges for large projects. As one of the new
emerged methodologies to these problems, TRISO-Model uses an integrated
three-dimensional structure to classify and organize the essential elements in
software development. In order to simulate and evaluate the modeling ability of
TRISO-Model, a new benchmark is created in this paper, called *SPW-2006 Example*, by extending the ISPW-6 Example. It may be used to evaluate other
software process models, and/or to evaluate software organizations, software
projects and also software development processes, particularly 3-D integrated
software development processes. With the *SPW-2006 Example* and its evolution
for quantitative evaluation to 3-D integrated software development processes, a
new approach of *TRISO-Model based assessment and improvement* is enabled.

1 Introduction

Software Process Workshop (SPW) provides an annual forum for assessing current
and emerging software process capabilities, and for obtaining insights into worthwhile
directions in software process research. TRISO-Model (TRidimensional Integrated
SOftware development Model), presenting a 3-D integrated software engineering
methodology, was proposed in the SPW 2005 held in Beijing, China [1]. Its main
objective is to deal with the problems caused by the increasing complexity and dynamic in current software development projects.

Process simulation is an effective mechanism for the study of the complexity and
dynamic of software development processes and has attracted the focus of both research and industry communities. An expression of the attraction is the annual workshop on software process simulation modeling (ProSim) from 1998, a leading event
for the simulation and modeling of software processes. In May 2006, ProSim will be
held jointly with SPW in Shanghai, China, co-locating with ICSE 2006.

A software process benchmark is used to understand the current status of a software project, to evaluate its modeling or the current practice gaps to the benchmark,
and to identify further process improvement opportunities. An assessment is used to
examine a software organization's processes against a reference model to determine

---

[*] Supported by the National Natural Science Foundation of China (Grant Number: 60573082).

Q. Wang et al. (Eds.): SPW/ProSim 2006, LNCS 3966, pp. 15–38, 2006.

the processes' capability or the organization's maturity, and to meet its quality, cost, and schedule goals.

In order to evaluate and improve integrated software development processes, this paper puts forward a new process benchmark; and presents a new process assessment and improvement approach.

The remainder of the paper is organized as follows. Section 2 summarizes the related work. Section 3 introduces TRISO-Model semantic specifications. Section 4 creates a new process benchmark *SPW-2006 Example* for effective evaluation of integrated software development processes. Section 5 presents a new approach of *TRISO-Model based assessment and improvement*. The paper is concluded in Section 6 with a summary and directions for future work.

2 Related Work

From the last 80s, some process modeling languages and corresponding tools, such as Little-JIL [2] and ADELE-TEMPO [3], have been designed to provide precise and comprehensive ways to represent various software process elements. Cost estimation methods, such as COCOMO II [4] and Web-COBRA [5], are invented to gain better predictability and quantitative control from the perspective of economics. Boehm's recent work on Value-Based Software Engineering [6] tries to further integrate value considerations into all of the existing and emerging software engineering principles and practices. The Personal Software Process (PSP) [7] and People Capability Maturity Model (P-CMM) [8] stress the factor of people, and provide a guide towards developing, motivating, and organizing the work force.

As Reifer lists in [9], the top challenges for nowadays developments fall into a large variety of interwoven areas such as technology, people, economy, change management and so on. CMMI [10] provides a framework covering most factors related to software development. MBASE [11] proposes a framework for avoiding model clash among different models (i.e. Process Model, Product Model, Property Model, and Success Model) in software development.

In SPW2005, the latest achievements on integrating different aspects of software development, besides TRISO-Model, are also presented by some researchers. Estublier relates processes, software production and humans in a pyramid framework to show and contrast the new and original potential uses of process technology [12]. Rombach proposes integrated software process & product lines (SPPL) [13] as a systematic way to choose both artifacts and processes needed for a given project. Osterweil [14] and Warboys [15] suggest different angle of views to integrate microprocess and macroprocess, respectively.

A simulation model is a computational model that represents an abstraction or a simplified representation of a complex dynamic system [16]. It offers the possibility of experimenting with different management decisions. Kellner et al. cluster the many reasons for using processes simulations into six categories of purpose, including [17]: strategic management, planning, control and operational management, process improvement and technology adoption, understanding, and training and learning.

Continuous modeling and discrete modeling are the two main approaches to build models in the simulation domain [18]. A continuous simulation model represents the interactions between key process factors, as a set of differential equations, where time is increased step by step. On the other hand, discrete modeling is based on the metaphor of a queuing network, where time advances when a discrete event occurs. Continuous modeling and discrete modeling only enhance the analysis of some aspects of the process, at a cost to other aspects [19]. A software process, however, shows both discrete system aspects (start/end of an activity, reception/release of an artifact by an activity) and continuous system ones (recourse consumption by an activity, percentage of developed product, percentage of discovered defects). It would be desirable to use a continuous modeling for the dynamic environment, and a discrete one for tasks and resources [20]. A combined model would allow investigation of the effects of discrete resource changes on continuously varying productivity. There are some other simulation techniques, like state based process models, rule based languages, petri nets [21], and agent-based simulation [22].

A benchmark is a test or set of tests used to compare the performance of alternative tools or techniques [23]. It usually has three components: motivating comparison, task sample and performance measures. A proto-benchmark is a set of tests that is missing one of these components. The most common proto-benchmarks lack a performance measure and are sometimes called case studies or exemplars. These are typically used to demonstrate the features and capabilities of a new tool or techniques. A software process benchmark is an average reference value that the process statistically performs in a given sector or a given region [24].

For the purpose of making comparisons between different software process technologies, the ISPW-6 Example [25] was proposed as a benchmark problem at the 6th International Software Process Workshop. It has been used successfully to exam the essential features of some main software process methods in the last 90s, e.g., OPSIS [26] applies a view mechanism to graph-based process modeling languages of type Petri-net; MVP-L1 [27] is oriented towards process-modeling-in-the-large to concentrate on the formalization of interrelations between individual processes; MERLIN [28] uses a PROLOG-based language as a basis of the process definition. It was later extended to incorporate teamwork and process change (ISPW-7)[29].

The ISPW-6 Example is mainly designed for assessing the software process modeling approaches, and as a reasonable simplification, pays less attention to some other software development critical factors. However, "change" is a much more complex problem in real-world software development [30]. Because of the complexity, even though the problem caused by requirements changes has been noticed quite a long time ago, it is still one of the most frequent reasons for project failure. Nowadays the paradigm has shifted to be driven by a set of interwoven factors, such as technology, management, quality, knowledge, and economic considerations, so some extensions should be made to the ISPW-6 Example from process-oriented perspective to a multi-perspective framework. Relevant factors, such as economy, technology, and human, as well as the interactions among these factors should be incorporated into the framework.

SPEM (Software Process Engineering Metamodel) [31] is a software process modeling standard put forward by OMG (Object Management Group). In SPEM, a common syntax and structure for software development process [32] is provided based on the abstraction of process models such as RUP. As an extension of UML [33], SPEM inherits the expressiveness and popularity. With the graphic notations, SPEM offers a comprehensive and documented view of the process model, which facilitates the communication of process stakeholders.

As a standard proposed by OMG aiming to be the unified software process modeling language, SPEM is being widely accepted. However, as a description language, the disciplines related to project management and analysis, process automation, etc. have not been involved. Furthermore, the dynamic semantics has not been addressed in SPEM.

MOF (Meta Object Facility) [34] is the meta-meta-model provided by OMG as the unified standard for domain metamodeling, and it provides common abstract syntax and semantic definition mechanism. MOF is suitable for constructing an integrated model of multi-dimension factors. However, a metamodel constructed in the MOF-based metamodeling method, as well as UML and SPEM, is an informal metamodel which has no precise semantics. Thus it is necessary to map it into another description using some formal method to reduce the ambiguity.

Figure 1 illustrates a segment (Review Design) of ISPW-6 Example represented by SPEM.

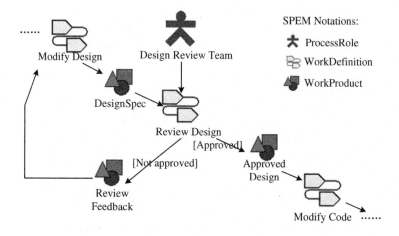

Fig. 1. Segment of ISPW-6 Example Represented by SPEM

CSP is developed by Hoare to address the concurrency and non-determinism in computing systems [35]. The basic idea is that those systems can be readily decomposed into subsystems which operate concurrently and interact with each other as well as with their common environment. As for the software process, Greenwood tentatively introduces CSP as a tool to model the software process [36]. LOTOS, another process algebra language similar to CSP, is employed to separate a whole software process into several concurrent subprocesses executed by different actors in [37]. But the actors and artifacts are just treated as communication channels, so it is difficult to present more information about those elements.

Using CSP, the segment (Review Design) of ISPW-6 Example in Figure 1 can be specified as follows:

$$ISPW\,6\,Part = ModifyDesign \parallel ReviewDesign$$
$$ModifyDesign = assigntodesigner \rightarrow designspec \rightarrow modifydesign$$
$$\rightarrow modifieddesign \rightarrow ModifyDesignLoop$$
$$ModifyDesignLoop = assigntodesigner \rightarrow designspec \rightarrow reviewfeedback$$
$$\rightarrow modifydesign \rightarrow modifieddesign \rightarrow ModifyDesignLoop$$
$$ReviewDesign = modifieddesign \rightarrow assigntoreviewteam \rightarrow reviewdesign \rightarrow$$
$$(approved \rightarrow approveddesign \rightarrow reportmeasurementdata \rightarrow SKIP \mid$$
$$notapproved \rightarrow reviewfeedback \rightarrow ReviewDesign)$$

3 TRISO-Model and Its Semantic Specifications

Based on the *Technology-Process-Human* triad conception and successful software engineering methodologies in the past, TRISO-Model presents a 3-D integrated methodology for software development processes, i.e. software development processes should be integrated improved from three perspectives of *technology*, *process*, and *human*. This expanded view incorporates the benefits gained from integrations among technologies, processes and humans.

TRISO-Model classifies the essential elements of the software development process into three dimensions: SE Technology, SE Process and SE Human. From the viewpoint of TRISO-Model, a software development process is thought of as a process driven by the interactions among the entities in the three dimensions.

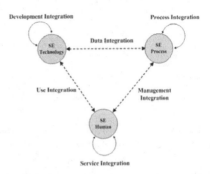

Fig. 2. Integrated Framework of TRISO-Model

The entities may be abstracted to the activities for SE Process, the actors for SE Human, and the input/output artifacts for SE Technology respectively. The interactions are modeled in Figure 2 as six integrations: (1) Development Integration; (2) Process Integration; (3) Service Integration; (4) Data Integration; (5) Management Integration; and (6) Use Integration. The former three are internal integrations; and the latter three are external integrations.

3.1 Static Semantic Specification of TRISO-Model

The static semantics of TRISO-Model is represented by the elements of the entities in the three dimensions and the relationships among them. A static structure of TRISO-Model is shown as Figure 3.

Figure 4 illustrates the core concept of SPEM. The main idea is that a software development process is a set of collaborations among ProcessRoles that perform WorkDefinitions in which the WorkProducts are operated.

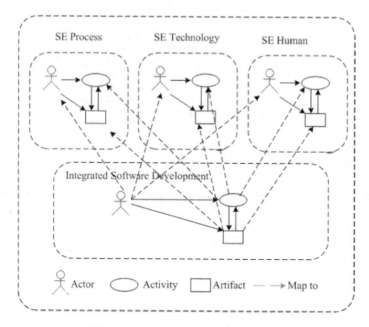

Fig. 3. Static Structure of TRISO-Model

The metaclasses in SPEM, ProcessRole, WorkDefinition and WorkProduct, may be viewed as the abstracted elements of *human* (or *actor*), *process* (or *activity*), and *technology* (or *artifact*) in TRISO-Model as shown in Figure 3. However, SPEM is over-simplified so that it cannot provide enough support to the integrated methodology. It has to be extended to describe the elements of entities in SE Human, SE Process and SE Technology dimensions of TRISO-Model and their relationships.

In TRISO-Model, an integrated soft-ware development process is expected to relate to the three dimensions.

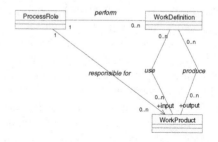

Fig. 4. Core Concept of SPEM

As an example shown in Figure 3, for each *actor* in the integrated process, there are corresponding *actors* in SE Process, SE Technology and SE Human dimensions; and it is the same with the *activities* and *artifacts*.

To support the idea stated above, we extend SPEM to *Integrated SPEM* (*I-SPEM* for short; more details will be introduced in another paper) with the metaclasses enhanced in three dimensions of SE Human, SE Process, and SE Technology. *I-SPEM* is defined as a M2 layer metamodel based on MOF, in which integrated elements in three dimensions and their relationships are specified in a consistent method as illustrated in Figure 5.

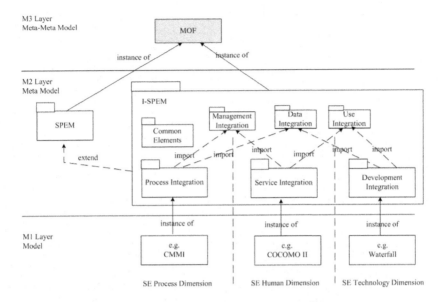

Fig. 5. Illustration of Static Semantics of TRISO-Model

In *I-SPEM*, there are six integration packages defined with the same names corresponding to Figure 2. The concepts and their relationships in three dimensions are defined in three internal integration packages; the integrations among the dimensions are defined in three external integration packages. The common elements and facilities are defined in the *Common Elements* package.

MOF, the M3 layer meta-metamodel, provides a consistent semantic base for every dimension specific metamodels in the framework of TRISO-Model. M1 layer models, the lowest abstraction level, are the instances of *I-SPEM* and the combination of discrete-type simulation, continuous-type simulation and analytical model. In Figure 5, CMMI, COCOMO II and Waterfall model are chosen only as the examples for the three dimensions. A different organization may have other choices. For instance, the ISO 9001 may be chosen to replace the CMMI.

3.2 Dynamic Semantic Specification of TRISO-Model

The dynamic semantics of TRISO-Model is represented by the evolutions of the entities in the three dimensions, and the communications and/or the coordination among them. A dynamic structure of TRISO-Model is shown as Figure 6. The *activities*, *actors*, and *artifacts* are the essential entities of the corresponding SE Process, SE Human, and SE Technology dimensions. Each entity has its own pattern of behaviors. It may communicate with other entities in the same dimension and/or coordinate with other entities in different dimensions through the synchronizations on some specific events.

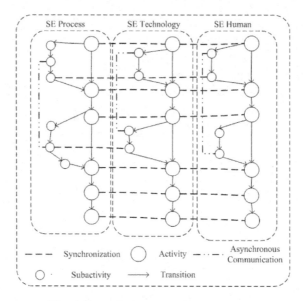

Fig. 6. Dynamic Structure of TRISO-Model

In the dynamic semantics, all the entities of TRISO-Model are mapped to three types of basic CSP processes, which are the *activity*, *actor*, and *artifact* processes. The three processes representing the three dimensions are combined together and coordinated by the synchronizations on some particular events. Each dimension is represented by a CSP process formed by the internal dimension integrations of the corresponding type of basic CSP processes. It can be taken as an agent possessing the necessary knowledge about how to evolve itself forward and having the exposed interfaces to synchronize with other dimensions.

Additionally, to make the content more comprehensible, all the illustrations presented in this section exclusively centralize on one problem, i.e., an abstracted software development process. The process is composed of the "requirement" and "design" activities only. The "requirement" activity begins with the requirements analysis and ends with outputting the requirements specification. In the "design" activity, the requirements specification is firstly input and then the system is designed. These two activities are sequentially arranged as those in the Waterfall lifecycle model. If the "requirement" activity and "design" activity are represented by two CSP processes, named *Requirement* and *Design* respectively, then the software development process can be denoted as:

$$DevelopemntProcess = req : Requirement; des : Design \tag{1}$$

To fully describe TRISO-Model, several aspects should be considered as the extensions on CSP, i.e. *CSP Extensions for TRSIO Model* (*CTM* for short; and will be discussed more in another paper). Firstly, CSP has to be extended to include asynchronous communication. In CSP, Hoare has chosen synchronized communications as basic. The synchronized communication means that a receiver blocks until a compatible agent is ready to send. Furthermore, CSP allows bi-party communications only.

Expression (1) cannot be implemented based on the synchronized communications, but it can be modeled by the following asynchronous communication. Secondly, in order to model the across dimension collaboration of TRISO-Model, a collaboration operator is needed. Two processes will be synchronized on the automatically inserted dummy actions indicated by the operator. Finally, a process in CSP is the behavior pattern of an entity. But the entity may have some attributes other than actions. In *CTM*, a process is extended with attributes that can be accessed by other processes.

The extension of asynchronous communication does not change the rule that the communications between processes are purely based on synchronizations. A buffer process is implicitly introduced between two communicating processes. The existence of the buffer process is transparent to the specifier. He or she can input or output any object freely without the need to considering the synchronization between the inputs and outputs. But the interactions among the inputting, outputting, and buffering processes are based on the synchronized communications. Here we recur to a *set* process to ease some constraints imposed by the buffer process. The *set* process, acting as the storage media, is one component of the environment. A *set* process based on the subordination operator is presented in [38].

Let the operator, !!, represent the asynchronous output. When using this operator, the specified object will be put into the set used for containing the artifacts of a software development process.

A *CTM* process outputting something to the environment can be set as:

$$\mathrm{Re}\,quirement_{CTM} = requirementanalysis \rightarrow !!requirementspec \rightarrow SKIP \tag{2}$$

where the subscript $_{CTM}$ means that the expression uses some notations that are defined in the *CTM*.

The above expression can be equivalently expressed in CSP notations as:

$$Requirement_{CSP} = (set : SET \,/\!/$$
$$(requirementanalysis \rightarrow set.add\,!requirementspec \rightarrow SKIP))$$

where *SET* represents the *set* process and *add* is the channel used for inserting an object into the set.

Let the operator, ??, represent the asynchronous input. It means that the process needs an input from the buffered *set* process. As an example, the design activity may use the *requirementspec* produced in (2):

$$Design_{CTM} = ??\,requirementspec\,!y \rightarrow design \rightarrow SKIP \tag{3}$$

where, *??requirement!y* means retrieve *requirementspec* from the *set* process and put the result into the variable *y*. (3) can also be described in CSP notations as:

$$Design_{CSP} = (set : SET \,/\!/$$
$$(set.isin\,!requirementspec \rightarrow set.result\,?\,y \rightarrow design \rightarrow SKIP))$$

where *isin* is a channel used for retrieving an object and the result can be got from the *result* channel. A minor change may be made on the definition of the *set* process presented in [38]. A *NIL* or a referenced object should be returned from the *result* channel instead of a Boolean value. When the needed object *requirementspec* does not exist, the *set* process returns *NIL*. The inputting process will be blocked and retested later.

The three dimensions are represented by *CTM* processes in TRISO-Model. The software development process is the combination of the three processes. It is the synchronizations among the three processes that seamlessly integrate the three dimensions. In the dynamic semantics of TRISO-Model, the alphabets of the three dimensions are not obliged to have common actions. Thus each dimension can be separately defined in a divide-conquer strategy. The synchronization is carried out on the automatically inserted dummy actions. It is implemented by the following collaboration operator.

The operands of the collaboration operator are two *CTM* processes. The operator, modeling the external integrations of TRISO-Model, is denoted as:

$$\Theta_{synchronizationname:\{\langle label1, label2\rangle,...\}}$$

where

synchronizationname	the name of the synchronization
$\{\{label1, label2\},...\}$	a set of synchronized points
$\{label1, label2\}$	a tuple representing a point
label1, label2	the lable of the subprocesses that should be synchronized in the operands

This operator ensures that each step of the two processes is synchronized on the automatically inserted dummy actions.

As examples, two processes are defined as:

$$P = P1; P2; P3 \quad \text{,and} \quad Q = Q1; Q2; Q3$$

then,

$$P\Theta_{utilize:\{\{p1,q1\},\{p3,q3\}\}}Q =$$
$$((p1.uitilize.q1 \rightarrow p1 : P1); P2; (p3.uitilize.q3 \rightarrow p3 : P3)) \parallel$$
$$((p1.uitilize.q1 \rightarrow q1 : Q1); Q2; (p3.uitilize.q3 \rightarrow q3 : Q3))$$

Here the representation of a dummy action is composed of the corresponding subprocesses, the name of synchronization, and the dots. But this does not violate the atomic property of an action in *CTM*.

It should be noted that two successive collaboration operators are syntactically legitimate. The synchronization points are the unions of the two operators. In this sense the two operators meet the communicative law.

4   3-D Integrated Software Engineering Process Benchmarking

As stated in Section 2, ISPW-6 Example is not competent in the face of the complex system nowadays, in which multi-dimension issues have to be considered. As the extension and improvement to ISPW-6 Example, we design a new benchmark, *a 3-D Integrated Software Engineering Modeling Example Problem*. It may be used to evaluate the emerging integrated software development models/methodologies like TRISO-Model. In correspondence with ISPW-6 Example, it could be called *SPW-2006 Example* in this paper.

4.1 SPW-2006 Example Problem

Extended from ISPW-6 Example, the *SPW-2006 Example* focuses on the various aspects that are affected by a change caused by a requirements change request. These aspects include not only the engineering process, but also the management process, support process, process improvement process, and so on. *SPW-2006 Example* extends ISPW-6 Example by:

- Expanding the problem to an integrated software development scenario in which *process*, *technology*, and *human* are all essential factors.
- Generalizing steps to *activities*; refining organizations to *actors*.
- Classifying steps into two categories, *component activities* that may occur step by step such as Review Design and *ongoing activities* that keep on going as Configuration Management
- Adding more steps/*activities* that may occur concurrently
- Adding more *actors* for expanding the organizational scope from development to the whole organization
- Extending constraints to *interactions*

In the following description, we use Italic font to differentiate the added or modified elements from those of ISPW-6 Example.

- ■ *Activities*
  - ◆ *Component Activities*
    - ✓ *Requirements Change Decision*
    - ✓ *Technical Solution Decision*
    - ✓ *Integration Test*
    - ✓ Schedule and Assign Tasks
    - ✓ Modify Design
    - ✓ Review Design
    - ✓ Modify Code
    - ✓ Modify Test Plans
    - ✓ Modify Unit Test Package
    - ✓ Test Unit
  - ◆ *Ongoing Activities*
    - ✓ *Configuration Management*
    - ✓ *Cost Estimation*
    - ✓ *Project Management (extended from "Monitor Progress" in ISPW-6 Example)*
    - ✓ *Measurement and Improvement (including "Process Change" in ISPW-7 extension)*
    - ✓ *Training*
    - ✓ *Knowledge Management and Reuse*
- ■ *Actors*
  - ◆ *SEPG*
  - ◆ CCB (Configuration Control Board)
    - ✓ *SCM*

- Project Team
  - ✓ **SQA (extended from "QA engineers" in ISPW-6 Example)**
  - ✓ **Knowledge Engineer**
  - ✓ **Estimation Expert**
  - ✓ **Requirements Engineer**
  - ✓ Project manager
  - ✓ Design engineers
  - ✓ Software engineers
- **User Representative**
- **Trainer**

■ Artifacts
- Input + Source (**Artifact**, **Actor**, or **Activity**) + Physical communication mechanism
- Output + Destination (**Artifact**, **Actor**, or **Activity**) + Physical communication mechanism

■ **Interactions (extended from "Constraints regarding step sequencing" in ISPW-6 Example)**
- **Teamwork (as mentioned in ISPW-7 extensions)**
- **Integration**

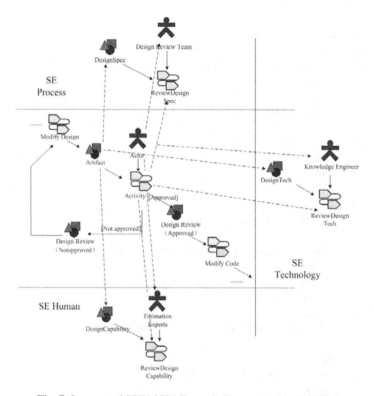

Fig. 7. Segment of SPW-2006 Example Represented by I-SPEM

Table 1. From ISPW-6 Example to *SPW-2006 Example*

	ISPW-6 Example	***SPW-2006 Example***
Actor	DesignReviewTeam	DesignReviewTeam
		KnowledgeEngineer
		EstimationExpert
Activity	ReviewDesign	ReviewDesignSpec
		ReviewDesignTech
		ReviewDesignCapability
Artifact	DesignSpec	DesignSpec
		DesignTech
		DesignCapability

In order to highlight the extension we made in *SPW-2006 Example*, comparing to ISPW-6 Example in Figure 1, we also use Review Design as the segment example in this section. Using *I-SPEM*, the problem is considered in the three dimensions of TRISO-Model, as shown in Figure 7. The *Actor*, *Activity* and *Artifact* are all expanded to groups of corresponding elements involved in the three dimensions. The mapping of these elements, from 1-D to 3-D, is illustrated in Table 1.

Using *CTM*, the dynamic semantics of the segment around the Review Design activity for the *SPW-2006 Example* is presented as follows:

$$SPW\_2006Part = ModifyDesign; ReviewDesign;$$
$$SKIP \ll approved \gg SPW\_2006Part; ModifyCode$$

A design is firstly modified and then the modified design is reviewed. If the modified design is not approved, the design should be modified again. Otherwise the source code will be changed according to the approved design.

An activity in TRISO-Model is described from the three dimensions. The following three processes are used for modeling an activity:

$$\begin{matrix} ProcessActivity & \text{describing the actions taken out by the activity;} \\ HumanActivity & \text{describing the involved actors;} \\ TechnologyActivity & \text{describing the involved artifacts;} \end{matrix} \quad (4)$$

As for the Review Design activity, the processes in (4) can be correspondingly defined as:

$$ProcessReviewDesign = rds : ReviewDesignSpec; rdt : ReviewDesignTech;$$
$$rdc:ReviewDeisignCapability$$
$$HumanReviewDesign = drt : DesignReviewTeam; ke : KnowledgeEngineer;$$
$$ee : EstimatonExpert \quad (5)$$
$$ArtifactReviewDesign = desspec : DesignSpec; dt : DesignTech;$$
$$dc : DesignCapability$$

Firstly, the SE Process and SE Human dimensions are combined together through the *Management Integration*. We have,

$$ReviewDesignMI$$
$$= ProcessReviewDesign \Theta_{MI:\{\{rds,drt\},\{rdt,ke\},\{rdc,ee\}\}} HumanReviewDesign$$

Then the *ArtifactsReviewDesign* process integrates this above process through the *Data Integration* and the *Use Integration*. Thus the *Review Design* activity is modeled as:

$$ReviewDesign = ArtifactReviewDesign$$

$$\Theta_{UI:\{\{desspec,drt\},\{dt,ke\},\{dc,ee\}\}}\Theta_{DI:\{\{desspec,rds\},\{dt,rdt\},\{dc,rdc\}\}}ReviewDesignMI$$

It should be noted that the order of the application of the three external integrations does not matter.

4.2 Evaluations with the *SPW-2006 Example*

S.Fogle et al proposed six phases of a benchmarking project [39]: project initiation, planning, benchmarking partner identification, data collection, data analysis, and reporting. D.Card and D.Zubrow summarized three critical factors to success [40]: well-defined objectives, careful planning and cautious interpretation. The *SPW-2006 Example* benchmarking may be conducted according to the following three steps:

(1) Planning: decompose the benchmarked object into the corresponding or relative elements in *SPW-2006 Example*, based on its evaluation goals;
(2) Benchmarking: compare the decomposed elements with those in *SPW-2006 Example*;
(3) Evaluating: analyze the benchmarked object's similarities and differences with *SPW-2006 Example* and report the result.

As defined in section 4.1, the *SPW-2006 Example* benchmark includes 4 aspects, 31 elements. We use three levels of satisfactions to identify the current practice gaps to the *SPW-2006 Example* benchmark: *Not Satisfied (N)*, *Partially Satisfied (P)* and *Fully Satisfied (F)*. A benchmarked element at *N* or *P* level indicates a further software development process improvement opportunity.

Table 2 illustrates the *SPW-2006 Example* evaluation result to TRISO-Model. All the decomposed elements in TRISO-Model are *Fully Satisfied (F)* in comparison with the elements in the *SPW-2006 Example* benchmark. It shows that TRISO-Model is a good model to describe 3-D integrated software development processes.

Like the ISPW-6 Example, the *SPW-2006 Example* is originally designed for assessing the software process modeling approaches, particularly for the evaluation of an integrated software development process model, i.e., TRISO-Model. Furthermore, it expands the problem from one dimension of *process* to an integrated software development scenario in which three dimensions of *process*, *technology*, and *human* are all essential factors. Thus, it also may be used to evaluate software organizations, software projects and software development processes.

Table 2 also shows the evaluation results to other models for software development processes, CMM [41]/CMMI [10], ISO 9001[42], and SEPRM[43], with the *SPW-2006 Example*. In Table 2, many elements of the ISO 9001 standard is labeled with *Partially Satisfied (P)* or *Not Satisfied (N)* for the reason that the corresponding elements are just discussed in a broad sense. The difference between TRISO-Model and the other two ones is minor. However, from an analysis to the similarities and differences between each one-to-one element in the benchmarked object and *SPW-2006 Example*, a consensus conclusion should be reached that the CMM/CMMI is suitable for a software process integrated process, project and engineering management, but not suitable for detailed technological support, knowledge-based solution and cost estimation; ISO 9001 is suitable for a general process control, but not

Table 2. Evaluations with the SPW-2006 Example

SEPRM	ISO 9001	CMM/CMMI	TRISO-Model				
F	P	F	F	*Requirements Change Decision*		*Component Activities*	*Activities*
P	P	P	F	*Technical Solution Decision*			
F	F	F	F	*Integration Test*			
F	F	F	F	Schedule and Assign Tasks			
F	P	F	F	Modify Design			
F	P	F	F	Review Design			
F	P	F	F	Modify Code			
F	P	F	F	Modify Test Plans			
F	P	F	F	Modify Unit Test Package			
F	P	F	F	Test Unit			
F	P	F	F	*Configuration Management*		*Ongoing Activities*	
F	N	F	F	*Cost Estimation*			
F	F	F	F	*Project Management*			
F	P	F	F	*Measurement and Improvement*			
F	F	F	F	*Training*			
P	N	P	F	*Knowledge Management and Reuse*			
F	N	F	F	*SEPG*			*Actors*
F	P	F	F	*SCM*	CCB		
F	P	F	F	*SQA*			
N	N	N	F	*Knowledge Engineer*	Project Team		
P	N	P	F	*Estimation Expert*			
F	F	F	F	*Requirements Engineer*			
F	F	F	F	Project manager			
F	F	F	F	Design engineers			
F	F	F	F	Software engineers			
F	F	F	F	*User Representative*			
F	F	F	F	*Trainer*			
F	F	F	F	Input + Source + physical communication mechanism			*Artifacts*
F	F	F	F	Input + Destination + physical communication mechanism			
F	P	F	F	*Teamwork*			*Interactions*
F	P	F	F	*Integration*			

Not Satisfied (N), Partially Satisfied (P), and *Fully Satisfied (F)* suitable for specific software process management; SEPRM is a very good software engineering process reference model integrated 3 process subsystems of organization, development and management, but still lack of enough support to technology, knowledge and economy. TRISO-Model is a fully support reference model for integrated software development processes from the three most important dimensions of *process*, *technology*, and *human* naturally.

TRISO-Model has many unique features that are beneficial to the performance, analysis, and improvement of software processes. In TRISO-Model, the interrelationships among the elements of the software development process entities can be represented in *I-SPEM*, which includes more stereotypes and suits the convenience of modelers; and all the entities are uniformly described in their behavior patterns and are mapped onto *activity*, *artifact*, and *actor* in three dimensions through *CTM*, which guides the performance of development processes with rigorous operational semantics. New techniques for the analysis of software processes can be put forward based on the formalism. With the description of *artifacts*, the technical factors that transform the user requirement into the final product are covered in TRISO-Model. As human constitutes the major part of the cost of a project, various models for measurement and cost estimation can be integrated into the model through the modeling of *actor*.

In a simulated world, *SPW-2006 Example* benchmarking only adopts pass/fail strategy. Some parts of *SPW-2006 Example* may be changed to a quantitative way for real applications, e.g., "*Measurement and Improvement*" element was developed to an effective measurement method [44], which can be used to help identifying, analyzing, and solving the problems arising during the development processes.

In terms of the seven desiderata for successful benchmarks presented by Sim et al. in [23], the *SPW-2006 Example* fared very well as follows: (1) Accessibility: the *SPW-2006 Example* is an extended ISPW-6 Example and easily to be understood, to be found and to be used. (2) Affordability: people may use it to have an overall assessment to integrated software development processes. The costs are caused by human efforts and tools support, depending on how details the assessment needs to be. (3) Clarity: *SPW-2006 Example* is clear enough to describe software development processes through the elements in the three necessary aspects of *activities*, *actors*, *artifacts* and their interactions. (4) Relevance: it can be used to assess not only a general software development process, but also some specific software engineering processes like requirement engineering, software measurement. (5) Solvability: it is a good example to evaluate other software process models, and/or to evaluate software organizations, software projects and also software development processes, particularly 3-D integrated software development processes. (6) Portability: it is of course easy to be implemented at a variety of platforms. (7) Scalability: it is an extended version of ISPW-6 Example and definitely may be further extended to more complicated examples or even to a commercial product.

5 TRISO-Model Based Assessment and Improvement

The purpose of the assessment process is to efficiently find evidence of key process areas and identify areas for improvement [45]. The essential process activities are:

plan the assessment, distribute assessment material, prepare for assessment meeting, conduct assessment, make changes for improvement, and follow-up. The input to an assessment is the work item (project) to be scrutinized, the relevant checklists enumerating the types of key process areas to be identified, and other documents such as procedures and standards. The output of an assessment is firstly the log of the key process areas uncovered and secondly the areas for improvement and thirdly a summary report showing the score.

Several software process assessment models have been developed, such as CMM/CMMI, ISO 9001, ISO/IEC 15504 [46], and SEPRM.

5.1 TRISO-Model Based Assessments

There are two kinds of TRISO-Model based assessments: *TRISO-Model Qualitative Assessment* and *TRISO-Model Quantitative Assessment*.

The *TRISO-Model Qualitative Assessment* provides a checklist-based assessment method. It is also a kind of benchmark-based assessment. The benchmark is *SPW-2006 Example* in this paper. By comparing each element in the given software development process with the one in *SPW-2006 Example*, a pass/fail checklist will be given and the final assessment result will be made according to the pass/fail information. It is a very simple assessment methodology. It may be used to evaluate whether an assessed integrated software development process is well defined or not. But it is not helpful in step-by-step process improvement.

The *TRISO-Model Quantitative Assessment* provides a flexible software development process assessment method, based on the evaluation to integrated capability maturity levels. It may be written in a triplet as follows:

TRISO-Model Quantitative Assessment = (*PCM Level, TCM Level, HCM Level*)

where *PCM* represents *Process Capability Maturity*, *TCM* represents *Technology Capability Maturity* and *HCM* represents *Human Capability Maturity*. The *PCM Level, TCM Level* and *HCM Level* mean its process capability maturity level or status, technology capability maturity level or status, and human capability maturity level or status, respectively, in an integrated software development process for a software organization or a software project.

Each of capability maturities in the TRISO-Model three dimensions may be modeled as some available assessment model or a new assessment model. The integration of the three assessment models will be the TRISO-Model quantitative assessment model.

Based on CMM/CMMI and P-CMM for *PCM Level* and *HCM Level* respectively, this section presents a *TRISO-Model Quantitative Assessment Reference Model*. Accordingly, there are five defined maturity levels in *PCM Level*: *Initial* focuses on competent people and heroics *(1)*, *Repeatable* focuses on basic project management *(2)*, *Defined* focuses on process standardization *(3)*, *Managed* focuses on quantitative management *(4)* and *Optimizing* focuses on continuous process improvement *(5)*; and five defined maturity levels in *HCM Level*: *Initial* initiates no processes *(1)*, *Repeatable* focuses on establishing basic workforce practices and eliminating problems that hinder work performance *(2)*, *Defined* addresses organizational issues, as the organization tailors its defined workforce practices to the core competencies required by its business environment *(3)*, *Managed* focuses on building competency-based teams and establishing a quantitative understanding of trends in the development of knowledge and skills and in the alignment of performance across different levels of the organization *(4)* and *Optimizing* covers issues that both the organization and individuals must address in implementing continuous improvements in their capability *(5)*.

Here we define the maturity levels in *TCM Level* on our own, also five levels to match *PCM Level* and *HCM Level*: *Initial* initiates software development *(1)*, *Repeatable* focuses on establishing necessary domain knowledge support *(2)*, *Defined* addresses technology standardization and tool support *(3)*, *Managed* emphasizes technology innovation and management *(4)* and *Optimizing* aims at a technological leadership and continuous technology improvement *(5)*.

Thus, an assessment result based on *TRISO-Model Quantitative Assessment Reference Model* will be the three numbers combination of the triplet between *(1, 1, 1)* and *(5, 5, 5)*. For an example, an assessment result *(4, 3, 4)* means that the assessed software development process achieved an integrated level *(4, 3, 4)*, with *Managed* process capability maturity level, *Defined* technology capability maturity level and *Managed* human capability maturity level, respectively. It performed a quantitative process management, used development tools support and possessed a good qualified team.

Table 3 shows a TRISO-Model based assessment form. The *TRISO-Model Quantitative Assessment* evaluates the assessed software development process from the three dimensions of *Process Capability Maturity (PCM) Level (1-5)*, *Technology Capability Maturity (PCM) Level (1-5)* and *Human Capability Maturity (PCM) Level (1-5)*, by assessing the six integrations as shown in Figure 2. It can be conducted through three steps as follows.

Table 3. TRISO-Model Based Assessment Form

	TRISO-Model Quantitative Assessment		
	PCM Level (1-5)	*TCM Level* (1-5)	*HCM Level* (1-5)
Process Integration		—	—
Development Integration	—		—
Service Integration	—		—
Data Integration			—
Management Integration		—	
Use Integration	—		
Assessment Result			

Firstly, it assesses the three internal integrations of *Process Integration, Development Integration* and *Service Integration*.

Secondly, it assesses the three external integrations of *Data Integration, Management Integration* and *Use Integration*. To assess *Data Integration*, factors in both process dimension and technology dimension have to be taken into account; and it is similar with *Management Integration* and *Use Integration*.

Finally, it accounts the assessment result to each dimensional capability maturity level, i.e., achieving the result of *Process Capability Maturity (PCM) Level* by accounting the three assessment scores of the internal *Process Integration* and the two relative external *Data Integration* and *Management Integration*; it is the same with the *Technology Capability Maturity (TCM) Level* and the *Human Capability Maturity (HCM) Level.*

From the viewpoint of model framework structures, Wang and Bryany observe the current assessment methods as three types [47]: (1) Checklist-based assessment, i.e., a software process assessment method that is based on a pass/fail checklist for each practice and process specified in a process model. The ISO 9001 model provides a checklist-based assessment method. (2) 1-D process-based assessment, i.e., a software process assessment method that determines a software development organization's capability from a set of processes in a single process dimension. CMM is an example of 1-D assessment models. (3) 2-D process-based assessment, i.e., a software process assessment method that employs both process and capability dimensions in a process model, and derives process capability by evaluating the process model against the capability model. ISO/IEC 15504 and SEPRM are examples of 2-D assessment models.

As the above discussions, the *TRISO-Model Qualitative Assessment* is a checklist-based assessment method; and the *TRISO-Model Quantitative Assessment* presents a new type of assessment method, i.e., a kind of "3-D" process-based assessment from the three dimensions of *process*, capability (*human* in TRISO-Model) and *technology*.

5.2 Improving 3D Integrated Software Development Processes

There are three key categories of philosophies underpinning software process improvement [47]: (1) Goal-oriented process improvement, i.e., a software process improvement approach by which process system capability is improved by moving towards a predefined goal, usually a specific process capability level. It is simple and the most widely adopted software engineering philosophy. ISO 9001 provides a pass/fail goal; CMM, ISO/IEC 15504, and SEPRM provide a 5/6-level capability goal. (2) Benchmark-based process improvement, i.e., a software process improvement approach by which process system capability is improved by moving towards an optimum combined profile according to software engineering process benchmarks, rather than a maximum capability level. It presents empirical indications of process attributes. This approach provides an organization with sufficient margins of competence in every process. (3) Continuous process improvement, i.e., a software process improvement approach by which process system capability is required to be improved all the time, and toward ever higher capability levels. Using this approach, software process improvement is a continuous, spiral-like procedure and there is no end to process optimization. It provides a basis for sustainable long-term strategic planning. The Deming Circle, plan-do-check-act, is a typical component of this philosophy.

Though there is a criticism that the goals for improvement are not explicitly stated in continuous process improvement philosophy and top management has to make clear the current goal, as well as the short, middle, and long-term ones, TRISO-Model is principally a continuous improvement approach with some staged goals or benchmarks to provide more precise assessment results.

There are three basic software process improvement methods [47]: (1) Assessment-based improvement, i.e., a software process improvement method in which a process system can be improved by basing its performance and capability profile on either a model-based or a standard-based assessment. Using this approach, the processes inherent in a software development organization are improved, according to a process system model with step-by-step suggestions like CMM, or a standardized process system model like ISO/IEC 15504. (2) Benchmark-based improvement, i.e., a software process improvement method in which a process system can be improved by basing its performance and capability profile on a benchmark-based assessment. Using this approach, the processes inherent in a software development organization are improved according to a set of process benchmarks. SEPRM is a benchmarked model, which provides an optimized and economical process improvement solution. (3) Integrated improvement, i.e., a combined model-based and benchmark-based software process improvement method in which a process system can be improved by basing its performance and capability profile on a integrated model-based and benchmark-based assessment. Using this approach, the processes inherent in a software development organization are improved according to a benchmarked process system model. SEPRM is designed to support integrated model- and benchmark-based process improvement, which inherits the advantages of both absolute and relative software process improvement methods.

TRISO-Model basically is a model-based process improvement methodology, but also it may introduce some benchmark-based improvement, and then to be an integrated improvement.

The conventional goal-based process assessment and improvement technologies have been widely accepted. However, its philosophy of "the higher the better" has been questioned in practice [24]. The determination of target capability levels for specific organization tends to be virtual, infeasible, and sometimes overshoot. Benchmark-based process assessment and improvement supports the philosophy of "the smaller the advantage, the better". CMMI continuous representation offers a flexible approach to process improvement [10]. An organization may choose to improve the performance of a single process-related trouble spot, or it can work on several areas that are closely aligned to the organization's business objectives; and to improve different processes at different rates.

TRISO-Model presents a new integrated improvement method. It adopts the philosophy of "the smaller the integrated goal, the better". The target capability maturity levels of given software development processes will be set relative to the next integrated goal, rather than to the virtually highest level as in a goal-based process assessment and improvement, or to the benchmarks of the software industry as in a benchmark-based process assessment and improvement.

For the given assessment result example (4, 3, 4) in section 5.1, it is a very good software organization if it focuses on international outsourcing. However, when it would like to evolve into a software product vendor, i.e., developing its own innovative technology or product, it has to improve its technology capability maturity firstly.

TRISO-Model is not only suitable for process improvement from process scope to project and organization scopes because it may provide precise measurement for every process at all the capability levels like ISO/IEC 15504 and SEPRM, but also very important for process improvement in technology scopes because it may provide advanced software technologies support to either software development processes for higher capability levels, or the project or organization's schedule/budget control.

As a simulation-based research up to now, also, more work is needed to mature the overall approach in order to make it a reliable, cheap, and easy-to-apply support tool for decision makers in software process improvement programmes, as Pfahl and Birk indicated in [48].

6 Conclusions and Future Work

TRISO-Model is developed to improve software development practices in the current complex and dynamic environment by describing and managing the elements contributing to project success in three interactive dimensions, i.e. SE Human, SE Process, SE Technology, and their integrations. With TRISO-Model, various aspects of projects, such as people, tools, and processes, can be modeled and managed systematically. The static semantics and the dynamic semantics of TRISO Model are specified by an extension of SPEM, *I-SPEM*; and by an extension of CSP, *CTM,* respectively. New techniques for the analysis of software development processes can be put forward based on the formalism.

In order to simulate and evaluate the modeling ability of TRISO-Model, we create a new process benchmark, *SPW-2006 Example*, by extending the ISPW-6 Example. Unlike the process-centered ISPW-6 Example, the *SPW-2006 Example* is not oriented to any specific single aspect of software development but it incorporates more aspects by adding more elements and interactions. It may be used to evaluate other software process models, and/or to evaluate software organizations, software projects and also software development processes, particularly 3-D integrated software development processes. The evaluation shows that the TRISO-Model approach is effective in modeling and managing different aspects and their complex interactions in today's software development.

With the *SPW-2006 Example* and its evolution for quantitative evaluation to 3-D integrated software development processes, we present two kinds of TRISO-Model based assessments: *TRISO-Model Qualitative Assessment* and *TRISO-Model Quantitative Assessment*. It enables a new integrated improvement method for software development processes.

The *TRISO-Model Qualitative Assessment* provides a checklist-based assessment method. It may be used to evaluate whether an assessed integrated software development process is well defined or not, based on the *SPW-2006 Example* benchmark. The *TRISO-Model Quantitative Assessment* provides a flexible software development process assessment method, based on the evaluation to integrated capability maturity levels of *process, technology* and *human*. It may be used in an integrated environment, as a continuous improvement approach with some staged goals or benchmarks to provide more precise assessment results.

Last, but not least, from the viewpoint of end-users (consumers) or investors (producers), software is always viewed as a true investment, not just a development activity, and therefore is evaluated in terms of the value created rather than only the functionality delivered. Thus, all the 3-D software development process assessment and improvement should be mapped into the return on investment (ROI) factor finally [49]. It is of course the next direction for further research.

Acknowledgements

The presentation was supported partly by the National Natural Science Foundation of China (Grant Number: 60573082). Also, I appreciate all the help offered by my colleagues (particularly to Qing Wang, Yongji Wang and Chen Zhao) and students (specially to Feng Yuan, Qiusong Yang, Jizhe Wang and Da Yang) in the Lab for Internet Software Technologies, Institute of Software at Chinese Academy of Sciences.

References

1. M.Li: Expanding the Horizons of Software Development Processes: A 3-D Integrated Methodology. In: Mingshu Li, Barry Boehm and Leon J. Osterweil (eds.), Unifying the Software Process Spectrum, Software Process Workshop (SPW2005; May 25-27, 2005). LNCS 3840, Springer-Verlag (2005) 54-67
2. A.Wise et al.: Using Little-JIL to Coordinate Agents in Software Engineering. In: Proc. of the Automated Software Engineering Conf. (2000) 155-163
3. N.Belkhatir et al.: Adele/Tempo: An Environment to Support Process Modeling and Enaction. In: A.Finkelstein et al., Software Process Modelling and Technology, John Wiley & Sons, Inc. (1994) 187-217
4. B.W.Boehm et al.: Software Cost Estimation with COCOMO II. Prentice-Hall (2000)
5. M.Ruhe, R.Jeffery and I.Wieczorek: Cost Estimation for Web Applications. In: Proc. of 25th Int. Conf. on Software Engineering (ICSE 25) (2003) 270-279
6. B.Boehm and A.Jain: An Initial Theory of Value-Based Software Engineering. In: A. Aurum et al.(eds.): Value-Based Software Engineering. Springer-Verlag (2005)
7. W.S.Humphrey: Introduction to the Personal Software Process. Addison-Wesley (1997)
8. B.Curtis et al.: People Capability Maturity Model. Addison-Wesley (2001)
9. D.Reifer: Ten Deadly Risks in Internet and Intranet Software Development. IEEE Software, March/April (2002) 12-14
10. M.B.Chrissis et al.: CMMI: Guidelines for Process Integration and Product Improvement. Addison-Wesley (2003)
11. B.Boehm and D.Port: Balancing Discipline and Flexibility with the Spiral Model and MBASE. Crosstalk, Vol.11(12) (2001) 23-28
12. J.Estublier: Software are Processes Too. In: Mingshu Li, Barry Boehm and Leon J. Osterweil (eds.), Unifying the Software Process Spectrum, Software Process Workshop (SPW2005; May 25-27, 2005). LNCS 3840, Springer-Verlag (2005) 25-34
13. H.D.Rombach: Integrated Software Process & Product Lines. In: Mingshu Li, Barry Boehm and Leon J. Osterweil (eds.), Unifying the Software Process Spectrum, Software Process Workshop (SPW2005; May 25-27, 2005). LNCS 3840, Springer-Verlag (2005) 83-90
14. L.J.Osterweil: Integrating Microprocess and Macroprocess Software Research. In: Mingshu Li, Barry Boehm and Leon J. Osterweil (eds.), Unifying the Software Process Spectrum, Software Process Workshop (SPW2005; May 25-27, 2005). LNCS 3840, Springer-Verlag (2005) 68-74
15. B.Warboys: Active Models: A Possible Approach to the Integration of Objective and Subjective Process Models. In: Mingshu Li, Barry Boehm and Leon J. Osterweil (eds.), Unifying the Software Process Spectrum, Software Process Workshop (SPW2005; May 25-27, 2005). LNCS 3840, Springer-Verlag (2005) 100-107
16. M.Ruiz et al.: A Dynamic Integrated Framework for Software Process Improvement. Software Quality Journal, 10 (2002) 181-194

17. M.I.Kellner, R.J.Madachy and D.M.Raffo: Software Process Simulation Modeling: Why? What? How? Journal of Systems and Software, 46 (2/3) (1999) 91-105
18. M.Ruiz et al.: Using Dynamic Modeling and Simulation to Improve the COTS Software Process. In: F.Bomarius and H.Iida (eds.), PROFES 2004. LNCS 3009, Springer-Verlag (2004) 568-581
19. P.Donzelli and G.Iazeolla: Hybrid Simulation Modeling of the Software Process. Journal of Systems and Software, 59 (2001) 227-235
20. R.H.Martin and D.Raffo: A Model of the Software Development Process Using both Continuous and Discrete Models. Software Process Improvement and Practice, 5 (2000) 147-157
21. H.Neu and U.Becker-Kornstaedt: Learning and Understanding a Software Process through Simulation of its Underlying Model. In: S.Henninger and F.Maurer (eds.), LSO 2002. LNCS 2640, Springer-Verlag (2002) 81-93
22. N.David et al.: Towards an Emergence-Driven Software Process for Agent-Based Simulation. In: J.S.Sichman et al. (eds.), MABS 2002. LNAI 2581, Springer-Verlag (2003) 89-104
23. S.E.Sim et al.: Using Benchmarking to Advance Research: A Challenge to Software Engineering. In Proc. of the 25th Int. Conf. on Software Engineering (2003) 74-83
24. Y.Wang and G.King: A New Approach to Benchmark-Based Process Improvement. In: Proc. of European Software Process Improvement 2000 (2000) 140-149
25. M.I.Kellner et al.: ISPW-6 Software Process Example. In Proc. of the First Int. Conf. on Software Process. IEEE Computer Society Press (1991) 176-186
26. D.Avrilionis et al.: OPSIS: A View Mechanism for Software Processes which Supports their Evolution and Reuse. In Proc. of the 18th Int. Conf. on Software Engineering (1996) 38-47
27. C.M.Lot and H.D.Rombach: A MVP-L1 Solution for the Software Process Modeling Problem. In Proc. of 6th Int. Software Process Workshop (ISPW 6) (1990)
28. G.Junkermann et al.: Merlin: Supporting Cooperation in Software Development through a Knowledge-based Environment. In Software Process Modelling and Technology. John Wiley & Sons, Inc. (1994) 103-127
29. N.Belkhatir, J. Estublier and W.L.Melo: Software Process Modeling in Adele: the ISPW-7 Example. In: Proc. of the 7th International Software Process Workshop (1991) 48 -50
30. F.P.Brooks: No Silver Bullet: Essence and Accidents of Software Engineering. Computer, Vol.20(4) (1987) 10-19
31. OMG: Software Process Engineering Metamodel Specification, Version 1.1 (formal/2005-01-06). (2005) (http://www.omg.org)
32. P.Kruchten: A Process Engineering MetaModel. (2001) (http://www.forsoft.de/zen/sdpp 02/papers/Kruc01.pdf)
33. C.Kobryn: UML 2001: A Standardization Odyssey. Communications of the ACM, 42(10) (1999) 29-37
34. OMG: MOF Core Specification, Version2.0 (ptc/2003-10-04). (2003) (http://www.omg. org)
35. C.A.R.Hoare: Communicating Sequential Processes. Prentice Hall International (1985)
36. R.M.Greenwood: Using CSP and System Dynamics as Process Engineering Tools. In Proc. of the 2nd European Workshop on Process Technology (Trondheim, Norway, Sept. 7-8, 1992). Springer-Verlag (1992) 138-145
37. K.Yasumoto et al.: Software Process Description Using LOTOS and its Enaction. In Proc. of the 16th Int. Conf. on Software Engineering (1994) 169-178
38. A.W.Roscoe: The Theory and Practice of Concurrency. Prentice-Hall Pearson (2005)

39. S.Fogle et al.: The Benchmarking Process: One Team's Experience. IEEE Software, Septeber/October (2001) 40-47
40. D.Card and D.Zubrow: Benchmarking Software Organizations. IEEE Software, Septeber/October (2001) 16-18
41. CMU SEI: The Capability Maturity Model Guidelines for Improving the Software Process. Addison-Wesley, Pearson Education (1994)
42. International Standard: ISO 9001 Quality Management System – Requirements (2000)
43. V.Chiew and Y.Wang: Software Engineering Process Benchmarking. In: M.Oivo and S.Komi-Sirvio (eds.), PROFES 2002. LNCS 2559, Springer-Verlag (2002) 519-531
44. Q.Wang and M.Li: Measuring and Improving Software Process in China. In: Proc. of 2005 International Symposium on Empirical Software Engineering (ISESE) (2005) 183-192
45. E.Gray et al.: An Incremental Approach to Software Process Assessment and Improvement. Software Quality Journal, 13 (2005) 7-16
46. International Standard: ISO/IEC 15504 - 1-9, Software Process Assessment – Parts 1-9 (2000)
47. Y.Wang and A.Bryany: Process-Based Software Engineering: Building the Infrastructures. Annals of Software Engineering, 14 (2002) 9-37
48. D.Pfahl and A.Birk, Using Simulation to Visualise and Analyse Product-Process Dependencies in Software Development Projects. In: F.Bomarius and M.Oivo (eds.), PROFES 2000. LNCS 1840, Springer-Verlag (2000) 88-102
49. K.E.Emam: The ROI from Software Quality. Auerbach Publications, Taylors & Francis Group (2005)

Ubiquitous Process Engineering: Applying Software Process Technology to Other Domains

Leon J. Osterweil

Laboratory for Advanced Software Engineering Research,
Department of Computer Science, University of Massachusetts, Amherst MA 01003 USA
ljo@cs.umass.edu

Abstract. Software engineering has learned a great deal about how to create clear and precise process definitions, and how to use them to improve final software products. This paper suggests that this knowledge can also be applied to good effect in many other domains where effective application of process technology can lead to superior products and outcomes. The paper offers medical practice and government as two examples of such domains, and indicates how process technology, first developed for application to software development, is being applied with notable success in those areas of endeavor. The paper also notes that some characteristics of these domains are highlighting ways in which current process technology seems to be inadequate, thereby suggesting ways in which this research is adding to the agenda for research in software process.

1 Introduction

In earlier papers we have argued that the processes that are used to develop software should themselves be viewed as software [1, 2]. We have suggested that software processes should themselves be developed by means of careful processes, starting with requirements specification, proceeding through architecture and design, and then defined precisely with languages that have execution semantics. We have argued that the execution of such *process programs* can effect the superior coordination of agents, both human and automated [1]. In more recent work we have also demonstrated that there can be considerable value in taking such executable processes as the subjects of dynamic analyses such as simulation runs [3] and as the subjects of static defect analyses [4, 5], [6]. Our view is that these analyses are essential components in continuous process improvement loops that 1) baseline existing processes, 2) use analysis to identify defects and shortcomings in these processes, 3) propose improvements to the processes, 4) use analysis to verify the value of the proposed improvements, and 5) deploy the improved processes, thereby creating the basis for the next improvement iteration. The ultimate goal of all of this is the establishment of a discipline of software process engineering in which the continuous enhancement of processes leads to increasing quality in final products, and increasing efficiency in producing them. In a previous paper [7] we have argued that more precise and comprehensive process definitions are more effective bases for the kinds of definitive analyses that lead more efficiently to successful improvement efforts. We referred to research aimed at such more precise and definitive languages and analyses as *microprocess* research.

Q. Wang et al. (Eds.): SPW/ProSim 2006, LNCS 3966, pp. 39–47, 2006.

Concurrently with these increasing understandings of the possible mechanics of continuous software process improvement, and the particular value of microprocess research, has come the realization that software development is only one of a multitude of diverse domains in which the continuous improvement of processes can lead to important benefits. We observe that processes are found universally in our society, and indeed that there are many domains in which the role of processes is at least as central as is the case in software engineering. Most of the work of government, for example, is essentially the creation and execution of processes. Likewise, medical care is centered importantly upon the devising and careful execution of processes. Processes are also at the core of such other domains as business, engineering, finance, dispute resolution, and law. Many other example domains can be identified quite readily. This observation immediately suggests, therefore, that the software process technologies that our community has developed have much to offer these other disciplines. Significantly, our preliminary investigations of these other areas has suggested that the notions of process in those domains are far less well developed than they are in software engineering, and that the rigor that we increasingly employ to good effect in software process engineering is lacking in process approaches in these other areas. Thus our current view is that these other domains have much to gain from the application of technologies that we have developed in software process engineering.

This paper explores that premise, indicating the sorts of process issues that we have encountered in other problem domains, and the ways in which we are finding software process technology to be relevant and effective. We also note that certain shortcomings of our process technologies have been highlighted in attempting to apply them in these other domains, suggesting areas for further research.

2   Goals and Motivations for Process Research

To understand the relevance of software process technology to other domains, it helps to note that the goals of all of these communities have quite a lot in common. In software process research, there is a very wide range of specific technologies and approaches, but the main goals are far smaller in number. These goals, some of which are elaborated upon briefly below, are generally shared by many other domains, as shall be indicated. This suggests that technologies that have been successfully applied in our domain of software development, should have relevance in the others. Here are some of the key goals of process technology.

Team Coordination. Much of the most difficult and challenging work in virtually all sectors of society requires synergistic collaboration among many diverse contributors. In software development, a product requires careful coordination among designers, coders, testers, managers, documentation specialists, and clerical personnel. In government, such activities as licensing, running elections, and legislation itself, require a similar sort of collaboration among bureaucrats, citizen volunteers, boards, panels, and elected officials. In both domains, a clear and precise specification of the processes to be carried out can improve the chances that all members of the team have the same view of what they should be doing, and how they are to interact with each other.

Efficiency Improvement. An immediate corollary of the previous goal is that improved understanding of the ways in which teams should coordinate their efforts facilitates the identification of bottlenecks and other obstacles to improved team efficiency. In emergency room medical care this is a particularly serious problem, as delays are pervasive, and can cause pain and loss of life. Identification of bottlenecks and inefficiencies, based upon a clear specification of how agents must coordinate their efforts can be used to identify where process changes, or resource reallocations can speed processing, and increase productivity.

Automated Support. Carrying the previous point further, we note that the performers in such processes need not always be humans. In software development, compilers, design tools, test automation tools, etc. can play useful roles. In medicine, medication dispensers, infusion pumps, medical records databases, and patient monitoring devices play similar roles. In both cases, an executable process definition can be used to delineate the exact roles of such automated devices, and to provide APIs and other interfaces that enable such automation aids to be coordinated with human activities. The executable process can then be used as an integration structure for the insertion (and incremental growth) of automation.

Education and Training. Process technology can be particularly useful in supporting the training and education of the humans who will participate in processes. Most large software organizations require that newcomers acquire indoctrination in the methods that their new organizations use to build software. In a similar way, commercial enterprises, such as banks and manufacturers also require such training to assure that new employees can become proficient at their jobs more rapidly. Process simulation technologies are an example of an approach that can provide strong support in this area.

Continuous Improvement. Highly visible activities such as the CMM [8], CMMI, and ISO 9000 [9] projects have emphasized the key role of process in effecting continuous improvement in software development. Other areas, such as manufacturing, have made similar observations. Indeed the use of such institutions as quality circles has resulted in impressive gains in quality and productivity in industry. In both cases, strong understandings of the current process, precise understandings of proposed improvements, and effective devices for measuring results are some keys to success in process improvement. A particularly key aspect of such improvement efforts seems to be effective analysis of both the current, and the proposed new, processes. Analysis that identifies defects is needed to trigger improvement, and analysis aimed at demonstrating that new processes actually achieve desired improvements (without creating new problems) is needed to carry the improvement processes further.

Reinvention. It has been suggested that, while steady incremental improvement is useful in software development, there must also be a place periodically for radical change, or reinvention. This is certainly also true in such areas as dispute resolution, where face-to-face negotiation is increasingly giving way to computer-mediated Online Dispute Resolution (ODR). In both domains, radical change can happen only after a firm understanding of the essentials of processes can be distilled. Such deep understandings are facilitated by the use of powerful formalisms, employing appropriate abstractions to suppress superficial detail and accentuate deeper conceptual issues. Thus, pursuit of formal process abstractions is useful in helping various domains seek and achieve radical change.

The foregoing has convinced us that the overarching goals that software process research seeks to address with its technologies are goals that are shared by medicine, government, business, and a wide range of other human endeavors. Thus we embarked upon a program of research aimed at determining the extent to which this is correct, attempting to apply software process technologies to specific problems in these other domains. In the following sections, we indicate how technologies originally developed for software process are now being employed in other domains where processes are also of central importance. In some of these domains, as had once been the case in software development, the centrality of process issues had been largely overlooked. But, with growing recognition of the centrality of process issues, the potential for important and fundamental contributions of process technology is growing rapidly.

3 Medical Safety

A highly influential report from the US Institute of Medicine [10] estimated that each year at least 97,000 people die from preventable medical errors in US hospitals. Far more suffer pain and non-lethal damage from such errors. The costs in money are far harder to estimate, but must be measured at least in hundreds of billions of US dollars each year. While there are many causes of the problems leading to these deplorable statistics, it seems clear that one of the most central is lack of control of the processes that are used to deliver medical care. A team consisting of University of Massachusetts software engineering researchers, and faculty from the School of Nursing, is working with administrators and workers at Baystate Medical Center in Springfield, Massachusetts, USA, to investigate ways in which process definition and analysis technologies might be effective in addressing medical care improvement goals. Our research team has identified three specific process areas as candidates for the application of process technology. In each area the goals are strikingly similar to software process goals, and the applicability of software process technology is proving to be correspondingly appropriate.

Emergency Room Operations. The Baystate Emergency Division is like most other Emergency Divisions in that patients must endure very long delays, and often simply leave without receiving care at all. We are investigating the use of process definition and simulation to determine how they might be used to improve efficiency in emergency room operations. Clearly scarcity of such resources as beds and physicians contribute to waiting. But process inefficiencies seem to exacerbate this situation. We are using process simulations to explore how different resources mixes (eg. providing additional doctors and/or nurses) can be expected to reduce waiting times and increase overall capacity to provide services, especially in response to disasters. We are also using these definitions and simulations to support the exploration of radical change in the operation of the Emergency Division. Languages and simulators originally intended for supporting software process studies are proving to be very appropriate and effective in this work, facilitating consideration not only of resource reallocation schemes, but also reinvention of the entire range of Emergency Division operations.

This research is, however, underscoring the difficulties in developing accurate definitions of highly concurrent processes. Emergency medical care is characterized by the need for promptness in acute medical situations, and the need for resources to be assigned to multiple tasks concurrently. These, and similar, reasons dictate that standard medical care procedures may need to be quite flexible, and yet must sill conform to some very basic procedural requirements. Our attempts to use software process definition languages to represent these processes are sharpening our understanding of the shortcomings of such languages in areas such as concurrency specification.

Chemotherapy Administration. We are investigating the use of precise process definition and analysis technologies to improve team coordination in chemotherapy administration, and to remove defects from the processes that those teams execute. A major focus of this work is the use of process definition and analysis techniques to identify process defects, and to incorporate continuous process improvement into the operations of the Chemotherapy Division of the Cancer Center. Chemotherapy is the process of using extremely powerful and dangerous drugs to destroy cancer cells, without causing undue harm to other cells in the body. Chemotherapy requires extremely careful measurements of the human body, and the very carefully monitored infusion of drugs over extended periods of time. The reaction of the patient's body to this regime must be monitored closely by diverse agents, and from different perspectives. Negative reactions must be noted and responded to appropriately, and interactions with other drugs that might be used to deal with other medical situations, must be continuously considered and adjusted for.

The processes for doing all of the above are complex, and require coordination among various doctors, nurses, pharmacists, clerical personnel, and the patient. One of the particularly noteworthy features of such processes is that they incorporate considerable amounts of redundancy, aimed at the prompt detection of errors and prevention of harm to the patient. Precise definition and analysis of these processes has helped the Chemotherapy Division to identify ways in which team coordination can be improved, and process defects can be detected. All of this has led to an understanding of how continuous process improvement can lead to overall benefits. One specific example is that our rigorous analysis of these processes has led to the identification of paths through the processes where some redundancy checking can potentially be bypassed, and other paths that seem to cause excessive amounts of redundancy checking.

Blood Transfusion. We are also investigating the use of process definition to improve the education and training of nurses in such processes as blood transfusion, and the use of process monitoring and analysis to reduce the incidence of such catastrophic errors as the infusion of incorrect blood types into patients. The goals here are improved team coordination, facilitation of training, detection and removal of defects, and continuous improvement. As in the cases of the other medical process projects, we are finding that much of our process technology is highly applicable. In particular, we have applied fault tree analysis to suggest such vulnerabilities as single points of failure in existing processes [11], suggesting ways and places were redundancy should be added.

4 Digital Government

The application of software process technology to the domain of government seems
no less appropriate, and our work is demonstrating that it should be quite effective
here as well. In this domain, such familiar goals of teamwork improvement, efficiency enhancement, defect removal, reinvention, and automation are also of great
importance.

License Renewal. In earlier work [12] we have demonstrated that precise process
definition can provide important benefits in the domain of license renewal. The US
state of Massachusetts, like most governmental units worldwide, is responsible for the
issuance of literally hundreds of different kinds of licenses. The processes for doing
this are more complex than is generally understood, typically involving the receipt of
a renewal request, the search of various records and archives (eg. for the existence of
complaints), the receipt of funds, and the issuance of the actual licensing materials.
All of these activities must take into account the possibility of various kinds of excep-
tional situations. We have applied precise process definition and analysis technologies to this problem area and have identified places where process details were lacking, places where increased redundancy was desirable, and ways in which computer
automation could be inserted, leading to transition strategies for digital (electronic)
government.

Election Processes. We note that elections are highly complex processes, starting
with voter registration activities, and continuing on through the conduct of actual
elections, the accumulation of results, and the need to administer recounts and various
dispute resolutions. Much attention in the US has been focused on elections since the
contentious 2000 Presidential election. Most of this attention has been directed to the
possibility of incorporation of electronic vote recording devices into election processes. While analysis of the soundness of these devices is clearly important, our own
work emphasizes the importance of assuring the soundness of the election processes
themselves, and the appropriate integration of electronic voting devices into these
overall processes [5]. We note that elections require the coordination of a wide range
of humans, as well as automated devices. We are starting to study these processes,
emphasizing the identification of defects, searching for appropriate levels of redundancy, appropriate use of electronic voting devices, and the vulnerability of election
processes to frauds and collusions. In this latter work, we have used our process definition technologies to represent the behaviors of fraudulent and collusive election
agents, as well as the election processes themselves. Early results of this research are
contained in a paper in these proceedings [5].

Labor-Management Dispute Resolution. We have also explored the application of
process technology to the domain of dispute resolution through a project involving
collaboration with the US National Mediation Board (NMB). While it may initially
seem that dispute resolution is an area in which rigorous process definition would be
unlikely to be effective, our initial research has indicated that this is not the case. As
with many other process domains, dispute resolution requires a great deal of human
ingenuity and initiative, but also a great deal of discipline and structure. The NMB
has long since recognized this and has over the years developed some structured

approaches to bringing disputants together in productive negotiation sessions. We have applied our rigorous process definition technologies to define these processes. In doing so, it has been easier to identify ways in which technology can support these processes [13].

In addition, our work with NMB has suggested the possibility of radical change to negotiation processes. For many years, NMB negotiations were carried out primarily in face-to-face sessions. But with the growth in the number of disputes to be resolved, and the increased availability of computer and communications technologies, NMB has become increasingly interested in augmenting or replacing face-to-face negotiation session with Online Dispute Resolution (ODR) approaches. In doing so, it has become increasingly clear that ODR requires more radical change to existing processes than simple replacement of some existing process steps with automation. Our process definitions have become the basis for the radical change to ODR that NMB needs to undertake.

The NMB project has also suggested another important goal for process technology, namely the involvement of broader stakeholder groups in the specification of requirements for processes, and indeed for the automated systems imbedded in them. NMB has noted that the acceptance of the agreements reached in dispute resolution is strongly enhanced when the parties to the dispute have had an active and effective role in designing the dispute resolution processes, and in monitoring that the processes have indeed been followed. The use of a clear, yet complete and precise, formalism for defining NMB's dispute resolution processes is being explored as just such a vehicle for developing processes that are sufficiently transparent that disputants will be more receptive to acceptance of dispute resolution outcomes [14]. We are currently engaged in work aimed at involving disputants in definition of ODR processes that will be used in resolving their disputes. Our technologies will also be used as the basis for displaying the progress through these processes to assure disputants that the agreed upon processes are indeed being followed.

5 Additional Domains

As noted above, many other domains seem equally appropriate for the application of process technology. Our own research has applied these technologies to the definition of processes that should be used in creating scientific datasets that are suitable for use by researchers other than those who have created these datasets [15]. Our work has indicated that many such datasets contain data that has undergone considerable complex transformation and analysis before being published. Scientists using these datasets for their own work are well advised to be aware of the various transformations that have been applied to this data, but generally documentation of such transformations is unavailable. Early work aimed at providing that documentation has indicated that the level of precision needed in order to assure safe reuse of these datasets require the use of process definition languages that employ strong semantic power. These process technology approaches resemble in striking ways approaches previously developed and applied in software process, especially as used in configuration management.

The application of process technologies to such other domains as manufacturing, banking, management, law, and military operations seems quite promising, and indeed has been begun in some cases. Software process researchers would do well to consider the benefits derived from applying the technologies in their grasp at present to these new domains.

As noted above, these domains will benefit from such work, but consideration of the applicability of these technologies will also lead to understanding of ways in which the technologies could benefit from extensions in directions indicated by the demands of these new application domains. We have already noted that defining processes in medicine has suggested the need for stronger language features for defining concurrency. Other process language and analysis shortcomings, such as the need for superior process abstractions, the importance of clearer artifact flow definition, and the need for improved support for specification of process properties, all have been underscored by this research, suggesting new roadmaps for software process technology research.

Acknowledgments

The author wishes to express his gratitude to numerous individuals who have participated in this research, and clarified the points made in this paper. Sandy Wise, a key architect of the Little-JIL process definition language, has supported every aspect of this work. My co-investigators, Lori A. Clarke, George Avrunin, and Beth Henneman have been key leaders of the work on Medical Safety. Special thanks go to Phil Henneman and Fidela Blank for support of the Emergency Division research, and Wilson Mertens and Lucy Cassels for their strong support of our Chemotherapy process research. My co-investigators, Ethan Katsh, Dan Rainey, and Norm Sondheimer have been key leaders in the Digital Government work. Many students have also supported this work. Special thanks go to Mohammed S. Raunak, Dave Miller, Irina Ros, Rachel Smith, Matt Goetz, Bin Chen, Matt Marzilli, Natalie Podrazik, and Dan Gyllstrom.

This material is based upon work supported by the US National Science Foundation under Award Nos. CCR-0427071, CCR-0204321 and CCR-0205575. The views and conclusions contained herein are those of the author and should not be interpreted as necessarily representing the official policies or endorsements, either expressed or implied, of The National Science Foundation, or the U.S. Government.

References

1. L. J. Osterweil, "Software Processes Are Software, Too, Revisited," presented at 19th International Conference on Software Engineering, Boston, MA, 1997.
2. J. Osterweil, "Software Processes are Software, Too," presented at Ninth International Conference on Software Engineering, Monterey, CA, 1987.
3. B. Chen, G. S. Avrunin, L. A. Clarke, and L. J. Osterweil, "Automatic Fault Tree Derivation from Little-JIL Process Definitions," Department of Computer Science, University of Massachusetts, Amherst UM-CS-2006-01, January 2006 2006.

4. M. S. Raunak and L. J. Osterweil, "Process Definition Language Support for Rapid Simulation Prototyping," presented at Proceedings of the Software Process Workshop, Beijing, China, 2005.

5. M. S. Raunak, B. Chen, A. Elssamadisy, L. A. Clarke, and L. J. Osterweil, "Definition and Analysis of Election Processes," University of Massachusetts, Amherst, Technical Report 2006-19, March 12, 2006 2006.

6. L. A. Clarke, Y. Chen, G. S. Avrunin, B. Chen, R. Cobleigh, K. Frederick, E. A. Henneman, and L. J. Osterweil, "Process Programming to Support Medical Safety: A Case Study on Blood Transfusion," presented at Proceedings of the Software Process Workshop, Beijing, China, 2005.

7. L. Osterweil, "Unifying Microprocess and Macroprocess Research," presented at Proceedings of the Software Process Workshop (SPW2005), Beijing, China, 2005.

8. W. S. Humphrey, "A Discipline for Software Engineering," in SEI Series in Software Engineering. Reading, MA: Addison-Wesley, 1995.

9. R. S. Pressman, Software Engineering - A Practitioner's Approach, Fifth ed. New York: McGraw-Hill, 2001.

10. L. T. Kohn, J. M. Corrigan, and M. S. Donaldson, "To Err is Human: Building a Safer Health System." Washington DC: National Academy Press, 1999.

11. B. Chen, G. S. Avrunin, L. A. Clarke, and L. J. Osterweil, "Automatic Fault Tree Derivation from Little-JIL Process Definitions," University of Massachusetts, Computer Science Department, Shanghai, China, Technical Report 2006-01, January 6, 2006 2006.

12. N. K. Sondheimer, L. J. Osterweil, C. Schweik, M. Billmers, D. Canavan, A. Kelly, C. Lee-Davis, C. Li, and J. Sieh, "Online License Renewal Analysis: Process Modeling and State Practice," Electronic Enterprise Institute and the Center for Public Policy and Administration, University of Massachusetts, Amherst May 7, 2002 2002.

13. E. Katsh, L. Osterweil, and N. K. Sondheimer, "Process Technology for Achieving Government Online Dispute Resolution," presented at National Conference on Digital Government Research, Seattle, WA, 2004.

14. L. J. Osterweil, N. K. Sondheimer, L. A. Clarke, E. Katsh, and D. Rainey, "Using Process Definitions to Facilitate the Specifications of Requirements," University of Massachusetts, Amherst, Technical Report UM-CS-2006-11, March 11, 2006 2006.

15. A. M. Ellison, L. J. Osterweil, J. L. Hadley, A. Wise, E. Boose, L. A. Clarke, D. Foster, A. Hanson, D. Jensen, P. Kuzeja, E. Riseman, and H. Schultz, "An Analytic Web to Support the Analysis and Synthesis of Ecological Data," submitted to Ecology/Ecological Monographs, 2004.

Dependencies Between Data Decisions

Frank G. Goethals, Wilfried Lemahieu, Monique Snoeck, and Jacques Vandenbulcke

F.E.T.E.W. – K.U.Leuven – Naamsestraat 69, B-3000 Leuven, Belgium
SAP-leerstoel Extended Enterprise Infrastructures
{Frank.Goethals, Wilfried.Lemahieu, Monique.Snoeck,
Jacques.Vandenbulcke}@econ.kuleuven.be

Abstract. In this paper we show that storing and transmitting data is a complex practice, especially in an inter-organizational setting. We found 18 data aspects on which heavy consideration and coordination is important during a software process. We present these data aspects and point out that these data aspects are dealt with at different levels within Extended Enterprises. A good software process embraces the idea that choices have to be made on these 18 data aspects, and it recognizes the dependencies between the aspects, and the dependencies between decisions made at different levels in the enterprise.

1 Introduction

Setting up an enterprise is a very complex matter. We distinguish between two views on an enterprise: *tasks* that change the state of an enterprise, and *data* that maintain the state of an enterprise (see Simon [1] and Hirscheim [2]). In this paper we draw attention to the data-side of the enterprise. The complexity of this side follows from the fact that many data-related decisions have to be made (18 'data aspects' are presented in this paper), and that many dependencies exist among these decisions. Decisions on these aspects should thus be aligned. This is, however, not the only complicating factor: the decisions reoccur along three dimensions (see Figure 1).

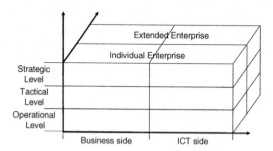

Fig. 1. Three dimensions along which the decisions re-occur (as discussed in [3])

First, decisions are made at the business-side and at the ICT-side of an enterprise. Secondly, decisions are made at strategic level (general principles and the like), operational level (decisions for a specific project), and tactical level (decisions valid

Q. Wang et al. (Eds.): SPW/ProSim 2006, LNCS 3966, pp. 48–55, 2006.
© Springer-Verlag Berlin Heidelberg 2006

for all projects). Thirdly, we need to acknowledge that companies nowadays integrate their systems with those of other companies. Data exchanges within so-called Extended Enterprises (EEs, i.e., *collections* of partnering companies [4]) are even more difficult to realize than internal data exchanges. Therefore, a third dimension in the picture shows decisions are made at the level of an individual enterprise and at the level of the collection of collaborating enterprises.

The decisions made in the boxes of this figure should be aligned. Every software development process should therefore recognize 1) the dependencies across different boxes, and 2) the dependencies among the decisions made within each single box. That is, decisions makers are *dependent* upon each other. Therefore, coordination is needed. Importantly, this is not only true when entirely proprietary software is used, but also in the case of (1) proprietary software using standards, or (2) Commercial Off-the-Shelf (COTS) software. (1) Standards are *the* coordination instrument in a Business-to-Business setting. However, standards hardly deal with all 18 aspects in all boxes of Figure 1, let alone that they would deal with the links between the different boxes. (2) While COTS software packages may deal with all 18 aspects at operational level at the ICT-side; a fit is still needed with decisions on the 18 aspects made in other boxes as well.

There are thus a big number of dependencies that need to be managed during the software process. We note that this 'dependency-view' is – at least theoretically – also acknowledged in the Enterprise Architecture way of working. However, in practice, the attention there often goes entirely to the architectural descriptions rather than to the *usage* of these descriptions to manage dependencies. The dependency-driven way of working suggested here is to be imbedded in an Enterprise Architecture-driven one. By doing that, it is acknowledged that architectural descriptions should be 'Enterprise'-wide in the broadest sense of the word: the descriptions are meant to manage dependencies across projects, across business- and ICT people, and across the individual enterprises that form an Extended Enterprise.

In what follows, we first discuss the link between Enterprise Architecture and dependencies in some more detail. Then we present the 18 data aspects and we illustrate why coordination on these 18 aspects is important by showing the (sometimes infinite) range of possible values. Finally, it is acknowledged that making decisions on all 18 aspects at once is unrealistic, and that 'decision-components' need to be made that are placed in some sequence to get a process.

2   Enterprise Architecture and Dependencies

Cook [5] states that architectural descriptions work like standards: they restrict people in choices they can make. Standards function as a coordination instrument (see Mintzberg, [6]). One key question is then 'what needs to be coordinated?', or stated differently: 'what dependencies need to be managed?' (see Malone and Crowston's definition of coordination [7]). We expected to find an answer to this question by assessing important Enterprise Architecture (EA)-frameworks, and the models they suggest to create (see e.g. [8, 9, 10, 11, 12, 13, 14]). Unfortunately, the answers we found were disappointing. The suggested models do not seem to be based on a thorough investigation of the dependencies that exist, and are as such far from complete.

The renowned Zachman-framework for example [8] is said to be comprehensive. We argue it is not. While other critique could be added, here we restrict ourselves to one line of thought. As we stated, there are basically two views on an Enterprise: *tasks* that change the state of an enterprise, and *data* that maintain the state of an enterprise. In Zachman's framework a 'data' model is something like an ER-diagram. For one thing, this neglects the fact that data is often not present in structured form, and often not even made explicit (i.e., implicit/tacit knowledge). More importantly, this neglects the fact that data *is not just there*: data is made by a system in a location at some moment and has to be transmitted using some medium at some moment to another location for use by another system and this has to happen in a timely, secure, ... fashion. Data dependencies do thus range much further than just knowing which data exists in which database so it can be reused in other projects. We note that such dependencies become particularly visible in an EE setting where different companies are dependent upon each other with respect to the decisions made on data aspects.

EA-frameworks do thus not seem to give a good overview of the dependencies they should manage. Unfortunately, classic dependency-theory [15, 16, 17, 18, 19, 20, 21, 22] seems to be scarcely out of the egg as well. The main focus of such theories is that one resource put out by one task is needed as an input for another task, and that a number of dependencies between tasks can therefore be suggested. Unfortunately, similarly as what we mentioned for Zachman's framework, classic dependency-theory only looks at *what* data is needed for (or created by) what task. It does not assess when data should be transported using what means to what location, etc.

Having a complete image of choices that need to be made and respected, and links between those choices is important not only to realize an effective system, but also to confront enterprise architects with the wide range of options they actually have. Companies who try to get competitive advantages have to be creative. Creativity should show in creative enterprise architectures, rather than in creative programming. While programmers know the building blocks to play with and are creative in using them, enterprise architects have a hard time to oversee their building blocks and thus to use them creatively. If one truly manages the building blocks, one will see that the building blocks can be arranged differently for different companies the company is doing business with. For example, imagine the case of a supplier with relatively expensive high-quality products, and who is assessing the 'data format' (see below) to be used. A long-term partner may get the price list in an xml format so it can easily be entered into his system. Other companies may get a nice graphical brochure with the prices. The latter 1) makes it harder for them to automatically compare prices across companies and 2) immediately shows them other information on the product: contents on which the supplier wants to compete.

In order to get a more complete image of the dependencies that do exist at the data side, we decided to study literature on diverse Business-to-Business integration (B2Bi) standards and B2Bi case studies. From this, we derived 18 data aspects that need to be dealt with. As such, these aspects can be seen as an extension to Enterprise Architecture frameworks, and to dependency-theory. The aspects are presented in the following paragraph.

3   The 18 Data Aspects

Space limitations make it impossible to deal with the aspects in detail. The first three aspects will be discussed in some more detail, to show the relevance of the three dimensions shown in Figure 1. We primarily point at issues that are interesting in a B2B situation.

1. Data content. Companies of course have to determine the content they want to share. While this may seem straightforward, it is not. For example, data content alignment is needed between different companies at a high level and at a low level. Alignment at a high level is for instance illustrated by Hansen, Nohria and Tierney [23]. They talk about two strategies for content management within companies. One strategy is to make information on the business itself explicit (to 'codify' information) so that it can be reused. Another strategy (the 'personalization' strategy) is to make information explicit about who knows what. They found that the content management strategies have to fit the business proposition of the companies. For example, companies like McKinsey and Bain primarily use the personalization strategy because they are strategy consulting firms. They are expected not to deal with standard solutions for standard problems, and thus not to store standard solutions. The market expects such practices, however, from Ernst & Young for example, which deals with the same problems over and over again. Once companies know what *type* of information they need to share, they can investigate what concrete information is needed (i.e. low-level alignment). Please note that in an Extended Enterprise setting, a collection of companies may want to appear to the outside world as one entity, and that the content they share with the outside world should reflect this. Also, in an Extended Enterprise it may be possible to create new content. For example, if an airline company, a car rental company and a hotel chain together offer trips they generally only have information on their own sales. By keeping the information together at the level of the collection of collaborating companies, data is available on how many customers booked an airplane seat as well as a hotel and a car. This data may then be linked to data on (individual/grouped) marketing campaigns and the like to do data mining.

2. Data format. Data has to be transmitted in some format. This first involves choosing between textual format or graphical format for example. If a textual format is chosen, it has to be decided whether a proprietary format or a standard format will be used. If a standard format is to be used, a concrete standard has to be chosen. For example, UBL, CBL, and cXML all offer standardized business documents. UBL (Universal Business Language) for example defines seven documents such as 'order', and 'invoice', and gives accompanying XML-schema definitions. Interestingly, specifications exist for automatically rendering a classic visual of the content of the XML documents, for example as a .pdf document, meant for human usage. This visual can serve as a boundary object between the business people of the different companies, while the XML files serve as a boundary object between their computer systems.

3. Roles. Different systems play different roles in a data exchange. In our research we have identified seven primitive roles. The Needy wants to process some data. The Needy may differ from the Initiation Event Originator. The latter is a node where an event originates (e.g., a 'request') that initiates the message transmission towards the

Needy. An Initiation Event Emitter (e.g., a 'requestor') is a party that transmits such an initiation event. This event can be sensed by an Initiation Event Sensor (e.g., an intermediary that groups requests from many parties). This party receives an initiation event from outside. The data that is needed by the Needy originates at the node of the Response Data Originator (e.g., the creator of a requested price list). A party that sends the data towards the Needy is called a Response Sender. A party that receives the data is called a Response Receiver. The roles are illustrated in the figure below.

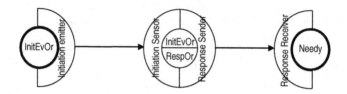

Fig. 2. The seven basic roles in an end-to-end transmission

In practice, one system may play several roles and one role may be played by several systems (and e.g., only vis-à-vis specific other systems). Roles may be discussed at the level of entire enterprises, departments within enterprises, specific people or computer systems within departments, etc.

4. Data distribution. Data may only be stored in one location, or in several locations. For example, in the health care industry the idea has arisen to share information on patients among authorized institutions if a patient enters one of these organizations for help. Because so many different institutions may have information on the patient, an institution needing information would need to contact all other institutions. Therefore, a central point has been entered in the network (an additional Provider role) where a Needy can request information. In the Netherlands, the central point itself does not have a copy of the patient's data. However, it has information on where information on some patient can be found. In the English set-up, however, the central point *does* contain information on the patients.

5. Exact physical system location. For each system that is involved, a specific physical location has to be determined. Data may for example be replicated on the premises of a close partner, or on the premises of a trusted third party. Also, it may all be stored together ('centrally'), it may be stored close to users, in a big city or not, etc.

6. Storage medium. Two angles can be considered per the storage medium: 1) the availability, reliability, capacity, security, transportability etc. of the medium, and 2) distinguishing between ICT-systems (ranging from Database-systems to CD-Roms and USB-keys), people (with knowledge in their minds), paper, etc.

7. Transmission network. Which nodes will be connected directly? For example, one could connect every node to every other node or connect every node only to one other node, or connect all nodes to a central node.

8. Transmission area. Through which geographical areas will connections pass? One may have to pay attention to 'hostile territories'.

9. Transmission medium. As for the storage medium, two viewpoints can be taken: 1) availability, reliability, capacity, security, etc. of the medium, and 2) distinguishing between specific media such as telephone, Internet, postal mail, etc. As an illustration, note that business people and ICT people may have a different perception of the medium (e.g., Internet telephony).

10. System availability. A data transmission can only happen during the 'operational time' of nodes and connections and if capacity is available.

11. Initiation events. Different (combinations of) events can initiate and inhibit a message transmission.

12. Initiator party. Initiating events may originate in different nodes. For instance, the sending-system (Response Sender) may initiate transmissions itself (e.g., when sending purchase orders), or initiations may happen by a Needy-system.

13. Immediately or postponed. A transmission may (have to) be started immediately or the transmission may be postponed for some time (e.g., because messages are not permanently being processed within the node).

14. Transmission relationships. Messages may be related to each other in different ways. In short, it has to be assessed whether a message sent to one system can/cannot/has to be sent to another system as well at the same moment or at a later moment (i.e., simultaneous start or arrival or not). Also, it should be investigated whether the transmission of message A can/cannot/has to be accompanied or followed by the transmission of a message B. In classic database systems development cardinalities get much attention. In a B2B context, putting cardinality requirements upon data transmissions rather than on the data itself seems more realistic. For example, if a supplier *receives* an order, this order has to be *forwarded* to his supplier (not knowing whether he will store the data persistently or not).

15. Unit/Batch. Data can be transmitted in units or in batches. We note this distinction is different from the one between sending data immediately and postponing transmissions (see 13. above), although both aspects are often grouped under the name 'real-time vs. batch'.

16. Coarse/Fine-grained. The data that is stored and transmitted may be fine-grained or coarse-grained. Different parties may want to use the data for different purposes and may desire different levels of granularity for those purposes.

17. Meta-data/Production-data. Data may be meta-data or production data. For example, an intermediary (e.g., playing the Initiation Event Sensor and the Initiation Event Emitter roles) may only have meta-data about where requested data is stored.

18. Authorizations. Authorizations may be related to the content that is transmitted, the party to who it is transmitted, the format, the timing, the location, etc. (i.e., authorizations are related to all issues mentioned above).

Now we know the 18 aspects on which coordination is needed, let us have a short look at their interdependencies.

4 A Dependency-Driven Software Process?

The fact that there are 18 data aspects makes it impossible for decision makers to deal with all aspects at once. Some order has to be taken, and only a small number of data aspects can be dealt with during every step. Interestingly, there are interdependencies between different decisions. Examples of interdependencies are the following:

(9→5)   *If a fast transmission medium is available a big distance is acceptable.*

(1→6)   *If data content is highly confidential use a very secure storage medium.*

(2→1)   *If you use some standard format (e.g. RosettaNet) then you may restrict yourself to transmitting only the content defined there.*

(6→11) *If the storage medium is human it is not desirable to fire a request for updates every minute, but rather to subscribe.*

Given the fact that there are dependencies between the different data aspects presented above, one would expect that some order could be given to the data aspects, or at least that some (highly interdependent) data aspects should be dealt with simultaneously, while others can be treated apart.

In our research we have tried to group data aspects on which decisions are highly interdependent. While looking for the interdependencies between the aspects we, unfortunately, found that most aspects are dependent upon most other aspects. Moreover, the degree of dependence is likely to differ from case to case. From this, it is clear that it is inappropriate to suggest the existence of components of data aspects that should be dealt with together in general. Therefore, we have created a 'tool' (actually an Excel-sheet) that shows the interdependencies between different data aspects. That is, for each of the aspects it is investigated how the choice of this aspect depends upon choices made for each of the other aspects. We have also suggested a value for each dependency (from 0 to 9). Remarkably, this value is likely to fluctuate from case to case. Assumed that values are given, an algorithm could evaluate all possible combinations of components of data aspects that should be dealt with together. Although forming components on such a basis is not academically correct, one needs to be pragmatic in this matter: companies cannot deal with all interdependencies at once, and need to make abstractions.

5 Conclusions

The contribution of this paper is that it identifies 18 data aspects that can be used creatively, and on which stakeholders throughout the Extended Enterprise need to reach agreement. While we cannot claim the 18 aspects are all the data aspects that actually exist, it seems very unlikely that any important ones would be missing. It is important to consider the 18 aspects and their interdependencies in every software process. Moreover, this paper acknowledges that the software process is not just taking place at the operational ICT level but is an integrated part of the entire Enterprise Architecture effort. Alignment is needed between business and ICT decisions; between strategic, tactical and operational decisions; and between decisions made for individual enterprises and those made for the collection of collaborating companies. Any software process that is not embedded in this philosophy is likely to result in software that is not aligned with the business, with other internal projects, or with other parts of the Extended Enterprise project that are being implemented by partnering companies.

Acknowledgements. This paper has been written as part of the 'SAP-leerstoel'-project on 'Extended Enterprise Infrastructures' sponsored by SAP Belgium.

References

1. Simon H.A. (1994). The sciences of the artificial (2nd ed). The MIT Press, Cambridge, Massachusetts, p 247.
2. Hirschheim, R., H. Klein and K. Lyytinen, "Control, Sense-Making and Argumentation: Articulating and Exploring the Intellectual Structures of Information Systems", Proceedings of the Fifth Australasian Conference on Information Systems, G. Shanks and D. Arnott (eds.), Melbourne, Australia, September 27-29, 1994, pp.1-25.
3. Goethals F., Vandenbulcke J., Lemahieu W., Snoeck M., Structuring the development of inter-organizational systems: Web Information Systems Engineering conference - Brisbane November 22-24, 2004. Springer LNCS-series, Volume 3306, pp. 454-465.
4. Goethals F., Vandenbulcke J., Lemahieu W., Snoeck M., Cumps B. (2005), Two Basic Types of Business-to-Business integration, International Journal of E-Business Research, 1(1), 1-15, Available at http://www.idea-group.com/downloads/samples/IJEBR.pdf.
5. Cook, M. (1996). Building Enterprise Information Architectures. Prentice-Hall, 179.
6. Mintzberg, H. Structure in Fives, Designing effective organizations. Prentice-Hall, Englewood Cliffs, New Jersey, 1993, p. 305.
7. Malone T.W., Crowston K. (1994). Towards an Interdisciplinary Theory of Coordination, Computing Surveys, 26(1), 1994.
8. Zachman J. (1987), A framework for information systems architecture, IBM Systems Journal, Vol. 26, No.3, pp. 276-292.
9. Kruchten P. (November 1995), The 4+1 View Model of Architecture, IEEE Software, pp. 42-50.
10. Soni, D., R.L. Nord & C. Hofmeister, 'Software architecture in industrial applications', in: R. Jeffrey, D. Notkin (eds.), Proceedings of the 17th International Conference on Software Engineering, ACM Press, 1995, pp. 196-207.
11. Tapscott D., Caston A. (1993), The New Promise of Information Technology, McGraw-Hill, pp. 313.
12. The Chief Information Officers Council (September 1999), Federal Enterprise Architecture Framework Version 1.1, pp. 41.
13. Department of Defense - C4ISR Architectures Working Group, (December 1997), C4ISR Architecture Framework Version 2.0, pp. 239. Retrieved from http://www.c3i.osd.mil/
14. Department of the Treasury, Treasury Enterprise Architecture Framework, Version 1, pp. 164. Retrieved from http://ustreasury.mondosearch.com/
15. Van de Ven, A.H., Delbecq, A.L., Koenig, R. Jr. 1976). Determinants of coordination modes within organizations. American sociological review, 41 (April), 322-338.
16. Tillquist J., King J.L., Woo C. (2002), A representational scheme for analyzing information technology and organizational dependency. MISQuarterly, Vol. 26 No.2, pp. 91-118.
17. Thompson, J.D. (1967). Organizations in Action: Social Science Bases of Administrative Theory. New York: McGraw-Hill.
18. Alexander E.R. (1995). How organizations act together. Gordon and Breach, p 384.
19. Chisholm Donald (1992). Coordination without hierarchy, informal structures in multiorganizational systems. University of California Press, p 273.
20. O'Toole L.J., and Montjoy R.S., 1984. Interorganizationl policy implements: a theoretical perspective, Public Administration Review 44(6): 491-503.
21. Pfeffer J., Salancik G.R., 2003 (1978), The external control of organizations. A Resource Dependence perspective. Stanford University Press, California.
22. Crowston, K. 2003. A taxonomy of organizational dependencies and coordination mechanisms. In T. W. Malone & K. Crowston & G. Herman (Eds.), The Process Handbook: 85–108. Cambridge, MA: MIT Press.
23. Hansen M.T., Nohria N., Tierney T. (1999). What's Your strategy for managing knowledge?, *Harvard Business Review*, March-April 1999, p.106-116.

Tailor the Value-Based Software Quality Achievement Process to Project Business Cases

Liguo Huang[1], Hao Hu[2], Jidong Ge[2], Barry Boehm[1], and Jian Lü[2]

[1] Computer Science Department, University of Southern California,
Los Angeles, CA 90089-0781, USA
{liguohua, boehm}@sunset.usc.edu
[2] State Key Lab for Novel Software Tech., Institute of Computer Software,
Nanjing University, Nanjing, 210093, China
{myou, gjd, lj}@ics.nju.edu.cn

Abstract. This paper proposes a risk-based process strategy decision-making approach. To improve the flexibility in applying the Value-Based Software Quality Achievement (VBSQA) process framework, we embed the risk-based process strategy decision-making approach into the VBSQA process framework. It facilitates project managers to tailor the VBSQA process framework to different project business cases (schedule-driven, product-driven, and market trend-driven). A real world ERP (*E*nterprise *R*esource *P*lanning) software project (DIMS[1]) in China is used as an example to illustrate different process strategies generated from process tailoring.

1 Introduction

1.1 VBSQA Process Framework

Value-Based Software Quality Achievement (VBSQA) process framework [1] is generated from the WinWin Spiral Model [2] and the theories of value-based software engineering [3]. It provides a general guideline to generate process instances in order to achieve stakeholder WinWin-balanced software quality requirements based on risk-driven concurrency. Instead of using one-size-fits-all metrics to measure software quality achievement, VBSQA process framework enables its users to elicit success-critical stakeholders' value propositions (i.e., prioritization, expected & desired values) with respect to quality (Q-) attributes. It also helps identify and resolve their value conflicts on Q-attributes through risk analysis, technology/architecture evaluation and milestone reviews. Note that we also consider schedule and cost as Q-attributes in software projects. Furthermore, the framework guides us to use real earned value to monitor and control the progress toward achieving the Q-attribute requirements. The top-level steps and anchor point stakeholder commitment milestones (bolded) of VBSQA process framework [1] are listed in Table 1.

---

[1] This DIMS project is anonymous for the sake of commercial confidentiality.

Q. Wang et al. (Eds.): SPW/ProSim 2006, LNCS 3966, pp. 56–63, 2006.
© Springer-Verlag Berlin Heidelberg 2006

Table 1. The top-level steps of VBSQA process framework

1.	Identify top-level mission objectives and stages – including quality (Q-) objectives
2.	Perform project cost/benefit analysis – Estimate project budget – Develop results chain to identify success-critical stakeholders and their top-level value propositions
3.	Stakeholders negotiate mutually satisfactory (Win-Win) quality (and other) goals and relevant mission scenarios.
4.	Concurrently engineer top-level Q-attribute and other requirements and solution tradeoff spaces.
5.	Identify top-level Q-risks, execute risk-mitigation spirals.
6.	Develop system top-level design and initial Feasibility Rationale Description (FRD).
7.	**Hold Life Cycle Objective (LCO) Review** – **Pass: go to 8. Fail: go to 4.**
8.	Concurrently engineer detailed Q-attribute and other requirements and solutions; resolve risks.
9.	Develop system detailed design and detailed Feasibility Rationale Description (FRD).
10.	**Hold Life Cycle Architecture (LCA) Review** – **Pass: go to 11. Fail: go to 8.**
11.	Construct, test, and deploy system – Use the mission scenarios and Q-attribute requirement levels as progress metrics and test cases – **Core Capability Demo (CCD)** – Monitor progress and change requests; perform corrective actions
12.	**Initial Operational Capability (IOC) Readiness Review**

1.2 Implications of Applying the VBSQA Process to ERP Software Development in China

VBSQA process framework covers all phases and milestones through the entire software development life cycle in the WinWin Spiral model [2]. It also includes various software development activities to incorporate the value-based consideration. For most ERP (*E*nterprise *R*esource *P*lanning) solution providers in China, different software quality assessment criteria are set based on different business cases [5] and different process strategies shall be selected to meet them. Three process strategies (schedule-driven, product-driven and market-trend driven) can be selectively applied in the ERP software development based on different business cases. Therefore a flexible process generation platform is expected to enable the trim or addition of the steps/milestones/activities in VBSQA process framework.

2 Process Strategy Decision-Making in VBSQA Process

In general, schedule-driven processes are lightweight processes that employ short iterative cycles while product-driven processes employ longer iterative cycles. Our risk-based process decision-making approach, summarized in Fig. 1, uses the project business case and risk analysis to tailor the VBSQA process into an overall software development strategy [4]. Embedding the risk-based process decision-making approach into VBSQA process framework provides a feasible solution to a flexible process generation based on project business cases. This approach relies heavily on project key stakeholder identification, project business case analysis and the collaboration of the core development team with other project stakeholders. Thus we insert the process decision-making point after Step 3 (stakeholders negotiate quality and other goals) in the current VBSQA process framework described in Table 1.

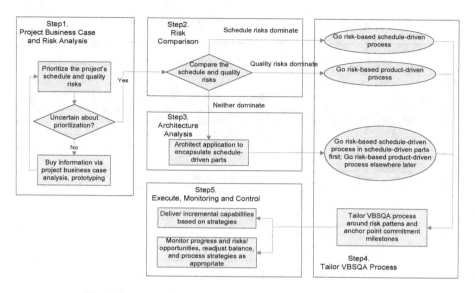

Fig. 1. Summary of risk-based process decision-making approach

Business case analysis aims to elicit success-critical stakeholders' value propositions. Risk analysis aims to identify and mitigate risks particularly associated with project schedule and software quality achievement. The results of risk analysis can be used to answer such questions as "How much software quality investment is enough?" by balancing the risk of investing *too little* on software quality with the risk of investing *too much*. Examples of such questions related to software quality achievement are "How much prototyping is enough?", "How much review is enough?", and "How much testing is enough?" As another aspect of quality achievement, we extend the approach to also consider the question "How much architecting and planning is enough?" Risk analysis is closely related to business case analysis in that project risks are prioritized based on the business case analysis by emphasizing the high-priority stakeholder value.

If schedule risks dominate quality risks, risk-based schedule-driven process is applied. If quality-risks dominate schedule risks, risk-based product-driven process is applied. If neither dominates, then architect the application to encapsulate the schedule-driven parts which applies the risk-based schedule-driven process and go risk-based product-driven process elsewhere. Based on this approach, we can tailor the VBSQA process framework and establish an overall project strategy by integrating individual risk mitigation plans [4].

Since no decision is perfect for all time, as indicated in Step 5 in Fig. 1, project management team needs to continuously monitor and control the performance of the selected process in order to adapt to changes in the project business case. In this way, we can always monitor and control the opportunity for realizing stakeholders' value.

3   Tailor VBSQA Process to Different Business Cases

Using the process decision-making approach embedded in the VBSQA process framework, we are able to tailor the VBSQA process to different project business cases when generating a process instance for a software project. When tailoring the process, we may skip some process steps/milestones, relax the deliverables/outputs of a particular process step/milestone, select a particular process activity or decide the participants of a process activity.

3.1   Characteristics of Three Example Business Cases

We first determine whether the project is dominated by schedule risks or quality risks before process tailoring. Table 2 compares the different characteristics of three typical business cases in ERP software projects. Then we use a real-world ERP software system, a Documents and Images Management System (DIMS) built by Neusoft, as an example to illustrate how to use the risk-based process decision-making approach to tailor the VBSQA process to three different business cases. Four success-critical stakeholder classes were identified in DIMS project, including the System Acquirer, DB Administrators, Software Maintainers and Developers.

Table 2. Characteristics of Three Example Business Cases in ERP Software Development

Business Case	Schedule-Driven	Market Trend-Driven	Product-Driven
Primary Objective	Rapid value by adding small extra functionalities	Rapid Market Share Occupation	Version upgrade with Q-attribute achievement: reliability, availability, performance, evolvability, etc.
Quality Risks	Low	Medium	High; major business losses
Schedule Risks	High; major business losses	High; market share loss	Low
Stakeholders	Single collocated representatives	Many success-critical stakeholders	Multiple success-critical stakeholders with various Q-attribute requirements
Requirements	1) A few specific and stable requirements; 2) Mostly functional	1) Goals generally known (e.g., platform changes); 2) Detailed requirements often vague, volatile and emergent; 3) Functional and non-functional [6]	1) Critical and conflicting Q-attribute requirements from various stakeholders; 2) Most requirements relatively stable; others volatile, emergent 3) Functional and nonfunctional;
Architecture	1) Extend from existing system architecture 2) Little architecting effort 3) Stakeholder high confidence	1) Brand new architecture; 2) Most architecting effort; 3) Stakeholder low confidence	1) Evolve based on existing product-line architecture 2) High confidence in some parts; low confidence in others
Refactoring	Inexpensive with skilled people	More expensive with mix of people skills	Very expensive, with mix of people skills

3.2   Tailor VBSQA Process to Schedule-Driven Business Case

Schedule-driven business case applies when rapidly accommodating a few minor product upgrading requirements from one or two departments within an organization. The examples of such requirements can be adding, deleting, updating certain attributes in the current DIMS database schema. Those functionalities are usually needed urgently. Delivering the functionalities on time becomes the stakeholders' highest-priority value proposition. Thus, we need to prioritize the process steps/activities and tailor the VBSQA process framework to only retain the most effective process steps/milestones/activities. In this case, system users are willing to tolerate some quality degradation and delay the Q-attribute requirements until the system operation.

Based on the schedule-driven business case in Table 2, the added functionalities are extended from the existing system architecture and stakeholders are more confident in the existing architecture. There is no need to propose or review several feasible architectural options. Requirements are specific enough to skip the high-level design and to proceed directly to the detailed design stage. In this case, process steps in Life Cycle Objective (LCO) stage are less effective than those in the Life Cycle Architecture (LCA) stage in VBSQA process framework. For the same reason, we may also skip the intermediate milestone Core Capability Demo (CCD) and proceed to Initial Operational Capability (IOC) Readiness Review. Since the quality risks are relatively low and developers only need to extend from the existing system architecture, *Selected Architectural Internal Review* within the developer team is performed in LCA stage instead of onsite *External Review* with the participation of all stakeholders in order to meet the delivery deadline. Fig. 2 shows an example of schedule-driven process strategy for DIMS project.

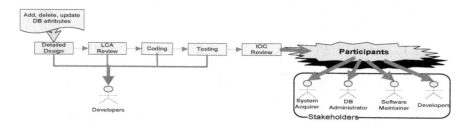

Fig. 2. An example of schedule-driven process strategy for DIMS project

3.3 Tailor VBSQA Process to Product-Driven Business Case

Product-driven business case applies when accommodating a system upgrading request to a higher version after aggregating common upgrading requirements from various departments. In this case, quality of the upgraded product is the process driver rather than meeting a delivery deadline. Quality risks are dominant compared with schedule risks as shown in Table 2. The requirements are relatively stable. Since the requirements are aggregated from various project stakeholders, the Q-attribute requirements may conflict with one another. An example is the DIMS version upgrade from 6.0 to 7.0. Functional requirements and their associated Q-attribute requirements were prioritized through stakeholder WinWin negotiation in Table 3.

Multiple project increments can be proposed based on the priorities of requirements. A process instance is generated for each increment. Fig. 3 shows an example of product-driven process strategy in DIMS upgrade project. R1, R2, R3 and R4 are grouped into the first increment due to their higher priorities and cohesion. R5 and R6 are grouped into the second increment. In product-driven business case, process instances of multiple increments can proceed concurrently since the functional and

Table 3. Prioritized requirements in DIMS upgrade from 6.0 to 7.0

Requirements	Description	Category	Priority
R1	Data migration from old DB platform to upgraded DB platform	Functional	High
R2	Data migration shall be completed within 1 day and within the storage space	Quality (Performance)	High
R3	Accommodate different DB platforms and schema in data migration	Quality (Evolvability)	Medium
R4	Add a printing function in DIMS system	Functional	High
R5	Build a unified log in user interface for different DIMS subsystems	Functional	Medium
R6	Improve search response time from 2 seconds to 0.5 seconds	Quality (Performance)	Medium

Q-attribute requirements are relatively stable. In each increment, process strategy shall place emphasis on involving stakeholders in identifying and resolving conflicting Q-attributes, concurrently identifying and mitigating Q-risks with architecture/technology evaluation and milestone reviews. Thus, its iteration cycle is longer than schedule-driven process in order to address the Q-risks and maintain the product-line architecture.

LCO/LCA reviews and CCD are all necessary to identify and mitigate Q-risks in each increment. It is also important to involve all success-critical stakeholders in the prototype evaluation and each milestone review (i.e., LCO, LCA, CCD, IOC). Therefore, performing onsite *External Prototype Evaluation, Architecture Options External Review* and *Selected Architecture External Review* with the participation of the System Acquirer, DB Administrators, Software Maintainers and Developers, is more effective than their internal counterparts within developer team.

3.4   Tailor VBSQA Process to Market Trend-Driven Business Cases

Market trend-driven business case applies when the upgrade of the product is driven by the market trend or competing companies' products, such as a change from Client/Server architecture to web-based architecture in the DIMS. In this case, providing superior capabilities to capture greater market share as early as possible is the key process driver.

The priorities of schedule risks and quality risks are comparable for market trend-driven business case as shown in Table 2. Therefore, the process strategy for market trend-driven business case is a mixture of the schedule-driven and product-driven process strategies. It is similar to schedule-driven process strategy in that it maintains the short iteration cycle in the first project increment to meet the product delivery deadline for capturing the market share early. However, since stakeholders are less confident in the web-based architecture, it is different from schedule-driven process strategy in that stakeholders should be closely involved in the prototype evaluation and each milestone review (LCO, LCA, CCD, IOC) as shown in Fig. 4.

It is similar to product-driven process strategy in that it emphasizes stakeholder involvement and multiple project increments can be proposed based on stakeholders' priorities of functional and Q-attribute requirements. However, it is different from product-driven process strategy in that only the top-priority capabilities can be

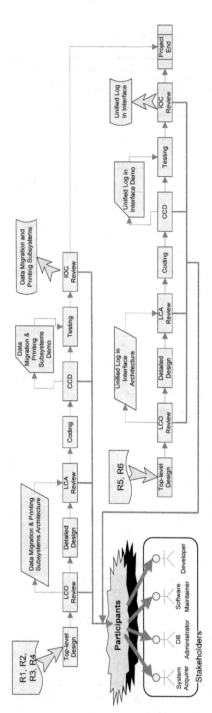

Fig. 3. An example of product-driven process strategy for DIMS version upgrade

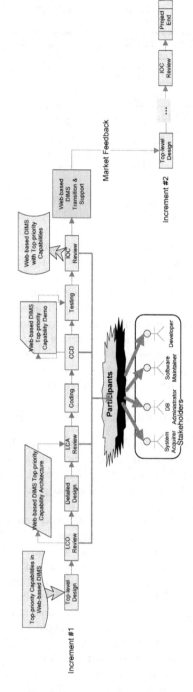

Fig. 4. An example of market trend-driven process strategy for changing from Client/Server-based DIMS to web-based DIMS

accommodated in the first increment (see Fig. 4) based on the Schedule/Cost/Quality as Independent Variable (SCQAIV) process strategy [7]. Stakeholders are usually willing to tolerate some quality (e.g., performance, evolvability) degradation at the initial trial of the system. In addition, the process strategy in the following increments heavily depends on the market feedback of the product delivered in the first increment. Thus, there is a gap between each increment to wait for the market feedback. As the operation of new platform becomes stable with sufficient market feedback, product-driven process strategy can be applied in the following increments.

4 Conclusion and Future Work

The risk-based process strategy decision-making approach embedded in VBSQA process framework enables us to tailor the process to various project business cases. It improves the flexibility in applying the process framework. Business case and risk analyses are critical success factors in selecting an appropriate process strategy.

We are investigating the interactive tool support for project managers to tailor the VBSQA process framework and generate an appropriate process instance for a specific project business case.

References

1. Huang, L.: A Value-Based Process for Achieving Software Dependability", Proceedings of International Software Process Workshop (2005), Beijing, China. LNCS, Springer Verlag
2. Boehm, B., Hansenzz, W.: Understanding the Spiral Model as a Tool for Evolutionary Acquisition", CrossTalk, May, (2001)
3. Boehm, B., Jain, A.: An Initial Theory of VBSE, in A. Aurum, S. Biffl, B. Boehm, H. Erdogmus, and P. Gruenbacher, Value-Based Software Engineering, Springer Verlag (2005)
4. Boehm, B., Turner, R.: Balancing Agility and Discipline, Addison Wesley, (2004)
5. Reifer, D.: Making the Software Business Case, Addison Wesley, (2002)
6. Chung, L., Nixon, B., Yu, E., Mylopoulos; J.: Non-Functional Requirements in Software Engineering, Kluwer, (1999)
7. Boehm, B., Port, D., Huang, L., and Brown, W.: Using the Spiral Model and MBASE to Generate New Acquisition Process Models: SAIV, CAIV, and SCQAIV, CrossTalk, vol. 15, no. 1, January, (2002), pp. 20-25.

Optimizing Process Decision in COTS-Based Development Via Risk Based Prioritization

Ye Yang and Barry Boehm

Center for Software Engineering, University of Southern California,
941 W. 37th Place, SAL 330,
Los Angeles, CA 90089 USA
{yangy, boehm}@sunset.usc.edu

Abstract. Good project planning requires the use of appropriate process model as well as effective decision support technique(s). However, current software process models provide very little COTS-specific insight and guidance on helping COTS-based application developers to make better decisions with respect to their particular project situations. This paper presents a risk based prioritization approach that is used in the context of COTS Process Decision Framework [6]. This method is particularly useful in supporting many dominant decisions during COTS-based development process, such as establishing COTS assessment criteria, scoping and sequencing development activities, prioritizing features to be implemented in incremental development, etc. In this way, the method not only provides a basis for optimal COTS selection, but also helps to focus the limited development resource on more critical tasks that represent greater risks.

1 Introduction

There is considerable consensus about the new technical, economical, and management challenges associated with COTS-based development (CBD) [1, 2, 4, 5]. However, traditional software process models fail to accommodate many of these challenges, because their process guidance is overly sequential (as with waterfall-based models [4]) or underdetermined (such as EPIC [2]). This often leads to the selection of best-of-breed but incompatible COTS products, without considering the increased costs and reduced benefits incurred by trying to integrate them together.

Extended from the general risk-driven Spiral Model [10], the CBD process decision framework [6] provides a value-based set of processes that helps CBD project teams avoid or minimize such value losses. It enables CBD projects to generate flexible process instances from its composable process elements that best fit their project situation and dynamics. However, making optimal process decision is never an easy job, and it requires a comprehensive evaluation of COTS costs, benefits, and risks within the feasibility analysis and project business case [8].

In the last two years, we have had the opportunity to instruct and apply framework to 13 e-services projects at the University of Southern California (USC) and observe their process execution. This environment provided us with a unique way of introducing, experimenting, validating, and improving the CBD process decision framework.

Q. Wang et al. (Eds.): SPW/ProSim 2006, LNCS 3966, pp. 64–71, 2006.

In this paper we introduce the CBD process decision framework, present the risk based prioritization strategy for improving its process decision support, and show three example scenarios where the strategy is used to generate flexible process instances.

2   CBD Process Decision Framework

Empirical analysis on both USC e-services and industry CBD projects has led us to develop and evolve a value-based CBD process decision framework as a COTS-specialized risk-driven Spiral framework. It consists of a set of composable process elements, accommodating concurrent CBD activities and frequent go-backs based on new and evolving stakeholder value propositions and risk considerations, as illustrated in Fig. 1. A CBD process instance starts by "walking" a path from start to deploy that connects activity areas (boxes) and decisions (ovals). The small circles with letters A, T, G, C indicate the assessment, tailoring, glue code, and custom code development process elements, respectively. Each activity area may enter and exit in numerous ways.

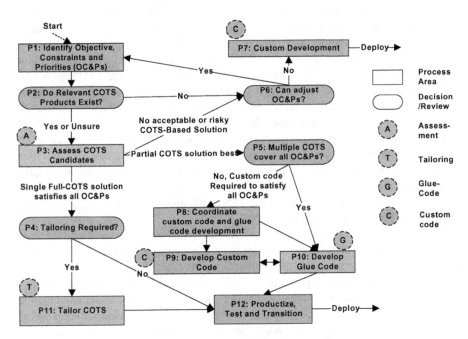

Fig. 1. CBD process decision framework

The framework emphasizes that stakeholders must be identified and their value propositions are prioritized (about features, platforms, performance, budgets, schedules, and so on) and a mutually satisfactory or win-win set of objectives, constraints, and priorities (OC&P's) is negotiated (P1). As the project progresses, risk considerations, stakeholders' priority changes, new COTS releases, and other dynamic considerations can alter the OC&Ps. In particular, if the team identifies no suitable COTS packages (P6), the stakeholders can change the OC&Ps and the process begins anew with these revised considerations. The framework looks sequential, but its elements support recursive and reentrant use to support the frequent go-backs involved in CBD processes. We've studied these and found frequently occurring ATGC patterns or "genetic codes" that characterize CBD processes [3].

3   Applying CBD Process Decision Framework to USC e-Services Projects

During the last two years, 13 USC e-service projects applied our CBD process decision framework in their development. At the same time, we use four other process drivers to help the development teams making their process decisions with respect to the volatile project situations. These include: the CBD Experience Base, cost estimation models (i.e. COCOMO II and COCOTS), key stakeholders' win-win negotiation, and COTS market watch. Each of these process drivers plays a different role in helping developers to generate appropriate process instances from the framework.

The CBD Process Decision Framework is used as a comprehensive baseline for generating a particular COTS process. The CBD Experience Base is a knowledge base of guidelines, patterns, and models that is empirically formulated and used to support the decision-making activity during CBD development. The Constructive COTS cost model (COCOTS) [1] is primarily used to estimate the COTS associated efforts. And the COCOMO II model is used to estimate the portion of custom development effort. The estimation results will be used during the cost/benefit analysis for choosing COTS options that produce the best life cycle expected cost-benefit. Different stakeholders have different expectations and priorities. Explicitly recognizing and involving them into win win negotiations will ensure all relevant areas are better identified and addressed. COTS market and COTS vendor are two important variation sources that introduce the most change factors. Therefore, it is critical for the developers to keep monitoring competitive COTS candidates by collecting and evaluating information from COTS market/vendor.

Using the information gathered from the 8 first year projects, we found that with applying the CBD process decision framework, the teams performed better than those who did not. More specifically, the statistical results show a factor of 1.28 in improving team performance and a factor of 1.6 in increasing client satisfaction. However, it is also found that a number of decision times where the framework and its guidelines were not sufficient enough in supporting developers' decision-making. This is mainly because most developers are computer science major graduate students who are skillful in programming but have little or no experience on project management, esp. risk management. Moreover, the framework is able to handle changes and provide guidance on what activity sequences the developers should follow in order to mitigate their risk, but nothing in the framework actually addressed how/how much one can do this.

4   Optimizing Decision Processes Via Risk Based Prioritization

To address this problem, we have developed a COCOTS Risk Analyzer [7] to auto-mate the COTS project risk assessment with the set of cost driver ratings that user enters to obtain a COCOTS cost/schedule estimate. The automated risk assessment workflow is shown in Fig. 2. It is based on an expert Delphi analysis of the relative risks involved in the most critical combinations of COCOTS cost driver ratings. Our previous study also showed that it has done an effective job of estimat-ing the relative risk levels of a sample of CBD projects.

With COCOTS Risk Ana-lyzer, risk based prioritization can be used as a fundamental strategy to structure decision

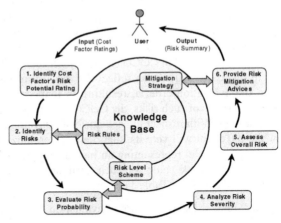

Fig. 2. COCOTS Risk Analyzer

procedures within our framework to prioritize both product and process alternatives that compete for limited resources. Table 1 summarizes how the risk strategy steps, spiral quadrants, and CBD process framework steps all relate to each other:

Table 1. Steps of Risk Based Prioritization Strategy

Risk Strategy Step	Spiral Quad-rants	CBD process Decision Frame-work Step	Description
S1	Q1	P1, P2	Identify OC&Ps, COTS/other alternatives
S2	Q2a	P3	Evaluate COTS vs. OC&Ps (incl. COCOTS)
S3	Q2a	P3	Identify risks, incl. COCOTS risk analysis
S4	Q2b	P3	Assess risks, resolution alternatives; If risks manageable, go to S7
S5	Q2b, Q1	P6	Negotiate OC&P adjustments; If none acceptable, drop COTS options (P7)
S6	Q2a	P3	If OC&P adjustments successful, go to S7; If not, go to S5
S7	Q3	P4 or P5	Execute acceptable solution

Next, we use four example scenarios to illustrate how to use this risk based priori-tization strategy in supporting decision processes.

4.1   Establishing COTS Evaluation Criteria

The small circle with letter A (i.e. P3) in Fig.1 represents the COTS assessment proc-ess element, which can be further decomposed into steps A1-A6 as elaborated in [6].

Establishing evaluation criteria is a major task included in step A1, where inexperienced CBD developers often report difficulty and problematic.

Selection of COTS products is typically based on an assessment of each product in light of certain product attributes as evaluation criteria. Inappropriate COTS selection can cause many late rework even project failure, therefore, it is very important to have an essential set of product attributes in the first place. To do this, follow risk based prioritization strategy starting with identifying an initial broad set of relevant attributes such as functionality, security, cost, etc. (A comprehensive list of COTS product attributes is defined in COCOTS [1], which can be used as a good starting point.).

In this case, major risks reflect the risk of not including certain product attributes into the evaluation criteria, resulting in inappropriate COTS choices. To assess the risk exposures of such risks, the COCOTS inputs include two types of voting (Step S2 in Table 1). With respect to each attribute, developers will vote its ease of evaluation; while the client will vote its importance to organization. The voted score is on a 0-10 normalized scale, representing an increasing degree of ease or degree of importance. And the risk rank value for each attribute is quantified according to the following equation (Step S3 in Table 1):

Risk rank = Degree of ease of evaluation * Degree of importance to organization

Therefore, attributes with higher risk rank values reflect those that are important to the organization and easy to evaluate. In general, as risk mitigation strategy, these attributes should have higher prioritization to be included to the evaluation criteria list. One thing needs to be mentioned here is that when conflicts exist among the votes (e.g. two extreme scores for the same attributes from different developers), the conflicts should be resolved first through further discussion before proceeding to finalize on evaluation criteria set.

4.2   Scoping COTS Assessment Process

Project teams often scope the COTS assessment process based on the COTS products' likely cost. A better scope criterion is to apply our risk based prioritization strategy to calculate the amount of risk exposure involved in choosing the wrong COTS combination. For example, a supply chain application started with an $80,000 effort on COTS initial filtering, using separate weighted-sum evaluations of the best-of-breed enterprise resource planning (ERP), advanced planning scheduling (APS), transaction management (TM), and customer relationship management (CRM) COTS package candidates based on documentation reviews, demos, and reference checking. The team quickly identified the best-of-breed COTS choices that seemed to be the strongest choices. However, there was a chance that the best-of-breed COTS combination could have many technical and business-model-assumption incompatibilities indicated by the COCOTS risk analysis results. For example, among the best-of-breed COTS combination, the COCOTS run (Step S2 and S3 in Table 1) for the COTS AB combination had an APCPX (interface complexity) rating of Very High and an ACSEW (supplier extension willingness) of Very Low, indicating a significant integration risk.

In this case, the risk based prioritization strategy suggests a better risk mitigation strategy that is to use the separate analyses (i.e. prototyping) to further assess the leading choices and identify the major interoperability risk exposures, then use the size of the overall risk exposure to scope a more detailed COTS interoperability assessment. The analyzed results showed that this would lead to a $3 million, eight-month overrun and associated system effectiveness shortfalls. Had they invested more than $80,000 in COTS assessment to include interoperability prototyping, they would have been able to switch to a more compatible COTS combination with only minor losses in effectiveness and without expensive, late rework. The CBD process decision framework accommodate this by two types of assessment tasks: initial filtering (A2) and detailed assessment (A3-A5) [6].

4.3 Sequencing COTS Integration Activities

Patterns exist between COTS activity sequences and their indicated risks [3]. Appropriately sequencing COTS activities following a pattern can be used as a valid means to mitigate its corresponding risk. However, it requires an overall evaluation with respect to a particular project situation.

In general, there are five types of risk mitigation strategies: buy information, risk avoidance, risk transfer, risk reduction, and risk acceptance [9]. In the above supply chain application example, the developers were actually using detailed COTS assessment to buy information to select a more compatible COTS choice. Considering the stakeholders may have different value propositions, Fig. 3 illustrates different risk mitigation strategies they can follow in terms of flexibly composing their COTS activity sequences, with the following stakeholder propositions in each situation:

- Risk avoidance: The team could use an adequate alternative COTS C and follow the sequence (a) to avoid the risk of COTS A and B not talking to each other.
- Risk transfer: If the customer insists on using COTS B, the developers can have them establish a risk reserve to be used to the extend that A and B cant talk to each other and follow the sequence (b).
- Risk reduction: If the customer decides to build the wrappers to get A and B talk through CORBA connections, the development cost will increase but the schedule delay will be minimized;
- Risk acceptance: If the developer prefers to solve the A and B interoperability problem, they will have a big competitive edge on the future procurements. "Let's do this on our own money, and patent the solution".

To illustrate these in our risk strategy, for example, if in steps S2 and S3, the COCOTS run shows the COTS AC combination had an ACPER (performance adequacy) rating of Low and an ACSEW rating of Very Low, also indicating a fairly significant risk. Then in Step S4, the developers prototyped the AB interface complexity state of nature and found that it incurred a significant added cost and schedule. Step S5 involves the developers and the customer evaluating the 4 risk resolution alternatives and determining an adjustment of the OC&P's that leads to an acceptable COTS solution in Step S6.

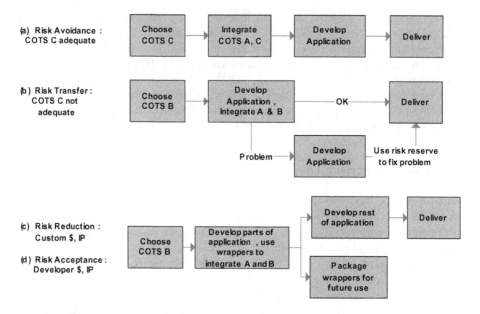

Fig. 3. Different risk mitigation resulting in different activity sequence

4.4 Prioritization of Top Features

Stakeholders win win negotiation plays an important role in converging on a mutually satisfactory set of product features to be implemented within 24 weeks schedule. In this case, COCOTS Risk Analyzer provides risk analysis that can be used in risk based prioritization for prioritizing the project requirements and converging on a feasible feature set. In an example USC e-services project, "Open source discussion board and research platform". During the win win negotiation, stakeholders agreed that the full operational capability includes three top-level features: discussion board, instant messenger, and other user management features supporting Internet Explorer, Mozilla, and Netscape Navigator web browsers. However, the development team only included 6 people and was under a strict schedule limit of 24 weeks. Using the COCOTS Risk Analyzer, the project followed the risk based prioritization strategy to find out that including support for Mozilla and Netscape Navigator web browsers would cause 6 weeks schedule overrun, and including instant messenger feature would cause 4 weeks schedule delay. Therefore, the stakeholders came into agreement to leave the feature of supporting other web browsers and instant messenger to the evolution requirements, which will be implemented in a later increment but still be used in determining the system architecture in order to facilitate evolution to full operational capability.

4.5 Discussion

In the second year, the risk based prioritization principle was experimented within the context of CBD framework on 5 projects, and an end-of-project survey was given to all developers to collect the usage data and feedback. Out of the total 24 responses, 19 commented that the framework is useful in preparing life cycle plan, and 21 reported that the risk based prioritization principle helped in their risk analysis. We believe that this is a satisfactory and encouraging indicator in evaluating the performance of the improved framework.

5 Conclusions

COTS-based applications pose unique development challenges that traditional process models can't anticipate. The CBD process decision framework can help developers to generate flexible process instances with respect to their particular project situations, providing a set of COTS-specific process areas and decision points.

This paper presented the risk based prioritization as a general principle for deriving optimal decision with the support of a tool named COCOTS Risk Analyzer. Using three critical decision scenarios, it also elaborated on the application of the principle. Statistical analysis results has shown that applying this principle within the CBD process framework can help steer CBD projects toward successful, cost-effective integration of components and applications. We will further investigate the effectiveness of this approach to improve decision support in CBD process framework.

References

1. C. Abts, B. Boehm, and E. Bailey Clark, "COCOTS: A Software COTS-Based System (CBS) Cost Model," *Proceedings, ESCOM 2001*, April 2001, pp. 1-8.
2. C. Albert and L. Brownsword, "Evolutionary Process for Integrating COTS-Based Systems (EPIC): An Overview," *Technical Report*, CMU-SEI-2002-TR-009, July 2002.
3. Y. Yang, "Process Patterns for COTS-Based Development," *Proceedings, SPW2006*, May 2005.
4. M. Morisio, C. Seaman, A. Parra, V. Basili, S. Kraft, and S. Condon, "Investigating and Improving a COTS-Based Software Development Process," *Proceedings, ICSE 22*, June 2000, pp. 32-41.
5. B. Boehm, D. Port, Y. Yang, and J. Buhta, "Not All CBS Are Created Equally: COTS-Intensive Project Types," *Proceedings, ICCBSS'03*, Ottawa, Canada, Feb. 2003, pp. 36-50.
6. Y. Yang, J. Buhta, B. Boehm, and D. Port, "Value-Based Processes for COTS-Based Applications," *IEEE Software*, July.Aug 2005.
7. Y. Yang, B. Boehm, and B. Clark, "Assessing COTS Integration Risk Using Cost Estimation Inputs", accepted by ICSE 2006.
8. D. J. Reifer, Making the Software Business Case. Addison-Wesley, September 2001.
9. Barry W. Boehm, Software Risk Management: Principles and Practices, IEEE Software, v.8 n.1, p.32-41, January 1991.
10. B. Boehm, A. Egyed, J. Kwan, D. Port, A. Shah, and R. Madachy, "Using the WinWin Spiral Model: A Case Study," *IEEE Computer*, July 1998.

Project Replayer – An Investigation Tool to Revisit Processes of Past Projects

Keita Goto[1], Noriko Hankawa[2], and Hajimu Iida[1]

[1] Graduate School of Information Science, Nara Institute of Science and Technology, Japan
keita-g@is.naist.jp, iida@itc.naist.jp
[2] Faculty of Management Information, Hannan University, Japan
hanakawa@hannan-u.ac.jp

Abstract. In order to help knowledge acquisition and accumulation from past experiences, we propose a KFC (Knowledge Feedback Cycle) framework among engineers and researchers. Three tools (Empirical Project Monitor, Simulator, and Replayer) are used to circulate captured knowledge in KFC. Project Replayer is a most characteristic tool used to review data of past projects derived from development logs; version control, bug reports and e-mails. With Project Replayer, past projects can be easily revisited and complicated phenomena of past projects can be investigated. As a result of preliminary experiments, we have confirmed that Project Replayer helps researchers construct and validate hypotheses of software process. We also confirmed that developers have acquired new knowledge about a certain problem extracted from past projects.

1 Introduction

Recently, software development scale becomes bigger, and software quality's impact to our society is significantly increasing. On the other hand, lifetime of software is getting shorter. In order to develop software with certain qualities in a limited time, developers require various knowledge such as cost estimation or risk management, as well as other software engineering techniques. Some of such knowledge should be extracted and accumulated through their own experiences. However, acquiring and accumulating such knowledge require long time and large efforts. In other words, it is very difficult for developers to become matured engineers in a short period.

In order to help knowledge acquisition and accumulation for novice software engineers, we propose a framework for *cycling* engineering and management knowledge among experienced developers, software engineering researchers and novice developers. We call this cycle KFC (Knowledge Feedback Cycle). In the KFC environment, knowledge, mainly concerning risk management and cost estimation, is extracted from past experiences for future reuse. Three tools, EPM (Empirical Project Monitor), Project Replayer, and Project Simulator, are used to capture and circulate knowledge in KFC. EPM [1] is a tool to automatically collect project data from source code repository, bug-reports and e-mails. Project Replayer is a tool used to review data of past projects. Project Simulator is used to provide actual feedback to developers. Developers can avoid mistakes that is not happened in their experiences but happened in other developers' experiences before.

Q. Wang et al. (Eds.): SPW/ProSim 2006, LNCS 3966, pp. 72–79, 2006.
© Springer-Verlag Berlin Heidelberg 2006

This paper mainly describes the concept of the KFC and features of Project Replayer. Section 2 shows related works. In section 3, we present a conceptual environment of KFC. In section 4, outline of Project Replayer and its feature are explained. In section 5, preliminary experiments to evaluate capability of the Replayer are shown. In section 6, we discuss experiment result. Finally, in section 7, conclusions and further work are shown.

2 Related Work

Recently, many works are published in the field of the software process simulations. Some of them focus to help understanding of process behavior and training of process management using software process simulators [2].

For example, Pfahl et al. present the system with integrated simulation component called CBT that is designed for software engineering education [3]. CBT provides an interactive environment using standard web browsers to learn knowledge of project management. The CBT simulation module employs the model to represent the characteristic of a project is generated by the event diagram based on a COCOMO model. RoleEnact is a tool to support simulation, evaluation and improvement of software development processes [4]. RoleEnact focuses on developers' roles. Once part of the existing process has been captured in the model generator, the model stepper and simulator evaluate the results of running process while RoleEnact revise the process.

Most of these works treat abstracted model to show behaviors of software processes, even though they are obtained from real project experiences. Though real project data is not directly handled by those systems, investigation of real project data is very important to understand the behavior of the project in detail. Real project investigation also plays a major role in construction and validation of process simulation models, especially when we construct organization-specific models based on their own experiences. Usually, project investigation is very time-consuming task, and reducing the cost of investigation task is the key factor of knowledge extraction.

3 Knowledge Feedback Cycle

The purpose of KFC environment is to circulate knowledge from experience of past projects to future projects. Developers are supposed to acquire new knowledge while experiencing software development projects. If such knowledge can be transferred to future projects at low-cost, it is quite valuable and helpful for the members.

To establish such cycle, KFC employs three tools; EPM, Project Replayer and Project Simulator (See Fig. 1). KFC also involves two human roles – software developers and software engineering researchers. Developers utilize the KFC environment in order to acquire new knowledge from past projects while researchers utilize the KFC environment in order to construct simulation models which are embedded to the Project Simulator.

A typical scenario in KFC would be as follows;

Step1: Various development data (records of code modification, bug tracking, and e-mails) is automatically captured by EPM during the project enactment (See "EPM" part of Fig. 1).

Step2: Researchers analyze collected data to construct various simulation models using Project Replayer and analysis tools (See "Researcher" part of Fig. 1).

Step3: Using Project Replayer, developers review past projects. Events and accidents that are not recorded by EPM are also clarified in interview with developers (See "Project Replayer" part of Fig. 1).

Step4: Regarding results of reviews and interviews, researchers refine their simulation models that were made in Step2. The models are embedded into the Project Simulator (See "Simulation Model" part of Fig. 1).

Step5: Using the Project Simulator, novice developers learn complicated phenomena in past projects. Developers can also utilize the Project Simulator to make their next project plans. The planned project is regarded as the target of Step1 of the next cycle (See "Project Simulator" part of Fig. 1).

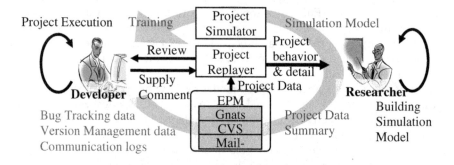

Fig. 1. Knowledge Feedback Cycle environment

The whole mechanism of the KFC environment is currently under development in our group, while a prototype of Project Replayer has been implemented at first to evaluate its capability. Following parts of this article describe the feature of Project Replayer and results of preliminary experiments using the Replayer.

4 Project Replayer

4.1 Purpose of the Tool

Project Replayer is a tool to *replay* project data collected by EPM in order to help understanding behavior of past projects. Project Replayer accelerates knowledge circulation by supporting both of two roles in KFC; developers can use Project Replayer to revisit their past projects for postmortem evaluations, while researchers can use Project Replayer to deeply understand and analyze dynamic behavior of the

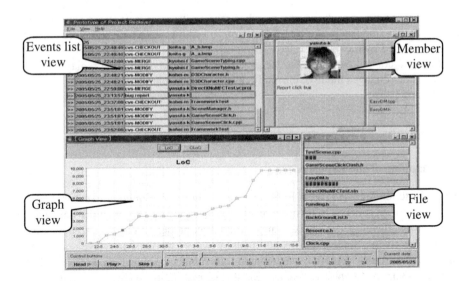

Fig. 2. Screen image of Project Replayer

projects. Replaying past real project is also important for education and training because simulators sometimes provide practitioners with quite less reality that is derived from abstract and ideal models. Project Replayer faithfully replays various behaviors of past projects. Developers are more familiar with the behaviors of past projects than behavior of the virtual projects.

4.2 Features

Current implementation of Project Replayer has four views (Event list view, File view, Graph view and Member view) and a time-control bar.

Event list view shows various (CVS: Concurrent Versions System, bugs, and e-mail) events collected through EPM are listed in order of time (See "Event list view" part of Fig. 2). The first column of each line works as a button to jump to the time of the event, which is indicated in the second column. The third column indicates the type of the event, the fourth column shows owner of the event, and the fifth column shows related filename.

File view presents source files in CVS repository (See "File view" part of Fig. 2). Each file item is shown with its name and progress bar. The progress bar shows rate of progress calculated as ratio of current CLoC (Cumulative modified Lines of Code) to the final CLoC. Graph view shows transitions of various data including total LoC (Line of code) and CLoC (See "Graph view" part of Fig. 2). Y-axis of the line chart indicates quantitative value such as LoC or CLoC, while x-axis indicates calendar time (days) of the project.

Member view lists project members with their role names and current actions (See "Member view" part of Fig. 2). The first row of a member item shows the member's name, the second row shows the member's portrait (or avatar), third row indicates current action s/he has performed, and fourth row shows active files that are currently being modified by the member.

The time control bar indicates the time (date) currently shown in replaying. Moving the slider changes the time currently displayed. The bar also provides buttons such as start and pause.

5 Preliminary Experiments

5.1 Planning of the Experiments

To evaluate features of Project Replayer, we conducted preliminary experiments. The aim of the experiments is to observe how Project Replayer's features help the researcher and developers to make a new simulation model and to acquire new knowledge respectively. Since experiments focused two viewpoints, i.e. developers' benefits, and researchers' benefits, we prepared four subjects; Subject0 is a researcher, and Subject1~3 are developers (graduate school students). Experiments form three phases, researcher's analysis, developers' review, and construction of simulation model by the researcher.

In the first phase, a researcher analyzes project's phenomena using Project Replayer. The researcher is requested to construct simulation models regarding the analyzed phenomena of the project. The researcher may have some questions about phenomena because information exposed by Project Replayer still does not include all detailed events that occurred in the project. Therefore, the researcher draws some questions about specific phenomena. The developers' answer to the questions, which is provided in the second phase, will help the researcher make a simulation model.

In the second phase, Project Replayer is used by developers to search answers to the questions. Project Replayer also helps to extract their recall. Originated questions are also important because they provide the developers with practical focus to deeply review the specific phenomena in past project. Just reviewing projects without any specific focus would be a very hard task.

In the third phase, the researcher tries to improve the simulation model according to the answer provided by developers.

The target project was for development of a typing-game. The project is operated for 24 days by six developers (students at NAIST). Program consists of 105 modules (.cpp files) and the final code size was 9,578 lines in total.

5.2 Results of the Experiments

In the first phase, the researcher (Subject0) made two hypotheses as follows;

(**H1**) If developers start to develop modules (.cpp files) on the end stage of project, the quality of the module is low.

(**H2**) If CVS's event behavior does not match to bug reports and e-mail data, the project is in confusion, and resulting software quality is low.

Meanwhile, the researcher also issued following questions about the phenomena of the projects:

(**Q1**) Why did not CVS data change from May 25th to June 5th?

(**Q2**) Why did the members delete many files from June 4th to 6th?

(**Q3**) How was the quality of these four modules: RankingScore.cpp, ScoreManager.cpp, ClickSocre.cpp, and GameSceneClickScore.cpp?

(**Q4**) Why was not CVS renewed during the last three days?

(**Q5**) How was the quality of the completed program?

In the second phase, the developers searched for the answers using Project Replayer. Resulting answers are shown as follows;

(**A1**: answer to **Q1**)

> Subject1~3: I remember that we had an examination in that period so we had to suspend the development.

(**A2**: answer to **Q2**)

> Subject1: I remember that we deleted image and sound files because it took long time to checkout from CVS repository.
>
> Subject2: We deleted image files because we changed image format from BMP to PNG. I confirmed deletion of many image files by the Replayer.
>
> Subject3: I think that some trouble occurred in the multimedia files, because the Replayer presented deletions of many image file and sound files.

(**A3**: answer to **Q3**)

> Subject1: **H2** is doubtful, because the Replayer shows that any modules were not changed after the module completion.
>
> Subject2: Most of them have good quality except of one module that was developed in only one day. Other modules were not revised once after they were completed. Therefore, the developers made carefully those modules, and those qualities were good. I confirmed this by the Replayer.
>
> Subject3: It is bad. I expected the modules were developed in a hurry at the end of project. I confirmed in Project Replayer.

(**A4**: answer to **Q4**)

> Subject1: Because the last three days were maintenance phase.
>
> Subject2: Maybe, the last three days were demonstration periods.
>
> Subject3: (No Answer)

(**A5**: answer to **Q5**)

> Subject1: I remember that the total quality is not high because bugs occurred in scoring functions.
>
> Subject2: The quality is not high. I remember there were bugs. I also found the existence of bugs using Project Replayer.
>
> Subject3: Not good. I realized that the LoC graph of Project Replayer indicates the growth of the curve was not to meet the deadline.

In the third phase, regarding provided answers, the researcher validated the hypotheses. The validation results and new findings are discussed in the following section.

6 Discussion

In this section, we discuss the validation of the researcher's hypotheses and the new finding in the experiments of Project Replayer.

At first, validation of the researcher's hypotheses is discussed. The first hypothesis **H1** was not clearly backed up by the developers' answers. Especially Subject2 said definitely that quality was good (See **A3**) though other subjects had doubt to the module quality. Therefore, we would say that the researcher should have to consider other factors, not just two factors, i.e. development period (only one day) and calendar time (the end of project). After additional analysis of the four modules in detail using Project Replayer, the researcher found that those were developed at the end of the project. Two of them that use other modules handling game-scores were assigned suddenly to two new developers, while game-scoring modules were completed later. It can be assumed that the two new developers didn't have sufficient knowledge about game-scoring specification. In fact, first two modules couldn't properly handle game-scores. Other two modules were assigned to another developer who developed game-scoring. Therefore, Hypothesis: **H1** should change to the following;

(**H1'**) If developers start developing modules at the end of project <u>and if the developers have little experience of developing the similar functions</u>, the modules' qualities are not good (This hypothesis may be regarded as a concrete case of Brooks' law that is "adding people to a late project makes it later"[5].)

Next, the second hypothesis **H2** is discussed. The researcher at once considered that the deadline was the 16th of June because CVS data was recorded until the 16th of June. Then the researcher set the hypothesis **H2** because it seems strange that the growth of LoC has stopped before the last day. After regarding the developers' answer **A4**, the researcher realized that true deadline was the 14th of June. With true deadline, no modification to the source code during June14th-16th seems quite natural now. Therefore, the researcher has withdrawn the hypothesis **H2**.

In general, researchers can validate their hypotheses in many projects with help of Project Replayer just like this way. After the hypotheses have been refined in many validations with Project Replayer, the hypotheses will be raised to simulation models.

Now, we discuss the usefulness of Project Replayer in the developer's viewpoint. The developers replayed past project using Project Replayer in search for the answers to the questions. The developers can review past projects when developers acquire new knowledge in past projects' phenomena. All developers successfully recognized the problem of the file size in BMP format in **Q2**. Subject2 and Subject3 identified this problem using Project Replayer. They will use different file format (PNG) to avoid the problem in future projects.

In addition, Subject1 and Subject3 noticed the problem of program quality in **Q3** and **Q5**. If the developers do not review past project, they would not have any rethinking about their program quality. Once the project has completed, the developer's matter of concern moves to other topics, or real engineers in industry do not have enough time to review past projects. Project Replayer provides developers with easy way to review past projects in very short time. Subject1 and Subject3 deeply re-thought the program quality. They searched logically, not intuitionally, for the problematic programs in short time. Project Replayer also helps the developers think logically in various situations.

7 Conclusion

We have proposed the KFC concept to circulate valuable knowledge acquired from past project processes. In the KFC concept, valuable knowledge is finally formalized as a simulation model that will be used in future projects. Project Replayer and Project Simulator are key tools of KFC to accelerate the knowledge circulation.

This paper mainly described features of Project Replayer. We also conducted preliminary experiments of Project Replayer, and showed that developers can acquire knowledge from past project with help of Project Replayer. Project Replayer was also applicable to support researchers make simulation models. In order to establish the KFC environment, we regard other tools such as Project Simulator also to be implemented and embedded. Moreover, we perform further evaluation and validation of the KFC's effectiveness by more controlled experiments in many organizations.

Acknowledgements

We would thank the anonimous reviewers for their valuable comments and suggestions to improve this paper. We would like to thank Kimiharu Ohkura in Software Design Lab. at NAIST for his contribution in implementation of the Replayer

This research was partially supported by the Japan Ministry of Education, Culture, Sports, Science and Technology, Grant-in-Aid for Scientific Research (C) 17500024, and also by the EASE project [6] in Comprehensive Development of e-Society Foundation Software program of the Japan Ministry of Education, Culture, Sports, Science and Technology.

References

1. Ohira, M., et al.: Empirical Project Monitor: A System for Managing Software Development Projects in Real Time. in Proceeding of ISESE2004, Vol.2 (2004) 37-38.
2. Navarro, O., E., van der Hoek, A.: SIMSE: An Interactive Simulation Game for Software Engineering Education. in Proceeding of CATE, (2004)12-17.
3. Pfahl, D., Klemm, M., Ruhe, G.: A CBT module with integrated simulation component for software project management education and training. The Journal of System and Software, No.59, (2001)283-298.
4. Henderson, P., et al.: A tool for evaluation of the software development process. The Journal of System and Software, No.59,(2001)355-362.
5. Brooks, P., F.: The Mythical Man-Month. Addison-Wesley Pub, 1995.
6. EASE Project, http://www.empirical.jp/

Software Process Measurement in the Real World: Dealing with Operating Constraints

Luigi Lavazza[1,2] and Marco Mauri[2]

[1] Università dell'Insubria – Varese, Dipartimento di Informatica e Comunicazione,
Via Mazzini, 5 – Varese, Italy
[2] CEFRIEL, Via Fucini, 2 - 20133 Milano, Italy
{lavazza, mmauri}@cefriel.it

Abstract. Process measurement occurs in an increasingly dynamic context, characterized by limited resources and by the need to deliver results at the pace of changing technologies, processes and products. Traditional measurement techniques (like the GQM) have been extensively and successfully employed in situations with little or no operating constraints. This paper reports about a measurement project in which –in order to limit the cost and duration of the activities– the team could not perform ad hoc measurements, but had to rely almost exclusively on the data that could be extracted automatically from development and measurement tools already in use. Exploiting the flexibility of the GQM technique, and with the support of a tool supporting the GQM, it was possible to define and execute the measurement plan, to analyze the collected data, and to formulate results in only three months, and spending a very small amount of resources.

Keywords: Process metrics, Product metrics Goal/Question/Metrics, Process quality assessment.

1 Introduction

The work described here was carried out in an organization of Banca Caboto in charge of the maintenance of a dozen banking applications, consisting mainly of Java code, SQL code, and HTML code. The size of the applications ranged from about 30 KLOCs (300 Function Points) to over 500KLOCs (over 9000 Function Points). The maintenance process employed 41 full-time people (13 employees and 28 people hired from external organizations) organized in three groups, each coordinated by a maintenance team leader.

The management of the organization needed to perform some basic evaluations of the process and products in order to support estimation activities and decision-making. For this purpose –having realized that objective quantitative data were needed– the management had started two measurement initiatives. The first one aimed at measuring the static properties of the managed software. For this purposed they adopted the CAST tool (http://www.castsoftware.com/). Measurement of the code was performed every three months on the whole set of applications. The collected data included for each application: LOCs, number of artifacts, backfired function points, number of files,

Q. Wang et al. (Eds.): SPW/ProSim 2006, LNCS 3966, pp. 80–87, 2006.

number of classes, average Java coupling and complexity, number of SQL artifacts, average SQL coupling and complexity, number of web pages. In addition, the difference between subsequent versions was assessed by measuring the variation of the aforementioned qualities. On the basis of these measures CAST computed a set of high-level indicators (most of which predefined), such as the "artifact granularity", functional size index, artifact coupling, technical complexity and standard violations. A second initiative consisted in measuring the Change Requests (CRs) stored in the tool adopted to keep track of changes (ClearQuest). The organization managed the CRs according to a standard lifecycle; transitions between lifecycle states were recorded by means of ClearQuest. The established measurement procedures provided the number of CRs per application and per state.

Although these initiatives provided the management with some useful data, they were not able to satisfy more complex evaluation needs, which the management expressed as a set of questions: *Are we doing our job well? Is the quality of the managed applications good? How good are the people in charge of maintenance?*

These questions were originated by the need to control, verify, estimate and evaluate the process and products, and ultimately to support management decisions.

The authors were asked to set up a measurement process that could deliver the required evaluation. It was thus decided to employ the GQM method [3, 4], which was suitable for converting the strategic goal into a measurement plan, and which had been previously successfully used by the authors [5, 9]. Throughout this paper we assume that the reader is familiar with the GQM.

The organization posed a few constraints that forced the GQM team to deviate from the standard GQM process. The constraints were:

- The measurement team had to provide results in three months. These could be initial results; however they had to be reasonably meaningful and reliable.
- The budget for data collection was quite limited.
- The measurement process had to be as non-intrusive as possible: the maintenance process was not to be disturbed. Only one project manager could be involved in the "manual" collection of data, and only for a very small fraction of her time.

The latter concern was originated by the need to keep the productivity of the maintenance process as high as possible –therefore people should not be distracted from their work– and by the awareness that the introduction of measurement programmes often generates resistance [7]: the management wanted to avoid problems with the acceptance of metrics programmes by developers.

The paper describes how the measurement activities were carried out in conformance of the constraints. We report what data it was possible to collect, how the original goals were affected by the limitations in measurement, and how it was necessary to redesign the GQM plan in order to fulfill the constraints.

The paper is organized as follows: Section 2 reports about the definition of the GQM plan. Section 3 describes the measurement phase; limits to the fulfillment of the GQM plan due to unavailable data are also described. Section 4 describes the data that it was possible to measure and the results that could be derived from such data. Section 5 illustrates related work. Finally, Section 6 summarizes the lessons learned and draws some conclusions.

2 The Planning Phase

The planning phase was carried out without taking into consideration any constraint. Although it was clear from the beginning of the work that only some of the required metrics were going to be collected, it was decided to build a complete GQM plan, i.e., a GQM plan that could in principle satisfy as thoroughly as possible the strategic goals. The rationale for this decision was twofold:

- It was not known in advance which metrics it will have been possible to collect. Excluding some metrics from the plan implied the risk of excluding metrics that actually could be collected without violating the operating constraints.
- The GQM team expected that the unconstrained GQM plan could provide a framework for assessing the relevance and quality of the available metrics, and for evaluating their meaning and reliability.

The strategic goals given by the management were translated –in a rather straightforward way– into the following set of GQM goals:

Goal 1: Analyze the maintenance process for the purpose of evaluating the quality of the product, from the point of view of the management of the organization.

Goal 2: Analyze the maintenance process for the purpose of evaluating the duration and cost of maintenance activities, from the point of view of the management of the organization.

Goal 3: Analyze the resources employed in the maintenance process for the purpose of evaluating their adequacy, from the point of view of the management of the organization.

The definition of the GQM plan was carried out employing the GQM tool [5, 10]. The tool supports the execution of GQM processes, by addressing both the generation of the GQM plan (including the precise definition of the metrics) and the successive phases of the process, namely data collection and analysis. The tool also integrates the measures database.

Given the very short time frame available for carrying out the whole GQM process, the availability of the GQM tool was fundamental. By employing the tool, the GQM team was able to define the GQM plan affectively and efficiently. In fact, in this phase the tool is particularly helpful in maintaining the GQM documentation in order, in identifying inconsistencies, redundancies and feasibility problems with the plan, and in generating the documentation for the management.

The GQM goals reported above were refined into abstraction sheets, questions and metrics according to the consolidated GQM practice. The complete GQM plan included 37 questions and 58 metrics.

The main object of the measurement activities was the execution and management of a Change Request. Therefore, most metrics concerned the CR. Every CR was characterized in terms of time and effort spent, type (defect correction or enhancement), lifecycle (i.e., the sequence of its states), application involved, amount and quality of the resources employed to perform the change, characteristics of the change (criticality, urgency, size, etc.).

3 The Measurement Phase

In order to produce reasonably sound and interesting results, while satisfying the constraints, the following operating criteria were adopted:

- Tools that were employed in the maintenance process had to be exploited to automatically derive as many measures as possible. This approach was expected to provide reliable data at a very low cost, and to provide measures as soon as the associated phenomena were available in the environment [9].
- Measurement tools that were already in place should have been exploited as well.
- Subjective data that did not require a big effort for collection (e.g., data that could be collected una tantum) were going to be obtained via interviews. For this purpose, the management designated one of maintenance team leaders to cooperate with the GQM team.

The analysis of the maintenance environment confirmed that the application of the criteria described above could result in deriving measures from CAST and from ClearQuest, and in obtaining some subjective data via interviews.

In order to ease the analysis phase, it was necessary to store all the collected data in a unique repository. ClearQuest records were initially extracted from the ClearQuest repository (currently implemented on top of an Oracle database) and inserted in a specifically designed Access database. All the measures corresponding to the GQM metrics were obtained by means of a step-by-step approach, which consisted of ad-hoc queries and some post-processing. In some cases the GQM team had to directly manipulate the contents of the tables. In the worst case, a simple Java program was needed to compute the relevant information concerning the durations of changes. The extraction of data from CAST was more difficult, since its internal repository was not designed (nor documented) in a way that allowed the final user to extract data from it. As a result, only some of the required data were extracted from the repository, while other data were obtained via the Web interface. Some of the data could not be obtained at all. Finally, all the collected data were inserted in an Access database, designed to store both measurements of code and data concerning difference between subsequent code versions. Differently from the CR information extracted from ClearQuest, no further post-processing activities were required.

When all the possible ways of extracting data from tools had been thoroughly explored, it appeared that the available data had a few quite serious limitations:

- The data was not at the required granularity level. In fact most of the metrics of the GQM plan were intended to capture the characteristics of each CR. On the contrary, the application code was measured every three months: thus the available data concerned versions that were "separated" by tens or hundreds of changes.
- It was not possible to retrieve the correspondence between every CR and the code modified in the execution of the request, since the ClearQuest records did not indicate which source files had been affected by the CR.
- Some fields in ClearQuest records were not regularly or consistently compiled. In particular, the indications concerning the estimated and actual effort required to manage a CR were often lacking or imprecise.

- Some subjective metrics were not collected, because the person that had to support the GQM team was too busy in her regular work to be able to dedicate enough time to the measurement activities.

As a consequence of these limitations it was quite clear that the original GQM plan could not be executed without modifications.

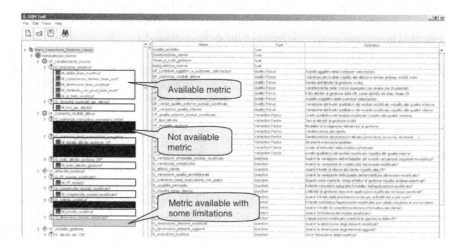

Fig. 1. Highlighting the available and not available metrics of the GQM plan

In order to understand the consequences of the unavailability of some metrics, and in particular in order to define a "simplified" GQM plan that could be successfully supported by the available metrics we proceeded as follows:

1. The metrics of the GQM plan were marked according to their availability. In Fig. 1 metrics are highlighted in different ways: boxed = available; blacked = not available; grayed = available with some limitations.
2. The structure of the GQM plan was exploited to understand the consequences of metrics unavailability: questions that had grayed or blacked metrics in their refinement could not be answered as planned. By considering the meaning of each gray and black element and its role in the GQM plan it was possible to assess to what extent the missing element could affect the goal.
3. On the basis of this assessment the whole GQM plan was revised in order to fit into the constraints. For instance the granularity of several questions changed: instead of referring to the management of the single CRs, they had to refer to the set of activities carried out in a three months period. As a consequence the involved goals did not change, but the associated results became less precise and accurate.
4. The GQM plan revision process was *dynamic*. In fact –also because of the short time available to complete the measurement process– it was not possible to fully understand what metrics were going to be collected before actually starting the collection phase. Therefore it was necessary to dynamically adjust the plan whenever a metric proved to be unavailable.

In summary, for goal 1, 14 questions out of 27 were modified and 2 were cancelled; for goal 2, 7 of 12 were modified; for goal 3, 4 of 13 were modified, and 2 cancelled.

4 Data Analysis and Results

The data collected from ClearQuest contained valuable information about the lifecycle of each CR. It was therefore possible to count the changes that were rejected, i.e., those that did not pass the acceptance test. It was found that the number of rejected changes was generally quite small, except for applications still under development.

Another type of analysis concerned the distribution in time of the CRs, according to their state. Fig. 2 shows the number of assigned, resolved and rejected changes per week. It indicates a generally good ability of the CR management process to satisfy the incoming requests, even in presence of peaks. However, it was not possible to estimate whether the volume of the work done to satisfy the CRs in a given time period was actually close to the amount required.

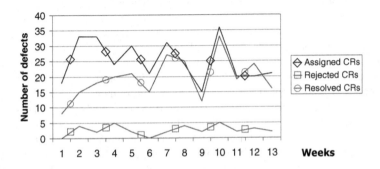

Fig. 2. Number of defect CRs per state in time

The GQM plan suggested also a type of analysis that was completely out of the scope of the previous measurement initiatives. In particular, the GQM plan indicated that the quality of the maintained product should be assessed in terms of defect density, which could be computed by combining the data derived from ClearQuest with the data derived from CAST. In particular, the dependency of the number of defects of an application from the characteristic of the application code was studied. It was thus found that no correlation could be established between the number of defects and the size (either measured in LOCs or in Function Points) of the applications. On the contrary, we found a good correlation between the number of defects and the number of Java classes contained in the code. In practice, data indicated that the object-oriented parts of applications were responsible for most defects.

Other results at the metric and question level are not reported here for space reasons. The results that could be obtained at the goal level are the following:

Goal 1. The maintenance process appears to be effective and the products of fairly good quality. Blocking defects and rejected changes are a small minority. Code changes do not affect quality.

Goal 2. Since it was not possible to collect measures on the "difficulty" of the CRs, nor on the effort required to perform changes, the part of the goal concerning costs could not be satisfied. The durations of maintenance activities appear reasonable and adequate with respect to priority.

Goal 3. The lack of data prevented the evaluation of the coherence between estimated and actual durations and costs. The resources appear generally adequate to satisfy the requests, preventing the creation of backlogs.

The results of the measurement process were presented (in much greater detail than given above) to the top management of Banca Caboto. They appreciated both the results and the method employed. They were also satisfied by the reusability of the measurement and analysis process and toolset in future measurement campaigns.

5 Related Work

Several experiences concerning "normal" usage of the GQM in industrial settings have been reported [5, 6, 13]. However, not much was reported about the usage of GQM in situations were data collection was severely constrained; in particular, we are not aware of any publication reporting the usage of the GQM as a tool easing the management of the operating constraints affecting the measurement process.

Actually, Mendonça and Basili [12] developed an approach combining the top-down GQM method with a bottom-up method based on a data mining. It is aimed at applying the principles of goal-oriented measurement in an environment that is already equipped with measurement practices. It aims at assessing if the user goals can be fulfilled by the data that is already being collected. Although this approach shares some objectives with ours, it is clearly more suitable for cases where large amounts of heterogeneous data are available. In our case, the identity and nature of the available data could be evaluated directly by the GQM team, who could assess whether user goals could be fulfilled by the available data and, when not, what modifications of the GQM plan were needed.

Concerning tool support, several articles address the problem of building frameworks specifically conceived to support measurement programmes [8, 2]. Unfortunately, it is often the case that a measurement programme has to be carried out in an environment that is not equipped with a suitable tool framework. Even worse, quite often the environment cannot be changed, or the allowed changes do not include the possibility of deploying new tools that could affect the development (or maintenance) process, e.g., changing the way developers (or maintainers) work.

Auer et al. evaluated tools that can be used in a measurement programme [1], but addressed rather low level issues, and considered only measurement tools, while other tools like ClearQuest can also play an important role as data providers.

6 Lessons Learned and Conclusions

A first observation is that tools (including development tools not specifically conceived for supporting measurement) can provide useful metrics. Data provided by tools –with the contribution of a small number of manually collected subjective data– can be sufficiently numerous and rich to support a whole measurement programme. Interestingly, tools provided the needed data in a quite non intrusive way.

In our case it was easier to extract data from a problem tracking tool than from a measurement tool: when selecting measurement tools, the possibility of exporting measures should be taken into due account.

The GQM tool was useful in organizing and documenting effectively the plan, and in supporting the identification of data unavailability and the evaluation of the consequences. For this purpose, the visibility "at a glance" of the plan, combined with the rigorous description of the GQM elements, greatly eased the task of revising the plan.

The GQM can provide a measurement framework that is useful even in presence of constraints that prevent several metrics from being collected. In the revision of the plan according to the data restrictions, the GQM was used –quite unusually– in a bottom-up fashion, as the decisions at the conceptual (goal/question) level were performed taking into account the situation at the operating (metrics/data) level.

In conclusion, the experience reported here can be seen as another confirmation of the value of the GQM, which performed well even in difficult and unprecedented operating conditions. Additional details on the work reported here can be found in [11].

References

1. Auer M., Graser B., Biffl S., A Survey on the Fitness of Commercial Software Metric Tools for Service in Heterogeneous Environments: Common Pitfalls, 9th International Software Metrics Symposium (METRICS'03), Sydney, Australia, September 2003
2. Aversano L., Bodhuin T., Canfora G. and Tortorella M., A Framework for Measuring Business Processes based on GQM, 37th Hawaii Int. Conference on System Sciences – 2004
3. V. Basili, GQM approach has evolved to include models, IEEE Software, vol.11, n.1, 1994.
4. Basili V., and Rombach H.D., The TAME project: towards improvement-oriented software environments, IEEE Transactions on Software Engineering, June, 1988.
5. Fuggetta A., Lavazza L., Morasca S., Cinti S., Oldano G., Orazi E., Applying G/Q/M in an Industrial Software Factory, ACM ToSEM, vol. 7, n. 4, October 1998.
6. Gresse C., Rombach D., and Ruhe G., Tutorial: A practical approach for building GQM-based measurement programs - Lessons learned from three industrial case studies, in Proceedings of 10th Brasilian Symposium on Software Engineering, Sao Carlos (Brasil), 1996
7. Hall, T. and Fenton N., Implementing software metrics — the critical success factors, Software Quality Journal, Kluwer Academic Publishers B.V., vol.3, n. 4, December 1994.
8. Kempkens R., Rösch P., Scott L., and Zettel J., Instrumenting Measurement Programs with Tools, in Proc. PROFES 2000, Oulu, Finland, June 2000, F. Bomarius and M. Oivo Eds. LNCS Vol. 1840
9. Lavazza, L., Providing automated support for the GQM measurement process, IEEE Software, vol. 17, n. 3, May-June 2000.
10. Lavazza, L. and Barresi, G., Automated Support for Process-aware Definition and Execution of Measurement Plans, ICSE 2005, St. Louis, May 2005.
11. Lavazza, L. and Mauri, M., Measurement tool support in the real world: a GQM experience, CEFRIEL Technical Report RT06001, March 2006.
12. Mendonça M.G. and. Basili V.R,, Validation of an Approach for Improving Existing Measurement Frameworks, IEEE TSE, Vol. 26, No. 6, June 2000.
13. van Solingen R., van Latum F., Oivo M., and Berghout E., Application of software measurement at Schlumberger RPS, in Proceedings of Sixth European Software Cost Modeling Conference, Paris, 1995.

Evaluation of Project Quality: A DEA-Based Approach

Shen Zhang[1,2], Yongji Wang[1,3], Jie Tong[1,3], Jinhui Zhou[1,3], and Li Ruan[1,3]

[1] Laboratory for Internet Software Technologies, Institute of Software,
The Chinese Academy of Sciences, Beijing 100080, China
{zhangshen, ywang, tongjie, jinhui,
ruanli} @itechs.iscas.ac.cn
[2] Key Laboratory for Computer Science,
The Chinese Academy of Sciences, Beijing 100080, China
[3] Graduate University, The Chinese Academy of Sciences, Beijing 100039, China

Abstract. The evaluation of project quality exhibits multivariable, VRS (variable return to scale) and decision maker's preference properties. In this paper, we present a Data Envelopment Analysis (DEA) based evaluation approach. The DEA VRS model, which handles multivariable and VRS effectively, is used to measure project quality. And the DEA cone ratio model, which utilizes Analytical Hierarchy Process (AHP) to constrain quality metrics with respect to decision maker's preference, is also adopted to analyze the return to scale of the projects. A case study, which assesses 10 projects from ITECHS and 20 "Top active" projects on sourceforge.net with the novel method, is demonstrated. The results indicate that our approach is effective for quality evaluation and can get accurate estimates of future possible improvements.

1 Introduction

Evaluation of project quality can lead to a better control of the schedule, cost and resources allocation, furthermore smooth the way for process improvement efforts. However, there are three characteristics embedded in the evaluation problem.

Firstly, defect, which is a key measure of software quality, consists of multiple attributes, such as defect severity, defect priority, etc. Thus, the quality evaluation has to deal with multi-attribute problem. Secondly, to evaluate project quality, we usually take software scale and defect attributes as input and output. However, as is stated in [5][6], the relationship between system size and the number of defects or defect-density is nonlinear. Thus, the problem of evaluation exhibits VRS (variable return to scale, i.e. the relationship between the input and the output is non-linear). Thirdly, generally speaking, the evaluation should be consistent with managerial goal of the organization. Thus, incorporating subjective managerial preference into quality assessment must be taken into account [2]. In a word, an efficient evaluation method is needed to fulfill these requirements of multivariate, VRS and decision maker's preference properties.

Data Envelopment Analysis (DEA) developed by A. Charnes and W. W. Cooper [12] in 1978 is a non-parametric mathematical programming approach. It can be used to evaluate the relative performance of a number of decision making units (DMU), which may have multivariate input and output. Henceforth, dozens of DEA extension

Q. Wang et al. (Eds.): SPW/ProSim 2006, LNCS 3966, pp. 88–96, 2006.

models have been brought into the world, Banker, Charnes and Cooper improved the basic theory and established the first DEA VRS model (BCC) [9] in 1984. Five years later, the C^2WH cone ratio model [11] with respect to "preference of decision maker" was brought forward by Charnes in 1989. At present, DEA has been widely accepted in the computing industry.

In this paper, we present a DEA-based approach to evaluate the project quality. The approach utilizes DEA CCR model and its extension models to calculate the quality score, which is the basis of the evaluation result. Since the datasets used for studies and analysis are collected from defect report and tracking systems, where cost and schedule information is insufficient, we only extract defect-related attributes from defect reports as input/output metrics in our approach. And then the quantitative results to measure the further possible improvements of low quality projects are discussed. Furthermore, the return to scale of each project with respect to decision maker's preference is also investigated.

2 Relate Work

[1] proposes to use DEA VRS model to measure the performance of ERP projects. Their method can handle multivariate data and VRS well, but doesn't take into account subjective managerial goal. Since they only evaluate the productivity as performance score, quality measurement is recommended to improve their work. Our work can be thought an extension of their study.

[10] presents a case study on an OSS(Open Source Software) development project, the FreeBSD project, and then compares the quality of OSS projects with that of commercial projects. But the evaluation only focuses on defect-density, which is the key quality metric, and ignores the impact brought about by other defect attributes. Also, their measurement can't deal properly with VRS.

J.C. Paradi et al. [2] introduce a DEA-based model to measure the performance of a group of software development projects and investigate the effect of quality on software maintenance projects. Decision maker's preference is incorporated into their model as well. However, the definition of quality used in their paper is quite narrow and omits other quality indicators, which can be easily extracted from defect reports.

In a word, compared with the existing models and methods for performance evaluation, our approach has the advantage of dealing with multivariate, VRS and decision maker's preference issues properly at the same time.

3 The DEA-Based Project Quality Evaluation Approach

In this section, we present our DEA-based project quality evaluation approach, which can be divided into four steps: constructing project dataset; establishing the input/output of DMUs; assessing project quality; analyzing Return to Scale. Figure 1 illustrates the flow chart of our approach.

3.1 Constructing Project Dataset

Constructing project dataset is to determine reference DMU sets. For the purpose of project quality measurement, we select each project under evaluation as a DMU. Moreover, because our DEA-based approach evaluates the relative quality among the similar DMUs, the basic requirement of the DMU selection is that the DMUs must be *homogenous*. The homogenous DMUs mean that they are project sets satisfying the same conditions, such as they are both object oriented projects and developed by the same language, so that the DMUs are comparable in quality.

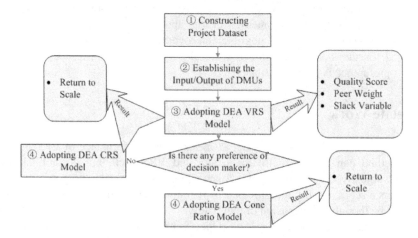

Fig. 1. DEA-based project quality evaluation approach

3.2 Establishing the Input/Output of DMUs

After constructing project dataset, we will establish input/output of DMUs [8] which largely depends on the selection of quality metrics.

Firstly, the defect reports specification of the projects under evaluation should be taken into account. It is because the selection of quality metrics is based mainly on the indicators provided by these defect reports. For example, when we choose quality metrics for the projects on sourceforge.net, we can't gather the information of defect priority and defect life-cycle, since defect reports on sourceforge.net don't provide any indicators of defect priority and defect life cycle at all.

Secondly, we must consider the relationship of the quality metrics. Because these metrics are not isolated, they may influence the cognizance of other variables. For example, we should discard a variable if its information has been covered by other several variables or has strong relationship with some other input/output variables.

Thirdly, we filter out the metrics that can't be quantified easily, for example, the customer satisfaction (corresponding to the comments submitted by customers in defect reports) and so on. Then we can generate the remaining metrics value for all the DMUs. Note that they are all positive values.

Fourthly, according to the efficiency ratio principle of DEA model, we prefer the smaller input values and bigger output values.

3.3 Assessing Project Quality

In order to evaluate the project quality, we adopt DEA VRS Model (BCC) [9] to deal with the nonlinear relationship inherent in the evaluation issue. The BCC model is written as:

$$
\left(D^{O}_{BC^{2}}\right)=
\begin{cases}
\max\left[\theta+\varepsilon\left(\sum_{i=1}^{m}s_{i}^{-}+\sum_{k=1}^{s}s_{k}^{+}\right)\right] \\[2mm]
\sum_{j=1}^{n}X_{j}\lambda_{j}+\sum_{i=1}^{m}s_{i}^{-}=X_{0} \\[2mm]
\sum_{j=1}^{n}Y_{j}\lambda_{j}-\sum_{k=1}^{s}s_{k}^{+}=\theta Y_{0} \\[2mm]
\sum_{j=1}^{n}\lambda_{j}=1 \\[2mm]
\lambda_{j}\geq 0,j=1,\ldots,n \\[1mm]
s_{i}^{+}\geq 0,i=1,\ldots,m \\[1mm]
s_{k}^{+}\geq 0,k=1,\ldots,s
\end{cases}
\tag{1}
$$

From (1) we calculate the quality score θ, the peer weight λ and slack variable s. The quality score is between 1 and $+\infty$, A project with quality score of 1 is of *relative high quality*, otherwise the project is of *relative low quality*. Each project can be presented by a linear combination of the DMU sets, such as: $DMU_{j0}=\lambda_{i}DMU_{i}+\lambda_{k}DMU_{k}+\cdots+\lambda_{j}DMU_{j}$. The peer weight λ_{i} provides the degree that high-quality project i for the relatively low-quality project j_{0} to emulate. The slack variable s can be divided into two parts: input slack variable s^{-} and output slack variable s^{+}. The former represents the over use of work effort scale, while the latter represents the insufficient quality metrics. Since we focus on defect elimination, we present the formula (2) to calculate the quantitative improvement of every quality metric for low-quality projects:

$$
\Delta=\theta y_{j0}+s_{j}^{+}-y_{j0}
\tag{2}
$$

3.4 Analyzing Return to Scale

After computing the results using DEA VRS model, we analyze return to scale between software scale and the quality metrics represented by defect attributes. For this purpose, we should take into account whether some specific managerial preference exists. When there is no impact of managerial preference, we can combine the results of DEA CRS model and VRS model to judge return to scale. First, calculate the quality score δ with DEA CRS model, then compare δ with θ, there are three conditions: 1) $\delta<\theta$, the project exhibits IRS ; 2) $\delta=\theta$, the project exhibits CRS; 3) $\delta>\theta$, the project exhibits DRS. —IRS (DRS) indicates that an increase in one unit's inputs will yield a greater (or less) proportionate increase of its outputs.

Otherwise, when it is necessary to incorporate subjective managerial preference in return to scale analysis, we should utilize the DEA cone ratio model [11] to fulfill managerial goals. In order to constrain the weights of quality metrics according to managerial preference, we adopt AHP (Analytical Hierarchy Process) [7]. Firstly, we gather opinions of several project managers on "the importance of each quality metrics", then establish the AHP Decision Matrix A_m and calculate the max latent root λ_{max} of A_m. Secondly, we construct weight constraint

$$\Gamma = \left\{ \mu \mid (A_m - \lambda_{max} E_m)\mu \geq 0 \right\} \tag{3}$$

where μ in Γ means the weights of quality metrics. Thirdly, incorporating Γ into DEA cone ratio model (4),(5) and calculate the parameter μ_0 which is the indicator of return to scale. There are also three conditions: 1) $\mu_0 < 0$, the project exhibits DRS; 2) $\mu_0 = 0$, the project exhibits CRS; 3) $\mu_0 > 0$, the project exhibits IRS;

$$\left(\hat{P}_{C^2R}\right) = \begin{cases} V_1 = \min(\omega^T X_0) \\ \omega^T X_j - \mu^T Y_j \geq 0, j = 1,\ldots,n \\ \mu^T Y_0 = 1 \\ (A_m - \lambda_{max} E_m)\mu \geq 0 \end{cases} \tag{4} \qquad \left(\hat{P}_{BC^2}\right) = \begin{cases} V_2 = \min(\omega^T X_0 - \mu_0) \\ \omega^T X_j - \mu^T Y_j + \mu_0 e^T \geq 0, j = 1,\ldots,n \\ \mu^T Y_0 = 1 \\ (A_m - \lambda_{max} E_m)\mu \geq 0 \end{cases} \tag{5}$$

4   Case Study

In this section, an empirical study is presented based on the sequence in Section 3.

Firstly, we construct the evaluation data sets. The first dataset consists of 10 projects from one single organization —ITECHS [3]. On the contrary, our second dataset consists of 20 "Top active" projects on sourceforge.net [4], which are developed by different organizations. These projects of the two datasets are all developed in Java. Especially the projects in the first dataset are all J2EE Web Applications, so the DMUs can be regarded as *homogenous*.

Secondly, according to the specification of defect reports of selected projects (13 metrics in total), we have chosen the following metrics for the first dataset. While only defect severity, system size and work effort are used in the second dataset as its Input/Output metrics.

Table 1. Input/Output metrics for evaluation

Metrics	Type	Meaning
Defect Severity	Output	Defects can be divided into four levels by severity: C,S,N,M.
Defect Life Cycle	Output	Defects can be divided into five class by the length of its life cycle: I,S,M,L,E
Defect Priority	Output	Defects can be divided in to three level by priority: H,M,L
System Size	Output	
Work Effort	Input	

Thirdly, the results of the quality measures on the ITECHS dataset using DEA VRS model are presented in Table 2. We observe that only two DMUs 6,7 are of relative low quality, while other eight DMUs are all of relative high quality. Moreover, the relative low quality projects can be improved under relative high quality projects' guidance in the future. For example, DMU6 can be shown in the following form: 0.06*DMU1+0.48*DMU2+0.25*DMU9+0.20*DMU10, so the DMU2 is of more benefit to help quality improvement since its peer weight is larger than others'.

Table 2. Quality scores and peer weights obtained from DEA VRS model (Dataset 1)

DMU	Quality score	λ_1	λ_2	λ_3	λ_4	λ_5	λ_6	λ_7	λ_8	λ_9	λ_{10}
1	1.00	1.00	0.00	0.00	0.00	0.00	0.00	0.00	0.00	0.00	0.00
2	1.00	0.00	1.00	0.00	0.00	0.00	0.00	0.00	0.00	0.00	0.00
3	1.00	0.00	0.00	1.00	0.00	0.00	0.00	0.00	0.00	0.00	0.00
4	1.00	0.00	0.00	0.00	1.00	0.00	0.00	0.00	0.00	0.00	0.00
5	1.00	0.00	0.00	0.00	0.00	1.00	0.00	0.00	0.00	0.00	0.00
6	1.36	0.06	0.48	0.00	0.00	0.00	0.00	0.00	0.00	0.25	0.20
7	1.22	0.15	0.31	0.00	0.00	0.00	0.00	0.00	0.00	0.00	0.55
8	1.00	0.00	0.00	0.00	0.00	0.00	0.00	0.00	1.00	0.00	0.00
9	1.00	0.00	0.00	0.00	0.00	0.00	0.00	0.00	0.00	1.00	0.00
10	1.00	0.00	0.00	0.00	0.00	0.00	0.00	0.00	0.00	0.00	1.00

In Table 3, the output slack variables s^+ can be used to calculate the margin of quality improvement for each quality metric. For example, in order to reduce the defects whose life-cycle is 6-10 days ("M"—Medium in defect life-cycle defined in table 1) in project 6, we combine the slack variable s_8^+ =217 with formula(2) in section 3.3, then calculate the $\triangle$= 9. The result means that the defects, whose life-cycle is "M" in project 6, can get an optimal reduction by 9 under the relative high quality projects' guidance in the future development.

Based on the Sourceforge dataset, we get the similar aggregate result. In Table 4, we only show the quality scores of the 20 projects.

Table 3. Slack variables obtained from DEA VRS model (Dataset 1)

DMU	Work Effort	System Size	Defect Severity				Defect Life-Cycle					Defect Priority		
			C	S	N	M	I	S	M	L	E	H	M	L
	s_1^-	$s_1^+, s_2^+,$ .... $, s_{13}^+$												
6	248	0	3	10	43	49	0	62	217	36	25	0	98	0
7	0	0	2	34	72	106	4	77	83	75	59	0	131	174

Table 4. Quality scores obtained from DEA VRS model (Dataset 2)

DMU	1	2	3	4	5	6	7	8	9	10
θ	3.79	5.59	5.38	3.02	3.65	1.00	1.98	2.78	7.39	6.53
DMU	11	12	13	14	15	16	17	18	19	20
θ	5.02	10.18	1.00	3.77	7.64	3.79	10.49	6.74	5.49	3.58

Fig.2 illustrates a comparison of two methods for quality evaluation of the two datasets. The first method is our DEA-based approach, while the second is to assess quality by defect-density (abbreviated as DD). In the chart, x-axis denotes project number, y-axis denotes quality score. Fig.2 reveals that DEA-based approach can make a more fair evaluation than DD, which can't handle VRS. For example, the third project in the second dataset is regarded as a project of the lowest quality by DD, since its defect-density is nearly 20 times greater than that of project 13, whose defect-density is the lowest. But using DEA-based approach, the quality score is only 5 times greater than that of the highest quality project. The reason for this is that project 3 is the biggest project with 409829 lines of code and 2113 defects, while project 13 has only 115144 lines of code and 43 defects. It is obvious that the comparison between a large project like 3 and a small project like 13 in defect-density is inappropriate, since the evaluation problem exhibits VRS. In general, it seems more reasonable to compare a project with other projects of similar size. So applying our VRS approach is more appropriate to solve the problem. Besides, as can be seen in Fig.2, the curve of dataset 1 is much smoother and closer to 1 than that of dataset 2 in our approach. It means that the process performance of ITECHS is significantly higher than that of the projects in dataset 2.

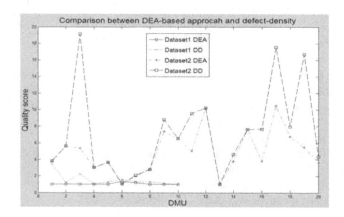

Fig. 2. Comparison between DEA-based approach and defect-density

Table 5. Return to scale obtained from DEA cone ratio model (Dataset 1)

DMU	1	2	3	4	5	6	7	8	9	10
V_1	2.04	1.00	1.38	1.17	1.46	1.86	1.61	1.44	1.35	1.35
V_2	1.00	1.00	1.00	1.00	1.00	1.42	1.31	1.00	1.00	1.00
μ_0	minus	0	minus	minus	minus	minus	minus	minus	minus	minus
result	DRS	CRS	DRS	DRS	DRS	DRS	DRS	DRS	DRS	DRS

In the last step, we present how to use our approach to analyze the return to scale of each DMU. As we have consulted several project managers from ITECHS for their preference on the quality metrics listed in table 1, we are convinced that the cone ratio

DEA model should be adopted to investigate the return to scale for the first dataset. After building the AHP Decision Matrix by incorporating the managerial goals, we use the modified model (4),(5) to calculate the results which is shown in Table 5. As we can see, all the projects except the second have DRS, which means the rate of various defects attributes in these projects increases quicker than the rate of the expending work effort. So the managers should consider of slowing down the scale expansion of these projects, then turn to make improvements in process efficiency.

5 Conclusion

The paper focuses on three intrinsic characteristics of project quality evaluation: multivariable, Variable Return to Scale (VRS) and preference of decision maker. To overcome the difficulties caused by these characteristics, we advocate a DEA-based approach which can fulfill these requirements. A case study illustrates the principle of our approach well. The results of the DEA-based approach is helpful to assess the project quality and estimate the margin of future possible improvement. The return to scale analysis can also help managers to make a decision on an expansion or a reduction in software scale.

Acknowledgements

This paper was partially supported by the National Natural Science Foundation of China (Grant Number: 60373053), 863 Program (Grant Number: 2005AA113140), the Plan of Hundreds Scientists in the Chinese Academy of Sciences, and the key program of the National High-Tech Research and Development Program of China (Grant Number: 2003AA1Z2220).

References

1. Stensrud, E., Myrtveit, I.: Identifying High Performance ERP Projects. IEEE Transaction on Software Engineering, 29(5) (2003) 387-416
2. Paradi, J.C., Reese, D.N., Rosen, D.: Applications of DEA to measure the efficiency of software production at two large Canadian banks. Annals of Operations Research 73(1997)91 – 115
3. http://itechs.iscas.ac.cn/
4. http://sourceforge.net/index.php
5. Malaiya, Y.K. Denton, J.: Module Size Distribution and Defect Density Software Reliability Engineering. Software Reliability Engineering, (2000)62-71
6. Rosenberg, J.: Some Misconceptions About Lines of Code. Software Metrics Symposium, (1997) 137-142
7. Golden, B.L., Wasil, E.A., Harker, P.T. (Eds.): The Analytic Hierarchy Process - Applications and Studies. Springer-Verlag (1989)
8. Liang L, CUI J.C.: Selection of Input-output Items and Data Disposal in DEA. Journal of Systems Engineering, 18(6) (2003) 487-490

9. Banker R.D., Charnes A., Cooper W.W.: Some Models for Estimating Technical and Scale Inefficiencies in Data Envelopment Analysis. Management Science, 30(9) (1984) 1078-1092.
10. Dinh-Trong T. Bieman J.M.: Open source software development: a case study of FreeBSD Software Metrics, Software Metrics, (2004) 96 - 105
11. Charnes A., Cooper W.W., Wei Q.L., etc.: Cone Ratio Data Envelopment Analysis and Multi-Objective Programming. International Journal of System Science, Vol. 20. 7 (1989) 1099-1118
12. Charnes A., Cooper W.W., Rhodes E.: Measuring the Efficiency of Decision Making Units. European J. Operational Research, Vol. 2. (1978) 429-444

A Pattern-Based Solution to Bridge the Gap Between Theory and Practice in Using Process Models

Antonio Amescua, Javier García, Maria-Isabel Sánchez-Segura,
and Fuensanta Medina-Domínguez

Computer Science Department, Carlos III Technical University of Madrid,
Avda. Universidad, 30, Leganes 28911, Madrid, Spain
{amescua, jgarciag, misanche, fmedina}@inf.uc3m.es

Abstract. In order to extend the use of software process improvement programs and to make it independent of organizational features, this work describes the results obtained using a knowledge based model and tool, and proposes a pattern-based solution, using a SPEM (Software Process Engineering Metamodel) extension, in order to improve the efficiency of use of the knowledge-based model proposed.

1 Introduction

The implementation of a software process improvement program is very expensive, especially for SMEs (Small and Medium Enterprises) and those organizations that first undertake an initiative of this type [1].

Due to the importance for organizations to develop improvement programmes in order to be competitive, their handicap in implementing them and the cost and time required, it is necessary to make improvement programmes accessible to most organizations, independently of the features of each organization.

The experience of the Federal Aviation Administration (FAA) of the United States of America indicates that knowledge management combines positively with process improvement, benefits the organization and the process improvement programmes [2]. Some other works, like the one published in [3], suggest that a knowledge infrastructure consisting of technology, structure and culture, along with knowledge process architecture of acquisition, conversion, application, and protection, are essential organizational capabilities or "preconditions" for effective knowledge management.

Knowledge management is based on four elements: *data-information-knowledge-innovation.* We believe that the knowledge management discipline can work together with software engineering in order to translate software engineering data and information, described as process models, standards, methodologies, etc., to knowledge and innovation once the knowledge of experts on process model, standards, methodologies, etc., is elicited and translated into a computable model. Therefore, a software system can deal with this knowledge in order to reduce the cost of process definitions and increase the maturity of the processes faster.

Data and information must be encapsulated to allow their subsequent recovery and reuse, and their evolution into knowledge. The artefact to encapsulate these data and

Q. Wang et al. (Eds.): SPW/ProSim 2006, LNCS 3966, pp. 97–104, 2006.

information is based on the concept of process patterns which define a general solution to a specific recurring problem [4]. The authors propose the concept *product pattern* that has been formalized using the SPEM (Software Process Engineering Metamodel) standard [5]. Knowledge management techniques will be used to recover and reuse the concept *product pattern*.

Although process improvement can be applied to a very wide range of processes, the importance of project management in the failure or success of a project is widely recognized [6] [7] [8]. This is why we are focusing on a specific set of project management processes improvement.

The research results included in this paper are divided into two main phases:

- The first represents the previous work of this research team to demonstrate the importance and the validity of working together in the fields of knowledge management and software process improvement. These results are illustrated in the paper through a brief description of the PIBOK-Model and the PIBOK-Tool as well as the results obtained from the use of both.
- The second is an improvement on the first and represents the current work, using the concept product patterns formalized with SPEM [5].

This paper is structured as follows: section 2 identifies some works related to the one presented in this paper; section 3 describes the PIBOK-Model in a static way, focusing on the model components and, in a dynamic way, explains how the model should be used. This section also summarises the results obtained using the PIBOK-model on real projects; section 4 describes the improvements under development with the version of PIBOK-Model presented, using the product pattern concept formalized with SPEM language; and finally section 5 presents the conclusions.

2 Related Works

Currently, there are no results in combining knowledge management discipline with software process improvement based on process patterns. There are some related works, however, where the concept of pattern has been used to support development processes [9][[10]. These works try to describe the process pattern in different ways.

In [9] the authors used templates for process pattern description; most of the fields in this template were described in natural language. This is a deficiency as the natural language is abstract and ambiguous.

The above deficiency was solved by proposing the Process Pattern Description Language, which embodies the concept process pattern without using natural language [11]. In [10], the authors also presented the metamodel PROPEL (Process Pattern Description Language) which provides concepts for the semiformal description of process pattern, but this metamodel is not a formalization of process patterns themselves. In this sense, we propose a process pattern formalization based on a conceptual model oriented towards defining processes called SPEM [5]. The purpose of SPEM is to support the definition of software development processes, specifically including those processes that involve the use of UML [5]. SPEM provides XMI (XML Metadata Interchange) that is based on the W3C's eXtensible Markup Language (XML). Therefore, SPEM provides a graphic language formalization.

In some related works [9][10], the process patterns are defined to support development processes as a general solution to a certain recurring problem. However, in the software development process, projects execute processes that produce software products. This is why we believe that the general solutions to be reused are not the processes but the software products, and we propose the concept *"product pattern"* to gather the knowledge of software engineering experts in order to obtain a specific software product. More details about product patterns can be found in section 4.

3   Previous Work: Software Process Improvement and Knowledge Management can Work Together

3.1   PIBOK-Model: A Knowledge Based Model Approach to Process Improvement

We believe, as well as the authors mentioned in section 1, that a knowledge-based approach can enhance the implementation of improvement programmes. This section is dedicated to describing the results obtained from the use of the PIBOK-Tool supporting the PIBOK-Model as well as the improvements to the above-mentioned model and tool after analyzing the data obtained from organizations.

With the description of the problem and our hypothesis, the main goals of the work achieved from 2002 to 2004 were:

1. to develop a knowledge-based software process improvement model (PIBOK-Model: Process Improvement Based On Knowledge management Model) and a support tool (PIBOK-Tool: Process Improvement Based On Knowledge management Tool) that would allow organizations to evaluate the current state of their processes and assist in defining their project management processes.
2. to determine the validity and ease of use of PIBOK-Tool in assessing and defining the organization's project management processes.

In order to provide the infrastructure needed to support the proposed PIBOK-Model we identified a set of components and defined how the PIBOK-model must be used. Fig. 1 summarizes both the components and the procedure for using the PIBOK-Model. It shows the logical architecture of the model.

PIBOK-Model is intended to improve software project management processes based on the standard PMBOK (Project Management Body of Knowledge) [12], software engineering reference models such as SW-CMM [13], CMMI [14][15], ISO 15504 [16], etc. and the most important project management methodologies such as Prince2 and Métrica3, DOIT, TenStep.

Each component of the model is identified with a number in brackets. The description of each component follows:

1. The PMBOK process framework configures the core of PIBOK-Model.
2. The PMBOK processes are detailed using experts' opinion and are based on the software reference models practices, for example, SW-CMM, CMMI, ISO 15504.
3. The process details are enhanced with the process assets of the most important project management methodologies, for example, Métrica 3, Prince2, TenStep.

4. The creation of a knowledge base that contains the meta software project management process definitions is the result of this model.
5. Using the PIBOK-Model, all the organization's process assets, which enhance the software project management process definition, are gathered during the process assessment phase. These software process definitions and their assessment information are stored in the knowledge base.
6. As an aid to improving the processes, PIBOK-Model also offers the possibility of adapting generic process assets, which are stored in the knowledge base and are taken from the most important project management methodologies. The standard software project management processes will be defined semi-automatically from the assessment results.
7. Once the organization has the standard definition of its software project management processes, the PIBOK-Model allows the standard processes to adapt to each concrete project.
8. The knowledge base also allows the products generated during the execution of management activities to be stored, thereby configuring a software project management historical data base within the organization.

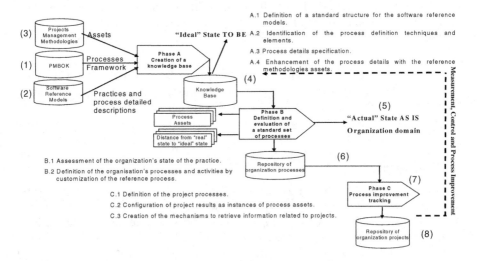

Fig. 1. Architecture of the PIBOK-Model

3.2 PIBOK-Model and Tool Experimentation and Results Obtained

PIBOK (Model and Tool) has been validated in several software organizations by training their high-level managers in the model concepts and their use in several software process improvement programs.

The aim was to determine the validity and ease of use of the PIBOK-Model for software process improvement.

During this validation phase, the researchers controlled the effort invested by seven groups (a total of 32 people) in charge of defining and implementing a software project management process using PIBOK-Model. This information was compared with the control data gathered from the six other workgroups (33 people) that had previously defined and implemented a software project management process without using PIBOK Model. The effort data used for this validation was computed using an effort registry form that had to be filled in each week by each member of the working groups. Table 1 shows the effort accumulated by the software project management processes definition and implementation work teams. For more information regarding the obtained results see the information in http://163.117.154.99/Patterns/ResultsPIBOKModel-Tool.htm

Table 1. Effort of Software Process Improvement activities

	Number of Groups	Time (minutes)	Average (minutes)
Without PIBOK-Tool	6	62099	10349,8
With PIBOK-Tool	7	44706	6386,5

4   Current Work: Using a Formalization of Pattern Concept

Despite the good results using the PIBOK-Model during the experimentation phase, there are some parameters we would like to focus on in an improved version. If we take a look at the results using PIBOK-Model and Tool, we realize that the efficiency of use and knowledge management capacity could be improved.

To achieve these, we are working on:

- improving the efficiency of use of the PIBOK-Model (understood as the number of tasks performed per time unit), moving from the actual ETVX (entry tasks verification exit) format to a graphical representation.
- achieving the next two knowledge management stages: knowledge and innovation.

The concrete changes, which have already been approved and in course, are described in detail below.

4.1   Changes to Process Definition Technique

The first change adopted is related to how to represent the definition of software processes. Currently, the processes are defined using an extended ETVX definition technique containing the following information items: Purpose, Preceding Processes/Activities, Subsequent Processes/Activities, Entry Criteria, Inputs, Activities/Tasks, Outputs, Exit Criteria, Practices, Tools and techniques, Metrics/Measurements, Interfaces with other processes, Roles and Notes.

The new way to define the processes is using SPEM [5]. SPEM is a conceptual model to define processes based on UML extensions. It provides a formal language, that is an XMI extension, and a graphical language to represent processes following UML basic diagrams.

In order to provide the functionalities related to process definition using SPEM, we are working on several adaptations related to:

- the modification of the internal structure of PIBOK-model repository to maintain specific information of processes considered in SPEM but not in extended ETVX.
- the adaptation of SPEM to PIBOK-Model needs. To satisfy all our requirements, SPEM model has to be extended to include information related to practices, lessons learned, metrics and measurements information.
- the modification of PIBOK-Tool user interface. Currently, the definition of a software process is exclusively based on text fields. SPEM provides a graphic language to represent the concepts to model software process, so the new user interface will be based on graphic components to draw the processes.

4.2 Changes to Process Definition Technique

In the last version of PIBOK-Model, the software processes are defined as a set of activities that are extracted from PM-BOK and enriched with information from software process reference models and the most outstanding software development methods.

In order to improve the knowledge management capacity of PIBOK-Model, the software process will now be defined in terms of the products to be elaborated and used during the process execution. All the products available to define the processes are also extracted from PMBOK and enriched with information from the most outstanding software development methods. We have defined a new concept called "product pattern" to determine how the products should be elaborated, updated and used during a software process.

The concept *"product pattern"* is a new term that comes from the Alexandrian Patterns [17], and is intended to gather the knowledge of software engineering experts to obtain a specific software product, understanding product as anything to be produced during the whole software development process. This product pattern is described in terms of the following fields:

- **Name:** name of the product pattern
- **Related patterns**
- **Initial Context:** Present situation where the project is being executed.
- **Resulting Context:** Future situation as a result of executing the pattern.
- **Problem:** Improvements to be achieved.
- **Forces:** Forces can come from different sources. We have identified the following sources of forces:
  - o Organization features
  - o Kind of system to be developed
  - o Kind of client
  - o Market Scope
- **Solution:** instantiations of products previously obtained in this context with this problem entailing these forces, including time for completion.
- **Roles**
- **Entries:** previously obtained products necessary to develop this one.
- **Lessons Learned**
- **Examples**

- **Exit:** Exit can come with the following attributes:
  - o   Name
  - o   Types of information content enclosed
  - o   A check box to specify whether or not the exit has configuration management.

The product patterns solution, entries and exit will be defined using SPEM. However, the rest of the information will be implemented using conceptual models.

These conceptual models are used because they allow the use of knowledge management recovery techniques and transformation of the experts knowledge in innovation. This transformation affects the component (4) in **Fig. 1**, which in the next version of PIBOK-Model, from now PIBOK-PB-Model, is represented as *product patterns* instead of ETVX format.

In the PIBOK-PB-Model, the selection of the concept *product pattern* as the element to encapsulate knowledge is based on the idea that a product is the minimum software engineering element to be obtained in any process model execution and the same product can be involved in different process model. This is why we believe that a "product" knowledge-based solution is more flexible and reusable than a knowledge-based process solution.

In order to execute a software project, the project manager will find the appropriate *product patterns* from (4) in **Fig. 1**, based on the following rule:

> If you find yourself in this context (and) with this problem (and) entailing these forces
> then
> map a product pattern in your project (and)look for product patterns

At present we are working with software engineering experts on the identification of the criteria that allows the appropriate classification and recovery of product patterns according to the context, problem and forces of the project to be developed in which the product patterns are being used. Some examples of the product patterns we are working on can be reached at http://163.117.154.99/Patterns/ProductPatternsExamples.htm

5   Conclusions and Future Trends

The work achieved from 2002 to 2004 allowed the definition and implementation of PIBOK-Model and Tool, and the validation demonstrated that software process improvement field and knowledge management techniques work well together. As the PIBOK-Model has been used in some organizations, this means that the proposed model is able to support improvement programs in SMEs.

The software engineering field has evolved a lot in the formalization of software processes, although today the proposed formalisms are difficult to use and their efficiency of use is very low. The proposed PIBOK-Model and tools represent a first step in bridging the gap between theory and practice in using software processes and, in general, software engineering formalisms.

The new version of PIBOK-Model will be able to incorporate the capability to help project managers implement an improvement program using a graphical interface. The efficiency of use of processes will also be incremented. In addition, the rapid technology evolution will allow us to go from the real version of PIBOK-Tool, which is web based, to a version based on collaborative web environments.

Acknowledgements

This work has been partially funded by the Spanish Ministry of Science and Technology through the TIC2004-7083 project.

References

[1] Pinto R. and Shoemaker D. "The Cost of CMM in a Conventional IT Organization: A Field Study", 2002.
[2] Burke, D., Howard, W. Knowledge Management and Process Improvement: A Union of Two Disciplines. The journal of defense software engineering. Jun 2005. Available at: http://www.stsc.hill.af.mil/crosstalk/2005/06/0506Burke.html
[3] Gold, A., Malhotra, A., and Segars, A. Knowledge Management: An Organizational Capabilities Perspective. Journal of Management Information Systems. (2001). Vol. 18 No. 1, pp. 185 – 214.
[4] Gnatz, M, Marschall, F., Popp, G, Rausch, A, and Schwerin, W. Modular Process Patterns supporting an Evolutionary Software Development Process. Lecture Notes in Computer Science. (2001). Vol. 2188.Pages: 326 – 340.
[5] OMG, Software Process Engineering Metamodel Specification (SPEM) Versión 1.1, January 2005
[6] White, D., Fortune, J., Current practice in project management – an empirical study. (2002). International Journal of Project Management. Vol. 20, Issue 1, Pp. 1-11.
[7] Nienaber, R., Cloete, E. A software agent framework for the support of software project management. (2003). Proceedings of the SAICSIT 2003. Pp 16-23.
[8] McConnell, E., Nine Deadly Sins of Project Management. From the Editor IEEE Software, (2001). Available at: http://www.stevemcconnell.com/ieeesoftware/iec19.htm
[9] Iida, H. Pattern-Oriented Approach to Software Process Evolution. (1999).
[10] Hagen, M,, Gruhn, V. Process Patterns - a Means to Describe Processes in a Flexible Way. (2004).
[11] Dittmann, T., Gruhn, V., Hagen, M. Improved Support for the Description and Usage of Process Patterns. (2002)
[12] Project Management Institute (PMI), "The Project Management Body of Knowledge (PMBOK)", Project Management Institute, Upper Darby, PA, (1987).
[13] Paulk M., Garcia S., Chrissis M., and Bush M. Capability Maturity Model for Software, Version 1.1, CMU/SEI-93-TR-24. Technical Report. Software Engineering Institute. Carnegie Mellon University, (1993).
[14] Software Engineering Institute. "CMMI for Systems Engineering, Software Engineering, Integrated Product and Process Development, and Supplier Sourcing (CMMI-SE/SW/IPPD/SS, V1.1)", Carnegie Mellon University, March, (2002).
[15] Phillips M. "CMMI V1.1 Tutorial". Software Engineering Institute. Carnegie Mellon University, (2003).
[16] Standard ISO/IEC 15504-5:1999 Standard for Information Technology-Software process assessment. (1999).
[17] Alexander, C. A Pattern Language: Towns, Buildings, Construction. Oxford University Pres. (1977)

On Mobility of Software Processes*

Mingshu Li[1,2], Qiusong Yang[1,3], Jian Zhai[1,3], and Guowei Yang[1,3]

[1] Laboratory for Internet Software Technologies,
Institute of Software, Chinese Academy of Sciences, Beijing 100080, China
{mingshu, qiusong_yang, zhaijian, yangguowei}@itechs.iscas.ac.cn
[2] State Key Laboratory of Computer Science,
Institute of Software, Chinese Academy of Sciences, Beijing 100080, China
[3] Graduate University of Chinese Academy of Sciences, Beijing 100039, China

Abstract. In this paper, the *mobility of software processes* is proposed
as a novel concept. It is defined as the structural change in a software
process resulting from interactions among linked process elements. The
concept addresses the essential change in a software process which brings
a high variability and unpredictability to process performance. Three
categories of the *mobility* that lead to the structural change are identified
and expounded upon. A reference model for describing the concept is put
forward based on the polyadic π-calculus. With the *mobility of software
processes*, it is possible to design a new PCSEE and associated PML with
increased flexibilities.

1 Introduction

The research on software processes is to enable people to produce high quality software systems and evolve them in an economic and timesaving fashion. The main stream of effort has been on concepts definition, languages and
complete process-centered software engineering environments (PCSEEs). The
process "culture" is widely recognized and adopted. However, existing PCSEEs
fail today in satisfying the market's evolution and the demand that may be summarized by [1]: the support of long lived and widely distributed, heterogeneous,
evolving and flexible processes. The notion of flexible process support costs an
extra price. The more flexible and adaptable PCSEEs are (in other words, the
wider the variety of processes which can be supported), the weaker is the support
for a concrete process [2].

A software process is still human intensive and almost impossible to be improved by a product view like in classic manufacturing. It is a set of activities
or operations that needs to always change for a variety of reasons. In order to
improve process support technology, we have to answer the following questions:

- What is the essential change in software processes?
- Based on the essential change, is it possible to define a novel concept?

* Supported by the National Natural Science Foundation of China under grant No.
60273026, 60473060, 60573082 and the Hi-Tech Research and Development Program
(863 Program) of China under grant No. 2004AA112080, 2005AA113140.

– Is there a reference model that can be devised to describe the concept?
– Can this model be used to design a PCSEE/PML (process modelling language) to support the essential change in software processes?

2   Mobility of Software Processes

It is widely accepted that the quality of software is related to not only the product, but the organization and the production process. According to Webster's dictionary, a *process* is "a series of operations performed in the making or treatment of a product" or "a series of actions, changes, or functions bringing about a result". Various definitions of the software process have been put forward from different angles:

– A software process can be defined as a set of activities, methods, practices, and transformations that people use to develop and maintain software and the associated products (e.g., project plans, design documents, code, test cases, and user manuals) [3].
– A set of partially ordered process steps, with sets of related artifacts, humans and computerized resources, organizational structures and constraints, intended to produce and maintain the requested software deliverables [4].
– A sequence of tasks, actions, or activities, including the transition criteria for progressing from one to the next, that brings about a result [5].

In this paper, a *software process* is defined as a set of process elements, links and interactions. The execution of a software process constitutes a trace of interactions among linked elements. Process elements are the basic entities of a software process, including activities, humans, artifacts, computerized resources, etc. A link is the abstraction of a certain type of relationship or a communication channel between two process elements. Each element can interrelate with other ones. The performance of a software process is a trace of interactions among interrelated elements. The ordering of those interactions is regulated by some constraints, methods, or practices. In addition, an interaction is carried out along a link for the purpose of sending a piece of data or some information for control between process elements. The control flow and the information flow of a software process are described through specifying its connecting structures and interactions types.

2.1   Conception of Software Process Mobility

The structure of a software process states the way in which the process elements are connected with each other through links, and the set of possible interactions that can be carried out among linked process elements. In fact, it may change during process performance as a result of interactions among process elements. It is possible that new process elements are added to a software process, existing ones deleted, and one process element replaced by another. For example, a new human agent (a process element) may be added for the enrollment of a new staff. On the other hand, a new link can be setup between two process elements who are unknown to each other in advance and two linked process elements may be disconnected. For example, a test engineer's affiliation with the test manager (a link) is shifted to a program manager when he or she is reassigned to the team for implementation. Furthermore, the set of possible interactions of a software process are altered correspondingly when the process elements or the links change. It is the essential change in a software process that its structure is altered during performance. It brings a high variability and unpredictability to software processes and may cause inconsistencies between process enactment and process performance.

Concerning the essential change in software processes, a novel conception, the *mobility of software processes* is proposed. According to Webster's dictionary, the word *mobility* means the "the quality of moving freely". The *mobility*'s synonyms within context are: changeableness, sensibility (and commonalty, motion). Thus, the *mobility of software processes* is defined as the structural change in a software process, resulting from interactions among process elements through links. As the logical relations among process elements remain immobile, the physical movement of a process element is not treated as the mobility of software processes. In addition, the situation that the internal state of a process element is updated or one process element seizes control from another is also not taken into account.

According to the definition of the mobility of software processes, it is the interactions that result in the structural change in a software process. On the other hand, the structure of a software process determines what interactions can be carried out along links connecting process elements. In the mobility of software processes, a software process is surveyed from the negativity of self-denial point of view and interactions among linked process elements constitute the momentum of process performance. Hence, based on the interactions among linked process elements, it is possible to describe the mobility of software processes in a modest but profound way.

2.2   Category of Software Process Mobility

Two basic categories of the mobility and a combination of them can be identified according to the mobile unit during an interaction:

- Element Mobility: A process element is mobile without links.
- Link Mobility: A link is mobile without process elements.
- Combined Mobility: Both process elements and the links among them are mobile.

Element Mobility. A process element is the mobile unit during an interaction. The received element will be connected with other ones existing in the new context. In addition, the creation of a new process element can also be expressed in the element mobility, in which a new element is added to the environment along the link between the element's producer and the environment. The behavior and the internal structure of the receiver can be dynamically updated.

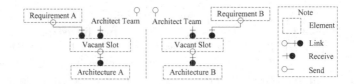

Fig. 1. An Example of the Element Mobility

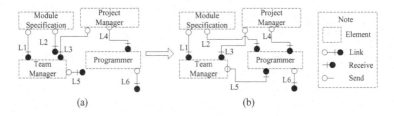

Fig. 2. An Example of the Link Mobility

In Fig. 1, there are more than one project that are simultaneously developed within an organization. But the architecture of each project is developed by the same **Architect Team**, responsible for devising an elegant architecture according to the given **Requirement**. In general, there is only one project that is scheduled for the **Architect Team**, which becomes mobile among those projects. Each project receives the **Architect Team** from a link and collaborates with it to produce an **Architecture**.

Link Mobility. It is a link to be mobile during an interaction. One process element sends a link, which is already connected to another element, to the third one. Thus, a new relationship can be set up between the latter two elements, who are unknown to each other in advance. The link mobility sticks to the fact that some process elements are dominated by some other ones or a meta-process which has the necessary knowledge to maintain a whole software process. It reflects the intrinsic dynamics in the control flow and information flow of a software process.

Fig. 2 denotes a demonstration on how the incremental definition of a software process is described in the link mobility. As shown in Fig. 2(a), a project manager assigns a programmer to a specific team and the team manager will have the programmer implementing a module according to the module's specification. As it is in a highly dynamic environment, neither the team manager nor the programmer is aware of the existence of the other before the performance of the software process. In Fig. 2(b), the project manager sends the link L5 to the programmer. The programmer establishes a new connection with the team manager through the link. The team manager sends the link L2 to the programmer and the programmer retrieves the module specification through the received link. Lastly, the programmer outputs the produced source code of the module through the link L6.

Combined Mobility. A fragment of a software process, including elements and links, is mobile. The combined mobility shows that a part of development

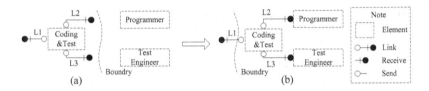

Fig. 3. An Example of the Combined Mobility

is delegated to a partner or a development team. The receiver of the fragment is responsible for establishing appropriate connecting structure for the received fragment. A fragment

In Fig. 3, the `Coding&Test` fragment is migrated along a link across the boundary. Connections can be constructed among the migrated fragment with those process elements on the other side of the boundary. A potential usage for the combined mobility is to present a process along with a software outsourcing contract. Thus, not only the milestones but also the development process adopted by the contractor can be fully specified. This provides a solution to problems caused by ineffective communication between contractors.

3   Formal Semantics

This section presents formal definitions of the mobility of software processes and three categories of the mobility. In addition, the polyadic π-calculus [6][7] proves to be a perfect candidate for constructing a new PCSEE supporting the novel concept.

Let a software process is represented as $SP = S\langle \mathcal{E}, \mathcal{L}, \mathcal{I}\rangle$, where, $\mathcal{E}$, $\mathcal{L}$, and $\mathcal{I}$ respectively represent the set of process elements, links and interactions of the software process, and S denotes the process's structure. In addition, $i\langle l\rangle$ represents an interaction along the link l between two linked process elements and m denotes the mobile unit during the interaction. Then, a formal definition of the mobility of software processes can be given as:

Definition 1 (Mobility of Software Processes). *The mobility of software processes is the structural change in a software process resulting from an interaction:*

$$S\langle \mathcal{E}, \mathcal{L}, \mathcal{I}\rangle \frac{i\langle l\rangle}{m} S'\langle \mathcal{E}', \mathcal{L}', \mathcal{I}'\rangle$$

where, $S \neq S'$ (S and S' are the structure of the software process before and after the interaction respectively).

The mobility of software processes is classified into three categories, i.e. *Element Mobility, Link Mobility, Combined Mobility*, according to the mobile unit m during an interaction. Let $RU(l)$ and $SU(l)$ denote a process element which respectively receives and sends a mobile unit from the link l. We then have three similar definitions but significant differences of mobile unit:

Definition 2 (Element Mobility). *Let* $n \geq 1$ *and* $e \in \mathcal{E}$ *denotes a mobile process element. The element mobility constitutes a series of interactions:*

$$\frac{i\langle l_1 \rangle}{e}, \frac{i\langle l_2 \rangle}{e}, \cdots \frac{i\langle l_n \rangle}{e}$$

where, $\forall i(i \geq 1 \wedge i \leq n-1)$, $RU(l_i) = SU(l_{i+1})$. *Then,* $RU(l_n)$ *instantiates the mobile process element* e *and sets up an appropriate connecting structure for it.*

Definition 3 (Link Mobility). *Let* $n \geq 1$ *and* $l \in \mathcal{L}$ *denotes a mobile link. The link mobility constitutes a series of interactions:*

$$\frac{i\langle l_1 \rangle}{l}, \frac{i\langle l_2 \rangle}{l}, \cdots \frac{i\langle l_n \rangle}{l}$$

where, $\forall i(i \geq 1 \wedge i \leq n-1)$, $RU(l_i) = SU(l_{i+1})$. *Then, a new link is set up between* $RU(l_n)$ *and the process element to which the link* l *is initially connected.*

Definition 4 (Combined Mobility). *Let* $n \geq 1$ *and* $l_{\&}e$ *denotes a set of linked process elements. The combined mobility constitutes a series of interactions:*

$$\frac{i\langle l_1 \rangle}{l_{\&}e}, \frac{i\langle l_2 \rangle}{l_{\&}e}, \cdots \frac{i\langle l_n \rangle}{l_{\&}e}$$

where, $\forall i(i \geq 1 \wedge i \leq n-1)$, $RU(l_i) = SU(l_{i+1})$. *Then,* $RU(l_n)$ *sets up an appropriate connecting structure for* $l_{\&}e$ *and existing links in* $l_{\&}e$ *are still there.*

In addition, the mobility of software processes and three categories of the mobility can be modelled in the polyadic π-calculus. With the formalism, it is fairly straightforward for working out a new PCSEE and associated PML supporting the concept. Based on the polyadic π-calculus, an process element is represented as a process in the untyped polyadic π-calculus (called π-process in this paper). A link between two process elements is modelled as a channel connecting the two corresponding π-processes. Interactions among process elements will be transformed into events of concurrently combined π-processes. With the operator of *abstraction*, a process element can be represented as:

$$\texttt{Element} \stackrel{def}{=} (\widetilde{ch}).\ (\nu \widetilde{g}, \widetilde{s})\ (U_p \langle \widetilde{g}, \widetilde{s}, \widetilde{0} \rangle \mid M_p \lfloor \langle \widetilde{g}, \widetilde{s}, \widetilde{ch} \rangle \rfloor) \tag{1}$$

$$U_p \stackrel{def}{=} (\widetilde{g}, \widetilde{s}, \widetilde{v}).\ (V \lfloor \langle g_1, s_1, v_1 \rangle \rfloor \mid \cdots \mid V \lfloor \langle g_m, s_m, v_m \rangle \rfloor) \tag{2}$$

$$V \stackrel{\triangle}{=} (g, s, u).\ (g(r).\ \bar{r}u.\ V \lfloor \langle g, s, u \rangle \rfloor) + s(v).\ V \lfloor \langle g, s, v \rangle \rfloor \tag{3}$$

$$M_p \stackrel{\triangle}{=} (\widetilde{g}, \widetilde{s}, \widetilde{ch}).\ (Action \langle \widetilde{g}, \widetilde{s}, \widetilde{ch} \rangle\ .\ M_p \lfloor \langle \widetilde{g}, \widetilde{s}, \widetilde{ch} \rangle \rfloor) \tag{4}$$

In (1), $\widetilde{ch}$ represents links connected to a process element. We assume that an element has a state and presents a certain type of behavior pattern (action). The two processes, U_p and M_p, represent the state and the action respectively. They share the channels $\widetilde{g}$ and $\widetilde{s}$. Thus in the body of the action, state variables can be respectively *get* or *set* through $\widetilde{g}$ and $\widetilde{s}$. The access to a variable is modelled by the process (3). In (2), processes for each variable are concurrently combined together to represent the private store of an element. The action of an element has the form $(\widetilde{g}, \widetilde{s}, \widetilde{ch}).P$.

A set of linked elements is also modelled as a π-process through the *application* notation. For example, a new linked element can be constructed from previously defined ones:

$$\texttt{ElementA} \stackrel{def}{=} (\langle in, out\rangle)\texttt{ElementABody}$$

$$\texttt{ElementB} \stackrel{def}{=} (\langle in, out\rangle)\texttt{ElementBBody}$$

$$\texttt{ElementC} \stackrel{def}{=} (\langle in, out\rangle)(\nu ch)(\texttt{ElementA}\langle in, ch\rangle|\texttt{ElementB}\langle ch, out\rangle)$$

As for the link mobility, it can be modelled by the name-passing of π-calculus. For example, the `Programmer` in Fig. 2 can be defined as:

$$Programmer \;=\; (\langle l_7, l_9\rangle)(l_7(l_8).\; l_8(l_5).\; l_5(content).\; coding.\; \overline{l_9}code) \qquad (5)$$

where, the state of a *Programmer* is not taken into account.

For the reason that an process element and a set of linked elements are both modelled as a π-process, the element mobility and the combined mobility are represented by the process-passing of high order π-calculus. For example, the equation

$$Fig3(b) \;=\; (\langle l_1, l_2, l_3\rangle)(l_0(codingest).codingtest\langle l_1, l_2, l_3\rangle) \qquad (6)$$

depicts Fig. 3(b) that the migrated `Coding&Test` is received and invoked. A high order π-calculus can be faithfully compiled down to the polyadic π-calculus (a first-order calculi) according to [7].

4   Implementation in SoftPM

In this section, an example is presented to show how a process for testing is expressed in SoftPM based on the mobility of software processes. SoftPM [8] is a toolkit for software process management and has been widely adopted in Chinese software organizations. The development teams of a customer are distributed across the whole city and there is one department, named *Quality Assurance Department*, who is responsible for testing all the projects within the organization. As an independent department assuming sole responsibility for its profits and losses, it is necessary to manage all testing activities by creating a new project in SoftPM.

However, it is difficult to predict the number of projects that are being tested in advance and the schedule of a test is heavily depends on the progress of the corresponding project. Thus, those process elements, including the project manager, developers, test cases, and source code, have to be dynamically allocated or deleted. In addition, to ensure that a bug is timely fixed, the tester conducts tests on the source code against given test cases and sends any identified bug to

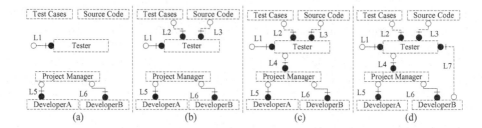

Fig. 4. A Process for Testing in the Link Mobility

the manager of the project being tested. Then, the bug is delegated to a developer according to its type. The developer fixes the bug and the result is fed back to the tester. The project manager and developers that a tester should communicate with are not prescribed and the relationships among them are difficult to be defined in a prescriptive manner.

The mobility of software processes surveys those problems from the angle that the structure of a software process may change as a result of interactions among process elements. In Fig. 4, the process for test is expressed in the link mobility. The process commences with Fig. 4(a), in which the `Tester` has not been assigned to a testing activity and is ready for accepting new tasks from the link `L1`. Then, the links to the `Test Cases` and the `Source Code` of the project to be tested is sent to the `Tester` along `L1`. New links, `L2` and `L3`, are set up as shown in Fig. 4(b). After the two previous interactions, a link to the project manager is also sent to the `Tester` along the link `L1`. As a result, the link `L4` between the `Tester` and the `Project Manager` is created in Fig. 4(c). Through the `Project Manager`, the link of the `Tester` is sent to the `DeveloperB` and the link `L7` is built up. In Fig. 4(d), a structure for communication among those process elements is appropriately configured. As you can see, the high variability and unpredictability of process performance is effectively addressed in the mobility of software processes.

5 Conclusion

In this paper, a software process is abstracted as a set of process elements, links and interactions. The execution of a software process constitutes a series of interactions among linked process elements. The intrinsically complex interrelationships among those entities involved during software development are described by the structure of a software process. The structural change imposed by interactions among linked process elements is considered as the essential change in a software process and brings a high variability and unpredictability to process performance. The mobility of software processes is presented as a novel concept to address the structural change. It reflects the fact that a software process is not static and it is changed through the negativity of self-denial driven by interactions. According the mobile unit during an interaction, three categories of the mobility are identified.

The mobility of software processes has a fundamental difference with the evolution of software processes [9][10]. The latter mainly focuses on solutions used for guiding how to apply an outer change request to a process or a model. The concept of evolution generally assumes that the structure of a software process is static, while the mobility states what a software process should be and exploits the momentum for structural changes. It is also different from the mobile software process described in [2] or [11][12], in which process parts, tools, participants tend to change their site allocation during the process or a process fragment is distributed in different workspaces. The dynamic ordering that the ordering of activities can be dynamically built and modified is an identified requirement for assessing a list of PCSEEs in [1]. However, the phrase is intended for expressing the non-determinism in the building constructs of PMLs.

As a novel concept, some aspects of the mobility of software processes can be exploited further:

- The mobility of software processes focuses on the structural change of a software process. The evolution of software processes can be taken as any change which takes place in software processes. In this way, the mobility of software processes can be thought of as a special type of evolution. However, as a novel concept, its correspondence with the evolution should be further clarified.
- It is necessary to exploit strategies and policies for managing the mobility of software processes. Inconsistencies between the process performance and the process enactment can be minimized with appropriate control criteria and policies for the mobility of software processes. A modelling approach based on the polyadic π-calculus can be further studied to support the novel concept. In particular, new techniques for analyzing software processes can be put forward based on the formalism. In addition, some other formalisms can also be examined to support the mobility of software processes.
- The mobility of software processes is classified into three categories according to the mobile unit during an interaction. It is possible that a new standard is adopted to produce different categories that define the extension of the concept.
- Moreover, a new PCSEE and associated PML can be developed based on the novel concept.

References

1. Arbaoui, S., Derniame, J.C., Oquendo, F., Verjus, H.: A comparative review of Process-Centered Software Engineering Environments. Annal of Software Engineering **14**(1-4) (2002) 311–340
2. Gruhn, V.: Process-centered software engineering environments, a brief history and future challenges. Annals of Software Engineering **14**(1-4) (2002) 363–382
3. Paulk, M.C., Curtis, B., Chrissis, M.B., Weber, C.V.: Capability maturity model for software, version 1.1. Technical Report CMU/SEI-93-TR-024, SEI, CMU (1993)
4. Lonchamp, J.: A structured conceptual and terminological framework for software process engineering. In: ICSP. (1993) 41–53

5. IEEE Std. 1220-1998: IEEE standard for application and management of the systems engineering process (1998)
6. Milner, R., Parrow, J., Walker, D.: A calculus of mobile processes – part I and II. Journal of Information and Computation **100** (1992) 1–77
7. Sangiorgi, D., Walker, D.: The π-calculus: a Theory of Mobile Processes. Cambridge University Press (2001)
8. Wang, Q., Li, M.: Software process management: Practices in China. In Li, M., Boehm, B.W., Osterweil, L.J., eds.: ISPW. Volume 3840 of LNCS., Springer (2005) 317–331
9. Conradi, R., Fernström, C., Fugetta, A.: Concepts for evolving software processes. In A. Finkelstein, J. Kramer, B.N., ed.: Software Process Modelling and Technology, John Wiley and Sons (1994) 9–31
10. Bandinelli, S., Nitto, E.D., Fuggetta, A.: Policies and mechanisms to support process evolution in PSEEs. In: ICSP. (1994) 9–20
11. Ben-Shaul, I.Z., Kaiser, G.E.: A paradigm for decentralized process modeling and its realization in the Oz environment. In: Proceedings of the Sixteenth International Conference on Software Engineering, IEEE Computer Society Press (1994) 179–188
12. Wang, A.I.: Support for mobile software processes in CAGIS. In Conradi, R., ed.: EWSPT. Volume 1780 of LNCS., Springer-Verlag (2000) 115–130

Software Process Fusion: Uniting Pair Programming and Solo Programming Processes

Kim Man Lui and Keith C.C. Chan

Department of Computing, The Hong Kong Polytechnic University,
Hunghom, Hong Kong
{cskmlui, cskcchan}@comp.polyu.edu.hk

Abstract. The role of pair programming process in software development is controversial. This controversy arises in part from their being presented as alternatives, yet it would be more helpful to see them as complementary software management tools. This paper describes the application of such a complementary model, software process fusion (SPF), in a real-world software management situation in China. Pair and solo programming are adopted at different stages of the process and according to the background of programmers, as appropriate. Unlike the usual practice of eXtreme Programming, in which all production code must written in pairs, all-the-time pair programming, the proposed model encourages programmers to design code patterns of their own in pairs and then to use these patterns to build sub-modules solo. The report finds that the longer team members work alone, the more code patterns they develop for reuse later in pairs.

1 Introduction

The success of a software development relies on not only a development paradigm but also people management. Programmer management remains more of an art form than an engineering principle. Pair programming (PP) is a form of teamwork in which two developers sit together and collaborate on a single computer [1]. One programmer, called the driver, controls the keyboard and implements the program while the other, the observer, continuously examines the work, identifying defects and thinking ahead. From this perspective, we may define a software process as being a pair process if a team is performed by pairs and as a solo process if it is performed by individual developers. It should be noted that pair programming includes not only programming but also design, system analysis, testing, and other typical programmer activities.

The benefits of pair programming processes may include job rotation/succession against personnel turnover, skills transfer for knowledge management, and, as a result of pairs being able to explore a larger number of alternatives than a single person [2], more creative thinking leading to better ways to solve problems. The processes of pair programming also raise issues of staff appraisal, economics, and productivity [3, 4, 5].

Many empirical studies [3, 4, 6, 7, 8] have shown higher that pair programming processes are more "productive" than solo programming process, particularly where they consider novice programmers. One report, however, recounts the development of highly negative attitudes towards management of professional programmers

Q. Wang et al. (Eds.): SPW/ProSim 2006, LNCS 3966, pp. 115–123, 2006.

implementing eXtreme Programming in real situations when software managers enforced 100% pairing [9]. Similarly, in our experience in China in which we had inexperienced programmers write production code pairs we found little evidence that programmers were either motivated by the practice or that they were more productive.

In this paper we are interested in the use of a mixed pair programming-solo programming method and its potential effect on the effectiveness and efficiency of the management of developers and, in particular, inexperienced programmers in China. We introduce the concept of Software Process Fusion (SPF) and propose its application with a case study of pair programming process and solo programming process that accounts not only for productivity but also considers staff motivation. It should be noted that although many programmers may from time to time work in pairs either willingly or out of necessity, at the moment we cannot say that this practice is well-defined, especially in terms of its role in the context of general professional practice.

This paper is organized as follows. Section 2 reviews the empirical studies on productivity in pair programming. Section 3 introduces the concept of SPF and a management case study in which inexperienced programmers are set to both pair programming and solo programming activities. Section 4 reports an industrial case of the use of SPF. The final section offers our Conclusion.

2　Pair Programming Process

All-the-time pair programming requires that all production code be written by pairs of programmers. It is the core of extreme programming [1]. In the past, many agile software practices individually proposed or re-introduced have been similar but have been called by different names. However, none of the practices has been alike to pair programming and this has made extreme Programming and pair programming so undividable.

Many software processes are usually regarded as team processes. The basic unit that forms the basis of a software team is an individual programmer, shown in (a) (b).

Fig 1.a. According to the team composition, we can categorize them as solo programming process. Alternatively, when software processes are adopted by a team formed by pairs as illustrated in (a) (b).

Fig 1.b, they are pair programming process. Collaborative Software Process by Williams is such software process [4].

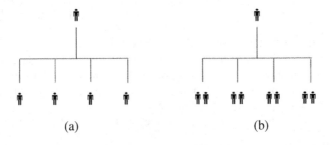

(a)　　　　　　　　　　　　　(b)

Fig. 1. Teams for solo programming process and pair programming process

This section reviews the literature on pair programming productivity. Two principles are reached in [3, 6, 7, 8]: The first principle is that a pair is much more productive and can work out a better solution than two individuals when the pair is new to design, algorithm, and coding of a program. The second principle is that pair programming can lose its productivity when a pair has prior experience of a task. Section 2.2 discusses an initial study in which pair programming is implemented as a way of assisting newly-hired programmers [10].

2.1 Control Experiments on Pair Programming

Two studies that favor pair programming have found that pair programming can speed up software development and at the same time produce better quality in terms of readability and maintainability than does solo programming. In 1998, Nosek [3] reported that full-time system programmers divided into five pairs and five singles were asked to write a UNIX script that performs a database consistency check (DBCC) in a Sybase database. On average, pairs took 42% longer than individuals on the same task; however, pair programming, in comparison with solo programming, reduced the elapsed time by 29% (i.e. $100\% - \dfrac{1+42\%}{2}$). In 2000, Williams [4] repeated the experiment in a similar setting using forty-one university students writing a challenging web-based program. The experiment showed that a pair took 15% longer than an individual on the same task; the elapsed time was reduced by 42,5% (i.e. $100\% - \dfrac{1+15\%}{2}$). In terms of productivity, the extra time was insignificant because pair programming achieves a higher quality.

In 2001, Nawrocki and Wojciechowski [11] reported experimental results unfavorable to pair programming, showing that pair programming consumed twice the time resources of solo programming. Subjects were asked to write four programs for (1) finding the mean and standard deviation of a sample of numerical data, (2) finding the linear regression parameters, (3) counting the number of lines in a program and (4) counting the total program LOC. The pairs took 100% longer than individuals. As the tasks of programming statistical calculations and counting the number of lines in a program were not new to the subjects, these experiments may indicate that pair programming is not as productive as solo programming when subjects are working on familiar tasks.

In 2004 Lui and Chan reported on a series of experiments called Repeat Programming in which pair and solo programmer subjects wrote the same program eight times [6, 7] or four times [8]. The purpose of this was to simulate the process in which a novice programmer develops expert familiarity with a task and to measure the change of productivity of pair programming versus solo programming. At the first round, pairs spent 7.5% longer than individuals on the same task, 23% longer on the second round, 40% on the third, deteriorating to 134% on the eighth. These results indicate just how much the relative productivity of pair programming depends on previous programming experience on a particular task. The less experience a pair has, the better it performs relative to the two similarly inexperienced individuals. Lui and Chan [7, 8] conclude that a pair is much more productive and can work out a better solution than two individuals when the pair is new to design, algorithm, and coding of a program. This advantage is lost, however, as subjects gain experience of the task.

2.2 Pair Programming for Newly-Hired Developers

Regarded as a process of learning and practicing, pair programming has a considerable pedigree in the area of learning theory. Active learning has been adopted in colleges [12]. It involves three processes: think-pair-share. Research into the effectiveness of pair learning relative to group learning [13] has shown that the group learning could be more effective than pair learning. Yet pair learning is still widely used in teaching. Research on learning in pair includes English Vocabulary [14], Physics [15], Mathematics [16], and recently, Computer Programming [17, 18]. When student programmers are compared to novice programmers, the success of pair learning formulates our research problem that pair programming can mentor less experienced programmers in industrial software development.

In 2003, a research student, Poff, conducted an empirical study was conducted in which two novice programmers in the company, TCMS, were selected to produce portions of an application for the verification of payload hardware prior to integration into the space shuttle at TCMS in the Kennedy Space Center [10]. The experiment lasted one month and the data collected was compared with historical data at TCMS. Two programmers were told that the experiment was of secondary priority; most important was successful and timely development of the application. The two programmers were then left to decide how often they would actually work together but were asked to work as a pair at least 33% of the time, but if they wished could work as a pair 100% of the time. The result was that the pair worked as a pair 50% of the time.

The author observed that a pair of novice-novice programmers could develop technical and environmental knowledge more quickly. Although the author did not mention a potential application of a mix of pair programming and solo programming, the case illustrates that pair programming and solo programming have been optimized in a reciprocal manner by a pair of newly-hired programmers.

Although Poff did not report the workspace layout, it should safely assume that those two programmers have their own machine so that they can do solo programming. If the two programmers are actually sitting closely and each other machine, they are doing is side-by-side programming proposed by Cockburn [19] in which the developers choose to work in pairs or solo on an ad hoc basis. In fact, two programmers may not have to sit side-by-side as suggested. As far as they are closed enough and can easily see both screens of each other which can be called "pseudo side-by-side programming", it probably achieve the same effect. In some cases, when an effective working rapport has been built between two programmers, they may sit a little far away or opposite to each other as far as they can easy talk and hear each other in a collocated place. It is the people collaboration that makes them productive and a workspace layout is just as a tool that facilities the collaboration.

In the Poff's experiment, whether the pair was practicing side-by-side, pseudo side-by-side programming or talk-and-hear programming, they cannot be considered as a disciplined software practice because there are no clear guidelines when they should pair up and split off. Section 3 will introduce Software Process Fusion (SPF). As an example of SPF, we will describe a combination of pair programming and solo programming.

3 Software Process Fusion (SPF)

The idea of software process fusion was brought from data fusion which is the process of combining two (or more) independent data sets in order to produce information to the user. As two data sets are independent, the challenging is to combine them by formulating common variables in mathematics [20]. In data fusion, one is a recipient set and the other is a donor set. The use of defined common variables allows the recipient set to be enriched with extra information from the donor set. For example in retail, a recipient set can be sales data and a donor set is a marketing survey.

In a similar fashion, A and B are two independent processes that can produce the same work products. One of the processes, say A, is a recipient process and the other, say B, is a donor process. It is possible to use the mechanisms of A and B to define a set of transfer conditions so that, over time, the recipient process can temporarily convert into the donor process for productivity and resource optimization.

In Software Process Fusion, we should start with and end in a recipient process. Although it may appear that two processes alternately change and become an alternating process (see Fig 2), the recipient process and the donor process cannot be mixed up because the transfer conditions are bound to this relationship. A fused process is a recipient process being merged with a donor process. We can draw an analogy between common variables in data fusion that bring two data sets together and transfer conditions in Software Process Fusion (SPF).

In Section 2.2, the real case reported by Poff would be Software Process Fusion as long as transfer conditions could be clearly established. Without those conditions, the alternating process in pair-and-solo programming appears uncontrolled and chaotic. The core of data fusion is to mathematically define common variables between data sets; the challenge in Software Process Fusion is to clearly establish a set of transfer conditions.

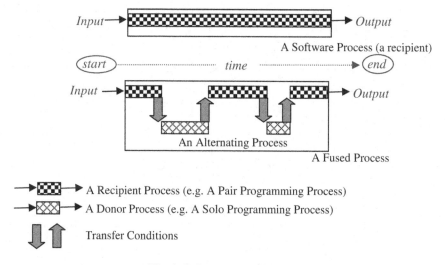

Fig. 2. Software Process Fusion

Fig. 2 shows an example of Software Process Fusion. Both a recipient process and a donor process can take and deliver the same input and output. Note that the recipient process is pair programming. In Software Process Fusion, we always start with and end at a recipient process. When the transfer conditions are satisfied during the pair programming process, it stops and initiates a donor process, i.e. the solo programming process. The donor process will not indefinitely take over the control and it will return to the recipient process if the transfer conditions for donors are met. Obviously, defining suitable transfer conditions is the key to the success of Software Process Fusion.

3.1   Transfer Conditions

In Section 2.1, previous studies have shown that it is productive for a pair of programmers to design algorithms, seek design patterns, and code. The productivity of pair programming will fall when the pair works on other modules in which the logic has been similar to the previous modules previously done as a pair [6, 7, 8]. In this case, to optimize resources, the pair should split off and the two individuals should complete those modules solo. Once they have finished, they should pair up again and review the overall task. This process is iterative until they complete their assignment.

Therefore, we define the transfer condition for a recipient process in Fig. 2 to convert into a donor process (i.e. solo programming process) is that a pair of developers has previously completed a similar task and they are individually able to solve the same problem again in the same way. Straightforwardly, the transfer condition for a donor process is for the individuals to pair up again after completing their solo programming tasks.

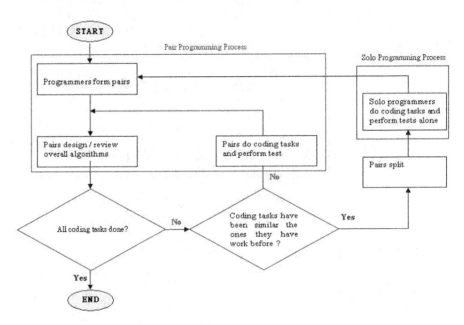

Fig. 3. Application of SPF for Managing Inexperienced Programmers

The transfer conditions can be regarded as a number of intermediate targets. We would like to reach such intermediate targets as many times as possible and hence the transfer conditions drive that fused process to (1) look for design patterns and implement them once in pairs, (2) reuse the same patterns in solo programming and (3) review overall progress and perform integration testing in pairs.

3.2 A Fused Process

A fused process not only is the sum of a recipient process and a donor process, but also includes necessary changes that come along with the transfer condition. This section will present a fused process: combining pair programming with solo programming processes. Fig. 3 illustrates the internal workflow of the fused process. It starts with a recipient process (i.e. a pair programming process) in which pairs work on design and algorithm and identify patterns of logic. Afterward, they code and test sub-programs in pair programming. The pairs then split up and code and test as solo programmers. Once those tasks are complete, they once again pair up, review their work, and perform integration tests.

4 Industrial Case Study

We introduced the work to Huida Technology Ltd in Huizhou, China in 2005. The company had seven technical staff, providing ERP/CRM solutions to their local customers. Two had four years experience and the other five all less than one year. The company would adopt what we proposed in this paper to work on their CRM project for one month. Of the five junior programmers, four paired up and the other worked as usual. Priority was given to the success of the inventory project, so that the company was free to terminate the proposed fusion process at any time. The results, shown in Table 1, were recorded and provided by two supervisory programmers.

The project was not an experimental test. It is a matter of happenstance that there were five staff available for the experiment, so the use of a single programmer was not intended to serve as a control group. Table 1 nonetheless provides for reference a comparison of the pair and solo teams. The programmers appeared to develop more (sub-) modules in terms of stored procedures and GUI. We are particularly interested

Table 1. Experimental Test in 2005

Item	Measurement Description	Huida Programmers		
		Pair	Pair	Single
1	Number of GUI Developed	7	6	2
2	Number of Stored Procedures Written	15	9	5
3.a	Programming Time (%)	49%	41%	40%
3.b	Testing Time (%)	26%	18%	20%
3.c	Debugging Time (%)	25%	31%	40%
4	Fusion Ratio	1.7	1.9	N/A
4.a	Pair Time (%)	37%	34%	N/A
4.b	Solo Time (%)	63%	66%	100%

in a fusion ratio, defined by the total time required for donor processes over the total time required for a recipient process. The fusion ratio was higher than Poff's measurement, which was around 1.0 [10].

The supervisors worked with those five programmers daily and knew them well. Their comments on the process are of interest.

1. They found that they were able to spend less time supervising the pairs as they tended to support and monitor themselves.
2. Coding standards were much better.
3. The fused process encouraged junior programmers to actively seek design patterns for reuse. This has rarely been seen before as the programmers just wanted to complete the program on time, rather than considering software reuse. Hitherto, it was common to see duplications of logic in the junior programmer's code as they had the habit of simply cutting and pasting code.

It has been reported that pair programming comes with pair pressure that a pair does not want to let its partners down and that this leads to pairs budgeting their time more wisely [4]. The supervisors failed to observe any signs of pair pressure; however, it was clear that programmers were glad to move on to solo programming as it demonstrated that they managed to discover reusable patterns of their own. The team had been motivated and influenced by its achievements of pattern discovery. In addition, the time that they split off demonstrated their supervisors that they were making progress.

5 Conclusions

The paper contributes to our understanding of software process fusion. Software methods/processes need not be defined as being in opposition or competition. Rather, they can be seen as complementary. We also presented a case study of the application of SPF in the management of inexperienced programmers in a real industrial project in China. The initial results and comments show that SPF is a promising software management approach.

Researchers on pair programming are divided. Some believe it is more efficient and effective than solo programming whereas others argue it doubles the resources that are consumed in software development. Perhaps, the truth lies between these two views. Software Process Fusion encourages not programming in pairs but working out coding patterns in pairs. Developers can pair up and split off. The proposed fused process has successfully been implemented in a small company in China.

References

1. Beck, K.: Extreme Programming Explained: Embraced Change (2nd Edition), Addison-Wesley, Boston, MA (2005)
2. Flor, N. and Hutchins, E.: Analyzing Distributed Cognition in Software Teams: A Case Study of Team Programming During Perfective Software Maintenance, In J. Koenemann-Belliveau, T. Moher and S. Robertson (Eds.), Empirical Studies of Programmers: Fourth Workshop, Norwood, NJ: Ablex (1991)

3. Nosek, J.T.: The Case for Collaborative Programming, Communications of the ACM, March (1998) 105-108
4. Williams, L.: The Collaborative Software Process, Ph.D. Dissertation, University of Utah, (2000)
5. Miller, M.M. and Padberg, F.: Extreme Programming from an Engineering Economics Viewpoint, In Proceedings of the Fourth International Workshop on Economics-Driven Software Engineering Research (2002)
6. Lui, K.M. and Chan, K.C.C.: When Does a Pair Outperform Two Individuals. In Proceedings of Extreme Programming and Agile Processes in Software Engineering, Italy (2003) 215-224
7. Lui, K.M. and Chan, K.C.C.: A Cognitive Model for Solo Programming and Pair Programming. In Proceedings of the Third IEEE International Conference on Cognitive Informatics, Canada (2004) 94-102
8. Lui, K.M. and Chan, K.C.C.: Productivity of Pair Programming: Novice-Novice and Expert-Expert, Tentatively Accepted by International Journal of Human Computer Studies (2006)
9. Stephens, M. and Rosenberg, D.: Extreme Programming Refactored: The Case Against XP, Apress (2003)
10. 10 Poff, M. A.: Pair Programming to Facilitate the Training of Newly-Hired Programmers, M.Sc. Thesis, Florida Institute of Technology (2003), Available online at http://www.cs.fit.edu/~tr/tr2003.html
11. Nawrocki, J. and Wojciechowski, A.: Experimental Evaluation of Pair Programming", Proceedings of the 12th European Software Control and Metrics Conference, England (2001) 269-276
12. Bonwell, C.C. and Eison, J. A.: Active Learning: Creating Excitement in the Classroom. ASHE-ERIC Higher Education Report. Washington, D.C. (1991)
13. Roth,V., Goldstein,E. and Marcus,G. : Peer Lead Team Learning A Handbook for Team Leaders. Upper Saddle River, NJ: Prentice- Hall, Inc. (2001)
14. Jones, M.S., Levin, M. E., Levin, J. R. and Beitzel, B. D.: Can Vocabulary-Learning Strategies and Pair-Learning Formats Be Profitably Combined? Journal of Educational Psychology, Vol. 92, No. 2 (2000) 256-262
15. Warnakulasooriya, R. and Pritchard, D.: Learning and Problem-Solving Transfer between Physics Problems using Web-based Homework Tutor. In Proceedings of World Conference on Educational Multimedia, Hypermedia and Telecommunications, Chesapeake, VA (2005) 2976-2983
16. Keeler, C.M. and Steinhorst, R.K.: Using Small Groups to Promote Active Learning in the Introductory Statistics Course, Journal of Statistical Education, [Online journal] (1995) available at
http://www.amstat.org/publications/jse/v3n2/keeler.html
17. McDowell, C., Hanks, B. and Werner, L.: Experimenting with Pair Programming in the Classroom, In Proceedings of the 8th Annual Conference on Innovation and Technology in Computer Science Education, Thessaloniki, Greece (2003)
18. McDowell, C., Werner, L., Bullock, H. and Fernald, J.: The Impact of Pair Programming on Student Performance, Perception, and Persistence, In Proceedings of the 25th International Conference on Software Engineering (2003) 602 – 607
19. Cockburn, A.: Crystal Clear: a human-powered methodology for small teams, Boston: Addison-Wesley (2005)
20. van der Putten, P., Kok, J.N. and Gupta, A.: Why the Information Explosion Can Be Bad for Data Mining, and How Data Fusion Provides a Way Out. In Proceedings of Proceedings of the Second SIAM International Conference on Data Mining (2002)

Towards an Approach for Security Risk Analysis in COTS Based Development

Dan Wu and Ye Yang

Center for Software Engineering, University of Southern California,
941 W. 37th Place, SAL Room 328,
Los Angeles, CA 90089-0781
{danwu, yey}@usc.edu

Abstract. More and more companies tend to use secure products as COTS to develop their secure systems due to resource limitations. The security concerns add more complexity as well as potential risks to COTS selection process, and it is always a great challenge for developers to make the selection decisions. In this paper, we provide a method for security risk analysis in COTS based development (CBD) based on Common Criteria and our previous work in identifying general risk items for CBD. The research result provides useful insights for developers in identifying security risks, so that it can be used to aid for the COTS selection decision.

1 Introduction

The use of Commercial-Off-The-Shelf (COTS) product(s) has become increasingly important in software system development. In more and more organizations, pressures from budget and schedule constraints force development teams to use preexisting components to implement security requirements such as encrypting, digital signing, access control, and authentication [1]. Generally speaking, the COTS product selection decision is made by considering many factors such as vendor maturity, customer support, product complexity and so on. With the addition of security concerns in large scale system development, the COTS selection process can become much more complex and risk-prone by adding some additional factors addressing application's security properties. Current state of practice in secure COTS selection is often in an ad hoc manner due to the lack of technique/method support. This usually leaves it a great challenge for developers to make decisions on selecting secure COTS as components for security sensitive systems and often results in wrong decision, tremendous rework, and schedule/cost overruns. Moreover, an inappropriate selection decision could bring the security vulnerabilities that will leave on your system no matter how perfect the glue codes are. While researchers have proposed some specific COTS-based development processes such as COTS selection and evaluation processes [2, 3]; very few of them have addressed issues to support the selection of secure COTS products for building systems with security concerns.

In contrast to the perception of most people, COTS-based development (CBD) is not a low risk development strategy. Many of the problems in CBD are a consequence

Q. Wang et al. (Eds.): SPW/ProSim 2006, LNCS 3966, pp. 124–131, 2006.

of poor appreciation of the risks involved and their management. This is especially true for building secure COTS-based systems. The black-box nature of COTS products, the lack of component interoperability standards, and complex implementation of security mechanisms often result in the accidental introduction of serious flaws into the system [4]. Hence, there needs to be a mechanism to help people evaluate and mitigate their risk.

In this paper, we propose a quantitative security risk analysis method to address the security issues in selecting secure COTS products. Our method integrates the Evaluated assurance level (EAL) concept in the Common Criteria (CC) [5], an internationally recognized standard for security requirements definition and evaluation for IT systems, with our previous work on COCOTS Risk Analyzer [6], a rule-based risk analysis method for analyzing COTS integration risks. The paper is organized as following: Section 2 introduces EAL and COCOTS Risk Analyzer; Section 3 presents 3 new cost drivers to address security in COTS based development for secure systems. Section 4 shows our analysis result of security risk items and the corresponding risk mitigation suggestions. Section 5 concludes our work and talks about the future plans.

2 Overview of Related Work

2.1 EAL

Evaluated assurance level (EAL) is a term brought in by Common Criteria (CC) [5] for providing confidence for security in secure systems. EAL can be viewed as a package of security assurance requirements (SARs). Different from security functional requirements (SFRs) that represent the security capabilities and strength of these functions in the system, SARs help provide the confidence about these SFRs, by defining executable actions for developers such as independent testing, using configuration management mechanisms, doing vulnerability assessment, etc. The higher EAL is, the more and stronger the included SARs are, which by other words, providing more confidence of security. By selecting SARs during early phase of the software development lifecycle (SDLC) and executing action items defined in SARs through out the SDLC, developer can claim the product that achieves the corresponding EAL. And a certified organization or center will evaluate the product within the chosen SARs to make the claimed EAL official. EAL adds another criteria in choosing secure COTS products, since it prevails some information that was invisible but important to users. EAL also has its big user group. National Institute of Standards and Technology (NIST) provides a list of secure products with their EALs, which is viewable online [7]. Secure products in that list are not only from general IT companies including Cisco, IBM, Microsoft, SUN, Apple, Oracle, etc, but also from security specific companies such as NetScreen Technologies, Inc., Symantec Corporation, McAfee, Inc., etc.

2.2 COCOTS Risk Analyzer

COCOTS is the acronym for the COnstructive COTS integration cost estimation model, which is a member of the USC COCOMO II family of cost estimation models. In our previous work of [6], the COCOTS risk analyzer enables the user to obtain a

COTS integration risk analysis with no inputs other than the set of glue code cost drivers the user enters to obtain a COCOTS glue code integration effort estimate. The risk assessment is based on an expert Delphi analysis of the relative risks involved in the most critical combinations of COCOTS cost driver ratings. We describe a risk situation as a combination of two cost drivers at their extreme ratings, and formulate such combination into a Risk Rule (RR). One example is a project condition whereby COTS products complexity (APCPX) is very high and the staff's experience on COTS products (ACIEP) is low. In such case, cost and/or schedule goals may not be met, since time will have to be spent understanding COTS, and this extra time may not have been planned for. Hence, a corresponding Risk Rule is formulated as:

IF ((COTS Product Complexity > Nominal)
AND (Integrator's Experience on COTS Product < Low))
THEN there is a project risk.

In order to capture and analyze the underlying relation between cost attributes and the impact of their specific ratings on project risk, several sets of mapping scheme and weighting scheme have been obtained through 2 rounds of expert Delphi survey. And finally, the overall project risk is calculated according to a normalized scale from 0-100. In this way, the COCOTS risk analyzer identifies and assesses risks in conjunction with COCOTS estimation and further provide mitigation advices to create mitigation plans based on the relative risk severities. Our preliminary evaluation result shows that it has done an effective job of estimating the relative risk levels of a sample of COTS-based e-services applications. Table 1 shows the 15 COCOTS cost drivers that are used to derive the risk identification and assessment in COCOTS Risk Analyzer.

Table 1. COCOTS Glue Code Submodel Cost Drivers

No.	Name	Definition
1	Glue Code Size	The total amount of COTS glue code developed for the system.
2	AAREN	Application Architectural Engineering
3	ACIEP	COTS Integrator Experience with Product
4	ACIPC	COTS Integrator Personnel Capability
5	AXCIP	Integrator Experience with COTS Integration Processes
6	APCON	Integrator Personnel Continuity
7	ACPMT	COTS Product Maturity
8	ACSEW	COTS Supplier Product Extension Willingness
9	APCPX	COTS Product Interface Complexity
10	ACPPS	COTS Supplier Product Support
11	ACPTD	COTS Supplier Provided Training and Documentation
12	ACREL	Constraints on Application System/Subsystem Reliability
13	AACPX	Application Interface Complexity
14	ACPER	Constraints on COTS Technical Performance
15	ASPRT	Application System Portability

As we can see, COCOTS provides 15 cost drivers to capture project characteristics of general COTS based development, however none of these drivers specifically addresses security. As security is becoming a more and more important, sometimes even critical concern in software development nowadays, extending COCOMO/COCOTS model to include security as a new cost driver is on the top of the Center for Software Engineering's (CSE) research task list. The security risk analysis approach that integrates the EAL with the COCOTS Risk Analyzer is a summary of our latest research progress in this direction.

3 New Security Drivers

As we already discussed before, EAL is well used in many organizations for measuring security assurance levels. During the collaborative development of the COCOMO security extension model [8], an ongoing research in CSE, there is a consensus among researchers and industry practitioners that EAL plays as a critical cost factor in the project development. Similar situation takes place in COTS based development. Hence in our approach, three new drivers derived from EAL are proposed to specifically address security properties:

- APEAL (Application Evaluated Assurance Level). This driver represents the future system's targeted EAL.
- ACEAL (COTS Evaluated Assurance Level). This driver represents the EAL for the COTS products that will be integrated for building the future system.
- ACPUF (percentage of COTS' unused features). This driver represents the percentage of COTS' features that are not directly or indirectly used in the integrated application.

Security risks due to lack of security functional requirements, such as a risk of losing confidentiality without using encryption on user-application compunctions, are not in the scope of our list of risk items. Risks related with SFRs are heavily relied on the system's environment and threats from outside, hence are unpredictable without the project-specific information such as domain types. For example, a database management system (DBMS) in bank has the risk as loss of account's integrity. While if a DBMS is in a military use, the risk becomes loss of information confidentiality instead. The assurance levels of COTS products and application are independent with those factors, hence security risks related with EALs are able to be generalized regarding different types of projects. For instance, risk exists if application targeting on higher EAL is built on COTS products with lower EALs. The mapping between rating levels of APEAL/ACEAL with CC EALS is shown in Table 2.

Table 2. Mapping between EALs and APEAL/ACEAL driver ratings

CC Evaluated Assurance Level	EAL 1,2	EAL 3	EAL 4	EAL 5	EAL 6	EAL 7
Rating Levels	Nominal	High	Very High	Extra High	Super High	Ultra High

The reason for including ACPUF is because it is critical to test these unused features of COTS products to make sure that they will not cause any vulnerability into the future application. Testing them indirectly affects the final system's assurance level. Only considering this factor, the more unused features it has, the bigger possibility that risk will be generated, hence the less cost effective it is to use this COTS product. The descriptions of ACPUF are shown in Table 3.

Table 3. ACPUF Driver Descriptions

ACPUF De-scriptions	<=15%	>15% && <=40%	>40% && <=65%	>65% && <85%	>85%
Rating Levels	Very Low	Low	Nominal	High	Very High

We use the similar rating level of APEAL/ACEAL as the security driver's (SECU) in COCOMO security extension model [8], since they all based on EAL. The rating level of ACPUF is derived from a mini-Delphi among the authors of this paper. These rating levels will be used to determine relative risk severity level later. For example, the risk of integrating two COTS product with ACEAL Nominal and Extra High is more serious that the risk of integrating two COTS products with ACEAL Very High and Extra High.

4   Security Risk Analysis

Our previous work [6] already identified 36 risk items when different COTS cost drivers have extreme driver ratings. However, none of them addressing security risks. In this paper, we will emphasize on the security risk items that need to be considered and mitigated during COTS product selection process as well as integration process. Following our definition in [6], security risks exist if there are conflicts or collisions between any pair of the 3 security drivers and the other 15 COCOTS cost drivers. The risk network in Figure 1 shows the initial list of our identified security Risk Rules, where each line indicating a potential risk condition.

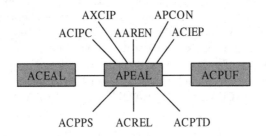

Fig. 1. Security Risk Items Network

COCOTS model groups its 15 cost drivers into three groups: Personnel, COTS product, and Application. We identify 11 security risk conditions and discuss the details of them by following the same classification.

4.1 Personnel Risks

- **APEAL vs ACIEP** Lack of experiences in COTS products may cause developers missing a particular feature that could leave a security hole in the future application. For example, there is a risk that the claimed broadness of testing is not satisfied due to this missing part, so that it fails to achieve the targeted EAL.
- **APEAL vs ACIPS** Low integrator personnel capability will directly affect the effectiveness of executing action items defined in SARs in the targeted EAL package. For example, EAL 6 requires developers to do automated configuration management (CM) using a configuration system (CS). Without some knowledge of CM and CS, this SAR action item cannot be executed.
- **APEAL vs AXCIP** Whether there is a formal integration process inside the organization, how good it is and developers' experiences with it will directly affect whether developers can achieve the targeted EAL. For example, EAL 5 requires developers to use a standardized life-cycle model for development.
- **APEAL vs APCON** Highly turnover rate brings security risks in two aspects: First, left person may intentionally or accidentally divulge the critical information of the system, however this kind of risks don't necessarily affect achieving the targeted EAL. Second, new coming people are most happen less familiar with the COTS product or application compared with left ones, which may bring risks as previously discussed ones.

4.2 COTS Product Risks

- **APEAL v ACPPS** Because of the limited information COTS products provide, product support is important for achieving high level of EAL. We can consider vendor of COTS product as one of the stakeholders, and there is a risk for lack of communication between stakeholders.
- **APEAL vs ACPTD** If a COTS product with very little documentation is chosen for implementing secure application, there are potential risks because all EAL requires documentation of user and administrator guidance. Furthermore, EALs higher than 4 require developers to provide formal/informal specification for low-level design of the application, and developers can hardly do it without enough COTS documentation.
- **APEAL vs ACEAL** It is a very tricky situation of choosing COTS products with lower EALs to implement the application with higher EALs. Though it is theoretically possible, the risks exist in increasing the EAL in COTS part may cause great effort. And there are risks that it does not practically work because of COTS products' black box properties.
- **APEAL vs ACPUF** Unused features of COTS products may bring vulnerabilities into future application. So besides necessary testing required for a certain EAL to provide the confidence for security, it takes extra effort to either turn off these features or wrap them off.
- **ACEAL vs ACEAL** Integrating COTS products with different EALs may have risks to lose the confidence of security in COTS product with higher EAL.

4.3 Application Risks

- **APEAL vs ACREL** If a failure of application could cause threat to mission critical requirements even safety critical requirements, the targeted EAL should be high enough to obviate any potential risk.
- **APEAL vs AAREN** Application architecture engineering directly affects the application EAL. All EALs require at least semiformal demonstration of the correctness of correspondence between architecture and security requirements. For example, there is a risk if the rating of AAREN is very low, i.e., no architecture validation is done.

The above 11 security risks provide an initial framework for developers in identifying and analyzing their project security risks. All that the developers need to do is just to check their ratings for the 18 cost drivers (3 new security driver plus the 15 COCOTS driver) to see if there is any pair of them having conflict ratings, i.e. violating the Risk Rules identified by our method.

4.4 Risk Assessment – Next Steps

To determine the relative risk severity levels and quantify overall project risk, similar weighting mechanisms as in [6] will be used for a quantitative risk analysis. And the overall project security risk is calculated using Eq-1.

$$\text{Project risk} = \sum \sum \text{risklevel}_{ij} \times \text{effort\_multiplier\_product}_{ij} \qquad \text{Eq.-1}$$

Finally, Table 4 shows some examples of risk mitigation suggestions for different types of security risks, which is not a full list at this time. We will keep evolving more detailed suggestions regarding each of the risk items in the future based on further, broader expert Delphi results and continuous literature review.

Table 4. Risk Mitigation Suggestions

Type of Security Risks	Personnel	COTS Product	Application
Examples of Risk Mitigation Suggestions	Training on necessary sets of knowledge	Use COTS products with high similarities as good references.	Establish rationale for architecture design.

5 Conclusions and Future Work

Beyond the risk items we identified in our previous work for COTS based development, we have further identified risk items for COTS based applications with security concerns. Developers need to consider them during the COTS selection process as well as the integration process and the COTS product selection decision should be driven by these security risks. The future work will be doing several rounds of Delphi to refine these new security drivers and calibrate effort multipliers for them. We will do the quantitative risk analysis using similar weighting scheme and calculation formula as we used in [6]. The mitigation approaches for different groups of risks will be refined to risk item level and stored in a knowledge base. Moreover, we want to automate our method to save developers more effort.

References

1. Devanbu, P. and Stubblebine, S.: Software Engineering for Security: a Roadmap. In the Future of Software Engineering. Special volume of the proceedings of the 22nd International Conference on Software Engieering – ICSE 2000, June 2000.
2. Kontio, J.: A Case Study in Applying a Systematic Method for COTS Selection, Proceedings of the 18th international conference on Software engineering May 1996, Berlin, Germany.
3. Brownsword, L.; Oberndorf, T.; Sledge, C. A. Developing New Processes for COTS-Based Systems. IEEE Software, July/August 2000.
4. Lindqvist, U. and Jonsson, E.: A Map of Security Risks Associated with Using COTS. In Computer, Vol. 31, No. 6, June 1998, pp. 60-66.
5. Common Criteria for Evaluation Criteria for IT Security V2.1. ISO/IEC 15408, National Institute of Standards and Technology, 1999.
6. Yang, Y., Boehm, B., and Wu, D.: "COCOTS Risk Analyzer", accepted by ICCBSS 20 06. Feb. 2006, Orlando, FL, USA.
7. http://niap.nist.gov/cc-scheme/vpl/vpl_type.html
8. Colbert, E., Wu, D., Chen, Y. and Boehm, B.: "Costing Secure Systems", in 18th International Forum on COCOMO and Software Cost Modeling, Los Angeles, CA, 10/2003.

COCOMO-U: An Extension of COCOMO II for Cost Estimation with Uncertainty[*]

Da Yang [1,2], Yuxiang Wan [1,2], Zinan Tang[1,2], Shujian Wu [1,2], Mei He [1,2], and Mingshu Li [1,3]

[1] Laboratory for Internet Software Technologies, Institute of Software, Chinese Academy of Sciences, Beijing 100080, China
[2] Graduate University of Chinese Academy of Sciences, Beijing 100039, China
[3] State Key Lab of Computer Science, Institute of Software, Chinese Academy of Sciences, Beijing 100080, China
{yangda, wanyuxiang, tangzinan, wushujian, hemei, mingshu}@itechs.iscas.ac.cn

Abstract. It is well documented that the software industry suffers from frequent cost overruns, and the software cost estimation remains a challenging issue. A contributing factor is, we believe, the inherent uncertainty of assessment of cost. Considering the uncertainty with cost drivers and representing the cost as a distribution of values can help us better understand the uncertainty of cost estimations and provide decision support for budge setting or cost control. In this paper, we use Bayesian belief networks to extend the COCOMO II for cost estimation with uncertainty, and construct the probabilistic cost model COCOMO-U. This model can be used to deal with the uncertainties of cost factors and estimate the cost probability distribution. We also demonstrate how the COCOMO-U is used to provide decision support for software development budget setting and cost control in a case study.

1 Introduction

Software development cost estimation is important as it is the basis for project bidding, budgeting and planning. Cost estimation is a practical part of any software development. Bad cost estimation causes problems while good cost estimation makes the whole process smoother. It can also be used to guide management, allocation of resources, modification of original plans, software process improvement, etc. But how to estimate the cost with high precision is still a largely unsolved problem. In the report of Standish Group [1], cost overruns averaged to 189% of the original cost estimate for all the projects in 1994 and remained as high as 45% in 2000. It is also indicated in a recent review of estimation surveys [6] that there has been little improvement in software cost estimation accuracy over the last 20 years.

We believe that one reason for this lack of improvement in software cost estimation is the overlook of inherent uncertainties of cost estimation. To better estimate cost, we

---

[*] Supported by the National Natural Science Foundation of China under Grant No. 60573082; the National High-Tech Research and Development Plan of China under Grant No. 2005AA113140.

Q. Wang et al. (Eds.): SPW/ProSim 2006, LNCS 3966, pp. 132–141, 2006.

need to better understand and deal with these uncertainties. For example, Kitchenham stated in [8] that managers do not understand how to use estimates correctly and particular they usually do not handle properly the uncertainty and risks inherent in estimates.

Among the large number of different cost estimation models been proposed over the last 20+ years, COCOMO II [4] is a well know and widely used one. The COCOMO II is a deterministic model, which takes deterministic values as input and estimates the most likely software development effort.

We believe at least two aspects of research can be done to improve the cost estimation practice:

- To explicitly incorporate the uncertainty information of cost factors into cost estimation.
- To explicitly assess the uncertainty of cost estimations and provide decision support for budget setting and cost control.

Given these two motivations, we will extend the COCOMO II for cost estimation with uncertainty in this paper.

2 Uncertainty in Cost Estimation

In software development, cost estimation uncertainty changes with time. It is illustrated in [4] that the uncertainty ranges of cost estimations present a decreasing trend as the software development lifecycle proceeds. Pendharkar [3] stated that software development is a dynamic process and a manager's beliefs about cost estimation are likely to change over the development life cycle. Practitioners also point out that many cost factors are uncertain at early phase of software life cycle and the early estimates are extremely inaccurate.

Kitchenham proposed four sources of estimate uncertainty as: measurement error about input variables, model error, assumption error of input parameters, and scope error [8]. It has also been proposed by Kitchenham that uncertainty can be better understood if costs are represented as a distribution of values [5]. Grimstad [11] proposes a probabilistic view about software development effort, which means that 'most likely effort', 'planned effort', 'budgeted effort', etc., are values (with different probabilities of being exceeded by actual effort) on an effort probability distribution. Jørgensen asserts in [9] that reflecting the underlying uncertainty of cost estimation will improve the budgeting and planning process.

COCOMO II takes the estimated project size and cost driver values as input, and estimates the amount of effort in person-months for a project by the formula:

$$PM = A \times Size^E \times \prod_{i=1}^{n} EM_i, \quad E = B + 0.01 \times \sum_{j=1}^{5} SF_j \qquad (1)$$

In the above formulas, 'Size' is the estimated size of software project measured in terms of KSLOC, A and B are constants that can be calibrated to existing project data; SFs are scale factors count for the relative economies or diseconomies of scale encountered for software projects of different sizes, and EMs are effort multipliers to adjust the PM. The COCOMO II has the Early Design and the Post-Architecture models, and the Early Design cost drivers are obtained by combining the Post-Architecture model cost drivers. The project size and other 22 cost factors are vital for COCOMO II cost estimation.

COCOMO II only takes deterministic values as input and thus can not explicitly assess the estimation uncertainty caused by the uncertainty of cost factors. Though COCOMO II also provides an uncertainty range of the estimation result besides the point forecast of the most likely effort, the uncertainty range is a static value determined by the phases and milestones at which the estimation is made, and it can not reflect the cause of uncertainty or the character of a certain project well.

BBN (Bayesian Belief Network) was introduced in [2] as a way of modeling uncertainty and causal relationships. The input of the BBN can be probabilistic values, and the output is a joint probability distribution and not a point forecast. A decision-maker can use the joint probability distribution information to estimate the probability or risk for that a budget will be overrun. Further, BBN provides a capability of updating the probability distribution.

As BBN is powerful at representing and modeling uncertainty, in this paper, we will use BBN to extend the COCOMO II for dealing with uncertainty.

The extension of COCOMO II named COCOMO-U can explicitly representing the uncertainty of cost factors and estimate the effort distribution. It proposes a three dimensional view of cost estimation: the first dimension of cost values, the second dimension of probability to reflect the uncertainty ranges of cost estimations, and the third dimension of time to reflect the dynamic changes of cost estimations during software life cycle. COCOMO-U can be used to model the uncertainties of cost estimation, continuously estimate the cost probability distributions when new information is available, and provide decision support for budget setting and cost control.

3   The COCOMO-U Cost Estimation Model

The extended COCOMO II named COCOMO-U is composed of three parts: the probabilistic inputs for measuring the uncertainty of cost factors, the BBN derived from COCOMO II Formula (1) for making estimation, and the probabilistic output for decision support.

As Fig. 1 illustrates, the COCOMO II takes deterministic values of project

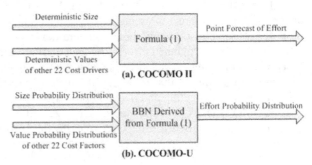

Fig. 1. COCOMO II and its Extension

size and other 22 cost factors as input, and uses Formula (1) to make a point forecast of effort. The extended COCOMO II will take probability distributions of the same cost factors as input, and use BBN derived from Formula (**1**) to estimate the effort probability distribution. From the estimated effort, we can calculate the cost of software development.

3.1 The COCOMO-U Input

The COCOMO-U takes the probability distributions of the estimated project size and other 22 cost factors as input.

In COCOMO II, the project size is an estimated value and there will be uncertainty to some extent in this estimation, but the model can't represent this uncertainty.

In our extension of COCOMO II, to represent the uncertainties or the confidence of the estimator with the project size estimation, we assume that the probability distribution of the log transformed size estimation (*ls*) is Normal [1] (Gaussian) ($ls \sim N(\mu, \delta^2)$). The μ stands for the most likely value of *ls*, and δ reflects the uncertainty of *ls* or the confidence of the size estimator.

As we assume that *ls* is Normal (Gaussian) distribution, given the estimated most likely project size and the estimators confidence, we can easily calculate the values of μ and δ. For example, an estimator makes an estimation of a project size as *mls* with 90% confidence that the real project size will within the interval [*mls*-deviate% $\times$ *mls*, *mls*+deviate% $\times$ *mls*]. When the size is log transformed, we transform this confidence interval into a balanced one for simplicity as: [ln(*mls*)-(ln(1+deviate%) - ln(1-deviate%))/2, ln(*mls*) + (ln(1+deviate%) - ln(1-deviate%))/2]. According to the property of Normal distribution (if x$\sim N(\mu, \delta^2)$ then p{ μ - $1.65\delta \leq x \leq \mu +1.65\delta$ } ≈ 0.9), we can easily calculate the value of μ and δ by the following formula:

$$\mu = \ln(mls) \quad \text{and} \quad \delta = (\ln(1 + \text{deviate\%}) - \ln(1 - \text{deviate\%})) \times 0.5 \times 0.606 \quad (2)$$

The COCOMO-U includes the 5 scale factors and the 17 effort multipliers defined in COCOMO II. Each of these factors has four to six ranks. In COCOMO-U, the values of these factors are also input as probability distributions to represent the uncertainty.

3.2 The COCOMO-U BBN-Based Cost Estimation Engine

The BBN-based cost estimation engine is derived form COCOMO II Formula (**1**) for estimating effort probability distribution from the input. The colored leaf nodes are the estimated project size, 5 scale factors, and 17 effort multipliers (further explanation of these cost factors can be found in [4]). They are all fed into to the BBN as probability distributions. To distinguish from the deterministic input in COCOMO II, we use the superscript """ to denote these cost factors of COCOMO-U.

---

[1] Though a skewed distribution such as Gamma distribution may be more general to represent the probability distribution of size and effort estimations, in this paper we only use the symmetrical Normal distribution to model the uncertainties with software size and effort estimations, as it is simple and easier to understand, calculate, and make inference.

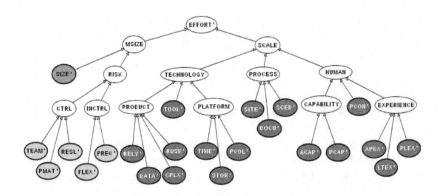

Fig. 2. Graph structure of the BBN-based Cost Estimation Engine

To limit the size of the NPTs for easily constructing it, we define each node to have no more than four parent nodes in the BBN. The graph structure of the BBN is illustrated in Fig 2:

The NPTs of the internal and output nodes are automatically calculated following the expressions in Table 1, which are derived from the COCOMO II Formula (**1**).

Table 1. Expressions for NPT construction

Nodes in BBN	Expressions for NPT construction
EFFORT'	MSIZE + SCALE
MSIZE	ln A + SIZE' × RISK
RISK	B + CTRL + INCTRL
CTRL	0.01 × (TEAM' + PMAT' + RESL')
INCTRL	0.01 × (FLEX' + PREC')
SCALE	ln(TECHNOLOGY × PROCESS × HUMAN)
TECHNOLOGY	PRODUCT × TOOL' × PLATFORM
PRODUCT	RELY' × DATA' × CPLX' × RUSE'
PLATFORM	TIME' × STOR' × PVOL'
PROCESS	SITE' × DOCU' × SCED'
HUMAN	CAPABILITY × PCON' × EXPERIENCE
CAPABILITY	ACAP' × PCAP'
EXPERIENCE	APEX' × LTEX' × PLEX'

3.3 The COCOMO-U Output

The output of COCOMO-U is the probability distribution of software development effort and not the most likely effort like what COCOMO II produces. We use *le* to stand for the log transformed effort estimation. As *le* will be the linear transformation of *ls* according to Formula (**1**), we assume that *le* is also Normal distribution ($le \sim N(\mu_1, \delta_1^2)$).

The software development effort probability distributions can provide decision support for budget setting. Given the estimated software development effort $le \sim N(\mu_1, \delta_1^2)$ and the probability p% with which project is required to be within a budget (*bgt*), as $\cdot (le - \mu_1)/\delta_1 \sim N(0,1)$ we can look up the statistical table [8] of standard normal distribution and get the interval $\left[-\infty, upbound\right]$ corresponding to possibility p%. Then we can decide a budget *bgt* according to the following formula:

$$\text{If } p\{\text{cost within budget}\} = p\% = p\{ le \le \mu_1 + \delta_1 \times upbound \} \text{ , then} \tag{3}$$
$$bgt \ge \mu_1 + \delta_1 \times upbound$$

The software development effort probability distributions can also be used for cost control. Once a budget has been set, we can calculate the possibility of cost overrun and check if the project is under cost control.

4 Case Study

In this section, we present a web-based application development using COCOMO-U for effort estimation. The developing team made two estimations of the project effort, one after the requirement analysis and the other after a requirement change during the development. We will demonstrate the use of COCOMO-U and compare it with COCOMO II.

4.1 Project Description

The customer of this software development project is a journal office. In the late 2001, the office began to use a web-based online system, which includes functions like online query, online paper transaction, etc. In late 2004, it decided to add new functions such as online reviewing of drafts by readers, automatic reminding of drafts reviewing, selecting readers by using keywords, etc. The selected project is well documented, and the team members are all interviewed to complete a retrospective case study.

4.2 The First Estimation for Budget Setting

When the team members began to gather information for estimating cost at the early phase of the project lifecycle, they found that some cost factors like RUSE, CPLX, RESL and SCED could not be determined by that time. For example, it was not decided if the codes in this system were to be reused in other journal web service systems, which made RUSE hard to determine. The project size estimation was also a great source of uncertainty. Considering the uncertainties of these cost factors, it seemed rather reasonable to use COCOMO-U to deal with the uncertainties and estimate the cost probability distribution.

Through group discussion, the team made an approximate estimation of the software size as 39ksloc, with 90% confidence that the fluctuation of this value would be under 30%. According to Formula (2), the estimated software size can be fed into COCOMO-U as Gaussian distribution $N(3.6636, 0.1876^2)$.

With these probabilistic inputs, the COCOMO-U then generated the logarithm effort probability distribution as shown in Fig. 3. With this result, the project team could set a budget (*bgt*) to ensure that with 80% probability the budget won't be exceeded.

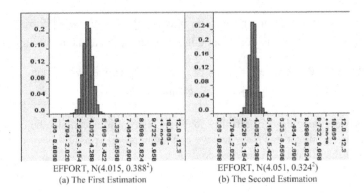

EFFORT, N(4.015, 0.388²)   EFFORT, N(4.051, 0.324²)
(a) The First Estimation   (b) The Second Estimation

Fig. 3. EFFORT Estimations

According to Formula (3), the *bgt* appeared to be $bgt \geq \mu_1 + \delta_1 \times upbound$ $= 4.015 + 0.388 \times 0.85 = 4.345$, and the budget effort was exp(4.345)=77.1 person months.

4.3 The Second Estimation for Cost Control

After a period of time, when developers submitted the prototype of the system, the customer raised new functional requirements. Based on the knowledge gained from the former development, developers gave a new estimated software size as 43ksloc, with 90% confidence that the fluctuation of this value would be under 10%. According to Formula (3), the size can be fed into COCOMO-U as N(3.7612, 0.0608²). Meanwhile, the former uncertain cost factors became deterministic this time (SCED=N, RESL=N, CPLX=N, RUSE=VH).

The COCOMO-U then estimated the effort probability distribution as N(4.051, 0.324²) which is shown in Fig. 3. As the budget was set to 4.345, we calculated out the risk of cost overrun to be 18%. This value was high enough to force the team to make some changes for the project. In fact, the developers took several measures to catch up with the schedule and make sure the project would be delivered on time, such as cutting some less vital functions, and working overtime.

4.4 Comparison of COCOMO-U with COCOMO II

For further explanation of our extension to COCOMO II, we made a comparison of the input parameters and the estimated results of COCOMO-U and COCOMO II. There are two main differences between the two estimation models.

1. When the cost drivers can not be determined accurately, COCOMO II adopts a deterministic rating value with an offset calculated by linear interpolation, while COCOMO-U adopts a probability distribution. Further more, COCOMO-U contains the uncertainty information of the estimated software size as input. (shown in Table 2)

2. COCOMO II produces the most likely value of project effort, while COCOMO-U yields the probability distribution of the estimated effort. As shown in Fig. 4,

COCOMO-U extends the COCOMO II to represent uncertainty information in the Probability Dimension.

The probability distribution measurably describes the risk of cost overruns and can help to set budget and control cost, which we have discussed in section 4.2 and 4.3. As shown in Fig. 4, the budget is a plane in the COCOMO-U view and the probability of cost overruns at a certain time is the areas of the cost probability distributions at the right side of the budget plane.

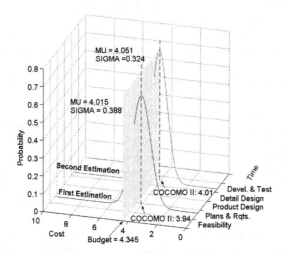

Fig. 4. Cost Estimations in the Three Dimension COCOMO-U View

Table 2. Input parameters comparison of COCOMO II with COCOMO-U

(a) The first estimation

Variable	COCOMO-U	COCOMO II	Variable	COCOMO-U	COCOMO II
PREC	100%H	2.48	PVOL	100%N	1.00
FLEX	100%H	2.03	ACAP	100%H	0.85
RESL	50%N, 50%H	3.54	PCAP	100%H	0.88
TEAM	100%VH	1.10	PCON	100%VH	0.81
PMAT	100%H	3.12	APEX	100%H	0.88
RELY	100%N	1.00	PLEX	100%H	0.91
DATA	100%N	1.00	LTEX	100%H	0.91
CPLX	40%L, 60%N	0.95	TOOL	100%H	0.90
RUSE	20%N, 50%H, 30%VH	1.08	SITE	100%N	1.00
DOCU	100%L	0.91	SCED	50%L, 50%N	1.07
TIME	100%N	1.00	SIZE	$N(3.6636, 0.1876^2)$	39
STOR	100%N	1.00			

(b) The second estimation (values same as that in (a) are omitted)

Variable	COCOMO-U	COCOMO II	Variable	COCOMO-U	COCOMO II
RESL	100%N	4.24	RUSE	100%VH	1.15
CPLX	100%N	1.00	SCED	100%N	1.00
SIZE	$N(3.7612, 0.0608^2)$	43			

5 Discussion and Conclusion

Although there are already many published or proprietary models available for cost estimation, the practice of software cost estimation still has much to be improved. The uncertainty of cost factors and the cost estimation deserves further research.

In this paper we use Bayesian Belief Network to extend the COCOMO II for cost estimation with uncertainty and construct the model COCOMO-U. We illustrate it in the case study that COCOMO-U extends COCOMO II by: 1) explicitly taking the probability distributions of cost factors as input for cost estimation, and 2) representing uncertainty information in the Probability Dimension and generating the cost probability distribution output. The COCOMO-U has been proved useful in helping us better understanding the uncertainty of cost estimations, and its effort probability distribution output can be used for budget determination, risk recognition, and cost control.

Our study also contributes to improve BBN cost estimation models in which we provide answers to the two questions: 1) how to construct a reliable BBN structure when taking into account the many critical cost drivers, and 2) how to determine the NPTs when increasing the node states to improve the outcome's precision.

As the BBN uses discrete node states to represent continuous variables, some loss of accuracy may occur when the number of node states is too small. Such error can be controlled and minimized by increasing the node states and adjusting the BBN structure.

Our model relies on the expertise of its users in terms of their ability to specify the uncertainty of the cost drivers. The influence of the cost drivers' uncertainty to the cost estimation result will depend on both the uncertainty range and the sensitivity of COCOMO II.

In our case study, the uncertainty information of cost drivers is assessed during group discussions among the team members before using COCOMO-U. As it has been reported that there is systematic bias in human judgment toward underestimation of the uncertainty of software projects [12], a more structured process [8] can be used when obtaining probability distributions from practitioners.

The research [13] on the sensitivity of COCOMO II indicates that the most critical input variable is size S, closely followed by effort multipliers EM_i, and the impact of error in determining exponent scale factors W_i is relatively small. As the COCOMO II is sensitive to Size and effort multipliers, adequate time and resources should be devoted to their accurate assessment. The scale factors are much less important and could be neglected (set to their nominal values) if necessary.

As discussed in section 2, for practitioners to handle properly the uncertainty and risks inherent in cost estimation, a cost estimation model can be evaluated with respect to the criteria: 1)explicitly take into account various kinds of uncertainty sources, e.g., uncertainty of input variables, model error, assumption error of input parameters, and scope error, 2)predict the uncertainty of the estimation result, and 3)represent the uncertainty information with the estimation results. COCOMO-U has made an initial progress towards the above goal, and it can be improved by incorporating and analyzing other uncertainty sources than uncertainty of input variables.

The COCOMO-U can be easily adapted to incorporate new information gained in the research on the cost estimation uncertainty. It can be further improved in several ways. For example, the uncertainty of project size and estimated cost can be represented with a more general probability distribution, like Gamma distribution, to reflect more features of the uncertainties. Other research results [10] about reasons for software effort estimation errors can also be included into COCOMO-U to accommodate the uncertainty of cost estimation.

Reference

1. Standish Group, Technical Report (2000), www.standishgroup.com/sample_research/ PDFpages/extreme_chaos.pdf
2. Pearl J., Probabilistic Reasoning in Intelligent Systems: Networks of Plausible Inference, Morgan Kaufmann Publishers, San Mateo, CA, (1988)
3. Pendharkar P.C., Subramanian G.H., Rodger J.A., A probabilistic Model for Predicting Software Development Effort, IEEE Transactions on Software Engineering, Vol. 31(7) (2005)
4. Barry W. Boehm, et al. Software Cost Estimation with COCOMO II, Prentice Hall (2000)
5. Kitchenham B., Pickard L.M., Linkman S., Jones P.W. Modeling Software Bidding Risks, IEEE Transactions on Software Engineering, Vol. 29(6) (2003)
6. Moløkken-Østvold K., Jørgensen M., A review of software surveys on software effort estimation, Proceedings of International Symposium on Empirical Software Engineering (2003) 223-230
7. Greene W.H., Econometric Analysis, Prentice Hall (2000)
8. Kitchenham B., Linkman S., Estimates, Uncertainty, and Risk, IEEE Software, May(1997)
9. Jørgensen M., Evidence-Based Guidelines for Assessment of Software Development Cost Uncertainty, IEEE Transactions on Software Engineering, Vol. 31(11) (2005)
10. Lederer A.L., Prasad J., A Causal Model for Software Cost Estimating Error, IEEE Transactions on Software Engineering, Vol. 24(2) (1998)
11. Grimstad S., Jørgensen M. and Kjetil Moløkken-Østvold, Software effort estimation terminology: The tower of Babel, Information and Software Technology, In Press, accepted 19 April 2005
12. Jørgensen, M., Teigen, K. H., et al., Better Sure than Safe? Overconfidence in Judgment Based Software Development Effort Prediction Intervals, Journal of Systems and Software, Vol. 70, no. 1-2, Feb. (2004)
13. Musílek P., Pedrycz W., Sun N., Succi G., On the Sensitivity of COCOMO II Software Cost Estimation Model, IEEE Symposium on Software Metrics (2002)

A Product Line Enhanced Unified Process

Weishan Zhang[1] and Thomas Kunz[2]

[1] School of Software Engineering, Tongji University,
No. 4800 Cao'an Highway, Shanghai, 201804, China
zhangws@mail.tongji.edu.cn
[2] Department of Systems and Computer Engineering, Carleton University,
1125 Colonel By Drive, Ottawa, Canada K1S 5B6
tkunz@sce.carleton.ca

Abstract. The Unified Process facilitates reuse for a single system, but falls short handling multiple similar products. In this paper we present an enhanced Unified Process, called UPEPL, integrating the product line technology in order to alleviate this problem. In UPEPL, the product line related activities are added and could be conducted side by side with other classical UP activities. In this way both the advantages of Unified Process and software product lines could co-exist in UPEPL. We show how to use UPEPL with an industrial mobile device product line in our case study.

1 Introduction

The Unified Process (UP) or Rational Unified Process (RUP) [6] is one of the most popular and complete process models that have been used by developers in recent years. The main characteristics of UP are:

1. Using iterative and incremental development that has a lifecycle consisting of several iterations;
2. Centering around software architecture, which is the highest-level concept of a system in its environment;
3. Embracing change by considering feedbacks from stakeholders and then make corresponding adaptations.

This architecture-centric approach is facilitating reuse for a single system development. Although it is claimed in RUP that "it also allows reuse on a larger scale: the reuse of the architecture itself in the context of a line of products that addresses different functionality in a common domain", in reality, it is very difficult to achieve this goal without the related supporting technology. There are no mechanisms in RUP to handle the technical issues for a software product line [1], for example variability management.

The current object-oriented technology and component-based development (e.g., with .NET™ or J2EE™), recommended in the RUP practice, provide many useful reuse mechanisms, but in many instances fail to achieve the desired reusability and maintainability. The main reasons come from the intrinsic problems of current programming languages and development methodologies [11].

Q. Wang et al. (Eds.): SPW/ProSim 2006, LNCS 3966, pp. 142–149, 2006.
© Springer-Verlag Berlin Heidelberg 2006

In this paper, we present an enhanced Unified Process called UPEPL (Unified Process Enhanced with Product Line) that incorporates the product line technologies implemented with XVCL (XML based Variant Configuration Language) [11]. The architecture of the underlying system(s) is implemented as a hierarchy of meta-components, which is called an x-framework in XVCL jargon. UPEPL was demonstrated with an industrial mobile device project in which we achieved good reusability, development and maintenance gains.

The rest of the paper is structured as follows: Section 2 presents the UPEPL process in which product line related activities are added and could be conducted side by side with other classical UP activities; then we demonstrate this process with the creation of a mobile game product line. In Section 4, we discuss our case study using the UPEPL process. The related work and concluding remarks end the paper.

2   Unified Process Enhanced with Product Line Technology

In UPEPL, the integration of the product line into the Unified Process may start from the end of the first iteration, or after the release of some products in the product family just like the typical process of product line engineering. Here we show the related activities in UPEPL starting from the early start of the inception phase.

There are four phases in the Unified Process, namely Inception, Elaboration, Construction, and Transition. The inception phase 'focused on ensuring that the project is both worth doing and possible to do', including the business case and the scope of the system. In the elaboration phase, the architecture is created and validated, which lays the foundation for the following activities. The construction phase focuses on the development of the system according to the baselined architecture. The product is delivered to the end user in the transition phase. As the transition phase is relatively simple, we will elaborate other three phases that incorporate product line related activities.

The activities shown in the following figures will follow the style defined in UP, with slight modifications where necessary, and activities and artifacts related to product line are shown with italic fonts. To make the figures clear and concise, the supporting activities, for example the change control, are not shown.

2.1   Inception

As shown in Fig. 1, besides the activities in a normal UP, the inception phase in UPEPL involves additional activities for product line visioning, for example, product line scoping to explore the degree of the commonality and variability, and conducting the initial domain analysis, in order to decide whether the product line is feasible or not.

The main artifacts produced in the inception phase are outlined software requirements, proof-of-concept software architecture, and initial domain feature model. Software requirements are organized in a use-case specification document, and a supplementary requirement document. As the non-functional requirements may appear both in the use-case specification and the supplementary requirements, and there are many similarities for a use case in different product line members, we are using the requirement x-framework to remove the redundancies as proposed in [8,9]. This will keep different documents in consistency.

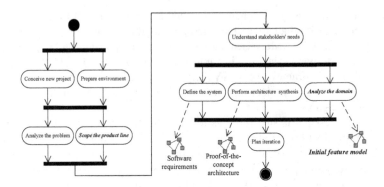

Fig. 1. Activities in inception phase

2.2 Elaboration

In the elaboration phase (Fig. 2), additional activities in UPEPL are related to the feature model refinement, product line architecture development, etc. The proof-of-concept architecture is refined to satisfy the requirements of the first product line member, and this serves as the foundation to develop the first-cut product line architecture (PLA).

More variants and commonalities could be identified during the process of the domain analysis in elaboration phase. This leads to the refinement of the product line requirement (represented as an x-framework), feature model, and product line architecture. The incorporation of the variants into various assets was discussed in previous work [4, 5].

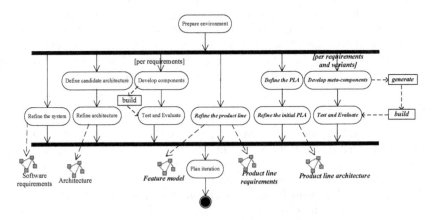

Fig. 2. Activities in elaboration phase

Meta-components for all kinds of assets (including requirements, models and code) are developed incrementally. The first set of meta-components may stem from a typical system and only address its own variants. As the developments proceeds, more variants will be added to make the meta-components more adaptable. And also the related meta-architecture becomes more evolvable as more domain variants are resolved.

Meta-components are used to generate specific components according to the specification for a product line member. Therefore an additional 'generate' process is added before the 'build' starts. The build activity may not be required if the generating process is not for code components, but for requirements, models and other documentary assets.

2.3 Construction

More meta-components are developed in the construction phase. After the product line is ready, the development of a new product line member may involve the selection of the meta-components from the meta-component repository. The selection process starts from the examination of the feature model in order to select the appropriate variants, and then adapting them by writing specification meta-components and modify related meta-components where necessary.

Unit testing and integration testing are also performed in this phase. The product is evaluated against the acceptance criteria in order to make a smooth transition to the end user. Activities in the construction phase are shown in Fig. 3.

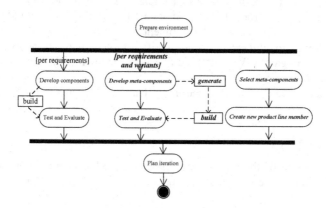

Fig. 3. Activities in construction phase

3   Case Study with a Mobile RPG Product Line

Mobile gaming is becoming increasingly popular. With a Role-Playing Game (RPG), the players take the roles of fictional characters and participate in the interactive story. The player's decision-making drives the story forward and the outcome varies depending on the players' actions.

For starting we will consider the **Climb** game (Figure 4) where the hero jumps up and down the floor (a bar in the following screen), in order to avoid falling down to the bottom of the mountain. Time elapsed and remaining is displayed with a thin bar on the top of screen.

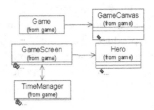

Fig. 4. Climb game screen shot   **Fig. 5.** Common concepts in mobile RPG domain

3.1 Inception

First we will consider four RPGs including Climb we just introduced; ***Kongfu*** where a young man learns kongfu skills from his 'master'; ***Feeding*** where the hero tries to pick up as much food as possible; In ***Hunt***, the hero shoots animals and monsters with arrows. All games are implemented with MIDP2.0 in J2ME platform.

When we look at all these RPGs, we do find some commonalities and variabilities among them. For the commonalities, we can find that there are always heroes in the game scenario, scores are increased or decreased, etc. It is very natural to consider these RPGs as a game product line. A mobile RPG product line should bring promised advantages over the classical development.

The initial examination into the code verified this as there are many similar code patterns inside the games. We analyzed this with our own code clone searching tool called JCloneMiner.

To save space, we do not show the initial feature diagram and other related documents here.

3.2 Elaboration

In the first iteration of the elaboration phase, we further analyzed the mobile RPG domain. The common concepts (implementation with MIDP) are illustrated with a UML class diagram (Fig. 5).

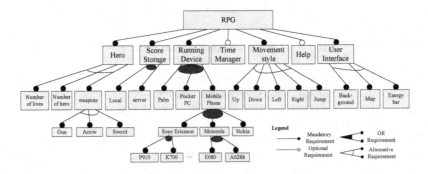

Fig. 6. Feature model for the mobile RPG product line

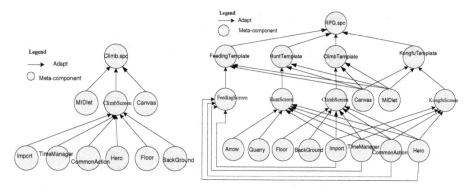

Fig. 7. the first-cut RPG PLA   **Fig. 8.** the final RPG PLA

The feature model is shown in Figure 6. Please note that the feature model may be refined as the iteration goes.

The first-cut RPG product line architecture (RPG PLA) was created by identifying and developing meta-components starting from the Climb game, as shown in Figure 7.

In the second iteration, more meta-components were developed. The first-cut PLA was refined to incorporate more domain commonalities and variants. During the creation of the meta-components and the refinement of the PLA, some of the optimizations were found and incorporated in the related meta-components, which will benefit all components generated from these meta-components. This was discussed in more detail in [10]. The final PLA is shown in Figure 8.

3.3 Construction

Since we have created the mobile RPG product line architecture, we can reuse it in the construction phase to develop a product line member. For example, assume we want to develop a game called **_Dig gem_** (Figure 9). The hero digs around the map to look for various kinds of gems. Different scores for different gems will be added to the total shown on the top. There may be traps and bombs which will consume the energy of the hero. Time elapsed and remaining is displayed with a bar on the top of screen.

Some of the meta-components, such as Hero, TimeManager, etc. could be reused. But other components, for example Cloud, PopUpMenu must be developed and added to the meta-component repository for future reuse.

Fig. 9. screen shot of the Gig gem game

4 Discussion of the Case Study

We first use the typical Unified Process (which is also part of UPEPL) to develop the four games, then we apply the UPEPL to incrementally build the mobile RPG product line. This process is summarized in the following table. The reduced lines-of-code (LOC) count is shown.

Table 1. The process of applying UPEPL to build the RPG product line

	Original LOC	Meta-components LOC	Reduced LOC	Reduced Percentage
climb	941			
feeding	463			
subtotal	1404	1154	250	17.8%
kongfu	720			
subtotal	2124	1579	545	25.7%
hunt	1286			
Total	3410	2547	863	25.3%

From the above table we can see that for a new product line member that is very similar to some of the existing members, the development efforts may decrease steadily. But for a member who has more differences, the reuse ratio may decrease a bit. In the case of the Kongfu game, as there are two heroes with different roles, the Hero meta-component was adapted two times in order to generate specific code components for the two heroes respectively. Therefore the reduced code percentage increases greatly.

In this process, the design and implementation of the mobile games could be unified, which is very important for software design and maintenance. The configurability from XVCL will make the changes to the related components in a consistent way.

6 Related Work

Gomaa presented PLUS method in his work [2]. PLUS is a design method for software product lines that describes how to conduct requirements modeling, analysis modeling, and design modeling for software product lines in UML. He also discussed the integration of PLUS with Unified Process. In essence, his method uses the same methodology as UPEPL. In UPEPL, we use a specific product line technology implemented with XVCL.

Massoni proposed RUPim [7] in order to support progressive and separate implementation of persistence, distribution, and concurrence control. This will reduce the impact of requirement changes, and simplify testing and debugging. UPEPL is aimed to improve the reusability and productivity hence, to inject the strong points of product line technology into the traditional UP.

Other extensions include RUPSec [3] dedicated to security system, where threats and security requirements can be captured and modeled by adding new Roles, Activities and Artifacts. If needed, such extensions could be added to UPEPL too to address specific application domain issues.

6 Conclusions and Future Work

We have proposed a product line enhanced Unified Process called UPEPL. The typical activities in the Unified Process could proceed side by side with product line related activities. UPEPL is demonstrated with a mobile RPG product line, in which four games were considered to build the RPG PLA. It shows that UPEPL is an efficient approach where both the advantages of Unified Process and software product lines can co-exist.

In the future, further applications of UPEPL will be conducted with other domains, such as the CRM systems. We are also considering developing an integrated development workbench, in which meta-component mining, smarting editing and debugging are all included. The UML modeling part are to use Rational Rose, where a plug-in should be developed to link them together.

Acknowledgements

This research is sponsored by "Excellent Young Teacher Funds of Tongji University". Thanks to Liu Wei and other participating develops from Meitong Co. Ltd.

References

1. Clements, P. & Northrop, L. "Software Product Lines: Practices and Patterns". Addison-Wesley, 2001.
2. Gomaa, Hassan.Designing Software Product Lines with UML: From Use Cases to Pattern-Based Software Architectures. Addison Wesley, 2004
3. Jaferian, P. Elahi, G., Reza, M., Shirazi, A., Sadeghian, B. RUPSec: Extending Business Modeling and Requirements Disciplines of RUP for Developing Secure Systems. Proc. of EUROMICRO-SEAA'05. Porto, Portugal, Aug. 2005
4. Jarzabek, S., Zhang, H.: XML-Based Method and Tool for Handling Variant Requirements in Domain Models. RE 2001: 166-173
5. Jarzabek, S., Wai Chun Ong and Zhang, H. Handling Variant Requirements in Domain Modeling. SEKE 2001: 61-68
6. Kruchten, Philippe. The Rational Unified Process, An Introduction, Second Edition. Addison Wesley Longman, 2000
7. Massoni, TL. A RUP-Based Software Process Supporting Progressive Implementation, in book 'UML and the Unified Process', Idea Group Publishing, 2003
8. Zhang W., et al. Software evolution with XVCL. A chapter for the book "Software Evolution with UML and XML", Idea Group Publishing, Dec. 2004
9. Zhang W. Architecturally Reconfigurable Development of Mobile Games. Proc. of the ICESS2005, Xi'an, China, IEEE CS, December 2005, pp 66-72
10. Zhang, W., Jarzabek, S. Reuse without Compromising Performance. Proc. of SPLC2005, Rennes, France, September 2005, Springer LNCS3714, pp. 57-69
11. XVCL homepage. http://fxvcl.sourceforge.net

Automatic Fault Tree Derivation from Little-JIL Process Definitions

Bin Chen, George S. Avrunin, Lori A. Clarke, and Leon J. Osterweil

Department of Computer Science, University of Massachusetts,
Amherst, MA 01003, USA
{chenbin, avrunin, clarke, ljo}@cs.umass.edu

Abstract. Defects in safety critical processes can lead to accidents that result in harm to people or damage to property. Therefore, it is important to find ways to detect and remove defects from such processes. Earlier work has shown that Fault Tree Analysis (FTA) [3] can be effective in detecting safety critical process defects. Unfortunately, it is difficult to build a comprehensive set of Fault Trees for a complex process, especially if this process is not completely well-defined. The Little-JIL process definition language has been shown to be effective for defining complex processes clearly and precisely at whatever level of granularity is desired [1]. In this work, we present an algorithm for generating Fault Trees from Little-JIL process definitions. We demonstrate the value of this work by showing how FTA can identify safety defects in the process from which the Fault Trees were automatically derived.

1   Introduction

A hazard in a safety critical system is "a state or set of conditions of the system that, together with certain other conditions in the environment, will lead inevitably to an accident" [2]. One fundamental requirement of developing a safety critical system, therefore, is to prevent or control the potential hazards. This requires an understanding of what hazards could occur in the system and how they could happen. A variety of hazard analysis techniques have been developed to identify potential hazards, assess their effect, and identify and evaluate the causal factors related to the hazards [2].

Fault Tree Analysis (FTA) [3] is a hazard analysis technique used to systematically identify and evaluate all possible causes of a given hazard. It has been well accepted and applied in many industries such as the nuclear industry [3] and the aerospace industry [4] etc. Given a potential hazard in a system, FTA deductively identifies events (component failures, human errors, etc.) in the system that could lead to the hazard and produces a fault tree, which provides a graphical depiction of all possible parallel and sequential combinations of those events. Once a fault tree has been derived, qualitative and quantitative analysis can be applied to provide information, such as specific sequences and sets of events that are sufficient to cause a hazard and overall system vulnerability to a hazardous outcome resulting from the occurrence of a particular event. This information can then be used as guidance for improvement of the design or implementation of the system.

Q. Wang et al. (Eds.): SPW/ProSim 2006, LNCS 3966, pp. 150–158, 2006.
© Springer-Verlag Berlin Heidelberg 2006

Many processes such as medical processes are also safety critical. In this paper, we discuss how FTA can help to identify the weaknesses in processes and provide guidance on how to improve processes to reduce their vulnerability to hazards. Since manual fault tree derivation is time-consuming and error-prone, we propose an algorithm that automatically derives fault trees from processes specified using the Little-JIL process definition language [5].

The rest of this paper is organized as follows. Section 2 provides background on the Little-JIL process definition language. Section 3 gives a brief description of FTA and uses a simple process to demonstrate how FTA can facilitate process improvement. Section 4 presents our automatic fault tree derivation algorithm. The final section presents conclusions and suggests future work.

2 Little-JIL Process Definition Language

Little-JIL is a visual language for coordinating tasks that are to be executed by either computation or human agents. A process is defined in Little-JIL using hierarchically decomposed steps, where a step represents some specified task to be done by the assigned agent. We first give a brief overview of the semantics and notation of Little-JIL. For a detailed description of Little-JIL, see the Little-JIL Language Report [5].

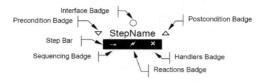

Fig. 1. Little-JIL step icon

Steps: Steps are the basic elements of Little-JIL processes. As shown in Fig. 1, each step has a name and a set of badges to represent the control flow, the interface, exceptions handled, etc. A step having no substeps is called a leaf step, and represents an activity that is to be performed by an agent, without any guidance or control from the process itself.

Step Sequencing: Every non-leaf step has a sequencing badge, which defines the order in which its substeps execute. For example, a sequential step indicates that its substeps are to be executed sequentially from left to right and is only completed after all of its substeps have completed. A parallel step indicates that its substeps can be executed in any (possibly arbitrarily interleaved) order. It, too, is only completed after all of its substeps have completed. A try step also indicates that its substeps are to be executed from left to right and it is completed as soon as one of its substeps is completed. A choice step indicates that any one of its substeps can be selected in order to complete the step.

Artifacts and Artifact Flows: Artifacts are entities that are used or produced by processes. Parameter declarations in the interface to a step specify artifacts read by the step as IN parameters and artifacts produced by the step as OUT parameters. Resources are special kinds of artifacts for which there is contention for access. They are managed by an external resource manager and their acquisitions need to be explicitly specified in step interfaces. After being acquired, resources can be passed as parameters like the other artifacts.

Exception Handling: A step in Little-JIL can throw exceptions when there are aspects of the step's execution that fail. A thrown exception is handled by a matching exception handler associated with the parent step of the step that throws the exception. An exception handler has an associated control-flow badge that indicates how the step catching the exception executes after the handler finishes. For example, the continue badge indicates that the step catching the exception should continue as if the substep that throws the exception completed successfully.

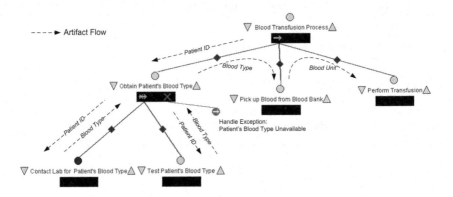

Fig. 2. Simple Blood Transfusion Process

Fig. 2 shows a simple Blood Transfusion Process. The root step "Blood Transfusion Process" is a sequential step, which means that its substeps, "Obtain Patient's Blood Type", "Pick up Blood from Blood Bank", and "Perform Transfusion", should be executed one by one, from left to right. Since "Obtain Patient's Blood Type" is a try step, it tries to execute step "Contact Lab for Patient's Blood Type" first. With the given patient ID passed as an argument, "Contact Lab for Patient's Blood Type" attempts to retrieve the patient's blood type from the lab. If the patient's blood type is available, it is returned as an argument to, and completes, step "Obtain Patient's Blood Type". Otherwise, an exception "Patient's Blood Type Unavailable" is thrown. This exception will be handled by an exception handler at "Obtain Patient's Blood Type". Since this handler is a continue exception handler as indicated by the right arrow, the process continues to execute "Test Patient's Blood Type" to get the patient's blood type. Once "Obtain Patient's Blood Type" is completed, the patient's blood type is passed to "Pick up Blood from Blood Bank", which acquires blood from the blood bank. Finally, blood is transfused at "Perform Transfusion".

3   Fault Tree Analysis for Processes

Event and Gates: The basic elements of a fault tree are events and gates. Events are used to represent faults, such as component failures, human errors, or other pertinent conditions in the system or environment. Fig. 3 shows symbols of several commonly used events and gates. Details about the others events and gates can be found in [3].

OR Gate   AND Gate   Basic Event   Undeveloped Event   Intermediate Event

Fig. 3. Symbols of commonly used gates and events

Basic events are basic initiating faults or conditions. Undeveloped events are events that are not developed any further, either because necessary information for deriving the fault tree leading to these events is unavailable or because these events are considered to have insignificant consequence. Basic events and undeveloped events are also called primary events because they require no further development. As opposed to primary events, intermediate events are events that need to be developed.

Each gate connects one or more input events to a single output event. The output event of an AND gate occurs if all of the input events occur. While the output event of an OR gate occurs if any of the input events occurs.

Fig. 4 shows a fault tree that represents combinations of faults in the simple Blood Transfusion Process that could lead to the hazard "The blood unit to be transfused is wrong".

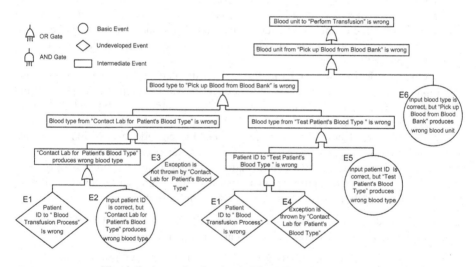

Fig. 4. Fault tree for the simple Blood Transfusion Process

Deriving Fault Trees: To derive a fault tree, the given hazard is represented as an intermediate event called the TOP event. Starting with this event, the fault tree derivation procedure proceeds to develop intermediate events until all leaf nodes in the fault tree are primary events. An intermediate event is developed by investigating the process, identifying the immediate, necessary, and sufficient events that cause this event, and connecting those events to it via a proper gate.

Analyzing Fault Trees: Once a fault tree has been derived, minimal cut sets (MCSs) for this fault tree can be computed automatically using Boolean algebra. A cut set is a set of primary events that ensure the TOP event to occur. A minimal cut set is a cut set that cannot be further reduced. For example, MCSs of the fault tree in Fig. 4 are: {E1, E3} {E2, E3} {E1, E4} {E5} {E6}. These MCSs indicate that the process is exposed to the single point of failure - the hazard will definitely occur if either E5 or E6 occurs. Therefore subsequent changes need to be made to the process to remove these weaknesses.

There are usually several options that could be applied to control or eliminate a hazard in a process, For instance, a failure-resistant agent could be assigned to some steps where major faults could occur. Additionally, consistency check steps could be added to well-chosen places in the process to stop the propagation of faults. Usually only a few of the most effective options can be applied because of resource limitations or other constraints. The effectiveness of an option can be decided by the reduction in the probability of the hazard, if the probabilities of primary events are available. More details about analyzing fault trees can be found in [3].

4 Automatic Fault Tree Derivation

Fault trees are usually derived manually based on a deep understanding of the process. Due to complicated interleavings of events and inter-process communication, manual fault tree derivation can be time-consuming and error-prone. Analysts might fail to identify some events or include events that could not lead to the given event. These errors directly affect the analysis results that decide the validity of decisions made to improve the system.

Two main difficulties in manual fault tree derivation are: 1) how to be sure that one has found all possible events that could occur in the various steps of the process and 2) how to be sure that one has accurately and completely identified all cause-consequence relationships among events. In Little-JIL process definitions, steps have simple uniform interfaces. Therefore we only need to consider a few kinds of events that could possibly occur in these steps. Moreover, cause-consequence relationships among Little-JIL steps follow several patterns, which can be captured using templates. With these events and templates, a simple algorithm can be applied to automatically derive fault trees from Little-JIL process definitions.

Events: Several kinds of events can be defined based on Little-JIL step interfaces. Four of them represent faults that might occur at that particular step. [1]

- *Resource r acquired at step S is wrong.* When a step is started, resources needed by that step are acquired from an external resource manager. Resources acquired might be wrong because of errors in the resource manager, which is not captured in the process. Therefore these kinds of events are defined as undeveloped events.
- *Artifact o to step S is wrong.* These kinds of events can be either undeveloped events or intermediate events. They are intermediate events if the wrong artifacts

---

[1] Without losing generality, we assume that no faults could occur during artifact passing. Unreliable artifact passing can be explicitly modeled using additional steps.

are passed from some step in the process. If wrong artifacts are passed directly from the environment, they are defined as undeveloped events,

– *Artifact o from step S is wrong.* Since these kinds of events are always directly caused by other events that occur in the process, they are defined as intermediate events that need to be developed further.
– *All inputs and resources are correct, but step S produces wrong output o.* These kinds of events can only occur at leaf steps and represent the possibility that designated agents fail to execute those steps as required. They are defined as basic events.

Two additional kinds of events are used to indicate conditions that decide where faults of a step could be propagated to. They are defined as undeveloped events.

– *No exceptions are thrown by S.* Faults of a step could be propagated to its immediate successors only if no exceptions are thrown by this step.
– *Exception e is thrown by S.* If a step throws an exception, its faults can only be propagated to the corresponding exception handling step.

According to [3], direct connections between gates should be avoided. Therefore temporary events are introduced to connect gates if necessary. They are intermediate events and do not change the semantics of fault trees. In the rest of this paper, temporary events are shown as rectangles drawn with dashed lines.

Templates: As noted above, *Artifact o to step S is wrong* and *Artifact o from step S is wrong* could be intermediate events that need to be further developed. To identify immediate events that could cause these events, several templates are defined based on Little-JIL semantics.

● Templates for *Artifact o from S is wrong*

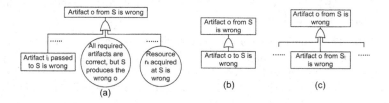

Fig. 5. Templates for Artifact o from S is wrong

If S is a leaf step, its OUT parameters are produced by S from IN parameters and resources. Therefore if o is an OUT parameter of S, it might be wrong if any input to S is wrong, any resource acquired at S is wrong, or S produces the wrong output although all required artifacts are correct, as shown in Fig. 5 (a). On the other hand, if o is not an OUT parameter of S, it cannot be changed by S. In this case, o from S is wrong only if the same wrong o is passed to S, as shown in Fig. 5 (b).

If S is a non-leaf step, S itself does not change artifacts that are passed through it. Any artifact that comes out of S is passed from its substeps. Therefore an artifact o from S is wrong only if o coming from one or more of the substeps of S is wrong, as shown in Fig. 5 (c). Since the template is defined to capture the immediate causes, S_i

in the figure should be a substep that could be the last substep of S to be executed. Such substeps can be decided according to the control badge of S.

- Templates for *Artifact o to S is wrong*

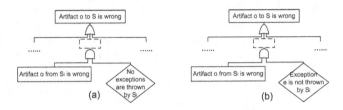

Fig. 6. Templates for Artifact o to S is wrong

As shown in Fig. 6 (a), if S is not an exception handling step, wrong artifacts to S might be propagated from a step S_i that might immediately precede S. Moreover, if S_i could throw exceptions, wrong artifacts can only be propagated to S if S_i does not throw exceptions. Steps that might immediately precede S can easily be calculated from the Little-JIL process definition.

For an exception handing step, it is executed only if the corresponding exception is thrown by some steps. Therefore, one step could propagate wrong artifacts to the exception handling step only if it throws the exception handled by the handler step, as shown in Fig. 6 (b).

Algorithm: With a given TOP event, the automated fault tree derivation algorithm keeps expanding the fault tree by applying proper templates to intermediate events that are leaf nodes until all leaf nodes are primary events. Applying this algorithm to the simple Blood Transfusion Process, we can get a fault tree semantically equivalent to the one shown in Fig. 4.

Limitations: The completeness a fault tree derived from a Little-JIL process by the algorithm depends on the completeness of the process. Thus, in cases where the Little-JIL process definition fails to completely represent steps in a real-world process that have an effect upon critical artifact flows, our algorithm will, accordingly, produce an incomplete fault tree.

Moreover, since Little-JIL processes do not specify how a leaf step produces its OUT parameters from its IN parameters and resources, our algorithm has to assume that any OUT parameter of a leaf step depends on all its IN parameters and resources. Thus, leaf steps that do not satisfy this assumption may cause the derived fault tree to contain superfluous subtrees.

Related Works: There exist several approaches for automatic fault derivation. Leveson et al. proposed a partially automated technique that derives fault trees from Ada programs based on templates [6]. We prefer the advantages of a fully automated approach. Another approach by Leveson et al. is a fully automatic fault tree derivation, but from the Requirements State Machine Language (RSML) specifications [7]. The approach by Pai et al. automatically derives fault trees from UML models [8]. This approach requires the dependency relationships to be explicitly specified. McKelvin et al. designed an algorithm that derives fault trees from Fault Tolerant Data Flow (FTDF) models [9]. These other automated approaches seem to us to suffer from their dependence upon modeling formalisms that lack semantics that are sufficient to represent complex processes clearly, completely, and precisely. Different from these approaches, some approaches, such as [10] and [11], use model checking to generate fault trees. They require explicit state machine models to represent the faults that can occur within components.

5 Conclusion

Fault Tree Analysis is a hazard analysis technique that is well accepted and applied to complex systems in various industries. FTA can also help to improve processes. To improve the efficiency and accuracy of FTA, fault trees can be automatically derived if processes are specified by languages that have precise enough semantics. In this paper, we present an automated fault tree derivation algorithm based upon Little-JIL process definitions. The superior clarity and precision of Little-JIL should result in more complete and definitive fault trees which should then subsequently lead to fault-tree analysis that should help us improve the Little-JIL processes.

Acknowledgements

We would like to thank Zongfang Lin and Sandy Wise for their many helpful suggestions with this work. This research was supported by the National Science Foundation under Award Nos. CCR-0204321 and CCR-0205575. The U.S. Government is authorized to reproduce and distribute reprints for Governmental purposes notwithstanding any copyright annotation thereon. The views and conclusions contained herein are those of the authors and should not be interpreted as necessarily representing the official policies or endorsements, either expressed or implied of The National Science Foundation, or the U.S. Government.

References

1. Clarke, L.A., Chen, Y., Avrunin, G.S., Chen, B., Cobleigh R.L., Frederick K., Henneman, E.A., Osterweil, L.J.: Process Programming to Support Medical Safety: A Case Study on Blood Transfusion. Proceedings of the Software Process Workshop (SPW2005), Beijing, China. (2005)
2. Leveson N.G.: Safeware: System Safety and Computers. Addison-Wesley. (1995)
3. Vesely, W.E., Goldberg, F.F., Roberts, N.H., Haasl, D.F.: Fault-Tree Handbook, Reg. 0492. US Nuclear Regulatory Comm., Washington, D.C. (1981)
4. Vesely, W.E. et al.: Fault Tree Handbook with Aerospace Applications. NASA (2002)
5. Wise, A.: Little-JIL 1.0 Language Report. Technical report (UM-CS-1998-024), Department of Computer Science, University of Massachusetts, Amherst, MA (1998)
6. Cha, S.S., Leveson, N.G., Shimeall, T.J.: Safety Verification in Murphy Using Fault Tree Analysis. ICSE '88: Proceedings of the 10th International Conference on Software Engineering, Singapore (1988) 377-386

7. Ratan, V., Partridge, K., Reese, J., Leveson N.G.: Safety Analysis Tools for Requirements Specifications. http://www.safeware-eng.com/index.php/publications/SafAnTooReq
8. Pai, G.J., Dugan, J.B.: Automatic Synthesis of Dynamic Fault Trees from UML System Models.13th International Symposium on Software Reliability Engineering (ISSRE'02) 243
9. McKelvin M.L.Jr., Eirea, G., Pinello, C., Kanajan, S., Sangiovanni-Vincentelli,A.: A Formal Approach to Fault Tree Synthesis for the Analysis of Distributed Fault Tolerant Systems. Procs. of the 5th ACM International Conference on Embedded Software (2005) 237-246
10. Liggesmeyer, P., Rothfelder, M.: Improving System Reliability with Automatic Fault Tree Generation. FTCS '98: Proceedings of the The Twenty-Eighth Annual International Symposium on Fault-Tolerant Computing (1998) 90
11. Bozzano, M., Villafiorita, A.: Improving System Reliability via Model Checking: the FSAP / NuSMV-SA Safety Analysis Platform. In Proceedings of SAFECOMP 2003, LNCS 2788, Edimburgh, Scotland, United Kingdom (2003) 49-62

Workflows and Cooperative Processes

Jacky Estublier and Sergio Garcia

LSR-IMAG, 220 rue de la Chimie BP53,
38041 Grenoble Cedex 9, France
{Jacky.Estublier, Sergio.Garcia}@imag.fr

Abstract. Workflows emphasize the partial order of activities, and the flow of data between activities. In contrast, cooperative processes emphasize the sharing of artefact, and its gradual evolution toward the final product, under the cooperative and concurrent activities of all the involved actors.

This paper contrasts workflow and cooperative processes and shows that they are more complementary than conflicting and that, provided some extensions, both approaches can fit into a single tool and formalism.

The paper presents Celine, a concurrent engineering tool that allows also to define and support classic workflows and software processes. We claim that the availability of both classes of features allows for the modelling and support of very flexible processes, closer to software engineering reality.

1 Introduction

Since the early 90s, it is a common belief that defining and supporting processes is a significant progress toward improving the predictability of the business at hand in term of quality, cost and delays. [2]

Workflow and software processes aim at modelling and automating processes, seen as a (partial) ordering of "steps", or "task" or "activities" leading to the realization of the business goal. In most workflow systems, the concept of activity is central. The goal can be a service, but most often it is the realization of an artefact. For that reason, most systems emphasize the fact that activities aim at creating or transforming a product [1]. For workflows systems, a process is a sequence of steps in which products are created/transformed; a process model is a graph where nodes are activities, and arcs a data flow/control flow between activities. Artefact versioning is usually not a central concern. The typical workflow is a simple sequence of activities as exemplified bellow. [3]

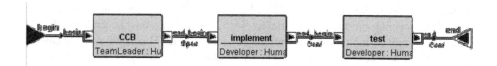

Fig. 1. Typical Workflow sequence

Q. Wang et al. (Eds.): SPW/ProSim 2006, LNCS 3966, pp. 159–166, 2006.
© Springer-Verlag Berlin Heidelberg 2006

By opposition, concurrent engineering emphasizes the fact that activities can be performed concurrently on the same artefact, and for that reason emphasizes the problems that can arise from concurrent modifications of the same artefact. Concurrent engineering often sees the process of producing an artefact as the continuous transformation of that artefact, performed simultaneously in multiple "workspaces". The concept of activity is not clearly identified, and the life cycle of a workspace is often undefined, and can last for the full duration of the process.[5][7]

The typical process is a star, where the centre is the artefact repository, and branches are concurrent workspaces contributing to the evolution of the artefact. Versioning of the shared artefact is a major concern.

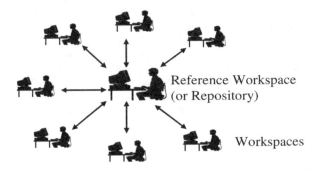

Fig. 2. Typical Concurrent Engineering process : the Star

The paper shows that, despite the differences, they are two complementary views of what is a process, and we propose a way to combine or reconcile these views.

2 Workflows and Processes

The concept of activity and artefact are central in all process support systems (PSS). In workflow, an activity is usually defined as taking some data in input, and producing, after a while, data as output. The duty of an activity is understood as the production of the output data, likely through the transformation of the input data, and possibly creating artefacts during its activity. An activity therefore starts in a "well defined" state of the process, and ends shortly after, when its duty is done.

The data provided to an activity is most often "owned" by the activity during its execution. Sharing and versioning are usually not supported, or at least not directly visible. This approach is a source of problems when it comes to handle concurrent activities working on the same artefact [8]. Most often, this is prohibited, and concurrent engineering on the same artefact is not possible. This is notably the case in PDM, where the artefacts are handled by a central database that does not allow concurrent changes to the same artefact.[4]

If the system allows concurrent changes on the *same physical* artefact, the semantics is often unclear since the combination of the actions performed should be clearly defined, which is often not the case. [9]

In most CSCW [12] systems, document authoring, and many commercial workflow like Staffware and COSA [6], there is only a single copy of the objects in a global store. In many cases a physical artefact is split in *independent logical artefacts* (e.g. in chapters for document authoring systems, or "composite blocks" in FLOWer[6], etc.), owned by each activity. We are in the same situation as before (no concurrency), at a lower granularity level.

If actions are undertaken simultaneously on the same logical document, a clear semantics can be defined only if the data structure and actions are extremely simple like inserting/deleting characters in a string. Blackboards, and some CSCW systems are pertaining to this class of systems. Most workflow systems that allow concurrent changes on the same logical document leave the problem of data consistency in the hands of the workflow designer (e.g. COSA [6]).

A last approach is to consider that each activity owns a different copy of the shared artefact. This solves the issue of concurrent changes, but since the whole process aims at producing a unique artefact, this approach raises the problem of data reconciliation. The problem of data reconciliation is tough; its semantics is very difficult to define, and this is why it is usually not supported by workflow systems. Conversely, this is the very goal in concurrent engineering. This approach is primarily found in Software Configuration Management. Unfortunately, SCM systems only provide workspaces and "mergers"; they do not provide concurrent engineering support, they do not allow to define concurrent engineering policies, and the processes they provide (like change control) are deterministic workflows that do not include any concurrency support. Concurrent engineering systems ambition is to extend the SCM approach with explicit, flexible and non deterministic concurrent engineering models and support.

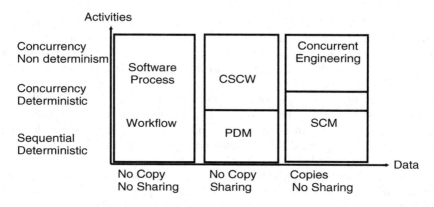

Fig. 3. The different approaches to support engineering activities and data

3 Cooperative Processes in Software Engineering

Tasks in SE (typically fixing a bug) require some time to be performed, and a fairly large, often unpredictable, fraction of the whole software [11]. Most often, being a consistent unit of work by itself, each task should be performed and its result tested individually. Consequently only two options are available : perform the work in sequence (like workflows), or provide each actor a complete copy of the software. The second case is supported in Software Engineering, using the concept of workspace.

Cooperative processes can be modelled by [5][7]:

1. *Concurrent engineering graph*, in which nodes are workspaces and arcs the data flow between workspaces. This graph defines how team work is structured and which paths the data can follow.

2. *Concurrent engineering policy*, which defines under which conditions the changes are allowed to flow along the cooperative graph.

3.1   Concurrent Engineering Graph

The typical concurrent engineering graph is the star presented above (fig 2), which is implemented in almost all SCM concurrent engineering systems. But other concurrent engineering graphs can be used like the following:

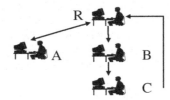

Fig. 4. Example of a workspaces graph

This graph may look like a workflow model, but it is not. Each icon represents a workspace, not an activity : each workspace, potentially, works simultaneously on the same data. Arrows are *only* data transfers between workspaces. At any point in time, any workspace may ask to be source or destination of a transfer, and after the transfer, to continue working or not.

Concurrent engineering is about producing a data in version Vn+1, from the same data in version Vn, and to iterate. It is therefore, intrinsically, a cyclic process, and concurrent engineering graphs reflect this property : at the beginning of a cycle, a well identified workspace, called the *reference workspace*, contains Vn, and eventually contains Vn+1 at the end of that cycle.

Therefore, cooperative graphs are not any graph, they are such that it exists a path between the reference workspace and any other workspace (to allow a workspace to get the latest common version), and conversely a path between any workspace and the reference workspace (for that workspace to promote its work). This characteristic of concurrent engineering graph is an important difference with usual workflows, since most workflow graphs do not match these characteristics, but it is common to repeat a process once terminated, which is a hidden cycle.

Using a UML like formalism, a concurrent engineering graph can be defined. The star graph (fig 2) is simply defined by :

Reference <->* Development

meaning that a single reference workspace is linked in both ways with an arbitrary number of development workspaces. The graph in fig 4 can be defined by : ***Reference<->*A; Reference->B; B->C; C->Reference***; meaning we have a star topology between Reference and A, and a simple cycle (Reference->B->C->Reference).

Fig 4 could model a Software Engineering process in which a star (Reference and A) develop changes on a product, and workspaces C and D are performing tests and validation in sequence (on Linux then on Windows for example). The coordination of all these workspaces is the duty of the concurrent engineering policy.

3.2 Concurrent Engineering Policies

Concurrent engineering emphasize the independent evolution, and reconciliation of multiple copies of the same artefact. But since changes can be conflicting, and the merge algorithm is unsafe, reconciliation, at least for software source code, is difficult to perform and can lead to erroneous results. To a large extend, it is the risk of inconsistent merge that makes concurrent engineering difficult; for that reason, *cooperative engineering is fundamentally about merge control*.

Concurrent engineering can be made safer if the risk related to merging can be controlled and reduced : it is the goal of concurrent engineering policies. A concurrent engineering policy should state :
  –   In which workspace(s) an artefact can be present / changed / created.
  –   In which workspace(s) changes on artefact A performed in workspace X and Y, can be merged.

For example, the usual CVS policy can be modelled as follows :

Graph : Reference <->* Development;
Read-only : Reference ;
Merge : Development, Development -> Development;

This policy means that the graph is a star (line 1), no changes are allowed in the *Reference* workspace (line 2)(it is the CVS data base), and that changes performed in *Development* workspaces can be merged in *Development* workspaces only, whatever the artefact (line 3). Another policy on a star graph could be :

Graph :   Reference (pull) < ->* Development (pull) ;
Merge :   Development, Development -> Reference (source)

This policy, in line 1, not only indicates that we have a star graph, but also that it is the person responsible of the *Reference* workspace that decides which work to integrate first (*Reference (pull)*), and developers who decide when to synchronize with the reference (*Developer (pull)*). Line 2 indicates that changes to the *source*[1] artefact, performed in *Development* workspaces are merged in the *Reference* workspace only. In this policy, all developers are working in parallel, but never perform any merge; it is the reference that is in charge of integrating their changes.

---

[1] The formalism proposed by Celine includes a data model definition allowing to define different policies for different artefacts. This is not presented here for lack of space.

Taking into account the read-only characteristic, different data models (logical objects), the different possible merges and transfers, even the simplest graphs (the star) can support many different policies, all easily defined in our formalism. Of course, less trivial graphs can support a very large range of concurrent engineering policies.

It is also possible to restrict the concurrency, using the "block" primitive, meaning that once a transfer is done, the source workspace is not allowed to continue its work, until the next loop. A policy could be :

Graph:Reference(push)->B; B(push)Block-> C; C(push) Block -> Reference; Merge : Reference;

This policy expresses that workspaces B and C are very much like workflow activities, they receive (*push*) the data they have to work on, and when they transfer their work, they are blocked (*Block*) until next loop. Workspace *Reference* continue working during the loop and can merge its activity with the one of the loop (and maybe with A activity, depending on the star policy definition).

A *transient* workspace is a workspace which is created by the first transfer where it is the destination, and deleted at the first transfer where it is the source.

4   Modeling Concurrent Engineering Workflows

In the Celine formalism, shortly introduced above, a traditional workflow can be modelled as a degraded case of concurrent engineering, where activities are transient workspaces, and control flow becomes workspace transfers. The reference workspace has to be added at the beginning and at the end of the model. Not having any concurrency, there is no merge and no need for any concurrent engineering policy.

Even if possible, we believe this kind of transformation, in general, is misleading : a workspace is not an activity, but a place containing artefacts, where activities can take place on these artefacts. In most our industrial experiments, a workspace has a very long life cycle and supports many successive activities. We believe instead, that workflows and concurrent engineering processes are complementary. The workflow model indicates what are the sequence of activities and actors involved, in a rather deterministic way. The concurrent engineering model indicates how artefacts are handled, what can be performed in concurrence on which artefact, who and when merges are to be performed, in a rather non deterministic way.

In its current form, the workflow tool is Apel; and the concurrent engineering tool is Celine. They have been designed to be totally autonomous, and indeed are used independently; the first one for activity and resource management, the second one for workspace and artefact management. We are in the process of developing the composition of Apel and Celine, at the level of their meta models, and composing workflow and concurrent engineering models.

4.1   Implementation and Validation

Technically, the Celine system is based on a "file system spy" that notifies when a file is changed or renamed. Celine can prohibit the change, or records who and when a given change has been performed. Prohibiting files to be changed is an implementation of a locking mechanism.

Celine implements concurrent engineering policies using locks on artefacts and prohibiting the execution of transfers between workspace, if they violate either the graph or the policy. This analysis is performed statically on the graph and policy definitions, and compiled into a lower level of locks and operation policy.

Celine relies on the spy and on an abstract versioning system for the storage of versions. Therefore, Celine is independent on both the platform (as long as a file system spy is available), the repository and the versioning system (currently available with CVS, Synchronicity, Subversion and Monotone). Celine works, since 2004, in industrial settings, on Windows and Unix systems (Linux and Solaris). The policy support presented above is under development.

5 Conclusion

It is our belief that concurrent engineering is poorly supported currently, mainly because concurrent engineering is not correctly understood, and addressed only at a very low level of abstraction. It is interesting to mention that even a simple policy is transformed into a fairly complex lock strategy, that is almost impossible to perform by hand. Therefore, concurrent engineering policies can be defined and enforced only if high level concepts are proposed, and transparently compiled into low level technical means. It maybe explains why concurrent engineering policies has not been implemented so far.

We believe that a first contribution of Celine is its very high level formalism for concurrent engineering definition. But the fact this formalism can be analysed statically and interactively during policy definition is another major contribution. Indeed, it helps the designer to identify the properties and drawbacks of the graph (process) and to find the policy best adapted to the desired graph, or vice-versa. It allows to computes the next action, and in some case to anticipate transfers and merges, allowing to improve performance, especially for large transfers. It allows to find out all the possible states in a system, and to show explicitly to the users what is the current states during execution, making users aware of the whole work and allowing them to anticipate (or avoid) future merges [5][10].

While classic workflows can be defined and supported in Celine, we resisted the temptation to develop THE unique universal workflow and concurrent engineering system. The reason is that we believe that activity and resource modelling on one side, and artefact and concurrent engineering modelling, on the other side, are two complementary visions of a process. Some parts of the real process are better described in one of these systems, while other parts require to be supported by a composition of the two systems, the workflow describing the activities, and the concurrent engineering system describing the fine grain cooperation between activities. And, of course, other parts of the real process are not described nor supported at all.

We believe this strategy allows to use the currently available workflow models and systems, and to complement them with the concurrent engineering support needed for a highly concurrent, but still safe, practice of concurrent engineering.

References

[1] Derniame J.-C., Kaba B., Wastell, D., "Software Process : Principles, Methodology and Technology". Springer-Verlag, Lecture Notes in Computer Science 1500, 1999.

[2] Georgakopoulos D., Hornick M.F., Sheth A.P., "An overview of workflow management-from process modeling to workflow automation infrastructure". Distributed and Parallel Databases 3(2) : 119-153, 1995.

[3] J. Estublier, S. Dami, and M. Amiour. "APEL: A graphical yet Executable Formalism for Process Modelling". Automated Software Engineering, ASE journal. Vol. 5, Issue 1, 1998.

[4] J. Estublier, J.M. Favre and P. Morat. "Toward an integration SCM / PDM". SCM8, Brussels, 20-21 July 1998. In LNCS 1439, Springer Verlag.

[5] J. Estublier, S. Garcia. "Process Model and Awareness in SCM". 12th Software Configuration Management Workshop. Lisboa, September 2005, Portugal

[6] N. Russel, A. H.M. ter Hofstede, D. Edmond. Workflow Data Patterns http://is.tm.tue.nl/research/patterns/download/data_patterns%20BETA%20TR.pdf

[7] Jacky Estublier, Sergio Garcia, German Vega. "Defining and Supporting Concurrent Engineering policies in SCM" SCM-11 May 2003, Portland, Oregon, USA

[8] Barghouti N. S., "Supporting Cooperation in the Marvel Process-Centered SDE", in: H. Weber (Ed.), Fifth ACM SIGSOFT Symposium on Software Development Environments, Vol. 17 of Special issue of Software Engineering Notes, Tyson's Corner VA, 1992, pp. 21-31.

[9] Charoy F., Godart C., Grigori D. COO-flow: a Process Technology to Support Cooperative Processes, International Journal of Software Engineering and Knowledge Engineering, Special issue: Best Papers from SEKE 2003, vol. 14, n°1, January 2004

[10] Sarma, A., Noroozi Z., Van Der hoek, A.: "Palantir: Raising Awareness among Configuration Management Workspaces". 25th International Conference on Software Engineering. 05 03 – 05, 2003. Portland, Oregon

[11] Dewayne E. Perry, Harvey P. Siy, Lawrence G. Votta. "Parallel Changes in Large Scale Software Development: An observational Case Study" ACM Transactions on Software Engineering and Methodology (TOSEM). Volume 10 , Issue 3 July 2001.

[12] Godart C., "Tutorial : Les outils du travail coopératif. Un point de vue ingénierie des données". 18ème Journées Bases de Données Avancées - BDA'02, Evry, France, October 2002.

Spiral Lifecycle Increment Modeling
for New Hybrid Processes

Raymond Madachy, Barry Boehm, and Jo Ann Lane

University of Southern California Center for Software Engineering,
941 W. 37th Place, Los Angeles, CA, USA
{madachy, boehm, jolane}@usc.edu

Abstract. The spiral lifecycle is being extended to address new challenges for
Software-Intensive Systems of Systems (SISOS), such as coping with rapid
change while simultaneously assuring high dependability. A hybrid plan-driven
and agile process has been outlined to address these conflicting challenges with
the need to rapidly field incremental capabilities. A system dynamics model has
been developed to assess the incremental hybrid process and support project decision-making. It estimates cost and schedule for multiple increments of a hybrid process that uses three specialized teams. It considers changes due to external volatility and feedback from user-driven change requests, and dynamically re-estimates and allocates resources in response to the volatility. Deferral
policies and team sizes can be experimented with, and it includes tradeoff functions between cost and the timing of changes within and across increments,
length of deferral delays, and others. Both the hybrid process and simulation
model are being evolved on a very large scale incremental project and other potential pilots.

1 Introduction

Our experiences in helping to define, acquire, develop, and assess 21st century SISOS
have taught us that traditional acquisition and development processes do not work
well on such systems [1][2]. We are using simulation modeling to help formulate and
assess new processes to meet the challenges of these systems.

The systems face ever-increasing demands to provide safe, secure, and reliable systems; to provide competitive discriminators in the marketplace; to support the coordination of multi-cultural global enterprises; to enable rapid adaptation to change; and
to help people cope with complex masses of data and information. These demands
will cause major differences in the current processes [2].

We and others have been developing, applying, and evolving new processes to address SISOS. These include extensions to the risk-driven spiral model to cover broad
(many systems), deep (many supplier levels), and long (many increments) acquisitions needing rapid fielding, high assurance, adaptability to high change traffic, and
complex interactions with evolving Commercial Off-the-Shelf (COTS) products,
legacy systems, and external systems.

The distinguishing features of a SOS are not only that it integrates multiple inde-
pendently-developed systems, but also that it is very large, dynamically evolving, and

Q. Wang et al. (Eds.): SPW/ProSim 2006, LNCS 3966, pp. 167–177, 2006.
© Springer-Verlag Berlin Heidelberg 2006

unprecedented, with emergent requirements and behaviors and complex socio-technical issues to address. Thus we have developed a system dynamics model because the methodology is well-suited to modeling these dynamic phenomena and their interactions [3].

1.2 The Scalable Spiral Model

The outlines of a hybrid plan-driven/agile process for developing a SISOS product architecture are emerging. It is a risk-driven balance of agility and discipline [4]. In order to keep SISOS developments from becoming destabilized from large amounts of change traffic, it is important to organize development into plan-driven increments in which the suppliers develop to interface specs that are kept stable by deferring changes, so that the systems can plug and play at the end of the increment. But for the next increment to hit the ground running, an extremely agile team needs to be concurrently doing continuous market, competition, and technology watch, change impact analysis, COTS refresh, and renegotiation of the next increment's prioritized content and the interfaces between the suppliers' next-increment interface specs.

The spiral model was introduced in 1986 and later elaborated for WinWin extensions [5]. It has continued to evolve to meet the needs of evolving development processes. We have been converging on a scalable spiral process model for SISOS that, for partial implementations to date, has scaled well from small e-services applications to super-large defense systems of systems, and multi-enterprise supply chain management systems.

Fig. 1 shows a single increment of the development and evolution portion of the model. It assumes that the organization has developed:

- A best-effort definition of the system's steady-state capability;
- An incremental sequence of prioritized capabilities culminating in the steady-state capability;
- A Feasibility Rationale providing sufficient evidence that the system architecture will support the incremental capabilities, that each increment can be developed within its available budget and schedule, and that the series of increments create a satisfactory return on investment for the organization and mutually satisfactory outcomes for the success-critical stakeholders.

As seen in Fig. 1, the model is organized to simultaneously address the conflicting challenges of rapid change and high assurance of dependability. It also addresses the need for rapid fielding of incremental capabilities with a minimum of rework, and the other trends involving integration of systems and software engineering, COTS components, legacy systems, globalization, and user value considerations.

The hybrid process uses a three-team cycle (lean, plan-driven, stabilized developers; thorough V&Vers; and agile, pro-active rebaseliners) that plays out from one increment to the next.

The need to deliver high-assurance incremental capabilities on short fixed schedules means that each increment needs to be kept as stable as possible. This is particularly the case for very large systems of systems with deep supplier hierarchies in

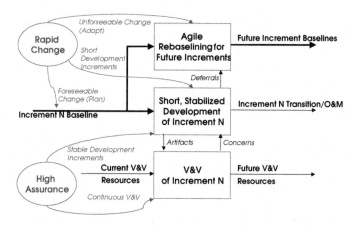

Fig. 1. The Scalable Spiral Process Model: Increment Activities

which a high level of rebaselining traffic can easily lead to chaos. The risks of desta-bilizing the development process make this portion of the project into a waterfall-like build-to-specification subset of the spiral model activities. The need for high assur-ance of each increment also makes it cost-effective to invest in a team of appropri-ately skilled personnel to continuously verify and validate the increment as it is being developed.

However, "deferring the change traffic" does not imply deferring its change impact analysis, change negotiation, and rebaselining until the beginning of the next incre-ment. With a single development team and rapid rates of change, this would require a team optimized to develop to stable plans and specifications to spend much of the next increment's scarce calendar time performing tasks much better suited to agile teams.

The appropriate metaphor for addressing rapid change is not a build-to-specification metaphor or a purchasing-agent metaphor but an adaptive "command-control-intelligence-surveillance-reconnaissance" (C2ISR) metaphor. It involves an agile team performing the first three activities of the C2ISR "Observe, Orient, Decide, Act" (OODA) loop for the next increments, while the plan-driven development team is performing the "Act" activity for the current increment. "Observing" involves monitoring changes in relevant technology and COTS products, in the competitive marketplace, in external interoperating systems and in the environment; and monitor-ing progress on the current increment to identify slowdowns and likely scope defer-rals. "Orienting" involves performing change impact analyses, risk analyses, and tradeoff analyses to assess candidate rebaselining options for the upcoming incre-ments. "Deciding" involves stakeholder renegotiation of the content of upcoming increments, architecture rebaselining, and the degree of COTS upgrading to be done to prepare for the next increment. It also involves updating the future increments' Feasibility Rationales to ensure that their renegotiated scopes and solutions can be achieved within their budgets and schedules.

A successful rebaseline means that the plan-driven development team can hit the ground running at the beginning of the "Act" phase of developing the next increment, and the agile team can hit the ground running on rebaselining definitions of the in-crements beyond.

As much as possible, usage feedback from the previous increment is not allowed to destabilize the current increment, but is fed into the definition of the following increment. Of course, some level of mission-critical updates will need to be fed into the current increment, but only when the risk of not doing so is greater that the risk of destabilizing the current increment.

1.2 System Dynamics Modeling Introduction

System dynamics is a simulation methodology for modeling continuous systems. Quantities are expressed as levels, rates and information links representing feedback loops. It provides a rich and integrative framework for capturing myriad process phenomena and their relationships. System dynamics is well-suited to deal with the complexities of SOS because it captures dynamic feedback loops and interacting phenomena that cause real-world complexity [3].

Fig. 2 serves as a model diagram legend showing the notation for system dynamics elements in a simple system. These notations and following brief descriptions of the elements may help understand the model described in Section 2.

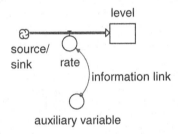

Fig. 2. System Dynamics Model Notation

Levels are the state variables representing system accumulations over time. They can serve as a storage device for material, energy, or information. Contents move through levels via inflow and outflow rates. Levels are a function of past accumulation of rates.

Sources and sinks represent levels or accumulations outside the boundary of the modeled system. Sources are infinite supplies of entities and sinks are repositories for entities leaving the model boundary.

Rates are also called flows; the "actions" in a system. They effect the changes in levels. Rates may represent decisions or policy statements. Rates are computed as a function of levels, constants and auxiliaries.

Auxiliaries are converters of input to output, and help elaborate the detail of stock and flow structures. An auxiliary variable must lie in an information link that connects a level to a rate. Auxiliaries often represent "score-keeping" variables.

Information links are used to represent information flow as opposed to material flow. Rates, as control mechanisms, often require links from other variables (usually levels or auxiliaries) for decision making. Information links can represent closed-path feedback loops between elements.

2 Model Overview

The primary portion of the system dynamics model diagram showing increment activities and the teams is in Fig. 3. It is built around a flow chain for capabilities and uses arrays to model multiple increments. The flow chains for the increment activities show multiple layers of levels and rates; these identify array elements that correspond to the increments. Thus the flow chain and its equations are arrays of five to model five increments (this preset number can be changed to model more or less increments).

Unanticipated changes arrive as a-periodic pulses via the *volatility trends* parameter. This is how they actually come on the projects vs. a constant level of volatility over time. The user can specify the pulses graphically (see the input for Volatility Profile in Fig. 4) or use formulas. The *capability volatility rate* will flow the changes into the corresponding increment for the current time.

From there they arrive in the level for *capability changes* and are then processed by the agile rebaselining team. They analyze the changes per the *average change analysis effort* parameter. Their overall productivity is a function of the *agile team size* (as specified by the user in Fig. 4) and the average analysis effort.

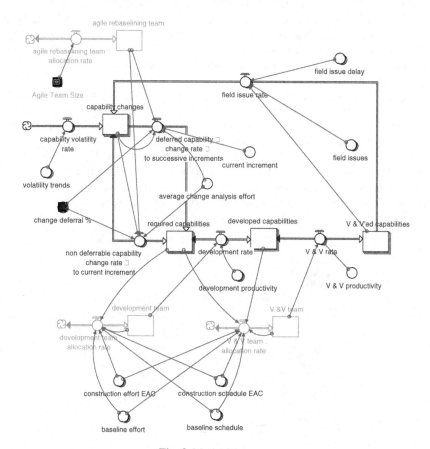

Fig. 3. Model Diagram

The *change deferral %* is a policy parameter to specify the percentage of changes that must be deferred to later increments via *deferred capability change rate to succeeding increments* to *required capabilities* for the appropriate increments. The remaining ones are non-deferrable that flow into the *required capabilities* for the current increment via the rate *non deferrable capability rate change to current increment*. The deferral policy parameter is also shown in the inputs in Fig. 4.

When an increment starts the *required capabilities* are developed by the development team at the *development rate* and flow into *developed capabilities* (all using the flow chain array index corresponding to the proper increment).

Similarly, the *developed capabilities* are then picked up the V&V team for their independent verification and validation. They do their assessment at the *V & V productivity rate* and the capabilities flow into *V & V'ed capabilities*.

The rates in the flow chain between *capability changes*, *required capabilities*, *developed capabilities* and *V & V'ed capabilities* are all bi-directional. This is a provision for capabilities to be "kicked back" or rejected by the various teams and sent back up the chain. For example, there are times when the developers have major concerns about a new capability and send it back to the re-baselining team. Likewise the V&V team might find some serious defects to be re-worked by the developers.

Finally there are user-driven changes based on field experience with the system. These are identified as *field issues* that flow back into the *capability changes* per the *field issue rate* at a constant *field issue delay* time. The *field issues* parameter represents the amount of concern with the fielded system and accounts for a primary feedback loop.

The agile baselining team is shown in the top left of the diagram. The size of the team can be specified as a constant size or a varying number of people over time via the inputs in Fig. 4. The *agile rebaselining team allocation rate* flows people in or out of the team to match the specified team size over time.

The development and V&V teams are shown at the bottom. Their allocation rates are based on the construction effort and schedule for the required capabilities known to-date. Currently the productivities and team sizes for development and V&V are calculated with a Dynamic COCOMO [6] variant. They are equivalent to COCOMO

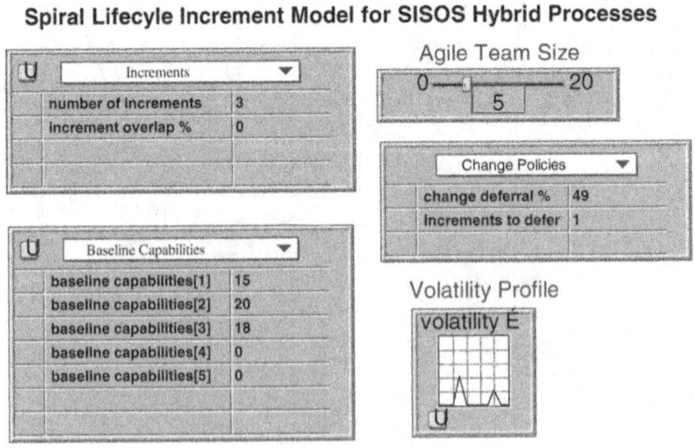

Fig. 4. Simulation Inputs

for a static project (the converse situation of this model context) and continuously re-calculated for changes. However, this aspect of the model whereby the team sizes are parametrically determined from size and effort multipliers will be refined so that constraints can be put on the development and V&V staff sizes.

An illustration of how the system responds to a volatility pulse in Increment 1 is in Fig. 5. In the figure legends, "[1]' refers to the increment number 1. An unanticipated set of changes occurs at month 8, shown as a *volatility trend* pulse. The changes immediately flow into the level for *capability changes*, which then starts declining to zero as an agile team of five people works it off per the average change analysis effort of four person-months.

The change is non-deferrable and it becomes incorporated into Increment 1, so the *total capabilities* for the increment increases. As the new capabilities become required for Increment 1, the development staffing responds to the increased scope by dynamically adjusting the team size to a new level.

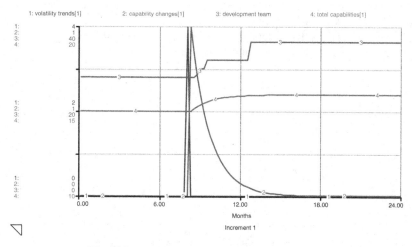

Fig. 5. System Response to Volatility – Increment 1

2.1 Tradeoff Functions

There are several functional relationships in the model that effect tradeoffs between deferral times and cost/schedule. For one, it is costlier to develop software when there is a lot of volatility during the development. If the required capabilities are added to an increment being developed, the overall effort increases due to the extra scope as well as the added volatility. The effort multiplier in Fig. 6 is used to calculate the construction effort and schedule based on a volatility ratio of total required capabilities to the baseline capabilities.

It is an aggregate multiplier for volatility from different sources. It works similarly to the platform volatility multiplier in COCOMO II [6], except in this context there may be many more sources of volatility (e.g. COTS, mission, etc.). This multiplier effect only holds for an increment when changes arrive midstream. If new changes are already in the required capabilities when an increment starts then it has no effect.

Additionally, the later a new capability comes in during construction the higher the cost to develop it. This is very similar to the cost-to-fix defects whereby the costs increases exponentially. Fig. 7 shows the lifecycle timing multiplier based on a ratio of the current time to the entire increment schedule.

Under normal circumstances, there is an additional cost of delaying capabilities to future increments because there is more of a software base to be dealt with and integrated into. Therefore we increase the cost of deferring to future increments by an additional 25% relative to the previous increment (this parameter is easily changed).

2.2 Dynamic Resource Allocation

In response to changes in the capabilities, the model calculates the personnel levels needed for the new increment size and interpolates for the amount of work done. If the increment has just started, then the interpolated staffing level will be closer to the higher level needed for the new Estimate-At-Completion (EAC). If the increment is mostly done, then it doesn't make sense to increase staff to the EAC level because almost all the work is done anyway.

A Rayleigh curve staffing version of the model intrinsically changes the staffing when changes occur with no interpolation necessary.

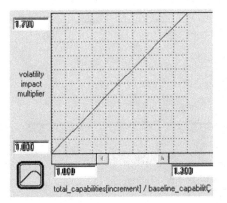
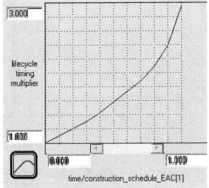

Fig. 6. Volatility Effort Multiplier   **Fig. 7.** Lifecycle Timing Effort Multiplier

2.3 Parameterizations

Since this is a macro model for very large systems, a capability is a "sky level" requirement measure. It is defined as a very high level requirement that we have made equivalent to 10 KSLOC for the purpose of estimation. The construction effort and schedule is currently calculated with a Dynamic COCOMO approach using the COCOMO II.2000 calibration [6].

The volatility impact multiplier is an extension of COCOMO for the SISOS situation. It is extrapolated from the current model and partially based on expert judgment. Other parameterizations relying on expert judgment include the average change analysis effort, lifecycle timing multiplier and amount of field issues. We are obtaining data on these and will be updating them based on the empirical data.

2.4 Sample Test Cases and Results

Table 1 shows the test cases results for varying the agile team size over two increments, each of 15 capabilities. The effort and schedule are for the development and V&V activities (the effort shown does not include the cost of the agile team, which does not account for substantial comparative differences). A change comes in at month eight (same as Fig. 5) and is processed by the agile team. The change is non-deferrable as it needs to be in Increment 1. However, the different team sizes will analyze the change at different rates.

The larger team size will process the change and incorporate it faster; hence the effort and schedule for Increment 1 improves with larger team size. However, if the team size is too small then it won't even make it into Increment 1. For team sizes of two and four it is processed too late and goes into Increment 2.

The total effort for four agile people is nearly equal to the total for a team size of ten (within 5%), since the change was effectively deferred and didn't incur lifecycle timing losses. However, the smaller team will also incur business value losses. These are not currently quantified in the model, but it is reasonable to assume that the value could far outweigh the 5% cost differential. Also not shown for the stretched out Increment 1 cases are losses due to late delivery.

Table 1. Test Case Results

Agile Team Size (People)	Increment 1		Increment 2		Total		Additional Losses
	Effort (PM)	Schedule (Mths.)	Effort (PM)	Schedule (Mths.)	Effort (PM)	Schedule (Mths.)	
2	728	32.3	2875	50.8	3603	83.1	Inc.1 business value
4	728	32.3	1171	37.8	1899	70.1	Inc.1 business value
6	1618	42	728	32.3	2346	74.3	
8	1448	40.5	728	32.3	2176	72.8	
10	1278	38.9	728	32.3	2006	71.2	

These results account for the lifecycle timing multiplier, volatility multiplier and increment delay losses. The model shows that a sufficient level of agile re-baseliners is necessary, or the cost and schedule for the project increases substantially. Enough must be on-board and productive enough to analyze the changes in a timely manner. Otherwise there could be a backlog of work to worry about at the beginning of a later increment that could have been resolved earlier by the agile team or other losses.

This set of test cases only varied agile team size, but another dimension to vary is the deferral percentage. Additionally we will simulate all five increments and have volatility occur in more than one increment in subsequent experiments.

3 Conclusions and Future Work

Processes need to rethought for current and upcoming SISOS, and the outlined hybrid process based on the scalable spiral model appears to be an attractive option. The dynamic model will help to further refine the hybrid process and determine optimized variants for different situations.

This first major iteration of the model already provides interesting results. It shows that if the agile team doesn't do their work, then developers will have to do it at a higher cost. Further experiments are underway to vary the deferral percentages, include rework, and constrain the staff sizes for development and V&V.

Both the hybrid process and the model will be further proven and evolved. Various improvements in the model are already identified and briefly discussed below, but further changes will come from users of the model. Additionally, empirical data to help calibrate and parameterize the model will come from users in the field and other data collection initiatives at USC.

This version of the model uses step function staffing profiles that adjust dynamically to changes. Another version uses Rayleigh curves for more realistic staffing patterns that adjust on the fly to midstream changes. These models will be integrated to allow the user to specify the type of staffing.

In the current test cases, only the optimum personnel levels are used for development and V&V, but in reality there may be staffing constraints. The model will be refined so users can constrain the development and V&V staff sizes. Another set of tests will compare tradeoffs between different agile team staffing policies (e.g. level-of-effort vs. demand-driven).

Patterns of changes and change policies will be experimented with. We will vary the volatility profiles across increments and demonstrate kick-back cases for capabilities flowing back up the chain from the developers or V&V'ers. Additionally we will model more flexible deferral policies across increments to replace the current binary simplification of allocating changes to the current or next increment.

As previously noted, the model currently does not account for business/mission value losses due to delays. Business value should be part of the overall process analysis, so provisions will be made to quantify the timed value of capabilities.

Parts of model have been parameterized based on actual empirical data, but not the change traffic. We will be getting actual data on volatility, change traffic trends and field issue rates from our USC affiliates and other users of the model. Data for the change analysis effort and volatility cost functions will also be analyzed.

After we get change data to populate the model and make other indicated improvements, we will be using it to assess increment risk for a very large scale SISOS program. It will also be used by contractors on the program in addition to our own independent usage to assess process options.

We also plan to apply it to other projects we are involved with, and the model will be provided to our USC-CSE industrial affiliates for assessing and improving their processes. They will also provide an opportunity to obtain additional empirical data for model parameters.

References

1. Boehm, B., Brown, A.W., Basili, V., Turner, R.: "Spiral Acquisition of Software-Intensive Systems of Systems", CrossTalk. May (2004)
2. Boehm, B.: "Some Future Trends and Implications for Systems and Software Engineering Processes", USC-CSE-TR-2005-507 (2005)
3. Madachy R.: Software Process Dynamics, IEEE Computer Society Press (2006)
4. Boehm, B., Turner, R.: Balancing Agility and Discipline, Addison Wesley (2003)
5. Boehm, B., Egyed, A., Kwan, J., Port, D., Shah, A., and Madachy, R.: "Using the WinWin Spiral Model: A Case Study" IEEE Computer, July (1998)
6. Boehm, B., Abts C., Brown A., Chulani S., Clark B.,Horowitz E., Madachy R.,Reifer D., Steece B.: Software Cost Estimation with COCOMO II, Prentice-Hall (2000)

Definition and Analysis of Election Processes

Mohammad S. Raunak, Bin Chen, Amr Elssamadisy,
Lori A. Clarke, and Leon J. Osterweil

Department of Computer Science,
University of Massachusetts,
Amherst, MA 01003, USA
{raunak, chenbin, samadisy, clarke, ljo}@cs.umass.edu

Abstract. This paper shows that process definition and analysis technologies can be used to reason about the vulnerability of election processes with respect to incorrect or fraudulent behaviors by election officials. The Little-JIL language is used to model example election processes, and various election worker fraudulent behaviors. The FLAVERS finite-state verification system is then used to determine whether different combinations of election worker behaviors cause the process to produce incorrect election results or whether protective actions can be used to thwart these threats.

1 Introduction

In previous work, we have demonstrated that it is possible to define complex processes with precision that is sufficient to support definitive demonstrations that the processes either do, or do not, have worrisome defects. Our preliminary work with healthcare processes [3], for example, shows that it is possible to identify potentially life-threatening defects, even in large complex medical processes. Our work with the US National Mediation Board has suggested that automating carefully defined processes that have been clearly understood by all stakeholders, can lead to increased trust and confidence in the workings of government.

This paper extends our previous process definition and analysis work to election processes. A novel aspect of this work is its approach to assessing the potential impact of fraudulent behavior. In our earlier work (e.g. with healthcare processes [3]) we assumed that participating agents (e.g. doctors and nurses) always try to perform assigned tasks correctly. We dealt with incorrect or inadequate performance through the use of pre- and post-condition checks and exception processing. But, in analysis of elections, we now attempt to deal with the consequences of the performance of tasks by agents whose actions may be intentionally incorrect or malicious. An interesting challenge of this work is how to represent such behaviors and assess how well processes defend against their negative effects. Early positive results of this work suggest the possibility of a discipline of election process engineering, in which costs and benefits of specific safeguards can be measured against specific election fraud risks.

Q. Wang et al. (Eds.): SPW/ProSim 2006, LNCS 3966, pp. 178–185, 2006.
© Springer-Verlag Berlin Heidelberg 2006

2 Related Work

There is now considerable interest in assuring the correct performance of elections. The 2000 US Presidential election yet again demonstrated that elections may have many and varied defects and loopholes [1], [4], [6], [8]. In response there have been many efforts to improve the conduct of elections [7], [9]. Most efforts focus on using electronic devices to record and tabulate votes and emphasize the potential for such devices to commit errors or frauds. Because electronic voting machines use software for vote recording and tabulation, software analysis is used to reason about the code in such machines. Our work differs in that it seeks to discover and correct defects in the overall processes of which voting machines are only a part. Elections generally have many different steps and activities, and are performed by many different agents (e.g. the voter, precinct officials, and district voting officials) in addition to just the actual vote recording device. Thus, opportunities for frauds and errors go far beyond those that can be accomplished by the software code in a voting machine. Our work employs analysis techniques and approaches that are applicable to reasoning about software code, and applies these techniques instead to rigorous definitions of overall election processes to demonstrate the presence or absence of specified defects and the resistance (or its lack) in specific processes to specific frauds.

3 Our Approach

For this research we used our process language, Little-JIL [2], [10] to define an election process. We used the resource specification and dataflow annotation features of Little-JIL to represent artifact flow and agent binding details in the process definition. We specified election security requirements as finite state automata, and then used our FLAVERS finite-state verification system [5] to identify vulnerabilities and to prove whether a process can defend against a particular type of fraudulent behavior or threat.

3.1 The Little-JIL Process Language

The Little-JIL language supports defining coordination amongst human and automated agents at different abstraction levels. It supports the definition of control flow, including the handling of exceptions, and it also supports the definition of artifacts and their flows. The central construct of a Little-JIL process is a step. Steps are organized into a hierarchy, whose leaves represent the smallest specified units of work, each of which is assigned to an agent.

Figure 1 shows the graphical representation of a Little-JIL step with its different badges and possible connections to other steps. The interface badge specifies artifacts either required for, or generated by, the step's execution as well as the resources needed to support step execution. Every step has a special resource, its 'agent', which is responsible for the step's execution. A step may also include pre- and/or post-requisite badges, representing steps that need to be executed before and/or after this step. On the left, inside the central black box of every non-leaf step, is a control flow badge that specifies the order in which the step's sub steps are to be executed. A child is connected to its parent by an edge, and artifact flows between the parent and child are indicated by annotations on this edge. On the right of the step bar is an X sign that represents the exception handling capabilities of the step. Attached to this badge by exception edges are handlers that deal with exceptions occurring in the step's descendants. Each handler is itself a step annotated to indicate the type of exception it handles. One of four exception continuation semantics define how process flow continues.

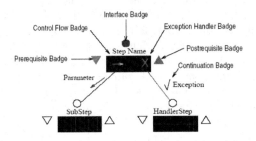

Fig. 1. A Little-JIL step construct

There are four different non-leaf *step kinds*, namely "sequential", "parallel", "try" and "choice". Children of a "sequential" step are executed one after another from left to right. Children of a "parallel" step can be executed in any order, including in parallel. A "try" step attempts to execute its children one by one from left to right. A "choice" step's agent chooses which of its children will comprise the step's execution.

A complete Little-JIL process definition also contains definitions of *artifacts* and *resources* to complement this coordination definition. *Artifacts* are entities such as data items, files, or access mechanisms that are passed between parent and child steps, much in the same way that parameters are passed in a procedure invocation in a standard programming language. Complete details about Little-JIL can be found in [10].

3.2 Process Verification

We used a finite-state verifier (our FLAVERS tool) to determine whether or not election soundness policies are violated by our election process definition. Given a property that represents a policy in terms of the states of process steps and the artifacts flowing between the steps, FLAVERS determines if this property always hold on all possible process executions. When properties may not hold for all executions, FLAVERS provides a counterexample execution showing where a violation occurs, thereby providing process-improvement guidance.

4 An Election Process Example

Our election process assumes that one single DRE (direct recording electronic) voting machine is being used at a precinct, that there is only one office for which an election is being held, and that there are two candidates (A and B) running for the office.

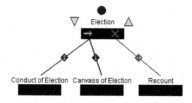

Fig. 2. Top level election process

At the top level, as shown in figure 2, the state-wide election process consists of *Conduct of Election*, followed by *Canvass of Election*, where state board officials aggregate precinct level election results, and a possible *Recount* if something major goes wrong. The child steps of the root step (*Election*) are elaborated in separate diagrams (e.g. Fig. 3 elaborates the details of *Conduct of Election*). The diagrams use yellow post-it notes to provide still more detailed elaboration.

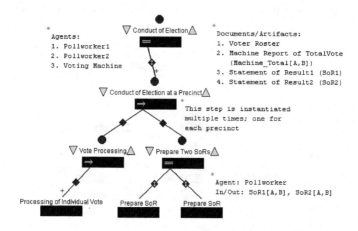

Fig. 3. Process model for *Conduct of Election*

Conduct of Election is a number of parallel activities taking place simultaneously at each precinct. *Conduct of Election at a Precinct* includes the processing of individual votes for each voter throughout the voting period and preparation of two copies of a precinct result summary called "Statement of Result" (SoR). *Processing of Individual Vote* is a reference to a step, which we have not elaborated in this paper due to space constraints. In that subprocess, an individual voter is first authenticated before being allowing to vote. A DRE is responsible for recording voter's exerted intent correctly, and the DRE keeps a running tally of the number of votes cast for each candidate.

At the end of the voting period, each of the two poll workers independently looks at the voting machine, and prepares a "Statement of Result" (SoR), consisting of the total votes for candidate A (Machine_Total[A]) and for candidate B (Machine_Total[B]). The two SoRs are then sent to the State Election Board for statewide aggregation and certification in *Canvass of Election*. Note that *Prepare SoR* is a task assigned to a poll worker agent. The agent can carry out the task honestly or may inadvertently or maliciously modify the numbers while preparing the SoR.

The State Election Board collects the precinct level result summaries (SoRs), validates the results reported in SoRs by matching them against each other, and aggregates the precinct summaries into a statewide summary-sheet that holds the total votes for candidates A and B. The State Election Board officials make sure that the totals reported in SoR1 match the totals reported in SoR2. If there is a mismatch, the officials examine the actual DRE to determine if one of the SoRs agrees with the machine. If so, the other SoR is corrected accordingly. These actions are part of the agent behavior represented by the *Handle Validation Fail* exception handling step. If neither SoR agrees with the DRE, the precinct officials are called in for consultation and both SoRs are corrected (these details are omitted from this example because of lack of space). Upon proper aggregation of the precinct results, including handling of any potential inconsistencies in the Statement of Results, the state board certifies the result and declares it official. Figure 4 shows the model for the last part of this process. The figure also shows how the Little-JIL system's inspector tools supports looking inside a step (*Statewide Aggregation* in this case) to reveal its resource and artifact definitions.

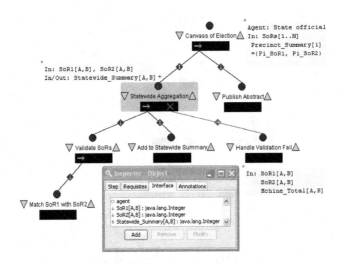

Fig. 4. Process model describing *Canvass of Election*

4.1 Analysis of Frauds

To analyze potential threats arising out of fraudulent agent behavior we use Little-JIL to model not only an election process, but also details of how an agent carries out tasks in this process. The analysis is applied to the process definition, potentially paired with different agent behavior definitions to see which properties hold when different processes are paired with different agent behaviors.

To demonstrate this, we consider the following property for our election process: *If two SoRs mismatch, the incorrect SoR gets detected and corrected before getting added to the Statewide Summary*. For this analysis, we paired the process described in section 4.1 with specifications of the behaviors of two different poll workers, exactly one of which is hypothesized to produce fraudulent SoR results. Space limitations prevent us from showing how we used Little-JIL to model the agents' performance of the *Prepare SoR* step. But, informally, we defined the fraudulent behavior by indicating that the observed machine vote totals were redefined by the poll worker. Our model of the performance of the correct poll worker showed that the totals reported were unchanged from the original machine totals.

Our process verification framework proved that the above property holds for this process/agent pairing. It also holds when both poll workers are honest. If we were to pair this process with two dishonest agents producing identical, yet incorrect SoRs, the process verification still proves, albeit misleadingly, that the property holds. This means that this property is not sufficient for verifying this additional incorrect agent behavior. This led us to develop a stronger property: *An SoR will never get added to the Statewide Summary if it is different from the Machine_Total.* A subsequent analysis showed that this new property is sometimes violated by the process when there are two dishonest poll workers. This led us to improve the process to have safeguards against this additional incorrect agent behavior.

In this iterative process improvement procedure, we specify a property, verify it holds for a process, specify a stronger property, attempt to verify the new property to identify where it fails and improve the process with additional safeguards and prove the strength of the new process through the verification of the new property.

In what follows we describe the detail of how the property verification works in our mechanism through the example of verifying the first property mentioned above. The formalism we used for specifying this property is a finite state automaton (FSA) shown in figure 5. For each poll worker, the following property should hold.

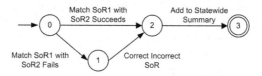

Fig. 5. A security property for the Election process

The labels associated with the transitions in this property representation automaton correspond to events in the process. The execution of a Little-JIL step is an event, but only some step execution events are germane to the property being analyzed. In the above property, the event "Match SoR1 with SoR2 succeeds" represents the execution of step *Match SoR1 with SoR2* is completed, while the event "Match SoR1 with SoR2 fails" represents the execution of step *Match SoR1 with SoR2* is terminated raising some exception. Similarly, the "Correct Incorrect SoR" transition represents execution of the step *Handle Validation Fail* is completed. Tools such as the FLAVERS system used here trace all possible paths through a process model and move the automaton from state to state as events in the automaton alphabet are encountered along a path. If the automaton is always in an accepting state after tracing all possible paths, then the property is verified. If not, it means FLAVERS has discovered a process execution path along which the property is violated.

We now show that for one honest poll worker and one dishonest poll worker, the property specified above holds. Since only one poll worker changes the SoR, two SoRs are not identical. Therefore when the execution goes to *Match SoR1 with SoR2*, exception "ValidationFail" will be thrown. The event "Match SoR1 with SoR2 fails" occurs and the property automaton goes to state 1. The exception is then handled by the exception handler *Handle Validation Fail*. When *Handle Validation Fail* step completes, the event "Correct Incorrect SoR" occurs and leads the property to state 2. Since the exception handler is a continue handler, the step *Add to Statewide Summary* will be executed. Completion of this step triggers the event "Add to Statewide Summary", which drives the property to state 3. The property remains in the accepting state 3 until the whole process completes. Thus the property holds.

The property may also hold if both poll workers are dishonest. When both poll workers change their SoRs, two SoRs could either be identical or different. If they are identical, when execution goes to step *Match SoR1 with SoR2*, no exception will be thrown. Thus event "Match SoR1 with SoR2 Succeeds" occurs and the property goes to state 2. Then *Add to Statewide Summary* step is executed and event "Add to Statewide Summary" occurs. The property goes to the accepting state 3 and remains in this state until execution ends. On the other hand, if two SoRs are different, the "ValidationFail" exception will be thrown by the step *Match SoR1 with SoR2*. The rest of the execution is the same as the one for only one dishonest poll worker, as shown above. In this case, the property is also in the accepting state when the execution ends. Thus the property may hold if both poll workers are dishonest.

The original property only detects a fraud if the poll workers produce different SoRs. Therefore the current process and analysis are inadequate to detect a fraud where the poll workers change both SoRs in the same way. We have to modify the process and/or include a more complex property to check for this kind of fraud. While it may be possible to verify these properties by careful inspection, we argue that such manual inspection quickly becomes infeasible as the process and agent behaviors grow larger and more complex.

5   Conclusion and Future Work

This paper describes how rigorous process definition and analysis can identify vulnerabilities introduced by agent behaviors. We verified an important property for a particular election process and a specific combination of agent behaviors, and indicated how to iteratively improve the process to make it robust against more complicated fraudulent behavior. We plan to model more complicated and elaborate election processes with many more agents and more complex fraudulent behavior. Modeling collusion among agents and developing processes to defend against such intricate frauds and collusions is an important direction in this work. These technologies seem to be the basis for a discipline of election process engineering and continuous improvement.

Acknowledgements

Matthew Goetz was very helpful at an early stage of this work. Prof. George Avrunin provided valuable feedback about the work. This research was partially supported by the National Science Foundation under Award Nos. CCR-0204321 and CCR-0205575. The U.S. Government is authorized to reproduce and distribute reprints for Governmental purposes notwithstanding any copyright annotation thereon. The views and conclusions contained herein are those of the authors and should not be interpreted as necessarily representing the official policies or endorsements, either expressed or implied of The National Science Foundation, or the U.S. Government.

References

1. Bannet, J., Price, D.W., Rudys, A., Singer, J., Wallach, D.S.: Hack-a-vote: Security issues with electronic voting systems. Security & Privacy Magazine, IEEE, Vol. 2(1). Jan.-Feb. (2004) 32 – 37
2. Cass, A.G., Lerner, B.S., McCall, E.K., Osterweil, L.J., Sutton Jr., S.M., Wise, A.: Little-JIL/Juliette: A process definition language and interpreter. In: Proc. of the 22nd International Conference on Software Engineering, Limerick, Ireland (2000) 754-757
3. Clarke L.A., Chen Y., Avrunin G.S., Chen B., Cobleigh R., Frederick K., Henneman E.A., Osterweil L.J.: Process Programming to Support Medical Safety: A Case Study on Blood Transfusion. In: Proceedings of the Software Process Workshop (SPW2005), Beijing, China, May 25-27 (2005), Springer-Verlag Lecture Notes in Computer Science, Vol. 3840, 347-359
4. Dugger, R.: Counting votes. Annals of Democracy. New Yorker Vol. 64 (38) Nov 7, 1988
5. Dwyer, M.B., Clarke L.A., Cobleigh J.M., and Naumovich G.: Flow Analysis for Verifying Properties of Concurrent Software Systems. ACM Transactions on Software Engineering and Methodology, October (2004) 359-430
6. Kohno, T., Stubblefield, A., Rubin, A., and Wallach, D.: Analysis of an Electronic Voting. System IEEE Symposium on Security and Privacy 2004. IEEE Computer Society Press, May 2004.
7. Robinson S.: Did Your Vote Count? New Coded Ballots May Prove It Did. New York Times, March 2nd 2004, http://www.nytimes.com/2004/03/02/science/02VOTE.html?ex=1084334400&en=88f5c6e6696ccdcf&ei=5070
8. U.S. presidential election, 2000: Wikipedia, http://en.wikipedia.org/wiki/U.S._presidential _election,_2000.
9. Verified Voting Foundation, http://www.verifiedvotingfoundation.org
10. Wise A.: Little-JIL 1.0 language report. Technical Report No. UM-CS-1998-024, Department of Computer Science, University of Massachusetts, Amherst, MA (1998)

The Design of a Flexible Software Process Language[*]

Beijun Shen[1] and Cheng Chen[2]

[1] Dept. Of Computer Science, Shanghai Jiaotong University, Shanghai 200240, China
bjshen@sjtu.edu.cn
[2] Wonders Information Co., Ltd., Shanghai 200230, China
chen_goodwin@yahoo.com

Abstract. We propose a flexible process language (FLEX) to specify both process model and meta-process model within a uniform framework based on process ontology. A process ontology and some kernel meta-activities are presented as the fundament for process support, such as modeling, enaction and evolution. In contrast to other process languages that only can evolve process model while encoding meta-process logic within PSEEs, our approach can also evolve meta-process model for adjusting process support mechanism flexibly.

1 Introduction

A process language should support the change of software process model in a flexible manner while the process is enacting, because there are full of indeterminacy during software project development. Furthermore the change of process representation may cause the change of related meta-processes. Conradi [1] remarked that "it is not possible to identify one universal meta-process for all possible process." So we believe that both process representation and meta-processes should also be user-defined and user-evolved.

In this paper, we propose a flexible process language (FLEX) to specify both process model and meta-process model within a uniform ontology-based framework, which also supports to specify customizable process enaction logic in meta-process model. The most significant feature of FLEX is the *process ontology*, which can be defined statically and modified dynamically through *operation primitives* during process evolution. It allows users to customize the representation of process elements and to define new operation primitive for extending the representation capability of language. On the other hand, general users can use it easily by pre-defined representation and operation primitives, so they needn't be involved in the detail of semantics. With this approach, we try to provide users customizable process language to reach the goals of flexibility, ease to use and semantic richness. Secondly, in contrast to most of PMLs, e.g. EPOS SPELL [1], Merlin [2], PEACE/PDL [3], SPADE/SLANG [4], that only specify process model while encoding meta-process logic within PSEEs, FLEX can obtain some significant advantages since it specifies meta-process model to support flexible process management. Based on some kernel

---

[*] This research is supported by the National Natural Science Foundation of China (No. 60373074).

Q. Wang et al. (Eds.): SPW/ProSim 2006, LNCS 3966, pp. 186–194, 2006.

meta-process models, we are able to define, enact and evolve software process model and meta-process model themselves continuously.

We introduce the concept of process ontology in Section 2. Section 3 proposes the fundamental process ontology, i.e. the pre-defined process modeling language, including the pre-defined operation primitives and the representation of process elements. Section 4 proposes the kernel of meta-process models and the mechanism of process enaction and evolution. We assess our approach and conclude in Section 5.

2 Process Ontology

In the view of AI, ontology is an explicit specification of a *conceptualization*: the objects, concepts, and other entities that are presumed to exist in some area of interest and the relationships that holds them [5]. Similar to ontology, we define process ontology as a specification of representation of process elements, i.e. the definitions of classes, relations, and semantics of process elements. There are several main parts in process ontology:

1) Super Ontology: This optional part specifies the super process ontology. Process ontology can inherit all observable process elements and related syntax and semantics from its super process ontology.

2) Syntax: It specifies the syntax of each process element with context-free grammar, which determines the representation of process elements user can use. We regard process model and its related process elements as a type system, which has some pre-defined types. We can define new types by some operations on those pre-defined types, i.e. *$boolean, $number, $string, $name, $time, $set*, and *$currency*. The name of process element is a particular pre-defined attribute with type *$name,* who can exclusively determine a process element in a process model. A process element should have explicit name while it may be referred by other process elements. For avoiding the name conflict in process model, we use the form *<process element name>.<attribute name>* to refer an attribute of a process element.

3) Semantics: It defines semantics of process elements and user-defined operation primitives by pre-defined operation primitives and system-supplied semantics.

There are six pre-defined operation primitives with implicit semantics in FLEX, which are *$relation, $consist, $derive, $alias, $semantic* and *$mask*.

– The primitive *$relation* implies that two process elements have some kind of relation.
– The primitive *$consist* defines the combination of process elements, and has the form of [A *$consist {A_1, A_2, ..., A_n}*], where A, $A_1, A_2, ..., A_n$ are process elements represented by their type descriptor.
– The primitive *$derive* defines the derivation of some defined process elements, has the form of [A *$derive* B], where A and B are process elements. We call that A is sub process element of B, and B is super process element of A. A process element can inherit all attributes and corresponding semantics from its super process element and keep the syntax of its super process element except its type descriptor.

- The primitive *$alias* defines the equivalence between two *semantic specifications*. The valid operation expression is remarked as semantic specification. Users can define new operation primitives by *$alias*.
- The primitive *$semantic* is similar to *$alias*. The difference between them is the left of *$semantic* should be a keyword in syntax and the right of *$semantic* should be a defined operation primitive. For example, let an operation expression (**consist** *$semantic $consist*), where **consist** is a keyword in syntax part of the process ontology, and its semantics will be equivalent to *$consist*.
- The primitive *$mask* makes some process elements and operation primitives to be invisible outside.

In addition, it also supports the form such as *first order predication, FAM, temporal operator,* and *DPDA* to specify semantics. Users can construct their detail semantic specification based on them.

3 Pre-defined Process Language

In the framework of process ontology above, we propose the fundamental process ontology for process model, meta-process model, and organization model. Organization models of different organization can have varied forms, but we prescribe that they must consist of the ontology of agent and skill.

For reaching the goal to describe process model in the following four views: function view, behavior view, organization view and information view, our pre-defined process language defines the attributes of process model in the following semantics:

Process Model $consist {Name, Interface, $set(Activity), $set(Product), set(Role),

$set(Trigger), $set(Pattern), $set(Conflict), $set(Relation), $set(Exception Handler), $set(SubProcess Model)}

1) Interface

Interface $consist {$set(Input Process Element), $set(Output Process Element)}

Input process elements are the external process elements used in the process model, and output process elements are the internal process elements that can be used in other process models.

2) Activity
It defines an atomic or composite step that contributes towards the achievement of a goal.

Activity $consist {Name, Interface, Precondition, Postcondition, Workload,

Planned Duration, State, State Transition Diagram, $set(Role), $set(Sub Activity), $set(Involved Sub Process Model)}

- Precondition and Postcondition are conditional expressions. The activity can be enacted while the Precondition becomes true, and can be finished successfully while the Postcondition becomes true. While the Precondition becomes true, the set of available products in input products is called the active product set of the activity. While the Postcondition becomes true, the set of usable product in output products is called the generated product set of the activity.

- State is a user-defined set {initial, ready, running, finished, aborted}.
- State Transition Diagram (STD) is a FAM, which defines state transition after performing an action. An action is a tuple $\hat{A}$ = <HA(R',o), o, A>, where o is an action name, which refers to meta-activity A', HA(R',o) is a human agent who is assigned to meta-role R' in meta-activity A', and A is type descriptor of an activity.
- Role is a tuple <R, HN>, where R is the role for enacting the activity, HN is the number of human agents of R needed in the activity.
- Involved Sub Process Model is a tuple <SA, SPMs>, where SA is the sub activity, and SPMs is a set that consists of the sub process models that SA is referred by.

3) Product
It defines a set of information that facilitates and supports the process.

Product $consist {Name, Identifier, State, State Transition Diagram, Tool Set, Sub Products, Involved Sub Process Models}

- State is a user-defined set {initial, available, submitted, unavailable}
- State Transition Diagram (STD) is a FAM, which defines state transition after performing some kind of operation.
- An operation is a tuple $\hat{O}$ = <HA(R,A), o, P>, where HA(R,A) is a human agent who is assigned to role R in activity A, P is a product that should be one of the output products of A, and o is an operator name, which refers to a meta-activity in corresponding meta-process model, two system-supplied operator is {r, w}.

4) Role
It defines a set of skills expected of an agent of the organization.

Role $consist {*Name, Skill Requirement*}

The latter is a set of Skill, which consists of skill type and degree. Skill and the relationship between Human Agent and Skill are specified in organizational model. Only those agents who reach the Skill Requirement can be assigned to the role.

5) Trigger
Trigger has the form of [*Condition* $\Rightarrow$ *Behavior*], or only [*Behavior*], which is a equivalence of [*true* $\Rightarrow$ *Behavior*]. *Condition* is a conditional expression. The *Behavior* can be

- [*do X*], where *X* is an action or operation, or

- [*{enable | disable} SX*], where *SX* is a set of patterns and conflicts.

6) Pattern and Conflict
In the domain of software process, there is no stable correctness criterion like serializable isolation in 2-phase lock because the transactions of software process are *long, open-ended, dynamic, iterative and cooperative*. Hence we allow user-defined correctness criterion.

Patterns and conflicts are used to define the correctness criteria for process model in detail, which specify the interleaving of actions/operations. Similar to [6], we express pattern by a set of rules that describe the grammar in **LR(0)** form. In these rules, we represent the nonterminals as script letters, e.g. **A**, **B**, with **S** reserved as the *start* symbol. The terminals are extended to action $\hat{A}$ of the form $<HA(R',o), o, A>$ or operation $\hat{O}$ of the form $<HA(R,A), o, P>$, which are defined above. A trigger can activate patterns and conflicts. An active pattern must be satisfied and an active conflict must be forbidden, otherwise an exception will be thrown.

5) Relation

We mainly focus on the relations between activities, between activity and product, and between products. Some operation primitives are given to define those relations, which can be transformed into temporal expression or some triggers, patterns, and conflicts.

- Relation between activities: $[T (C_1, C_2)]$, where T can be 'before', 'after', 'contains', C_1 and C_2 are conditional expressions. It means that T_1 {before | after | contains} T_2, where T_i is the time interval when the value of C_i is true. Some predefined relations are *follow, synchronization*, and *concurrent*. For example, $(A_1$ follow $A_2)$ $\$alias$ (after $(A_1.state = running, A_2.state = finished)$)
- Relation between activity and product is specified by a 3-tuple $<A, P, o>$, where A is an activity, P is a product and o is the operation to P. It can be transformed into a pattern PA_1 and a conflict CF_1. Both of them have only one production:

PA_1	$S \rightarrow <HA(R, A), o, P>$, where R is free
CF_1	$\overline{S \rightarrow <HA(R, A), o, P>}$, where R is free

They construct the semantics that only those who participate the activity A can perform operation o to product P. There are two pre-defined operations: r (read) and w (write).

- There is a pre-defined relation between products: depends. Its semantics is
  $(P_1$ depends $P_2)$ $\$alias$ ($\exists A(<A, P_1, generate> \wedge <A, P_2, use>) \wedge$ **enable** $PA)$
  Where PA is a pattern that has the following production:

	$S \rightarrow <M, w, P_2>$ **B**, where M is free
PA_2	$B \rightarrow <HA(R, A_1), r, P_2>$, where R is free, A_1 satisfies $<A_1, P_2, use>$
	$B \rightarrow <HA(R, A_1), w, P_1, reject>$ **B**, where R is free, A_1 satisfies $<A_1, P_2, use>$

6) Exception Handler

Like the form of trigger, exception handler has the form of $[$**handle** $E \Rightarrow Behavior]$, where E is the name of an exception, and *Behavior* is $[$**do** $SEQ_X]$, where SEQ_X is a sequence of actions and operations. For example, if one conflict occurs and it throws an exception E_1 while enacting activity A_1, the simplest treatment is to abort the activity. The logic can be expressed as

$$\textbf{\textit{handle }} E_1 \Rightarrow \textit{do abort } A_1.$$

7) Meta-Process Model

Meta-process model is also a process model. For distinguishing it from process model, we note activity, product and role in meta-process model as meta-activity, meta-product, and meta-role. An instance of meta-product is some kind of process element, identified by its type descriptor. *Action* is the reference to the meta-activity that is no interaction with human agents. Through invoking an action, process model can invoke corresponding meta-activity. Meta-activity mainly deals with activity and product, and we also call the reference to the latter as *operation*. Action can be regarded as traditional transaction because it suits ACID properties.

4 Process Management Mechanism

There is a system-supplied kernel meta-process model, which contains some popular meta-process activities, such as process modeling, process enaction and process evolution, and is enacted by FLEX interpreter. In this paper, we focus on the mechanism of process enaction and evolution based on the initial process language and kernel meta-process model.

4.1 Process Enaction Mechanism

There are five key meta-activities and corresponding actions in process enaction, the form of those actions are specified in the following:

- r, read a process element.
- w, write a process element.
- *start*, start to enact an activity/meta-activity and translate its state to 'running'.
- *commit*, finish the enaction of an activity/meta-activity, commit the influence of the enaction to system, and translate its state to 'finished'.
- *compensate*, withdraw the influence of committed or un-committed activity/meta-activity, consist of necessary compensation to related activities/meta-activities.

Those actions will be executed in the constraint of some general correctness criteria, such as:

- (CC_1) If an activity A_1 writes product P_1, any other activities can't write P_1 before A_1 is committed.

CC_1	PA_1	$S \rightarrow <HA(R, A_1), w, P_1>$ **B**, where R is free
		$B \rightarrow <HA(R', commit), commit, A_1>$, where R' is free
		$B \rightarrow <HA(R, \overline{A_1}), w, P_1, reject>$ **B**, where R is free

- (CC_2) Let activity A_1, A_2 and product P_1, A_1 generates P_1 and A_2 uses P_1. If A_1 writes P_1 again after A_2 has read P_1, A_2 must read P_1 again before it commits or writes anything.

CC_2	PA_2	$S \to <HA(R, A_2), r, P_1>$ **B**, where R is free
		$B \to <HA(R, A_1), w, P_1>$ **D**, where R is free
		$D \to <HA(R, A_2), r, P_1>$, where R is free
		$D \to <HA(R', commit), commit, A_2, reject>$ **D**, where R' is free
		$D \to <HA(R, A_2), w, X, reject>$ **D**, where R and X is free
CC_3	CF_1	$S \to <HA(R, A_1), w, P_1>$, where R is free

- (CC_3) Any activity can not write its input products. Let activity A_1 and product P_1, A_1 uses P_1.

CC_3	CF_1	$S \to <HA(R, A_1), w, P_1>$, where R is free

The execution of an action consists of three parts. Firstly, PSEE should judge whether the action can be executed, based on the patterns and conflicts user-defined or system-generated. Then PSEE can perform the meta-activity corresponding to invoked action. In the end, if the action is performed successfully, the process scenario should be calculated. In this section, we assume that the process model is stable.

Definition 1 (*action history*). Let $A = \{A_1, ..., A_n\}$ be a set of actions. An action sequence AS over A is a 2-tuple $<A, \leftarrow>$, where $\leftarrow$ is the partial order on A. $\leftarrow$ must satisfy all of the correct criteria. Action history AH is the action sequence from enacting the model.

Definition 2 (*process scenario*). Let PM be a process model, $PA = \{PA_1, ..., PA_n\}$ be the set of patterns of PM, and $CF = \{CF_1, ..., CF_m\}$ be the conflict of PM. Process scenario PS is a set of 2-tuple $<Ci, SC>$, where $Ci \in PA \cup CF$, and SC is a stack of Ci, that contains nonterminals of accepted partial production.

Because we extend the definition of terminal in LR(0) grammar of patterns and conflicts, we propose an operation primitive *suit* to judge whether an action is matching to required terminal.

Operation primitive 1 (*suit*)
Let action history AH, process scenario PS, expected terminal Ti of Ci, current action $a = <M, o, O>$, where M is a member, o is an action name, O is an object identifier.

(a suit Ti) \$alias (((Ti = <HA(R,A), o', P>) $\land$ (M $\in$ HA(R,A)) $\land$ (o = o') $\land$ (O = P)) $\lor$ ((Ti = <HA(R',A'), o'', A>) $\land$ (M $\in$ HA(R',A')) $\land$ (o = o'') $\land$ (O = A)))

Now we propose the pseudo-program of performing an action.

Algorithm 1 (Perform an action)

> let a set *SA*, which contains values with type $number;
> for each *Ci* in current *PS* begin
> > for all *Ti* that *a suit Ti*, look the *SC* of *Ci* and get the matching production **Pr** of *Ci*;
> > > if (*Ci* is a conflict) and (**Pr** is **S**) and (*SC* is empty), reject the action;
> > > otherwise add the subscript of *Ci* into *SA*;
>
> end;
> for each *Ci* in *SA* begin
> > invoke *a*;
> > calculate the expected terminal *Ti* of each production;
> > push the left non-terminal of **Pr** into *SC*;
>
> end

4.2 Process Evolution Mechanism

Almost anything in FLEX, including process ontology, process model, meta-process model, and organization model, can be evolved continuously. In this paper, we only give a simple example to show the process evolution.

Suppose an organization, which uses FLEX for their process management, wants to enhance an activity state, such as '*suspended*'. The requirement can be reached by the following steps:

1) add '*suspended*' value into the activity state set in process ontology;
2) create two meta-activities: *suspend_activity* and *resume_activity*, to suspend or resume an activity;
3) create two actions: *suspend* and *resume* to refer to *suspend_activity* and *resume_activity*;
4) add necessary correctness criteria in corresponding meta-model to reject any actions to the activity, except *resume*, to be performed while an activity state is '*suspended*';
5) modify the STD of activity in process ontology.

5 Conclusions

We have proposed a flexible process language FLEX as an approach to specify process model and meta-process model within a uniform framework, based on process ontology. FLEX has some features that can meet the requirement of software process domain:

- *Semantic Richness and Ease of Use.* FLEX proposes process ontology as the framework to specify process elements. On the one hand, experts can customize the attributes and representation of process elements and can define new operation primitives to extend the capability of process management. On the other hand, general users can work with the PSEE easily because FLEX provides them with pre-defined and expert-defined operation primitives, so that they must not be involved in the detail of semantics of process management.

- **_Flexible._** Not only the representation of process elements, but also the process management logic is flexible to be customized. Customizable meta-process model allows users to control process in different way, and to adjust process control mechanism as expected during process enaction. Furthermore, each process model has a set of patterns and conflicts that define its own correctness criteria to control the sequence of actions over the process model.
- **_Reflective._** We regard meta-process model as special process model, so the functions of meta-process model can be applied to themselves. For example, user can define a meta-process model by invoking *process modeling* and following the same step of defining a process model. Both process model and meta-process model can be evolved through invoking *process evolution*.

Now we have developed FLEX interpreter and a prototype of PSEE based on FLEX. Further research will focus on a formalism foundation for FLEX.

References

1. Conradi, R. et al.: EPOS: Object-Oriented and Cooperative Process Modeling. In: Software Process Modeling and Technology. Research Studies Press Ltd. (1994)
2. Derniame, J.C., et al.: Software Process: Principles, Methodology, and Technology. Lecture Notes in Computer Science, Vol. 1500. Springer-Verlag, Berlin Heidelberg New York (1999)
3. Arbaoui, S., Oquendo, F.: PEACE: Goal-Oriented Logic-Based-Formalism for Process Modeling. In: Software Process Modeling and Technology. Research Studies Press Ltd. (1994)
4. Bandinelli, S., et al.: SPADE: An Environment for Software Process Analysis, Design, and Enactment. In: Software Process Modeling and Technology. Research Studies Press Ltd. (1994)
5. Genesereth, M.R., et al.: Logical Foundations of Artificial Intelligence. San Mateo, CA: Morgan Kaufmann Publishers (1987)
6. Nodine, M.H., et al.: A Cooperative Transaction Model for Design Databases. In: Database Transaction Models for Advanced Applications. Morgan Kaufmann (1992)
7. Kirk, D.: A Flexible Software Process Mode. Proceedings of 26th International Conference on Software Engineering (2004)
8. Zhao, X.P., et al.: Applying Agent Technology to Software Process Modeling and Process-centered Software Engineering Environment. Proceedings of ACM Symposium on Applied Computing (2005)

Building Business Process Description and Reasoning Meta-model M_{bp} in *A-Prolog*

Hai Wan[1,2], Yunxiang Zheng[1], Yin Chen[3], and Lei Li[1]

[1] Software Research Institute, Sun Yat-Sen University, Guangzhou, 510275, PRC
[2] Computer Science & Tech Department, Sun Yat-Sen University, Guangzhou 510275, PRC
whwanhai@163.com
[3] Computer Science Department, South China Normal University, Guangzhou 510631, PRC

Abstract. In order to elicit and describe business processes of *Complex Information System* (*CIS*) in requirements analysis phase definitely, avoid inconsistent or ambiguous process definitions, and help reasoning, checking and planning processes, *Business Process Meta-model M_{bp}* in *A-Prolog* is proposed, which is composed of three hierarchical representations: interactive multi-business processes *Multi-pro*, business process *Pro*, and business *Bus* cored by *Role-Action-Form*. This paper presents the applicability of *A-Prolog* to the representation of business process and multiple aspects of reasoning about processes and effects. Finally, based on *BPPA* system (*Business Process Planning based on A-Prolog*) which has been applied in *CIS* development, an example of applying business process reasoning to workflow planning demonstrates that M_{bp} can simplify and improve business process representation and analysis of *CIS* reasonably and effectively.

Keywords: Business process, Meta-model, A-Prolog, Requirements analysis.

1 Introduction

Eliciting and describing business processes precisely and accurately is critical and important to develop *Complex Information System* (*CIS*), typically: *Enterprise Resource Planning* (*ERP*), *Workflow System, e-business* or *e-government system,* etc., also the main task and aim of *CIS* requirements elicitation and analysis [1].

Because of the complexity and variety of business processes in *CIS*, a variety of different methods and tools have been developed to represent, model, and analyze business processes, then map into software process, which can be cataloged as: *Object-oriented* (such as *OOA, OOSE,* or *UML,* etc.), *Process-oriented* (such as *SA, SADT,* or *VDM,* etc.), *Data-oriented* (such as *JSD* or *ER*), *Control-oriented* (such as *DFD*), *Goal-oriented, Aspect-oriented, Model-driven,* etc [6]. Letier has discussed how to reason about partial goal satisfaction for non-functional requirements in [3].

However it is inappropriate to apply these methods and tools in *CIS* requirements elicitation and analysis directly, the reasons of which are as following: ① many factors concerned in representing business logic, such as relationship between roles, data, forms, and actions, etc., which may confuse requirement staffs or system users and lead to indefinite or imperfect requirements specification;② because of difficulties in communication with users, requirements boundary definition, iteration in requirements

Q. Wang et al. (Eds.): SPW/ProSim 2006, LNCS 3966, pp. 195 – 203, 2006.

phase, business process specification is often unavoidably incomplete, inconsistent, or ambiguous;③ lake of inference engine is the main deficiency in requirements tools, is it possible to represent processes of reasonable size involving complex effects of actions, and is there an available inference engine to compute solutions in an efficient manner?

This paper proposes applying *A-Prolog* to elicit, describe and reason business process, which is the research branch of applying the methods of *artificial intelligence* to solve the problems of requirement analysis. Business process is meant to be represented in formal specification, with which business logic can be described more declarative and unambiguous by reducing the errors caused by misunderstanding.

The paper is organized as follows. In the next section, we depict the syntax and semantics of *A-Prolog*, and business process paradigms in *CIS*. Section 3 considers business process from meta-model perspective and defines M_{bp}. Section 4 proposes formalization and reasoning methods of business process in *A-Prolog* with theorems and proofs. Finally, based on *BPPA* system, an example of applying business process reasoning to workflow planning is presented, which demonstrates that M_{bp} can simplify and improve process representation and analysis of *CIS* reasonably and effectively.

2   *A-Prolog* and Business Process Paradigms

A-Prolog extends "classical" *Prolog* [8] by *classical negation* and *disjunction* for representing commonsense knowledge related with nonmonotonic reasoning or negation in logic programming, and is a declarative logic programming and new programming paradigm based on *Stable models / Answer sets semantics*, allowing the encoding of *defaults* and various other types of knowledge contained in dynamic domains, typically, the representation of actions, action sequence and effects [4, 5].

Definition 1 *A-Prolog program*. *A-Prolog* is a pair $\{\Sigma, \Pi\}$, where Σ is a signature and Π is a collection of rules over Σ;

‑‑‑ *Signature* $\Sigma = <T,C,F,P>$, where *T, C, F,* and *P* are sets of symbols, members of the set *T* are called *types*, the set *C* contains *object constants* for each type in *T*, symbols from sets *F* and *P* are typed *functions* and *predicate* constants, respectively. *Term* is either a typed object constant, or a string of the form $f(t_1,..., t_n)$, where $t_1,...,t_n$ are terms of *T*, and *f* is a typed function of *F*. *Atom* is a sting of the form $p(t_1,...,t_n)$, where $t_1,...,t_n$ are terms of *T*, and *p* is a typed predicate of *P*. *Literal* is either an atom (*positive literal*), or an atom preceded by ¬ called *classical negation* (*negative literal*).

‑‑‑ *Rule* of Π is a statement of the form:

$$l_0 \leftarrow l_1, ..., l_m, \textbf{\textit{not}} \; l_{m+1}, ..., \textbf{\textit{not}} \; l_n \quad \text{\scriptsize (} n \geq m \geq 0, \text{and } l_i\text{'s are literals over } \Sigma \text{)}} \qquad (1)$$

where *not* is a logical connective called *negation as failure or default negation*.

Definition 2 *Answer set of A-Prolog program*. Set *S* is an *answer set* of Π if:

$$S = Cn(\Pi^S) \qquad (2)$$

where Π is an arbitrary ground program in *A-Prolog*, for any set *S* of ground *literals* of its *signature* Σ, let the *reduct* of Π relative to *S*, denoted Π^S, be the program obtained by deleting from Π: ①each rule that has a *negative literal* in its body belonging to S; and ②all *negative literals* in the bodies of remaining rules; if Π^S satisfies: ① closed under the rules of ground Π, and ② if Π^S contains an atom p and its negation $\neg$p, then Π^S contains all ground literals, denoting Π^S as $Cn(\Pi^S)$, i.e., program Π with at least one consistent answer set $Cn(\Pi^S)$.

From definition 2, we assume the sets of all *ground literals* over Σ as $lit(\Sigma)$, then a *literal* $l \in lit(\Sigma)$ is *true* if $l \in Cn(\Pi^S)$; l is *false* if $\neg l \in Cn(\Pi^S)$; otherwise, l is *unknown*; it is easy to see that programs of *A-Prolog* are nonmontonic, which is important for the representation of knowledge of business processes and gives the means for reasoning about actions, processes and effects. We can show this by example 1.

Example 1. Assume that the signature Σ_1 contains two object constants $\{a,b\}$, with program $\Pi_1:\{q(a). ;\neg p(X) \leftarrow not\ q(X). \}$. From definition 1,$\Pi_1$ has the unique answer set $S = \{ q(a), \neg p(b)\}$, i.e. $\Pi_1 \models \neg p(b)$; however, if some new information, $q(b)$ is added into Π_1, it forces the withdrawal of the previous conclusion $\neg p(b)$, i.e., the new program $\Pi_1 \cup \{q(b)\}$ has the unique answer set $\{q(a), q(b)\}$.

Answer set semantics of *A-Prolog* belongs to a higher level of computational complexity and has more expressive and very useful for nonmonotonic reasoning. *A-Prolog* is a new form of declarative logic programming, interpreting a logic program as a constraint on sets of literals, just as a propositional formula can be viewed as a constraint on assignments of truth values to atoms. The idea of *A-Prolog* application is to represent a given computational problem as a logic program and apply answer set solver to find answer sets. *A-Prolog* has been applied in several combinatorial problems, including planning, wire routing, and phylogeny reconstruction, etc. [2, 4].

Currently, several systems have been developed, which can be applied to compute the answer sets of a logic program based on answer sets semantics, such as *DLV* and *SMODELS* [2]. *SMODELS* has two parts, *smodels* and *lparse*. The first part, *smodels* is the actual logic programming engine doing all the hard work and *lparse* work as variable grounding which maps a subset of variables of a rule into ground terms.

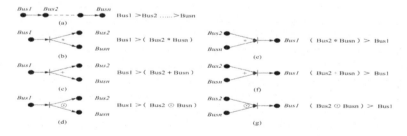

Fig. 1. Relationship between *Bus*s in *single business process*

Business process representation is critical to depict users' requirements and should identifies process actions, transitions, participant specification, relevant data, and processes interaction, etc., which may be complicated to requirement staffs and system users. This paper assumes business process paradigms can be simplified and divided into 2 categories based on whether there exist communications or interactions between processes: one is *single business process*, the other is *multi-business process*.

Assuming *basic unit* in *single business process* is *Bus*, based on relationships between *Buss*, *single business process* can be classified as 7 categories(Fig.1). There are
4 logic connective symbols between *Buss:Sequence* > ,*And* *,*Or* +,and *Exclusive or* ⊙.

Multi-business process depicts message or data transition between two or more
single business processes, based on difference of interactive types: synchronization or
asynchronism, it can be classified as 4 types (as show in Fig.2)

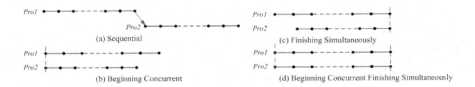

Fig. 2. Interactive types of *multi-business process*

3   Business Process Meta-model M_{bp}

As indicated in the *business process* paradigms, process model includes various entities whose scope may be complicated, such as, participants, actions, and relevant data,
etc. By defining *Business Process Meta-model M_{bp}*, business process can be represented hierarchically, helping analyzing various entities simply and reasonably.

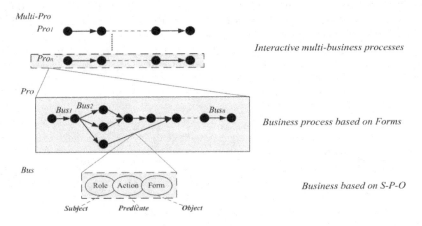

Fig. 3. Framework of *Business Process Meta-model M_{bp}*

The M_{bp} is generally composed of three architectural levels (shown in Fig.3). The top
level describes interactive multi-business processes *Multi-pro*, comprised of business process
Pro based on *Forms* in second level. As describing in section 2, the *basic unit Pro* is *Bus*,
consisting of three parts: *Role*, *Action* and *Form*, which we have described iconically
as *Subject*, *Predicate* and *Object* respectively in [9].

Definition 3. *Business Bus*: can be specified by a triple:

$$Bus = <Role, Action, Form> \tag{3}$$

where *Role* represents all the roles in relative business, *Action* is a set of actions performed by *Role*, and *Form* is various data forms *Role* processes. *Bus* describes which *Role* can do what *Action* to what data in which *Form*. Address *Bus* in detail:

Role =<*Dept,User*>, where *Dept* represents relative department, *User* is the staff, organization, or system in   *Dept*. *Action*∈ACTION, ACTION is atom action sets, consisting of *Access, Delete, Add, Update*. *Form*=<*Field,Forms*>, where *Forms* represent various data forms (real or virtual forms) and *Fields* are the items of *Forms*;

The *Bus* in *Pro* can be figured as directed graph (shown in Fig.3), in which node represents *State S* expressed by first-order predicate logic formula regarding *Field* in *Forms* as *Term*, and edge represents *Bus*. Assuming *C* as conversion condition and *E* as event which triggers *Pro* converts from *S* when satisfying *C*, then *Bus conversion* definition can be given as following (shown in Fig.4):

Definition 4. *Bus Conversion*: has two type formulas:

$$Cause\ \textbf{\textit{bus}}\ \textbf{\textit{if}}\ \textbf{\textit{s}}\ \wedge\ \textbf{\textit{e}}[\textbf{\textit{c}}] \tag{4}$$

$$Impossible\ \textbf{\textit{bus'}}\ \textbf{\textit{if}}\ \dot{\textbf{\textit{s}}}\ \wedge\ \dot{\textbf{\textit{e}}}'[\textbf{\textit{c}}'] \tag{5}$$

mean when condition *c* is satisfied, and event *e* is triggered, *bus* should be converted from state *s* to next state *s'*; or when condition *c'* is satisfied, and event *e'* is triggered, *bus'* should not be converted from state *s* to next state *s'*.

Fig. 4. Conversion relationship of *Bus*s and *State*s

Based on *Bus conversion* we can represent relationships between *Bus*s in *single business process* definitely as shown in Fig.2.

Definition 5. *Business Process Pro*: can be specified by:

$$Pro = < form,\ s,\ bus,\ t,\ s_\vartriangle,\ s_\square > \tag{6}$$

Pro is related with a specific *form* and composed of state set *s*, business set *bus* and bus conversion set *t*, in which $s_\vartriangle$, $s_\square \in s$, $s_\vartriangle$ is beginning state, $s_\square$ is ending state.

Definition 6. *Process Message Msg:* can be specified by:

$$Msg = < Pro,\ Pro',\ bus,\ bus',\ e,\ type,\ data> \tag{7}$$

Pro and *Pro'* are two interactive business processes; *bus and bus'* are business in *Pro* and *Pro'* respectively; *e* is event which triggers *Msg*; *type* means type of *Msg*, there are two *types*: synchronization and asynchronism; *data* is the content of *Msg*.

Based on definition of *Bus*, *Pro*, and *Msg*, we can present M_{bp} in the top level.

Definition 7. *Business Process Meta-model M_{bp}*: can be specified by:

$$M_{bp} = < PRO, MSG > \tag{8}$$

Where *PRO* is business process set in M_{bp}, and *MSG* is process message set in M_{bp}. If $Msg_{(pro,pro')} \in MSG$, *pro, pro'* $\in PRO$, there exists interaction between *pro* and *pro'*.

According to *Business Process Meta-model M_{bp}* above, we can definitely elicit business process easily, because the processes are related with specific forms and can be represented clearly and definitely.

4   Business Process Formalization and Reasoning in *A-Prolog*

Given business process description *P* based on M_{bp}, it can be translated into *A-Prolog* $\Pi(P)$ consisting of domain facts and constraint rules describing *Role, Action,* and *Form* respectively, and then find the answer sets of $\Pi(P)$, allowing us to reason and do some checking or planning work. *Business process description $\Pi(P)$* over a signature Σ is a collection of atoms: • *role(r_i,d_i).* (role r_i belongs to department d_i); • *action(a_i).*(atom action a_i); • *form($field_i, forms_i$).*(field $field_i$ belongs to form $forms_i$); • *bus($forms_i,t$).*(t business *bus* related with $forms_i$); • *s($forms_i,t$).*(t state *s* related with $forms_i$); • *pro($forms_i$).*(process *pro* related with $forms_i$);• *msg(m).*(message *msg*).

By an *observation*, $O(\Sigma)$ means a set which depicts business:

{*occ(bus($forms_i,t$): role(r_i, d_i), action(a_i), form($field_i, forms_i$))*}   -- denotes that *bus (forms_i,t)* is composed of role *role(r_i,d_i)*, action *action(a_i)*, form *form($field_i,forms_i$)*.

In order to represent the relationship between business *bus* and state *s*, we need to define state and transition relation $<s_0,bus,s_1>$, where s_1 is the state after *bus* is processed in previous state s_0, and relation ***holds(F,T)*** denotes fluent *F* holds at step *T*.

$O(\Sigma)$ indicates three types of definition paradigms: *static constraint law* (expressed by ***g if f***), *dynamic casual law* (expressed by ***a causes f if g***, as shown in formula 4), and *commonsense of law of inertia* (i.e. normally, things tend to stay as they are).

By *domain description $D(P,\Sigma)$*,i.e.$D(P,\Sigma)$ =$\Pi(P) \cup O(\Sigma)$,we can depict business process, which is the base of business process checking and planning.

We demonstrate reasoning method with theorems as following:

Theorem 1. *Let set S be the set of all the answer sets of the $D(P,\Sigma)$.If S=ϕ, then some inference rules are wrong or missed.*

Proof. According to *A-Prolog* semantics, if there is no *answer set* for a logic program, it means that through the domain facts and inference rules none of the atoms can be found by answer set solver i.e. each atom can be proved true by the resolution mechanism. Suppose f is hold at the beginning and goal is g, so we find the answer sets by 'compute all *{f,g}*'. Here *f(g)* is a fluent which can be roles or forms. If there is no *answer sets*, there is no way to reach to goal state from the initial. It is impossible for business process reasoning and some inference rules must be wrong or missed.   ∎

In this situation, reasonable plan can not be derived, so we must check business process specification and find the wrong rules and modify it.

Theorem 2. *Let set S be the set of all the answer sets of the D(P,Σ). if (S) ≥ 2, where (S) means the number of elements S contains, ambiguity may exists.*

Proof. Consider this example: if a program contains these two rules in the action part and they are both possible at time T: *occ(a1,T) :- not occ(a2,T)* ; *occ(a2,T) :- not occ(a1,T)*. Apparently, we will get at least two answer sets, for we can't decide which action will occur at time T. We need some constraints for this case. ∎

When this happens, i.e. there are more than one answer sets for a program; we may need to check our business processes specification.

Business process reasoning has two aspects in detail: ① *Business process* planning for workflow design; ② Checking errors in *business process* specification, such as: relationships between *roles* and *departments*, data origin relationships between *forms*, operation-data relationships between *actions* and *forms*, etc.

5   Example and Experience

In this section we demonstrate an example: *EOrder Main Process* of applying business process planning for workflow design, which is illustrated in [7].

Example 2. *EOrder Main Process* takes a formatted string as an input and returns a string that indicates whether the order was confirmed or rejected (as shown in Fig.5)

EOrder Main Process in Fig.5 confuses control and data flow, besides, without solver to help workflow planning. So we design **BPPA** system (*Business Process Planning based on A-Prolog*), which represents business process in M_{bp} with

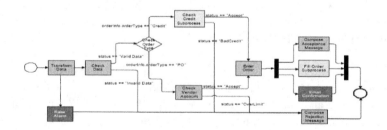

Fig. 5. *EOrder Main Process*

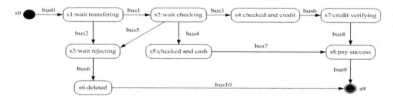

Fig. 6. Improved *EOrder Main Process* based on M_{bp} in *A-Prolog*

graphical interface, written in *Java*, allowing users to (1) draw business process diagram, (2) automatically translate a process drawing to *A-Prolog*.

The improved *EOrder Main Process* based on M_{bp} in *A-Prolog* is showed in Fig.6. After *BPPA* translating process drawing into *A-Prolog* program based on *SMODELS* solver, we can easily plan business process to show reasonable workflows.

```
%% State fluent
   { s(fsu,0,I) }:-time(I). ......
%% Business fluent
   { bus(fsu,0,I) }:-time(I). ......
%% Transformation
   :-ns(fsu,0,I),s(fsu,0,I),time(I). ......
   s(fsu,1,I+1):-s(fsu,0,I),bus(fsu,0,I),time(I).
   ns(fsu,1,I+1):-not s(fsu,0,I),time(I).
   ns(fsu,1,I+1):-not b(fsu,0,I),time(I). ......
%% An state may not be valid at the same time
   :2(s(fsu,0,I),s(fsu,1,I),s(fsu,2,I),s(fsu,3,I),s(fsu,4,I),s(fsu,5,I),
   s(fsu,6,I),s(fsu,7,I),s(fsu,8,I),s(fsu,9,I)),time(I).
   :-2(bus(fsu,0,I),bus(fsu,1,I),bus(fsu,2,I),bus(fsu,3,I),bus(fsu,4,I),
   bus(fsu,5,I),bus(fsu,6,I),bus(fsu,7,I),bus(fsu,8,I),bus(fsu,9,I),
   bus(fsu,10,I)),time(I).
%% Define the time steps
   time(1..length).
%% Iinitial state
   s(fsu,0,1).
%% Planning Goal
   compute {s(fsu,9,time)}.
```

Limited by page sizes, we only present above part of *A-Prolog* program translated from *EOrder Main Process* shown in Fig.6, by which there are four derived planning workflow as following with S_0 as beginning state $s_\triangle$ and S_9 as ending state $s_\square$.

```
(1) %0-3%0-3%1-3%1-3%4-3%5-3%6-3%7-3%8-3%9-3.
(2) %0-3%0-3%1-3%1-3%2-3%5-3%7-3%8-3%9-3.
(3) %0-3%0-3%1-3%1-3%2-3%3-3%6-3%10-3%9-3.
(4) %0-3%0-3%1-3%1-3%2-3%6-3%10-3%9-3.
```

BPPA system has been applied to elicit, describe and plan business processes in developing *Vantage ERP System of Zhongshan*, *Digital Platform of Donghua Campus*, and *Resource Scheduling System of Guangdong Telecom*.

6 Conclusion and Future Works

This paper has presented a new approach and business process description and reasoning meta-model M_{bp} in *A-Prolog*, described how to apply this model to business process planning and checking with answer sets solver *SMODELS* in detail. M_{bp} is composed of three hierarchical representations: *Multi-pro, Pro, Bus* cored by *Roles-Actions-Forms*. In addition, an example on representing business process and reasoning suitable workflow demonstrates that M_{bp} can simplify and improve business process Description and Reasoning in *CIS* requirements analysis phase reasonably and effectively. There are several issues to be addressed: M_{bp} and the framework are to be formalized and followed by the validation of requirements specification to some extent.

Acknowledgments. This effort is supported by *PH.D Subject Construction Project* of *Sun Yat-Sen University* in the Software Field.(35000-3253201). Many thanks to our colleagues and the same thanks to the anonymous reviewers for their helpful suggestions that improved the quality of this paper.

References

1. Andrés Silva. Requirements, domain and specifications: a viewpoint-based approach to requirements engineering. *In Proceedings of the 22rd International Conference on Software Engineering, ICSE 2002,* pp.94-104, Orlando, USA. ACM 2002.
2. Esra Erdem. Theory and Applications of Answer Set Programming. *Ph.D Dissertation,the University of Texas* at Austin,2002 August.
3. Emmanuel Letier and Axel van Lamsweerde. Reasoning about Partial Goal Satisfaction for Requirements and Design Engineering. *In proceedings of 12th International ACM SIGSOFT Symposium on the Foundations of Software Engineering (FSE-12),Newport Beach, Califonia, USA,* Oct.31-Nov.5, 2004 pp.53-62.
4. M.Gelfond and N.Leone. Logic Programming and Knowledge Representation – An A-Prolog perspective. In *Artificial Intelligence,* 138(1-2), pp.3-38, June 2002.
5. M.Gelfond. Representing Knowledge in A-Prolog, *Computational Logic: Logic Programming and Beyond, Essays in Honor of Robert A. Kowalski,* volume 2408, Part II,pp.413-451, Springer-Verlag, Berlin, 2002.
6. LU Mei and LI Ming Shu. Review of Methods and Tools of Software Requirements Engineering. (in Chinese with English abstract). *Computer Research & Development* Jan. 1999 Vol.36, No.11 pp.1289-1300.
7. WfMC(Workflow Management Coalition). Workflow Process Definition Interface - XML Process Definition Language(Ver1.0).*Document Number WFMC-TC-1025.*October 25,2002.
8. S.Ceri, Gottlob, L.Tanca, Logic Programming and Database, Springer-Verlag,1990.
9. Yunxiang Zheng, Hai Wan, Lei Li. A New Software Requirement Method Based on Subject- Predicate-Object Logic. *Software Process Workshop* 2005, Beijing, China, May 25-27,2005.

A Process-Agent Construction Method for Software Process Modeling in SoftPM[*]

Qing Wang[1], Junchao Xiao[1,2], Mingshu Li[1,3], M. Wasif Nisar[1,2],
Rong Yuan[1,2], and Lei Zhang[1,2]

[1] Laboratory for Internet Software Technologies, Institute of Software,
The Chinese Academy of Sciences, Beijing 100080, China
{wq, xiaojunchao, mingshu, wasif, yuanrong,
zhanglei}@itechs.iscas.ac.cn
http://www.cnsqa.com
[2] Graduate University of Chinese Academy of Sciences, Beijing 100039, China
[3] Key Laboratory for Computer Science, The Chinese Academy of Sciences
Beijing 100080, China

Abstract. Software development, unlike manufacturing industry, is highly dependent on the capabilities of individual software engineers and software development teams. SEI presents PSP and TSP to establish personal and team capabilities in the software process, to maintain them and assist organizations in conducting CMMI-Based process improvement. Thus, executors' capabilities should be taken into account as a key issue of the software process modeling method. ISCAS conducts research on Organization-Entities capabilities- based software process modeling and presents a corresponding method. The Organization-Entities have definite capabilities and are called Process-Agents. The modeling method applies Agent technology to organize the basic process units and to establish the project process system self-adaptively according to the special project goal and constraining environment. In this paper, we present the method for constructing the Process-Agent. Each Process-Agent is comprised of two parts: Firstly, the infrastructure to describe Process-Agent's knowledge, and secondly the engine driven by external environment, used for reasoning Process-Agent's behavior based on its knowledge.

1 Introduction

Software processes are knowledge-intensive and one of their characteristics is their high dependence on the capabilities of individual software engineers and software development teams. However, process resources especially capabilities of human resource that mainly impact the process, have not been well considered. Traditional methods, such as activity-based method [1] [2], artifact-based method [3] and role-based method [4] were known to have resulted in the instability and unpredictability in regards to the execution process, leading to some extent, the loss in significance of process modeling.

---

[*] Supported by the National Natural Science Foundation of China under grant Nos. 60473060, 60273026 as well as the Hi-Tech Research and Development Program (863 Program) of China under grant No. 2004AA112080.

Q. Wang et al. (Eds.): SPW/ProSim 2006, LNCS 3966, pp. 204–213, 2006.

Several researches have been conducted into the capabilities of engineers and teams in the software process, e.g. SEI presented PSP [5] and TSP [6] to see the possibility of improved performance for the two above, in regards to efficacy linked to products and hence helping organizations improve the CMMI-Based [7] process.

Other attempts have been made to apply the agent technology to process modeling. They focus on business processes modeling and their automation by adopting multiple kinds of agents [8] [9] [10] use software agent in representing the flexible organization structure of the software development process model [11].

In [12], ISCAS presents a solution for software process management and also implements a toolkit: SoftPM. Process-Agent was used to organize the Process Assets and, based on it, a process modeling method [13] [14] called Organization-Entity Capability Based Software Process Modeling (OEC-SPM) was presented to model standard processes. OEC-SPM considers the Organization-Entity's capabilities a decisive factor for determining what a software process can do, how it can be done and how many resources are needed. Thus it can better reflect the essence of software process.

This paper aims to introduce most importantly, the method that defines and constructs a Process-Agent. Each Process-Agent comprises two parts: the Infrastructure and the Engine. The infrastructure contains the descriptive knowledge, the process knowledge and the experience of a Process-Agent. Process-Agent can determine what it can do by using descriptive knowledge, how to do by using process knowledge, and how many resources would be needed. The engine provides a working mechanism for the Process-Agent, it is used to reason the Process-Agent's behavior based on the infrastructure and driven by environment where the Process-Agent resides.

2 Process-Agent in OEC-SPM

As we know, most software process modeling methods focus on establishing an appropriate process network according to what processes can do. However, software development is a special kind of production process that is highly human sensitive. Different performers would produce productions with varying quality and quantity even in a same software process. It is not enough to consider only the relationships among processes, but also take into account the three aspects of the above-mentioned process:

(1) What can the process do?
(2) How does the process work?
(3) How many resources, such as cost, schedule etc., are needed?

Process capabilities are determined by devices' capabilities in traditional methods. These methods usually consider the first aspect rather than the second, and rarely the third. Focusing on the special characters of the software process, OEC-SPM takes into account not only the first two aspects but the third aspect as well. It constructs an organization entity with definite capabilities (e.g. a java coding team with definite productivity) as a Process-Agent. All the historical data, experience and knowledge of this entity are encapsulated in the Process-Agent that can determine its specific capabilities and performance baseline based on these data as well as its self-learning mechanism. Based on Process-Agent, OEC-SPM is able to consider not only relation-ships among process elements, but also capabilities of process. It guarantees the stable and predictable performing of process network as a result and that effectively sup-ports quantitative process management.

In SoftPM, Process-Agent is used in the organization and management of the proc-ess asset, based on that, OEC-SPM establishes and maintains standard processes and project processes, as denoted in Fig.1.

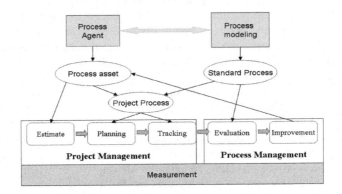

Fig. 1. OEC-SPM in SoftPM

When project process under a specific environment requires establishment, the Process-Agent can respond actively and autonomously to the software process envi-ronment and self-adaptively establish the project process henceforth achieving the goals of software development. During the process execution, the process data will be collected by the Process-Agents in order to optimize and improve their capabilities. The process is denoted in Fig. 2.

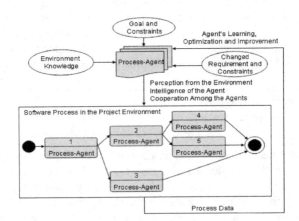

Fig. 2. OEC-SPM Process

The OEC-SPM comprises of a set of process goals with their constraints, knowledge in the goals' context and a group of Process-Agents. It can be defined as a triple. OEC-SPM = (G, EK, PA), here:

1. G represents a set of environment goals under specify constraints, $G = \{g_1, g_2, ..., g_n\}$; each g_i in G can be defined as a triple. $g_i = (gs_i, gse_i, gc_i)$:
   a) gs_i is the goal statements, it is a string and describes what the goal is;
   b) gse_i is the goal size estimation;
   c) gc_i is a set of goal constraints that realize the goal g in Process-Agent, such as TC (Time Constraint), CC (Cost Constraint), QC (Quality Constraint), LC (Language Constraint), etc.
2. EK is the environment knowledge that comprises a number of facts as the basis to realize goals and the premises to know the world.
3. PA is a group of Process-Agents, $PA = \{pa_1, pa_2, ..., pa_n\}$.

3   Construction Method of the Process-Agent

As an agent, Process-Agent is defined as a duple, PA = (PAI, PAE), where PAI is the Infrastructure which describes the knowledge of the Process-Agent and is used as the basis for PAE, while PAE is the Engine which reasons the behavior of Process-Agent based on its PAI and is driven by external environment. The structure of a Process Agent is shown in Fig. 3.

Actually, the method focuses on problem solutions in the software process modeling. The three parts of knowledge are used to determine

- What the Process-Agent can do with its descriptive knowledge
- How to do with its process knowledge
- How many resources will be needed with its experience data.

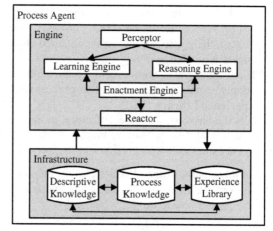

Fig. 3. Structure of the Process-Agent

In addition, the engine of Process-Agent will help reason and make these decisions.

3.1   Process-Agent Infrastructure (PAI)

PAI is defined as a triple, PAI = (DK, PK, EL), that is, the Descriptive Knowledge (DK), the Process Knowledge (PK) and Experience Library (EL).

- **Descriptive Knowledge (DK)**

DK describes what the Process-Agent looks like and can be used to determine what the Process-Agent can do, it is composed of 6 elements, DK = (BA, AG, CRM, SK, RC, AEG):

(1) In the **BA** part, some basic attributes of the Process-Agent are taken into account **BA = (EN, PAN, Description)**, where **"EN"** is the name of the entity which the Process-Agent represents, **"PAN"** is the Process-Agent's Name and **"Description"** shows what the Process-Agent is.

(2) **AG** is composed of a goal string; it describes the Process-Agent's goal, that is, it's intention and end goals.

(3) **CRM** is the control rule model, inclusive of the pre-conditions (PreC) and post-conditions (PostC) whose function is behavioral control of the Process-Agent.

(4) **SK** is the skills set which the Process-Agent has, SK = {sk_1, sk_2, ... , sk_n}, among this, sk_i = **(Type, Name, Level)**, where, **"Type"** is the skill type, e.g., "Language" . **"Name"** is the skill e.g. C++ or Java. **"Level"** is the skill rank which may be High, Medium, Low or NONE.

(5) **RC** is the resource constraint of the Process-Agent; it is the schedulable resource of the Process-Agent. RC can have different kinds of constraints, for example, constraint of time resource (tr), human resource (hr), tool resource (tlr), etc.

(6) **AEG** is the resources estimation on the goal, and it shows the estimate of Time (**T**), Human Resource (**HR**), Cost (**C**), Quality (**Q**), etc., to realize the given goal, these estimations can be obtained on the basis of the given goal and EL.

- **Process Knowledge (PK)**

PK describes the Process-Agent's realization of its goal. It is composed of policy, procedures, templates, rules, and other process related knowledge.

- **Experience Library (EL)**

EL is the basis for resource utilization in the process of realizing the goal. It comprises historical data such as the time, cost, defect, etc. On the basis of EL, each Process-Agent can establish and refine its process performance baseline.

The three parts of the PAI are closely interwoven. Actually, DK and PK are dependent on EL. They use the data and experience to determine if it can meet the requirements and how to do it.

3.2   Process-Agent Engine (PAE)

PAE is used to reason the behaviors based on its knowledge. PAE has five functional modules, it can be defined as PAE = (P, R, LE, EE, RE), among this:

1. **P** is the Perceptor of the Process-Agent and it can perceive the environment knowledge, goals and their constraints from the environment.

2. **R** is the Reactor of the Process-Agent. It will generate the action of the Process-Agent.

3. **LE** is the Learning Engine of the Process-Agent whose provisions include the learning mechanism to facilitate Process-Agent efficacy in terms of intelligence.

4. **EE** is the Enactment Engine, controlling the other modules to realize the intelligent behaviors of the Process-Agent.
5. **RE** is the Reasoning Engine. It performs some reasoning in the behavior judgment of Process-Agent.

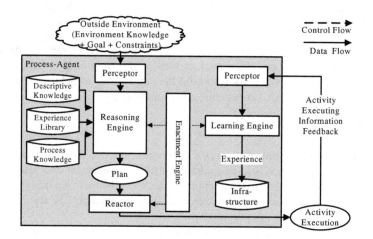

Fig. 4. Behavior Reasoning Process

Fig. 4 shows the process of behavior reasoning. In the Engine, EE is the core of the implementation mechanism and is used to control the other modules. Firstly, the Process-Agent perceives the outside environment, goals, and constraints. Then, RE will enact the following reasoning process to generate the plan for the perceived environment goal:

Step1: Judge whether the Process-Agent's goal matches the description of the environment goal.
Step 2: Determine whether the Process-Agent's pre-conditions can be satisfied
Step3: Judge whether the Process-Agent's skills can satisfy the goal's constraints.
Step 4: Estimate the resources needed to realize the goal by the Process-Agent. Based on EL and the environment goal's size estimation; RE uses the estimating function to give the value of AEG.
Step 5: Compare whether the estimated resources of Process-Agent meet the environment goal's constraints.
Step 6: Generate the local plan for realizing the environment goal.

If any of the above reasoning conditions are not satisfied, the Process-Agent lacks the capabilities to perform the current given goal and will terminate the behavior reasoning process.

At last, the processes executing information will be perceived by the Perceptor and relay feedback to the Process-Agent. The information will be inclusive to the PAI through LE and improve the knowledge of the Process-Agent.

4 An Example

As we may well know, coding plays a crucial role in the software process. In order to explain the intention of each part of the formation of a Process-Agent in a software process, we establish a software process that realizes coding by making use of several typical Process-Agents to illustrate what the functions of each part of the infrastructure of a Process-Agent are, how every components of the engine are working based on the knowledge of the Infrastructure. Thereby makes the Process-Agent able to realize the perception to the given goal as well as the reasoning to behaviors, ultimately makes the Process-Agents who hold the capabilities of achieving the goal to produce the project software process that achieves the goal.

4.1 Hypothesis

We suppose in the environment there is a goal requiring code in Java. The size of the goal is 12KLOC and it needs to be realized between January 1st and March 15th in 2006. The knowledge in the environment indicates the existence of a design document for realizing the goal. The goal g and environment knowledge EK are described as follows:

1. g = (gs, gse, gc), here:
   a) gs = "Coding", i.e., the goal is to code an application;
   b) gse = "12KLOC", i.e., size estimation is 12KLOC;
   c) gc = {TC=[2006-01-01, 2006-03-15], LC="Java"}, here:
      ■ TC is time constraint of the goal, meaning the goal must be realized before 2006-03-15;
      ■ LC is language constraint of the goal and its value is "Java", that means Java is the language that must be used to realize the goal.
2. EK = {DesignDoc(g)}, is indicative of the presence of a design document in the environment for realizing the goal g.

In brief supposition let us picture that there are three Process-Agents relating to coding. These three Process-Agents have different characteristics in aspects of skills and resource restriction, thereby reveal different capabilities. The descriptive knowledge of three Process-Agents is illustrated in table 1.

Table 1. Descriptive Knowledge of Process-Agents

DK\Process-Agent		PA1	PA2	PA3
BA	EN	XIELIZI	ZHANGLEI	LIUDAPENG
	PAN	PA1	PA2	PA3
	Description	programmer with Java	programmer with C++	programmer with Java
AG		Coding	Coding	Coding
CRM	PreC	$\exists DesignDoc(x) \wedge (x \in G)$	$\exists DesignDoc(x) \wedge (x \in G)$	$\exists DesignDoc(x) \wedge (x \in G)$
	PostC	$Code(x) \wedge (x \in G)$	$Code(x) \wedge (x \in G)$	$Code(x) \wedge (x \in G)$
SK (sk0)		(Language, Java, Middle)	(Language, Java, NONE)	(Language, Java, High)
RC	Tr	[06-01-15,2006-04-20]	[06-02-10,2006-03-10]	[06-01-20,2006-01-30]
AEG		--	--	--

AEG will be determined by the perceived environment goal and Process-Agent's EL and expressed here with "--".

In EL, according to its historical data, we only present the baseline of productivity, which is shown in table 2.

Table 2. Baseline productivity of the Process-Agent

EL\ Process-Agent	PA1	PA2	PA3
Productivity(KLOC/PDay)	0.4	0.1	0.6

4.2 Behaviors Reasoning

On the basis of goal coding, environment knowledge and self-capabilities, Process-Agent PA1, PA2, and PA3 independently and automatically reason their behaviors, determining their respective actions in this process, analyzing the resources needed, and finally generating the plan to realize the coding goal:

Step1: Match Process-Agent's goal: if the Process-Agent's AG has the same meaning as the environment goal's gs, then AG matches the description of goal.

∵ PA1.PAI.DK.AG = g.gs, ∴ PA1's goal matches the environment goal.

Similarly, PA2's and PA3's goal matches the environment goal.

Step 2: Determine whether the pre-condition of the Process-Agent can be satisfied: if the environment knowledge makes its pre-conditions that are described in CRM to be true, then the Process-Agent's process can be executed.

Since there exists DesignDoc(g) in the EK, so $\exists$DesignDoc(x)$\wedge$(x$\in$ G) is true, i.e., pre-condition of PA1, PA2 and PA3 are all satisfied

Step3: Judge whether the Process-Agent's skill can satisfy the goal's constraints: if the Process-Agent has the skills described by the goal' constraints, then it satisfies the goal's skill constraints.

For Process-Agent PA1:

(DK.SK.sk0.Type = = "Language") $\wedge$ ((DK.SK.sk0.Name = = g.gc.LC)

$\wedge$ (DK.SK.sk0.Level != NONE)) $\rightarrow$ PA1's skill satisfies the goal's constraint

Similarly, PA2 does not satisfy and PA3 satisfies.

Step 4: Estimate the executing time based on Process-Agent's EL and the environment goal's size

PA1: AEG.T = g.gse/EL.Productivity= 12KLOC/(0.4KLOC/PDays)= 30 PDays

PA3: AEG.T = g.gse/EL.Productivity= 12KLOC/(0.6KLOC/PDays)= 20 PDays

Step 5: Compare AEG with the Process-Agent's time resource

For PA1, from environment goal, the time constraint is 53 workdays from [06-01-01, 06-03-15]), PA1 need 30 person-day and it has only one person. From its available starting date, '06-01-15'+30 = 06-02-13, it satisfies.

Similarly, for PA3 it can be reasoned that there is not ample time to facilitate this goal.

Step 6: Generate the local plan of the Process-Agent for realizing the environment goal.

After the behavior reasoning process, PA1 meets all the constraints and gets the authority to perform the coding task. PA1 will generate its local plan on the basis of its

PK and EL knowledge and this local plan will be merged into global project plan as shown in Fig. 5.

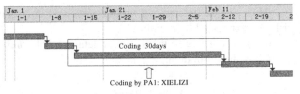

Since PA1 has the capabilities to achieve the goal, the project software process generated on the basis of its

Fig. 5. Global Project Plan

capabilities that is used to achieve the goal can be executed by the Organizational-Entities who have proper capabilities, so it makes the result of the execution stable and predictable.

4.3 Perform and Monitor in SoftPM

After reasoning and generating the project plan, it will be under the process management of SoftPM, as is shown in Fig. 6. When significant deviation occurs, the related Process-Agent will perceive the change requirements and constraints in decision making regarding supports based on its knowledge and reasoning.

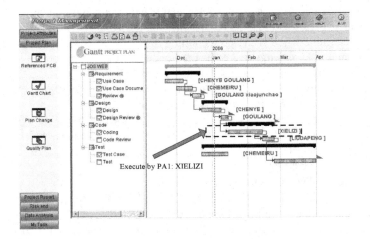

Fig. 6. Plan Perform and Monitor in SoftPM

The actual perform data will be collected with SoftPM and fed backed to Process-Agent. SoftPM also uses this data to evaluate the Process-Agent and improve them continually.

5 Conclusions

This paper presents a method for defining and constructing the Process-Agent. For each Process-Agent, it organizes and describes its knowledge such as goal, skill, resource, experience, etc. in PAI, and reasons and determines its capabilities to meet the given goal by PAE. With this method, the Process-Agent can determine what it can do, how to do, and how many resources are needed self-adaptively. On the basis of the Process-Agent and its modeling method, SoftPM can organize the process asset as an appropriate form and granularity, providing the capabilities and performance of process predictability and stability in regards to the quantitative process management. According to its self-learning, the Process-Agent can make self-improvements continually.

References

1. S. Bandinelli, M. Braga, A. Fuggetta, L. Lavazza.: The Architecture of the SPADE Process-Centered SEE. B. Warboys, ed.: Proceedings 3rd European Workshop on Software Process Technology (EWSPT'94), Villard-de-Lans, France, 1994, pp. 15-30.
2. A. G. Cass, B. S. Lerner, E. K. McCall, L. J. Osterweil, S. M. Sutton Jr., A. Wise: Little-JIL/Juliette: A Process Definition Language and Interpreter. Proceedings of 22nd International Conference on Software Engineering, Limerick, Ireland, 2000, pp. 754-757.
3. G. Cugola, and C. Ghezzi, Design and Implementation of PROSYT: A Distributed Process Support System, Proceedings of IEEE 8th International Workshops on Enabling Technologies: Infrastructure for Collaborative Enterprise, Palo Alto, California, 1999, pp. 32-39.
4. L. Briand, W. Melo, C. Seaman, and V. Basili: Characterizing and Assessing A Large-Scale Software Maintenance Organization. D. Perry ed., Proceedings of the 17th International Conference on Software Engineering, ACM Press, Seattle, Washington, 1995, pp. 133-143.
5. W. S. Humphrey: A Discipline for Software Engineering. Addison-Wesley, 1995
6. W. S. Humphrey: Introduction to the Team Software ProcessSM. Addison-Wesley, 2000.
7. SEI: Capability Maturity Model Integration (CMMISM) version 1.1 CMMI-SE/SW Continuous Representation. Technical Report CMU/SEI-2002-TR-001, Software Engineering Institute, Carnegie Mellon University, 2002.
8. A. I. Wang: A Process Centered Environment for Cooperative Software Engineering. Proceedings of SEKE' 02, ACM Press, 2002, 457-468.
9. H. Gou, B. Huang, W. Liu, Y. Li, S. Ren: Agent-Based Virtual Enterprise Modeling and Operation Control. Proceedings of IEEE International Conference on Systems, Man, and Cybernetics, IEEE Press 2001, 1053-1057.
10. L. Zeng, A. Ngu, B. Benatallah, M. O. Dell: An Agent-Based Approach for Supporting Cross-Enterprise Workflows. Proceedings of Australiasian Database Conference, Gold Coast, Queensland, Australia, 2001, pp.123-130
11. N. Glaser, J-C. Derniame: Software Agents: Process Models and User Profiles in Distributed Software Development. Proceedings of 7th International Workshop on Enabling Technologies: Infrastructure for Collaborative Enterprises, California, USA, 1998, pp. 45-50.
12. Q. Wang, M. Li: Software Process Management: Practices in China. M. Li, B. Boehm, and L.J. Osterweil (Eds.): SPW 2005, LNCS 3840, pp. 317–331
13. X. Zhao, M. Li, Q. Wang, K. Chan, H. Leung: An Agent-Based Self-Adaptive Software Process Model. Journal of Software, Vol. 15, No. 3, 2004, pp. 348–359.
14. X. Zhao, K. Chan, M. Li: Applying Agent Technology to Software Process Modeling and Process-Centered Software Engineering Environment. The 20th Annual ACM Symposium on Applied Computing (SAC'05), Santa Fe, New Mexico, USA, 2005, pp. 1529-1533

Applying Little-JIL to Describe Process-Agent Knowledge in SoftPM

Junchao Xiao[1,2], Leon J. Osterweil[3], Lei Zhang[1,2], Alexander Wise[3], and Qing Wang[1]

[1] Laboratory for Internet Software Technologies, Institute of Software,
The Chinese Academy of Sciences, Beijing 100080, China
{xiaojunchao, zhanglei, wq}@itechs.iscas.ac.cn
http://www.cnsqa.com
[2] Graduate University of Chinese Academy of Sciences, Beijing 100039, China
[3] Department of Computer Science University of Massachusetts,
Amherst, MA 01003-4610 USA
{ljo, wise}@cs.umass.edu

Abstract. In a software process modeling method based upon the Organization-Entity capability, the Process-Agent is a well-defined unit whose role is to encapsulate an entity's knowledge, skill etc. The Process-Agent's infrastructure comprises descriptive knowledge, process knowledge and an experience library. The process knowledge is represented by process steps, whose execution determines the behaviors of the Process-Agent. This causes Process-Agent knowledge to be precisely described and well organized. In this paper, Little-JIL, a well-known process modeling language, is used to define a Process-Agent's process knowledge. Benefits for process element knowledge representation arising from Little-JIL's simplicity, semantic richness, expressiveness, formal and precise yet graphical syntax etc., are described.

1 Background

Software processes are highly people-dependent and they rely on the capabilities of a group of developers and their creative work. In a software organization, the executers of the process are the Organization-Entities who have the needed capabilities. These entities generally display dynamic, autonomous and active behaviors whose precise definition would seem to be a requisite element in software process modeling.

In [1], ISCAS presents a solution and implements a toolkit, SoftPM, for software process management. The concept of Process-Agent is used to organize the Process Assets in SoftPM. A process modeling method [2] [3] called Organization-Entity Capability Based Software Process Modeling (OEC-SPM) has been presented as the basis for modeling the software process, and for subsequent process management. A Process-Agent is an abstract model of an Organization-Entity that has definite capabilities. The entity's experience, skill, and historical data are all encapsulated as a Process-Agent in order to assure that the Process-Agent has the knowledge to determine what it can do, how to do these things, and how many resources are needed. Obviously, the way in which this knowledge is described and organized has a most important impact upon the power of a Process-Agent.

Q. Wang et al. (Eds.): SPW/ProSim 2006, LNCS 3966, pp. 214–221, 2006.

Little-JIL [4] is process language that offers simplicity, semantic richness and expressiveness, formal and precise yet graphical syntax etc. Thus, using Little-JIL as the vehicle for describing the knowledge of a Process-Agent seems to offer advantages such as graphic depiction of a process specification, control over activity implementation, etc.

This paper tries to use Little-JIL to describe the knowledge of a Process-Agent. The method uses Little-JIL semantics to describe the process knowledge and organize it through a precise construction.

2   Little-JIL Language Overview

Little-JIL was developed to coordinate software development processes [5]. But it has also been used to define complex processes in robotics, data mining, e-commerce and complex data analysis processes [6]. These process definitions have generally been clear, detailed, and precise. Space limitations prevent presentation of full details about Little-JIL (the details can be found in [4]). Therefore, we instead suggest key language features only very briefly here. Process steps in Little-JIL are represented visually by a step name that is positioned directly above a bar that is surrounded by several graphical badges that represent aspects of step semantics. The leftmost element in the bar indicates how substeps are to be executed. For example, a sequential badge (an arrow) indicates that substeps are executed in order, left to right, while a parallel badge (two parallel lines), indicates that substeps may be performed simultaneously.

A Little-JIL step may also have a prerequisite and/or postrequisite, represented by triangles on the left and right of the step name, respectively. The body of the requisite is a separately specified step possibly containing multiple substeps. This feature supports the ability to program processes that perform internal runtime checks for the validity of evolving results. When exceptions are thrown, exception handlers may handle them elsewhere in the process. Exception handlers are attached to the right side of a step bar. Exception handlers may be simple or complex subprocesses, represented by additional substeps, and may integrate with the nominal control flow in multiple ways. This affords latitude in responding to unexpected results. Examples of Little-JIL process definitions will be incorporated into subsequent sections of this paper.

3   Knowledge in Process-Agent

The OEC-SPM uses the concept of an Organization-Entity based Process-Agent to encapsulate an entity's knowledge, skill etc. as a well-defined process unit and uses the Process-Agent as the basic unit for modeling processes. When a process system needs to be developed as a component of a process environment, the Process-Agent is able to determine what it can contribute by examining properties such as its skills, comparing them to required goals, and analyzing how to realize the goals, including determining an estimate of how many resources will be required. In order to do this, the Process-Agent must contain three types of knowledge:

- **Descriptive Knowledge (DK):** describes what the Process-Agent looks like and what it can do;
- **Process Knowledge (PK):** describes how the Process-Agent can proceed to realize its goals by means of process steps organized into defined sequences;
- **Experience Library (EL):** constructed from historical data generated by the previous executions of steps by this Process-Agent. This experience can be used to estimate how many resources are likely to be required in order to achieve the process goals.

PK consists of a potentially large and complex set of process elements and the relationships among these elements. It determines the goals of the Process-Agent and the ways in which Process-Agent will attempt to achieve them. The Process-Agent determines what it can do based on its capability as described in DK. After this determination, it will decide what it can do to realize its goal by using PK. PK is captured as a group of steps that are the abstract representation of the Process-Agent's activities given its particular knowledge level.

In particular, we define the **Process Knowledge** as PK= {st_1, st_2, ..., st_n}. Each step st_i in PK is an 8-tuple, $st_i = (SID_i, SD_i, R_i, SCRM_i, IP_i, OP_i, IMP_i, PRI_i)$, here:

(1) SID_i is the identification of the process step;
(2) SD_i is the form of natural language, informal, descriptive words of the process step;
(3) R_i is the role being played by the Process-Agent while executing the step, e.g., if the type of the step is review, then R_i is "QA".
(4) $SCRM_i$ is the step's control rule model. It comprises pre-conditions and post-conditions, such as constraint specifications on the process elements (e.g. the existence of artifacts or resource constraints etc.) The process step can be executed only if all preconditions are satisfied, and the step can be successfully completed only if all postconditions are satisfied; thus the $SCRM_i$ controls the behaviors of the process step and conditions under which it will be executed.
(5) IP_i is step's input parameters, such as the artifacts needed for executing the step;
(6) OP_i is step's output parameters, such as the artifacts produced by the step's execution;
(7) IMP_i describes the way the step is implemented. A step can be directly implemented by Process-Agent (DIRECT), or assigned to other Process-Agents as a cooperative goal (SUBPROCESS).
(8) PRI_i is the priority of the step, if several steps in a Process-Agent have the same behaviors, the step that has the highest priority will be performed.

4 Applying Little-JIL to Describe Process Knowledge

As the definitions above show, process knowledge is step-based knowledge. As PK is composed of steps, the description of PK is essentially the description of steps and their organization. Thus the specificity we seek in agent behavior definition would seem to be best supported by a language whose fundamental semantics focus on the concepts of a step and organization of steps into structures. The Little-JIL language draws on the lessons of the work of [7] using the "step" as the central abstraction and capturing process coordination structure by using such semantic features as scoping and hierarchy. In the next sections we will discuss in detail how to apply Little-JIL to the definition of PK.

4.1 Step Elements Description

The steps in PK can be represented by Little-JIL steps, and, in particular, each tuple in st_i can be represented by available Little-JIL semantic features:

(1) The "**Step Name**" uniquely identifies the step and it is used to represent the SID in PK.
(2) "**Annotation**" in Little-JIL facilitates the specification of **SD**. Annotations are associated with a step, and they are identified by their type [8]. We can represent the description (SD) of the process knowledge step (st) by creating and associating a document type of annotation with st.
(3) Because a specific step can only be executed by a certain role, the **R** in a st is described by a Little-JIL "**pre-requisite**" that is checked before step execution and assures that the step is being executed by the right role.
(4) As **requisites** provide the mechanism for defining guards on the entry to, and exit from, steps, they seems very well adapted to represent **SCRM**: we represent pre-conditions and post-conditions included in SCRM respectively by two Little-JIL steps that are referenced as **prerequisite** and **postrequisite** from the Little-JIL step that represents st. **Fig. 1** depicts an example. Sticky notes placed beside the requisite badges of st are used to provide descriptive material about the pre/post-requisite of the step.

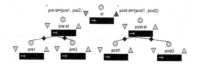

Fig. 1. Single Condition   **Fig. 2.** Multiple Conditions

If the SCRM has multiple complex pre- or post-conditions, Little-JIL steps that represent each of these can be specified separately, but then can be grouped under a higher-level step. This higher-level step can specify sequential step decomposition if the order of evaluation is known and significant. Parallel step decomposition can be specified if the order of evaluation is not important. **Fig. 2** depicts an example of sequential precondition representation.

(5) Since "**Parameters**" in a Little-JIL step have the same meanings as IP and OP in PK's step, according to the parameter passing mode, IP and OP are represented by the In parameter and Out parameter respectively.
(6) "**Annotation**" is adapted to be applied to **IMP**. In particular, an annotation type "ImplementationWay" can be created and associated with st. Its value is utilized to represent the meaning of IMP, e.g. if st_i must cooperate with

another Process-Agent to pursue a cooperative goal its "ImplementaionWay" value is set to "SUBPROCESS"; otherwise its value is set to "DIRECT".

(7) We can also apply **annotation** to describe **PRI** by creating an annotation type "PRI".

4.2 Step Organization Description

The executions of the steps in a PK definition are not completely independent of each other. They collaborate via mechanisms defined through **SCRM**. Little-JIL is adept at representing the ways in which steps and the agents executing them are supposed to coordinate their efforts. Specifically, Little-JIL's four step kinds, "sequential," "parallel," "try," and "choice", facilitate far more precise and articulate specification of activity sequencing. By the sequencing, the steps in PK can be organized as follows:

1) If a group of steps $st_s = \{st_j, st_k, st_l, \ldots st_n\}$ in PK have the relationship that post-conditions of st_j are precisely the pre-conditions of st_k and post-conditions of st_k are precisely the pre-conditions of st_l.... till st_n, thus, these steps imply the sequential relationship of st_j: st_k : st_l : ... :st_n. A new Little-JIL "sequential" step will be created as the parent of these steps, making the sequential relationship of these steps clear and explicit. The parent step must satisfy qualifications that pre-conditions of st_i are precisely the pre-conditions of st_j and post-conditions of st_n are precisely the post-conditions of st_i and so on. Fig. 3 shows this transformation.

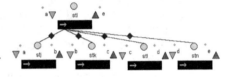

Fig. 3. Sequential

2) If several steps in PK have the same pre-conditions, these steps can be implemented concurrently. A new Little-JIL **"parallel"** step can be created as the parent step of these steps to construct such a relationship, it has the same prerequisites as its sub-steps' and its post-requisites is the conjunction of the post-requisites of all sub-steps. Fig. 4 shows the relationship.

3) If several steps have the same SCRM and PRI, they have a "choice"-like relationship, the Process-Agent will only choose one of them to perform in order to realize the goal. A new Little-JIL "choice" step can be created as parent step of these steps to make the relationship clear and explicit, and this parent step has the same pre-requisites and post-requisites as its sub-steps'. Fig. 5 shows this relationship.

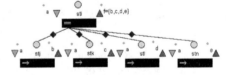

Fig. 4. Parallel

4) If several steps have the same SCRM but different PRI, they have a "try"-like relationship. The substeps should

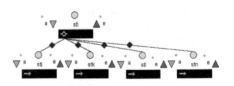

Fig. 5. Choice

be arranged so that their priorities are in decreasing order from left to right. Little-JIL semantics require that the Process-Agent must select steps in order from left to right assuring that they will be tried in the correct priority order. Thus a new Little-JIL "Try" step can be created as the parent step of these steps to make such relationship clear and explicit; this parent step has the same pre-requisites and post-requisites as the sub-steps'. Fig. 6 shows this relationship.

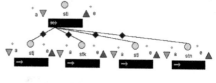

Fig. 6. Try

5) No sub step connection will be created between step st_i and steps in sts= { st_j, st_k, st_l ... st_n} unless they are related to each other according to the conditions listed in 1), 2), 3), or 4). Fig. 7 depicts one example of this rule.

Fig. 7. An example where steps are not related by any of the conditions listed in 1), 2), 3),4)

5 An Example

Here we present an example of a simple software module development to illustrate how Little-JIL is applied to describe the step elements and organization in a Process-Agent's knowledge.

A Process-Agent *Dev-Team* holds process knowledge about how to develop a simple software module, where the knowledge is captured in the form of the steps described in the table below:

SID	SD	SCRM		IP	OP	IMP	PRI
		Pre	Post				
Requirement	Requirement Analyze	G	RD	G	RD	DIRECT	0
OOD	Object Oriented Design	RD	DD	RD	DD	DIRECT	0
SOD	Structure Oriented Design	RD	DD	RD	DD	DIRECT	0
Coding		DD	CD	DD	CD	DIRECT	0
By Tester	Write test cases by tester	RD	TC	RD	TC	DIRECT	1
By Coder	Write test cases by coder	RD	TC	RD	TC	DIRECT	0
Test		TC; CD	AM	TC; CD	AM	DIRECT	0

*Annotation: **RA**-Requirement Analyze; **Imp**-Implementation; **PM**-Product Manager; **AH**-Architect; **PE**-Program Engineer; **TE**-Test Engineer; **G**-Goal; **RD**-Requirement Document; **DD**-Design Document; **CD**-Code; **TC**-Test Case; **AM**-Accomplished Module; **Pre**-Pre-Condition; **Post**-Post-Condition*

We can see from the SCRM that this is a complex process with multiple controlling structures. Representing such a process clearly yet precisely requires a method that is semantically concise, expressive, and precise. Little-JIL has these characteristics, and thus provides a powerful capability for representing an Agent.

Fig. 8 depicts the Little-JIL representation of the process knowledge using step elements and process knowledge step organization. The Little-JIL description seems to provide a representation that is both precise and graphically clear in representing the process knowledge in this simple software module development for the Process-Agent *Dev-Team*.

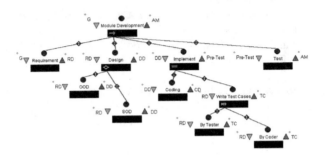

Fig. 8. Little-JIL representation of Process Knowledge for Process-Agent *Dev-Team* on a simple software module development

6 Future Work Discussions

This paper has presented a method that uses Little-JIL to specify the process knowledge of a Process-Agent in SoftPM. This method makes use of Little-JIL semantics to describe process elements, and takes advantage of Little-JIL's language constructs to combine behaviors of Process-Agents. And by using Little-JIL, behaviors of Process-Agents can be determined effectively and precisely. Hence it seems that this is a particularly powerful approach to Process Asset definition in SoftPM.

However, the use of Little-JIL to represent Process-Agents still presents several potential problems that suggest possible research issues:

- **Description of the Role and its Capability:** In a process modeled by Little-JIL, we can express easily what a role should do but there is no mechanism provided to express whether the selected role has the capabilities that are necessary in order to perform it. Process-Agents in OEC-SPM take into account the capabilities of entities in the process model and assure that the entities have desired capabilities; hence using OEC-SPM in conjunction with using Little-JIL as a process model can help to assure that appropriate capabilities participate in the process execution.

- **More Precise Control of Concurrency:** Concurrency in Little-JIL can be defined using the parallel step, whose semantics are essentially "fork and join". But there are cases in which more precise control of the interleaving of concurrent steps might be needed. For example, in Fig. 9, the completion of steps A, B and E will be sequential; C and D, the children steps

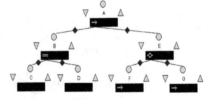

Fig. 9. Reverse Dependent

of B could be executed concurrently; one of F and G, the children steps of E will be selected to execute. While we know that F (or G) cannot be executed until both C and D have completed, we may wish to assure that F immediately follows execution of C, for example, without any intervening execution of D, while if G is selected, we may not care. Thus, our preference with respect to the order of execution of step D may need to depend on the execution decision of a step that comes after step D; we refer to this situation as "reverse dependent". There is no easy way in Little-JIL to deal with this potentially important issue. It is a specific case of the need for more powerful concurrency constructs in Little-JIL.

Acknowledgments

This research was supported in part by the National Natural Science Foundation of China under grant Nos. 60473060, 60273026 as well as the Hi-Tech Research and Development Program (863 Program) of China under grant No. 2004AA112080. It was also supported by the National Science Foundation under Award Nos. CCR-0204321 and CCR-0205575. The U.S. Government is authorized to reproduce and distribute reprints for Governmental purposes notwithstanding any copyright annotation thereon. The views and conclusions contained herein are those of the authors and should not be interpreted as necessarily representing the official policies or endorsements, either expressed or implied of The National Science Foundation, or the U.S. Government.

References

[1] Q. Wang, M. Li: Software Process Management: Practices in China. M. Li, B. Boehm, and L.J. Osterweil (Eds.): SPW 2005, LNCS 3840, pp. 317–331

[2] X. Zhao, M. Li, Q. Wang, K. Chan, H. Leung: An Agent-Based Self-Adaptive Software Process Model. Journal of Software, Vol. 15, No. 3, 2004, pp. 348–359.

[3] X. Zhao, K. Chan, M. Li: Applying Agent Technology to Software Process Modeling and Process-Centered Software Engineering Environment. The 20th Annual ACM Symposium on Applied Computing (SAC'05), Santa Fe, New Mexico, USA, 2005, pp. 1529-1533

[4] A, Wise. Little-JIL 1.0 Language Report. Technical Report 98-24, Laboratory for Advanced Software Engineering Research, University of Massachusetts, Amherst. 1998-04-16

[5] A. G. Cass, H. Lee, B. S. Lerner, L. J. Osterweil: Formally Defining Coordination Process to support Contract Negotiations. Department of Computer Science, University of Massachusetts, Amherst, MA 01003, June 1999. (UM-CS-1999-039)

[6] D. Jensen, Y. Dong, B. S. Lerner, E. K. McCall, L. J. Osterweil, S. M. Sutton, Jr., A. Wise: Coordinating Agent Activities in Knowledge Discovery Processes. Proceedings of Work Activities Coordination and Collaboration Conference (WACC 1999), San Francisco, CA, 1999, pp. 137-146

[7] S. M. Sutton, Jr. and L. J. Osterweil. The design of a next generation process language. In Proc. of the Joint 6th European Software Engineering Conj and the 5th ACM SICSOFT Symp. On the Foundations of Software Engineering, pages 142-158. Springer-Verlag, 1997.

[8] LASER Process Working Group. Getting Started With Little-JIL Using Visual-JIL. 2002, Laboratory for Advanced Software Engineering Research, University of Massachusetts, Amherst.

Reusable Model Structures and Behaviors
for Software Processes

Raymond Madachy

University of Southern California Center for Software Engineering,
941 W. 37th Place, Los Angeles, CA, USA
madachy@usc.edu

Abstract. An organization of increasingly complex system dynamics model structures and behaviors has been developed to promote modeling reuse for software processes. It uses an object-oriented framework for describing structures in a class hierarchy with inheritance relationships. This original approach provides a set of common assets that can be referenced for a "product line" of software process models. The structures and their behaviors are process patterns that frequently occur, and the recurring structures are model building blocks that can be reused. They provide a framework for understanding, modifying and creating system dynamics models regardless of experience. Previous work can be understood easier and the structures incorporated into new models with minimal modification. A goal of this work is to help accelerate software process modeling and simulation activities. Experience indicates that the model assets scale from small to large, complex models. Examples of the constructs and executable versions of associated models are also available.

1 Introduction

This work organizes system dynamics model structures and behaviors for software processes starting with elemental components, incorporating them into basic flow structures and building up to larger infrastructures. The taxonomy and process representations provided generalized and adaptable "plug and play" components of varying complexity. This is similar to the domain engineering results for a software product line, but in this case the product line consists of software process models for anyone to build.

The structures and their behaviors are process patterns that frequently occur. The recurring structures are model "building blocks" that can be reused. They provide a framework for understanding, modifying and creating system dynamics models regardless of experience. With access to reusable formulations that have been repeatedly proven, previous work can be understood easier and the structures incorporated into new models with minimal modification.

System dynamics was developed by Forrester [1], from which this work is ultimately derived. Since the pioneering work of Abdel-Hamid to create an integrated software project model [2], many system dynamics applications have been developed for software processes. However, the modeling task may be difficult and time consuming for new or even experienced modelers. This work attempts to fill the knowledge gap for the software domain, and make the modeling easier.

Q. Wang et al. (Eds.): SPW/ProSim 2006, LNCS 3966, pp. 222–233, 2006.
© Springer-Verlag Berlin Heidelberg 2006

Previous work for classifying system dynamic structures was been done in [3], where relatively small scale "modeling molecules" are described. Simulation packages often come with usage examples, such as [4] which provides descriptions of common building blocks. However, no other work has examined and provided a comprehensive taxonomy for a specific domain. Nor has an object-oriented framework been used to categorize inheritance properties of the structures. This presentation of the modeling craft is intended to resonate with software engineers.

This paper is a highly condensed summary from work to be published in [5] which contains further detailed illustration of all the structures, relevant equations and model outputs. Due to the space limitations of this paper, only a few short examples are shown that lead up to an integrated model of Brooks's Law phenomena. The book [5] also describes a system dynamics modeling process that leverages on the reusable structures. Additionally, applied examples of the structures are shown for different software process aspects. Executable models are provided for the smaller infrastructures up through large, complex application models [5].

2   Background and Overview

Below is an overview of terminology related to model structures and behavior:

- *Elements* are the smallest individual pieces in a system dynamics model: levels, rates, sources/sinks, auxiliaries and feedback connections.
- *Generic flow processes* are small microstructures and their variations comprised of a few elements, and are sometimes called *modeling molecules*. They are the building blocks, or substructures from which larger structures are created and usually contain approximately 2-5 elements.
- *Infrastructures* refer to larger structures that are composed of several microstructures, typically producing more complex behaviors.
- *Flow chains* are infrastructures consisting of a sequence of levels and rates (stocks and flows) that often form a backbone of a model portion. They house the process entities that flow and accumulate over time, and have information connections to other model components through the rates.

Not discussed explicitly are *archetypes*. They present lessons learned from dynamic systems with specific structure that produces characteristic modes of behavior. The structures and their resultant dynamic behaviors are also called patterns. Whereas molecules and larger structures are the model building blocks, archetypes interpret the generic structures and draw dynamic lessons from them. Senge discusses organizational archetypes based on simple causal loop diagrams in *The Fifth Discipline* [6].

2.1   A Class Hierarchy

An object-oriented software framework is convenient to understand the model building blocks and their inheritance relationships described in this chapter. Consider a class or object to be a collection of model elements wired in a way that produces characteristic behavior. Fig. 1 shows the model structures in a class hierarchy with inheritance. Object instances of these generic classes are the specific structures used for software process modeling (e.g. software artifact flows, project management policies, personnel chains, etc.).

The specific structures and their respective dynamic behaviors are the inherited attributes and operations (likened to services or methods). The hierarchy in Fig. 1 also shows multiple inheritance since some infrastructures combine structure and behavior from multiple generic classes. Not shown are the lower levels of the hierarchy consisting of specific software process instances that all inherit from this tree.

The simplest system is the rate and level combination, whereby the level accumulates the net flow rate (via integration over time). It can be considered the super class. The next level of structures include the generic flow processes, which are all slight variants on the rate and level system. Each of them adds some structure and produces unique characteristic behavior. For example the compounding process adds a feedback loop from the level to the rate with an auxiliary variable that sets the rate of growth. The new behavior derived from this structure is an exponential growth pattern.

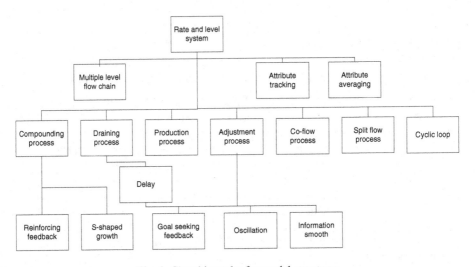

Fig. 1. Class hierarchy for model structures

This hierarchy only includes systems explicitly containing rates and levels. There are also structures using auxiliary variables instead of levels that can produce similar dynamics. For more on how the object-oriented modeling concept can be extended and automated see [5].

3   Model Structures and Behaviors

Next is a review of the basic model elements, generic flows and infrastructures. Specific structures for software process models and some behavioral examples will be identified. All of the software process structures are derived from one or more generic structures. Each structure can be represented with a diagram, summary of critical equations, and behavioral output. All of these are provided in [5].

3.1 Model Elements

The basic elements of system dynamics models are levels, flows, sources/sinks, auxiliaries and connectors or feedback loops. Fig. 2 serves as a legend showing the standard notation of these elements in a rate and level system with an auxiliary variable connected to the rate via an information link. Next the standard elements are briefly reviewed with sample instantiations for software processes.

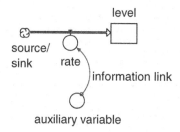

Fig. 2. Model Notation Example of a Rate and Level System

Levels are the state variables representing system accumulations. Typical state variables are software work artifacts, defect levels, or personnel levels. These examples may be broken out further per the following:

- <u>work artifacts</u> – these may include tasks, requirements, design, lines of code, test procedures, UML models, reuse library components, documentation pages, etc. These can be new, reused, planned, actual, etc. Sub levels like high-level design could be differentiated from low-level design, etc.
- <u>defect levels</u> – these can be per phase, activity, severity, priority or other discriminator.
- <u>personnel levels</u> – often segregated into different experience or knowledge pools (e.g. junior and senior engineers).

Other level examples include effort and costs expenditures, schedule dates, personnel attributes such as motivation, staff exhaustion or burnout levels, process maturity, key process areas and process changes.

Sources and sinks represent levels or accumulations outside the boundary of the modeled system. Sources are infinite supplies of entities and sinks are repositories for entities leaving the model boundary. Typical examples of software process sources could be requirements originating externally or outsourced hiring pools. Sinks could represent delivered software leaving the process boundary or personnel attrition repositories for those leaving the organization.

Rates in the software process are necessarily tied to the levels. Levels don't change unless there are flow rates associated with them. Some examples include software productivity rate, software change rate, requirements evolution, defect generation, personnel hiring and de-allocation, and learning rate.

Auxiliaries often represent "score-keeping" variables. Example for tracking purposes include the percent of job completion or other progress measures, percent of tasks in certain states, calculated defect density, other ratios or percentages used as independent variables in dynamic relationships.

3.2 Generic Flow Processes

Generic flow processes are the smallest, essential structures based on a rate/level system that model common situations and produce characteristic behaviors. They consist of levels, flows, sources/sinks, auxiliaries and sometimes feedback loops. See Table 1 for a summary of generic flows and example applications.

Table 1. Generic flow processes and example software process applications

Example	Description
Rate and Level System	The simple rate and level system (also called stock and flow) is the primary structure from which all others are derived. This system has a single level and a bi-directional flow that can fill or drain the level. It can be considered a super class for subsequent structures, because each one builds on top of this basic structure with additional detail and characteristic behavior.
Flow Chain with Multiple Rates and Levels	The single rate and level system can be expanded into a flow chain incorporating multiple levels and rates. It can be used to model a process that accumulates at several points instead of one, and is also called a cascaded level system. A generic flow chain within itself does not produce characteristic behavior without other structure and relationships.
Compounding Process	The compounding structure is a rate and level system with a feedback loop from the level to an input flow, and an auxiliary variable representing the fractional amount of growth per period. A compounding process produces positive feedback and exponential growth in the level. Modeling applications include cost-to-fix trends, user bases, market dynamics, software entropy, social communication patterns (e.g. rumors, panic), etc.
Draining Process	Draining can be represented similarly as the compounding process, except the feedback from the level is to an outflow rate and the auxiliary variable indicates how much is drained in the level. Draining is a common process that underlies delays and exponential decays. Personnel attrition, promotion through levels, software product retirement, skill loss and other trends can be modeled as draining processes.
Production Process	A production process represents work being produced as a rate equal to the number of applied resources multiplied by the resource productivity. It typically has an inflow to a level that represents production dependent on another level in an external flow chain representing a resource. It can also be used for pro-

	duction of other assets beside software artifacts.
Adjustment Process	An adjustment process is an approach to equilibrium. The structure for it contains a goal variable, a rate, level, and adjusting parameter. The structure models the closing of a gap between the goal and level. The change is more rapid at first and slows down as the gap decreases. The inflow is adjusted to meet the target goal. This basic structure is at the heart of many policies and other behaviors.
Co-Flow Process	Co-flows are a shortened name for coincident flows; flows that occur simultaneously through a type of slave relationship. The co-flow process has a flow rate synchronized with another host flow rate, and normally has a conversion parameter between them. This process can model the co-flows of software artifacts and defects, it can be used for personnel applications such learning or frustration, resource tracking such as effort expenditure, or tracking revenue as a function of sales.
Split Flow Process	The split flow process represents a flow being divided into multiple sub flows, or disaggregated streams. It contains an input level, more than one output flow, and typically has another variable to determine the split portions. Applications include defect detection chains to differentiate found vs. escape defects (i.e. defect filters), or personnel flows to model dynamic project resource allocation at given organizational levels.
Cyclic Loop	A cyclic loop represents entities flowing back through a loop. The difference from non-closed chains is that a portion of flow goes back into an originating level. This structure is appropriate to represent iterative software development processes, artifact rework, software evolution and other phenomena.

3.2.1 Example Generic Flow for Production Process

Fig. 3 shows an example of a classic production structure. The *production rate* is the number of applied *resources* multiplied by the *productivity* per Equation 1. This

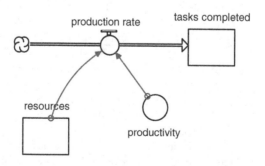

Fig. 3. Example Production Structure

structure is what associates personnel entities with task production in a model. The level for resources is typically contained in another flow chain for personnel resources (the single level in Fig. 3 doesn't show its associated flow rates), as demonstrated in the integrated example in Section 4 that builds upon this generic structure.

$$\text{production rate} = \text{resources} * \text{productivity} \tag{1}$$

3.3 Infrastructures and Behaviors

The infrastructures in Table 2 are based on one or more of the generic flow types with additional structural details. The additional structure typically leads to characteristic dynamic behaviors. A few of the structures herein do not cause specific dynamic behaviors, but instead are used for intermediate calculations, converters or instrumentation of some kind. The examples listed for the infrastructures are provided in [5].

Table 2. Example infrastructures and behaviors with examples

Example	Description
Exponential Growth	Growth structures are based on the generic compounding flow process. Examples are defect cost-to-fix over time or software entropy growth.
S-shaped Growth and S-curves	An S-shaped growth structure contains at least one level, provisions for a dynamic trend that rises and another that falls. There are various representations because S-curves may result from several types of process structures representing the rise and fall trends. Examples are cumulative effort or knowledge diffusion.
Delays	Delays are based on the generic draining process. An example is a hiring delay. Exponential decay results when the outflow constant represents a time constant from a level that has no inflows. The decay declines exponentially towards zero. A higher order delay behaves like a connected series of first order delays.
Balancing Feedback	Balancing feedback (also called negative feedback) occurs when a system is trying to attain a goal, such as reaching a hiring goal.
Oscillation	Oscillating behavior may result when there are at least two levels in a system. Normally there is a parameter for a target goal that the system is trying to reach, and the system is unstable as it tries to attain the goal. Examples are oscillating personnel systems.
Smoothing	An averaging over time. Random spikes will be eliminated when trends are averaged over a sufficient time period. An example is perceived quality.
Production and Rework	The classic production and rework structure accounts for incorrect task production and its rework. Work is performed, and the percentage done incorrectly flows into undiscovered rework. Rework occurs to fix the problems at a specified rate. The work may cycle through many times. This structure is also related to the cyclic loop, except this variant has separate sources and sinks instead of directly connected flow chains. A number of other

	structures can be combined with this, such as using the production structure for the task development rate.
Integrated Production Structure	This infrastructure combines elements of the task production and human resources personnel chains. Production is constrained by both productivity and the applied personnel resources external to the product chain. The level of personnel available is multiplied by a productivity rate.
Personnel Learning Curve	The continuously varying effect of learning can be modeled via a classic feedback loop between the completed tasks and productivity, to account for becoming more proficient at a task. It can be a representation where the learning is a function of the percent of job completion, or the learning would be expressed as a function of the volume of tasks completed.
Rayleigh Curve Generator	The Rayleigh generator produces a Rayleigh staffing curve. It contains essential feedback that accounts for the work already done and the current level of elaboration on the project, producing the familiar hump shaped curve. The manpower buildup parameter sets the shape of the Rayleigh curve. The Rayleigh curve is also frequently used to model defect levels.
Attribute Tracking	Important attributes to track are frequently calculated from levels. They can be used as inputs to other model portions, such as a decision structure. For example, defect density can be calculated by dividing the software size by the total number of defects.
Attribute Averaging	A structure for attribute averaging (similar to attribute tracking) calculates a weighted average of an attribute associated with two or more levels. It can be easily extended for more entities to average across and for different weighting schemes.
Effort Expenditure Instrumentation	Effort or cost expenditures are co-flows that can be used whenever effort or labor cost is a consideration. Frequently this co-flow structure serves as instrumentation only to obtain cumulative effort and does not play a role in the dynamics of the system. It could be used for decision making.
Decision Structures	Infrastructures for decision policies that frequently determine rates. Some common decision structures relevant to software processes [5] include: • Desired Staff • Resource Allocation • Scheduled Completion Date • Defect Rework Policies.

3.3.1 Example Infrastructure and Behavior for a Delay

An example structure for a first order delay is shown in Fig. 4 that models outflow from a level as introduced in Table 2. Equation 2 expresses the outflow rate as a function of the level and average delay time. It produces the characteristic exponential

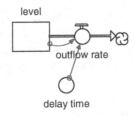

Fig. 4. Example Delay Structure

decline shown in Fig. 5 for a starting level of 10 and average delay time of 20 days. The integrated example in Section 4 incorporates this delay structure to model personnel assimilation on a project.

$$\text{outflow rate} = \text{level / delay time} \tag{2}$$

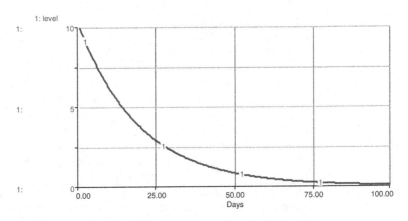

Fig. 5. Example First Order Delay Behavior

3.4 Software Process Chain Infrastructures

This section identifies flow chain infrastructures related to software processes consisting mostly of cascaded levels for software tasks, defects and people. These infrastructures can be used as pieces in a comprehensive software process model, or could serve as standalone base structures for isolated experimentation.

The chains represent basic flows pervasive in software processes. When applying system dynamics, the question must be asked: *What is flowing?* Determination of what kinds of entities flow through a software process is of primary importance to identify the chains to build models on top of. As always when modeling with system dynamics, the level of aggregation used in the chains depend on the modeling goals and desired level of process visibility. Applied examples of these chains from past modeling applications are highlighted in [5] to illustrate the concepts.

Software products are software artifact sequences modeled as conserved flows, where each level has the same unit, or in non-conserved flow chains where product transformation steps are modeled using distinct artifact types. Each level has different units in non-conserved chains. An elegant aspect of system dynamics is the simplification of using conserved flows; hence many models employ a generic "software task". But if the process and modeling goals dictate that sequential artifacts be modeled in their respective units then non-conserved flows are used. An example product flow chain is in the integrated model in Section 4 and shown in the top of Fig. 6.

Defects are an important process measure that can provide many insights. There are a number of ways to represent defects including their generation, propagation, detection and rework. Defects are the primary focus in the chains, but are inextricably tied to other process aspects such as task production, quality practices, process policies to constrain effort expenditure, various product and value attributes, etc.

Examples infrastructures related to defects detailed in [5] include, defect generation, defect co-flows, Rayleigh defect generation, defect detection (filters), defect detection and rework, defect amplification and defect categories.

People flows are conserved flow chains traditionally accounting for experience pools. Chains for personnel are mainstays of models that account for human labor and may also correspond to attributes for different skillsets, labor grades, or other differentiators requiring more detail than auxiliaries or single levels can provide. Frequently the chains contain two or more experience levels. Varying degrees of detail and enhancements are possible, such as adding chain splits for attrition from any experience level. See [5] for examples of personnel chains with increasing levels of detail. An example personnel chain is in the model in Section 4 and at the bottom of Fig. 6.

4   Integrated Example: Brooks's Law Model

A model for Brooks's Law phenomena in Fig. 6 illustrates integrating the aforementioned components to model the effects of adding people to a late project [5]:

- **Product chain** with *requirements* being developed in *developed software* per the *software development rate*
- **Personnel chain** where *new personnel* are added when the project is late through the *personnel allocation rate* and they assimilate into *experienced personnel*
- **Production structure** with a composite productivity formula for the *software development rate* accounting for communication overhead, training overhead and differences in productivity between new vs. experienced people
- **Delay structure** for the assimilation of *new personnel* to *experienced personnel* per the *average assimilation delay*.

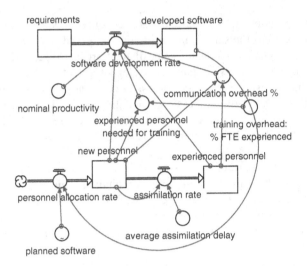

Fig. 6. Brooks's Law Model

There is also an information feedback loop from *developed software* to compare to *planned software* for the decision to add people. The resulting behavior in Fig. 7 for varying the personnel added once to catch up on schedule indicates the optimum is adding 5 people in this case. See [5] for more details of the model and its behavior.

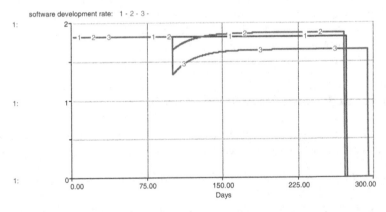

Fig. 7. Sensitivity of Software Development Rate to Varying Personnel Allocation Pulses (1: no additions, 2: add 5 people on 110th day, 3: add 10 people on 110th day)

5 Summary and Conclusions

Models are composed of building blocks, many of which are generic and can be reused. Model elements can be combined into increasingly complex structures that can be incorporated into specific applications. There are few structures that have not already been considered for system dynamics models, and modelers can save time by leveraging existing and well-known patterns.

This work provides reusable knowledge of those patterns specifically tailored for the software processes domain. The hierarchy of model structures and software process examples can be likened respectively to classes and instantiated objects. Characteristic behaviors are encapsulated in the objects since their structures cause the behaviors.

Generic flow processes, flow chains and larger infrastructures are examples of recurring structures. Generic flow processes have structural detail to model compounding, draining, production, adjustment, co-flows, splits and cyclic loops.

The structures all have multiple applications for software processes. Common main chain infrastructures are centered on products (software artifacts), defects, and people. Decision structures are also important to represent, such as policies to allocate staff, adjust project goals/estimates as a project progresses and defect rework policies.

The generic structures can be combined in different ways and detail added to create larger infrastructures and complex models. This was illustrated when integrating a few simple structures into the Brooks's Law model of complex and interacting effects.

The reusable structural/behavioral assets have been the result of culling many software process applications. Experience has shown that they are useful for creating new applications. The assets are further detailed and provided in [5] as executable models. Students, researchers and practitioners are encouraged to use and experiment with them.

References

1. Forrester JW: Principles of Systems. Cambridge, MA: MIT Press (1968)
2. Abdel-Hamid T, Madnick S: Software Project Dynamics, Englewood Cliffs, NJ, Prentice-Hall (1991)
3. Hines J: Molecules of Structure Version 1.4, LeapTec and Ventana Systems, Inc. (2000)
4. Richmond B, et al.: Ithink User's Guide and Technical Documentation, High Performance Systems Inc., Hanover, NH (1990)
5. Madachy R.: Software Process Dynamics, IEEE Computer Society Press (2006)
6. Senge P: The Fifth Discipline, Doubleday, New York, NY (1990)

Organization-Theoretic Perspective for Simulation Modeling of Agile Software Processes

Levent Yilmaz and Jared Phillips

M&SNet: Auburn Modeling and Simulation Group
yilmaz@auburn.edu
Computer Science and Software Engineering,
Auburn University Auburn, AL, USA

Abstract. Software development is a team effort that requires cooperation among individuals via task allocation, coordination of actions, and if necessary avoidance and/or management of conflicts among members of the organization. This perspective contrasts with the production focused view of software development. That is, interaction becomes the central activity, not a side-effect of a method's prescription. Understanding the principles and components of organizational behavior for inclusion in software process models improves the level of fidelity and credibility of existing process simulations. Furthermore, there are strong connections between the neo-information processing view of organizations and agile software development. This paper introduces the conceptual basis for an agent-based simulation modeling test-bed, Team-RUP, which is based on an organization-theoretic perspective for simulation modeling of agile software processes.

1 Introduction

Software production methods are enacted via interactions of software teams that cooperate to build software (Sawyer 1994). As such, organizational dynamics can have significant effect on project coordination. Software development is carried out by teams of people that have to be coordinated within an organizational structure. Therefore, it is critical to pay attention to complex interrelations between technical, product-oriented activities and organizational factors that affect the performance of software processes. The lack of conceptualization and inclusion of human, social, and organizational dynamics in software process models is a critical obstacle in exploring socio-technical aspects of software processes [1]. Hofstede [2] and others [3] point out that organizational culture can have significant effect on project coordination, and yet, this is not reflected in current project management paradigms applicable to software development [4].

This paper presents a strategy for developing software process simulation models from an organization-theoretic perspective, and it illustrates the utility of the framework using an agent-based simulation test-bed (Team-RUP), which is originally developed for studying cooperative team behavior in software development organizations that exercise agile processes such as Rational Unified Process (RUP). Agile processes promote communication among team members. Communication is a

Q. Wang et al. (Eds.): SPW/ProSim 2006, LNCS 3966, pp. 234–241, 2006.

fundamental part of any software development project. When a project is developed in pieces, understanding how the pieces fit together is vital to creating the finished product. There is more to integration than simple communication. Quickly integrating a large project while increments are being developed in parallel requires collaboration. As such, the premise of the presented strategy is based on the following observations: Human organizations, including software development organizations, (1) continually acquire, manipulate, and produce artifacts through joint cooperative activities and (2) they are comprised of multiple distributed agents (i.e., software engineers) that exhibit collective properties via communication, interaction via collaboration and coordination. Furthermore, the characteristics of agile processes (i.e., iterative, time-bound, parsimony, adaptive, incremental, convergent, people-oriented) impose new challenges on model design. Team-RUP focuses on these challenges in terms of a novel task and organizational model.

Human organizations are the subject of study of organization theory, and our framework is grounded in the science of organizations (contingency theory [5] and computational organization theory [6]). In our work, the organization-theoretic perspective to simulation modeling of software processes entails characterizing the components of organizational design, as well as established types of organizational paradigms [7,8,9]. We present the conceptual basis and design aspects underlying the agent-based simulation test-bed, called Team-RUP.

The rest of the paper is organized as follows. Section 2 presents the basic organizational concepts used during the conceptualization of Team-RUP. Section 3 provides a brief synopsis regarding the realization of these concepts within the design and implementation of the model. Finally, in section 4 we conclude by discussing potential avenues of further research.

2   Organizational Concepts for Software Process Simulation

To design an organization we must first know what are the components and features of the organization we can select and combine. Figure 1 presents the partial conceptual model that can be used to specify the conceptual models of organizations.

Organization Design: The structure of the organization includes a set of relations between its members (i.e., agents), skills, and resources, task-resource, task-skill, resource access, task-precedence, and task assignment [6] are among the fundamental elements of organizational structure. In a software development organization, we are also interested in the execution of a complex function that can be decomposed into sub-functions, so that the agents capable of solving, distributing, and routing subtasks and sub-results can collectively and cooperatively solve the problem. The specification of this function is defined here as the behavior of the organization. The functions that designate the behavior of an organization constitute the primitive and composite tasks. Each task requires a number of skills provided by agents that play certain roles such as project manager, designer, and tester.

Organizational Behavior Moderators: Behavior moderators or stressors [6] such as time pressure, deadlines, turnover, trust, reward mechanisms, influence the observed behavior of a software process. As variations in technology [6] and human dynamics such as anxiety, stress, emotions, and personality continue to be embedded with software process models, the fidelity and variability of simulations will improve.

Organizational Roles and Intelligent Agents: Most recent advancements in computational organization theory are being achieved through the agent-based modeling methodology. Agent-based simulation modeling is well-established as a method for simulating Complex Adaptive Systems, i.e., those with many participants, (often many kinds of participants), whose behavior both adapts to, and influences emerging conditions. The purpose of agent-based models is not necessarily to predict the outcome of a system, rather it is to reveal and understand the complex and aggregate system behaviors that emerge from the interactions of the various individuals involved.

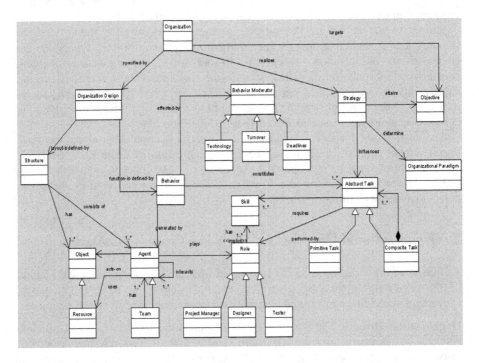

Fig. 1. Partial Conceptual Model of Team-RUP's Organizational Design

Organizational Strategy and Paradigms: The strategy of an organization is its future intention of how it will attain its objectives that are designated by the organizational performance model. A strategy is realized in terms of cooperation mechanisms that require coordination and collaboration among the members of the organization. A strategy can be realized in terms of coordination mechanisms such as planning, rules, mutual agreement, and hierarchy. Constantine [7] outlines a comprehensive framework that he calls organization paradigms. In this framework organizational paradigms are viewed as the mechanisms by which groups control and coordinate their efforts on a common task. Four types of paradigms are identified [7]. Tasks can be coordinated by a traditional hierarchy (closed teams), by reliance on individual initiative and innovative independence (random teams), by collaborative discussion and negotiation (open teams), or by virtue of harmonious alignment (synchronous teams).

Task-Environment Model: The task-environment model refers to the environmental and task characteristics that affect the performance of the organization. These characteristics include type, size, rate of change, uncertainty, interdependence, complexity, and granularity of tasks.

Performance (Objective) Model: To maximize the applicability of the results across the vast diversity of software development objectives and constraints, efficiency and effectiveness are used as common performance indicators. Often, organizational efficiency is measured in terms of productivity and staff utilization, while effectiveness is viewed as a combination of timeliness and software quality.

3 Team-RUP: A Test-Bed Toward Next-Generation Software Development Organization Models

Team-RUP is an agent-based simulation model that is used to explore cooperative behavior in software development organizations that employ Rational Unified Process. The model focuses on three levels of organizational character and the feedback loop they produce: process activities via an explicit task model, organizational design, and various team archetypes.

3.1 Organization Design

As connoted by its name, Team-RUP provides a test-bed for studying collaboration and coordination among teams at multiple resolutions guided by the Rational Unified Process [10]. The organizational model addresses the structure of the organization and agents, the coordination of tasks, and agent collaborations. The structure of an organization modeled in the Team-RUP framework is shown in figure 2. As is most common among software development organizations, the Team-RUP is structured as a hierarchy of agents. It consists of a project manager, a design manager, and teams of engineers. The remainder of the software development organization, including an independent testing group, acts as a hook point and is implemented via parameterized components so that detailed models can later be plugged in to the Team-RUP framework.

3.2 Organizational Paradigms Used in Team-RUP

To represent cooperation at the team level, Team-RUP considers four group archetypes based on characteristics resulting from collaboration and coordination techniques. Ferber [11, p. 80] defines a collaboration technique as "being of those that enable agents to distribute tasks, information and resources (among themselves) in the advancement of a common labour." We classify teams in terms of the degree of autonomy afforded by such strategies. In particular, team collaboration strategies are classified as top-down or bottom-up. As the former entails step-wise refinement, a large degree of oversight is required, which diminishes autonomy. The latter, however, provides more flexibility since the structure of the final integrated product is not entirely preconceived. These categories are further subdivided in terms of coordination. According to Ferber [11, p. 400], coordination of actions means "the articulation of the individual actions accomplished by each of the agents in such as way that the whole ends up being a coherent and high-performance operation." We classify team behavior according to the degree of concurrency realized through coordination. In particular, teams can function sequentially or concurrently.

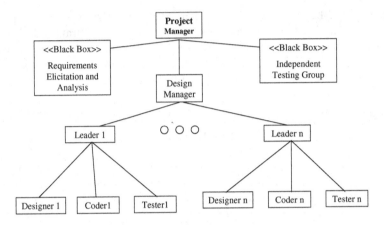

Fig. 2. Team-RUP Organizational Structure

3.3 The Team-RUP Task Model

In accord with RUP, the development of software in Team-RUP is viewed as a multi-stage transformation. During a series of time-boxed iterations, the design manager and its subordinates map the analysis model into a design model and implementation. Construction begins with the analysis model being passed to the project manager, who forwards it to the design manager. During a series of time-boxed iterations, the design manager and its subordinates map the analysis model into a design model and implementation. For simplification purposes, the latter two artifacts are not syntactically distinct entities in the model. As will be evident later, both are sub-lists of the same (semi-) sorted list. To reflect RUP's incremental nature, testing occurs during each iteration. We recall that in the Rational Unified Process, software projects are completed through a sequence of time-boxed iterations, each of which may comprise design, implementation, and/or testing. Development organizations using RUP should complete some subset of the final system at the end of each iteration. Because of its iterative nature, RUP allows an organization to cope with requirements changes. RUP also stipulates that those parts of the project involving greater risk should be addressed in early iterations so that overall risk to the project can be mitigated. To model this incremental and iterative process, the organization sorts integer arrays using a variation of a well-known iterative sorting algorithm; namely, Shell sort. In the Team-RUP framework, an array of integers represents a project configuration, and problem facets are modeled as ordered pairs of elements. The set of all possible facets pertaining to a configuration C (and hence a project) is the following set:

$$\{(x_i, y_j) \in C \times C | i < j\}$$

Suppose (x_i, y_j) is a problem facet corresponding to a configuration C and let z_k be an element of C. If $k \geq j$, comparing x_i and z_k translates into performing a task associated with (x_i, y_j). Similarly, if $k \leq i$, comparing z_k and y_j is also analogous to performing a task associated with (x_i, y_j). Clearly, many tasks can be accomplished via a single comparison. As in the real world, not all facets of a problem need to be addressed to accomplish a given project; certain tasks can remain undone. Team-RUP classifies tasks according to two categories. A supporting task does not reverse the order of a problem facet pair. Principal tasks are the second form of task, and they address a special form of problem facet. Team-RUP represents requirements in terms of inversions; that is, pairs of array elements that are out of order. A single inversion is interpreted as a principal, *atomic* task yet to be performed. Thus, a set of inversions is an incomplete requirement fulfillment (*ie.* principal task), and removing a set of inversions corresponds to fulfilling a requirement. Sets of inversions can be decomposed into subsets just as a task can be decomposed into subtasks. With this mapping of tasks to inversions, Shell sort provides a strong analogy for RUP for several reasons. Obviously, the algorithm's approach of removing inversions in phases coincides with RUP iterations. Of greater significance is the fact that a Shell sort phase does not undo work performed in earlier phases: 2-sorting a 5-sorted list generates a 5-sorted (as well as 2-sorted) list. This reflects the fact that each RUP iteration produces part of the final system rather than draft-quality, throw-away workproducts. Recall that Shell sort initially swaps unordered elements that are far apart and decreases with each phase the distance between the elements it compares. Because it eventually sorts the set of adjacent elements, the algorithm is guaranteed to sort the entire list. Since inversions inserted by an outside entity during the execution of Shell sort will ultimately be removed by later phases, the algorithm reflects RUP's ability to cope with changing customer requirements.

As mentioned before, we interpret Shell sort phases to be RUP iterations. In each phase of Shell sort, the base array is partitioned into sub-arrays whose lengths are determined by a particular increment sequence. Each of these sub-arrays is sorted using some secondary sorting algorithm (typically insertion sort) (Weiss, 1999). By varying the way this secondary sorting occurs, we use this feature of Shell sort to model alternative team behaviors. That is, the sorting is performed by agents cooperatively and consistent with the specific sorting strategy. Comparing array elements and performing element exchanges represent the design and implementation phases performed by agents. Ascertaining the number of inversions in sub-arrays is seen as testing. Several sub-arrays can be tested during each iteration. Thus, in accordance with RUP, our model organization avoids a linear lifecycle approach. The project ends when the originally proposed deadline for the final time-box expires, regardless of the state of the array.

3.4 The Team-RUP Design, Implementation, and Experimentation

Team-RUP framework is developed using the Repast Agent Simulation Toolkit. Figure 3 illustrates a screenshot of the GUI during a simulation run. The lower left-hand window displays the current state of the list being sorted. In particular, it shows a Cartesian coordinate system in which ordinates increase from top to bottom and abscissa increase from left to right. Suppose L is the list of n integers being sorted. The dots are plots of the points in the set

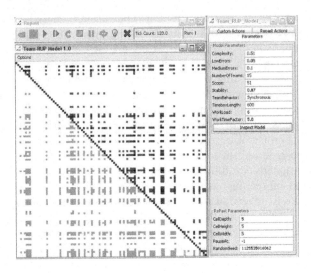

Fig. 3. Team-RUP GUI

$$S \equiv \{(x_i, y_j) \in L \times L | 1 \le i < j \le n\}$$

Let $(x_k, y_l) \in S$ be given. If $x_k < y_k$, then (x_k, y_l) is not an inversion and corresponds to a green dot. If $x_k > y_l$, then (x_k, y_l) is an inversion and corresponds to a red dot. In the case of an inversion, darker dots represent greater values of the difference $l - k$. The information shown in the right window of Figure 3 displays the simulation run's model parameters. The complexity value is the percent of inversions found in the initial list. *LowErrors* and *HighErrors* provide upper bounds on inversion percentages used by the testing department to classify work products. *NumberOfTeams* refers to the number of engineering teams in the software construction team. The scope is the size of the list to be sorted. Stability relates (inversely) to the percent of insertions injected into the list at the end of the first iteration. This value decreases as simulation time progresses. Obviously, the team behavior parameter takes on the values shown in Figure 3. In the Team-RUP model, the nature of collaboration varies with the selection of team behavior. While always centralized due to organizational constraints, task allocation possesses characteristics from both the imposed and brokered paradigms [11]. Task assignments involving the project manager are imposed. In contrast, the design manager can exhibit trader qualities. For example, Synchronized teams query the design manager to ascertain the team whose skill set matches a service needed by the inquiring team. Likewise, Agile teams consult the design manager to discover which team manages a particular requirement. In contrast, imposed allocation characterizes the autonomous team behaviors. Team interaction, another aspect of collaboration, exhibits even greater diversity among behaviors.

4 Conclusions

With its extensive tool set and corporate support, the Rational Unified Process has garnered large support from software developers. Understanding its interaction with human agents, therefore, is extremely important. We believe our current implementation will serve as a test-bed for a larger scale project. The value of the work so far is found in our demonstration that team culture can indeed be simulated. In the past, software developers have relied solely on "folk-wisdom" heuristics or studies bound by historical circumstance. Simulation provides software development organizations a tool for understanding why a project progresses the way it does. More importantly, it affords the opportunity to try new avenues for improvement in a risk-free environment.

References

1. Acua, T. Silvia and N. Juristo (2005). *Software Process Modeling* (page xix). Springer Science and Business Medias Inc.
2. Hofstede, G. (1998) *Identifying Organizational Subcultures: An Empirical Approach, Journal of Management Studies,* Vol. 35, pp. 32-49.
3. Cabrera, A., Cabrera, E. F. and Barajas, S. (2001) 'The key role of organizational culture in a multi-system view of technology-driven change', *International Journal of Information Management,* Vol. 21, pp.245-261.
4. Boehm, B. W., Abts, C., Brown, A. W., Chulani, S., Clark, B. K., Horowitz, E., Madachy, R., Reifer, D. and Steece, B. (2000) *Software Cost Estimation with Cocomo II,* Prentice Hall PTR, Upper Saddle River, New Jersey.
5. Scott, W. R. (1992). Organizations: Rational, Natural, and Open Systems, third edition. Englewood-Cliffs, N.J. Prentice Hall.
6. Carley, M. K. and L. Gasser (1999). "Computational Organization Theory, "In *Multi-Agent Systems: A Modern Approach to Distributed Artificial Intelligence.* (Ed. Weiss G.). The MIT Press.
7. Constantine, L. (1993) "Work Organization: Paradigms for Project Management and Organization," *Communications of the ACM,* Vol. 36, No. 10, pp.35-43.
8. Armour, G. P. (2004). *The Laws of Software Process: A New Model for the Production and Management of Software.* Auerbach Publications.
9. Dyba, Tore (2000). "Improvisation in Small Software Organizations,"*IEEE Software* September/October 2000. pp. 82-87.
10. Krutchen, P. (1999). *The Rational Unified Process: An Introduction.* Reading, MA: Addison Wesley Longman.
11. Ferber, J. (1999). *Multi-Agent Systems: An Introduction to Distributed Artificial Intelligence.* New York, NY: Addison Wesley Longman Inc.

Semi-quantitative Simulation Modeling of Software Engineering Process

He Zhang[1,2] and Barbara Kitchenham[2]

[1] School of Computer Science and Engineering, UNSW
[2] National ICT Australia
{he.zhang, barbara.kitchenham}@nicta.com.au

Abstract. Software process simulation models hold out the promise of improving project planning and control. However, purely quantitative models require a very detailed understanding of the software process, i.e. process knowledge represented quantitatively. When such data is lacking, quantitative models impose severe constraints, restricting the model's value. In contrast, qualitative models display all possible behaviors but only in qualitative terms. This paper illustrates the value and flexibility of semi-quantitative modeling by developing a model of the software staffing process and comparing it with other quantitative staffing models. We show that the semi-quantitative model provides more insights into the staffing process and more confidence in the outcomes than the quantitative models by achieving a tradeoff between quantitative and qualitative simulation. In particular, the semi-quantitative simulation produces a set of possible outcomes with the ranges of real numeric values. The semi-quantitative model allows us to determine the solution boundaries for specific scenarios under the conditions of limited knowledge.

1 Introduction

In the late 80's, Abdel-Hamid and Madnick (AHM) proposed the use of quantitative System Dynamics models to simulate the dynamic aspects of software projects [1]. Since then, other researchers have continued their work and extended their approach. This approach is intended to attain a detailed understanding of project behavior, improving both project planning and project control. Although it has shown great promise, in practice, it is not frequently used.

One major problem with quantitative simulation models is that they require very detailed understanding of the processes to be simulated. Such models require reliable data for their initial construction, and additional data to tailor the general model to the specific practices of a particular organization. When the knowledge of software process is limited or inadequate, quantitative simulation models impose strict constraints on the models which results in deterministic outcomes that neglect other possibilities.

As an alternative to the quantitative approach, qualitative simulation has been introduced to model and simulate software processes. Ramil and Smith developed qualitative models with reference to the quantitative models to extract the high-order qualitative trends of software evolution [2]. Zhang *et al.* developed a qualitative simulation model of a software staffing process, and presented a new approach to examine

Q. Wang et al. (Eds.): SPW/ProSim 2006, LNCS 3966, pp. 242–253, 2006.

the Brooks' Law [9]. So far, these are the only examples of software process modeling using qualitative simulation.

Semi-quantitative simulation involves combining incomplete quantitative and qualitative knowledge. It provides a smooth transition between qualitative and quantitative modeling. In this paper, we introduce a semi-quantitative model of the staffing process of software project and apply it to develop a QSIM+Q2 simulation. The simulation displays a set of behaviors which display all possible quantitative outcomes when team size changes. We examine the generated behaviors of our model by comparing them with the results of other quantitative models.

Section 2 introduces semi-quantitative simulation modeling. We address the qualitative constraints and quantitative bounds of the software staffing process model in Section 3. Then, we illustrate the model results of the EXAMPLE project (Section 4), followed by the comparison with the previous models and discussion of the relevant factors (Section 5). Finally, Section 6 presents our conclusions and intentions for future work.

2 Semi-quantitative Simulation

Semi-quantitative simulation can be implemented in two stages, i.e. qualitative simulation and quantitative constraint propagation. In this section, we briefly introduce their mechanisms.

2.1 Qualitative Simulation

Qualitative models represent systems in the real world at an abstract level. Fewer assumptions are required than for quantitative models. Qualitative simulation is implemented in the QSIM tool [4].

A system is normally modeled as a set of ordinary differential equations (ODEs), which involves quantitative information. At a higher level, a qualitative differential equation (QDE) represents a large set of possible ODEs, for example, each $M+$ (or $M-$) function represents the set of all monotonically increasing (or decreasing) functions. When only incomplete knowledge is available, we can replace ODEs with QDEs to represent the relationships and values of system variables qualitatively [3].

A QDE is the input constraint model to QSIM. The values of its variables are given relative to sets of qualitatively significant landmarks, e.g. 0 and infinity.

Qualitative simulation starts from a given initial system state. The output generated by QSIM is a set of possible qualitative behaviors and each behavior consists of a sequence of states. Each state in a behavior describes an open temporal interval or a time point. These qualitative states represent graphically the system behavior from its initial state to its final state. Time is treated as a qualitative variable in QSIM. Its landmarks are produced by QSIM when necessary, they indicate critical points of other variables [4].

2.2 Q2 Extension

Semi-quantitative simulation uses bounding intervals to represent partial quantitative knowledge. Q2 (Qualitative + Quantitative) is the basic semi-quantitative reasoner implemented as an extension to QSIM [4].

The qualitative behaviors generated by QSIM provide the framework for semi-quantitative reasoning. Given interval bounds on the values of some landmarks and envelopes on the monotonic functions, its QDE defines a constraint-satisfaction problem (CSP). A solution to this CSP is an assignment of an interval to each landmark consistent with the constraints. Because a few qualitative behaviors cover a wide range of real possibilities, a contradiction refutes a qualitative behavior and all the real possibilities it describes [3]. Fig. 1 shows how a system described by single QDE implements a semi-quantitative simulation (QSIM+Q2).

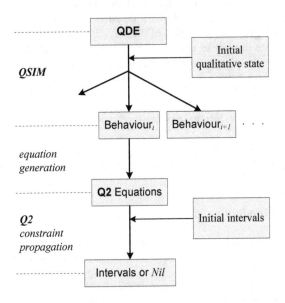

Fig. 1. Overview of QSIM + Q2

3   QSIM+Q2 Model for Staffing Process

Several previous researches have investigated the software staffing process using quantitative and qualitative models. This section first gives a brief description of these models, and then presents our semi-quantitative (QSIM+Q2) model for this process.

3.1   Related Models

Abdel-Hamid and Madnick (AHM) modeled the basic process of software human resource management as a part of their integrated model [5]. They assumed two workforce levels, i.e. "newly hired workforce" and "experienced staff", and then formulated the assimilation process as a first-order exponential delay.

Madachy developed a software staffing model to examine the Brooks' Law [6]. He simplified AHM's model by focusing on the assimilation procedure, i.e. "new project personnel" is transformed into "experienced personnel" at "personnel allocation rate".

Both of these staffing models were System Dynamics models and used to verify Brooks' Law. Unfortunately, these models were built using a set of specific numeric values, which were selected from the literature or historical data of company projects, to represent the factors in the models. Further, they simulated the process with the data from specific projects or example as inputs.

Stutzke developed a simple model in order to perform a similar investigation [7]. He believed that the added burden of communication was a second-order effect.

Zhang *et al.* extracted the basic qualitative assumptions of the staffing process and developed a qualitative model [9]. The qualitative simulation generated all possible behaviors that arise when the workforce changes during a project. This paper extends their work by combining the qualitative model with partial quantitative knowledge.

3.2 Qualitative Modeling

Both AHM's and Madachy's models are quantitative simulation models which consist of a set of ODEs. To develop the semi-quantitative model, a qualitative model has to be created first on the base of a minimal set of assumptions of the staffing process. We refine Zhang's qualitative model and combine the quantitative extensions later.

3.2.1 Qualitative Abstract Elements
The qualitative model is derived from some basic assumptions, including the unstated assumptions in previous models. We summarize these assumptions and extract the corresponding qualitative constraints in Table 1.

Table 1. Basic Assumptions of Staffing Model

Assumption	Constraint
1. no changes of requirements S_P	*constant* S_P
2. reworking is included in S_P	
3. S_P is transformed to product by R_{SD}	$S_C + S_R = S_P$, $R_{SD} = d(S_C)/dt$
4. workforce WF_{TL} consists of WF_{EX} and WF_{NW}	$WF_{TL} = WF_{EX} + WF_{NW}$
5. R_{ND} is the product of productivity PD and WF	$R_{EXD} = PD_{EX} * WF_{EX,}$ $R_{NWD} = PD_{NW} * WF_{NW}$
6. increasing WF_{TL} increases R_{CM} due to an increase in L_{CM}	$L_{CM} = \boxed{M+}(WF_{TL})$, $R_{CM} = R_{ND} * L_{CM}$
7. R_{SD} is difference between R_{ND} and R_{CO}	$R_{SD} = R_{ND} - R_{CM}$
8. PD_{EX} is constant on average, and higher than PD_{NW}	$PD_{NW} < PD_{EX}$, *constant* PD_{EX}
9. more WF_{NW} need to be trained by more WF_{ET}	$WF_{ET} = \boxed{M+}(WF_{NW})$,
10. WF_{NW} are assimilated into WF_{EX} by R_{AS}	$WF_{ET} + WF_{ED} = WF_{EX,}$ $R_{AS} = d(PD_{NW})/dt$

Based on these assumptions, the qualitative abstract structure was created to visualize the qualitative constraint structure of software staffing process as shown in Fig.2.

As time progresses, the *remaining size* (S_R), initially equal to the requirements (S_P), decreases until it becomes equal to *completed size* (S_C). The project will be completed when S_C equals the initial requirements, or, equivalently, S_R drops to zero.

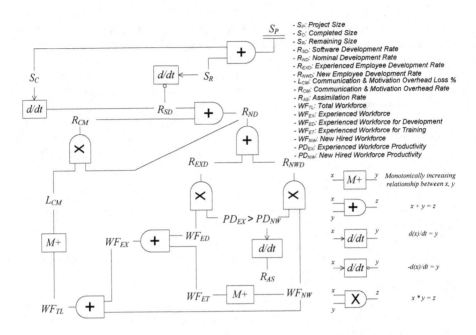

Fig. 2. Qualitative Abstracting Structure of Software Staffing Process

The *experienced workforce* (WF_{EX}) and the *new workforce* (WF_{NW}) work at different productivities. When the new employees join the project ($WF_{NW} > 0$), a portion of experienced staff (WF_{ET}) have to leave their original tasks to train the new personnel.

There are two major differential components in this model. The first one is the *software development rate* (R_{SD}), which represents the development speed of the software project. It is determined by two factors: the *nominal development rate* (R_{ND}), and the equivalent *communication and motivation overhead rate* (R_{CM}). The R_{ND} can be further decomposed into development rate contributions from the experienced workforce (R_{EXD}) and the newly hired workforce (R_{NWD}). The second differential relation is the *assimilation rate* (R_{AS}) of the new employees, which indicates how quickly their productivity increases to the level of experienced staff by the training process.

3.2.2   QDE Programming

Two QDEs are developed to convert the qualitative abstract model (Fig. 2) to constraint programs. One QDE is used to describe the normal software development process, and the other to describe the interaction and relations in the assimilation process.

Normal Software Development QDE

The constraint clauses of this QDE are shown as below. It represents the normal software development process without new employees hired. All the constraints are based on the first seven assumptions in Section 3.2.1.

```
(constraints (add Sc Sr Sp)(constant Sp)(d/dt Sc Rsd)
   (constant WFnw 0)(constant WFex)(add WFex WFnw WFtl)
   (constant PDex)(Mult PDex WFed Rexd)(constant Rnwd 0)
   (add Rexd Rnwd Rnd)(M+ WFtl Lcm)(Mult Rnd Lcm Rcm)
   (add Rsd Rcm Rnd))
```

Assimilation Process QDE

The assimilation process can be refined in two different ways.

Refinement 1: The newly hired workforce will be gradually transferred into the experienced staff pool at the *assimilation rate* (R_{AS}). WF_{NW} will be reduced to zero when the assimilation process finishes. The productivity of new staff stays at the initial low level during assimilation. Because of the positive monotonic relationship, the *experienced workforce for training* (WF_{ET}) reduces to simultaneously with WF_{NW}.

Refinement 2: The newly hired workforce are transferred into the experienced staff pool only when the assimilation process finishes. However, their average productivity will be increasing until it reaches the *experienced workforce productivity* (PD_{EX}). The amount of experienced trainers required (WF_{ET}) does not change.

Refinement 2 is consistent with AHM's enhanced model, which separated the assimilation procedure into four stages with the different productivity levels of new staff [5]. We use this refinement in this paper. The new and changed constraints from the first QDE required to represent the assimilation process are highlighted below.

```
(constraints (constant WFnw)(add WFed WFet WFex)
   (M+ WFnw WFet)(d/dt PDnw Ras)(Mult PDnw WFnw Rnwd))
```

Two transition functions are used to switch between the QDEs. One triggers the assimilation procedure at a particular time point during development. The other monitors the increase of the new employees' productivity until it equals the experienced level. Then it switches the simulation back to the first QDE.

3.3 Quantitative Extension

The qualitative model can be extended by Q2 equations for semi-quantitative simulation. Q2 equations, including parameter intervals and envelope functions, are representations of incomplete quantitative knowledge and uncertain scenarios.

3.3.1 Parameter Intervals

Variable units and unit conversion were not addressed in the qualitative model because the landmark values are symbolic names with unknown real values (like algebraic variables). All quantities are assumed to have appropriate and compatible units. However, because some quantitative interval bounds are involved in semi-quantitative simulation, the units must be explicitly denoted for the interval arithmetic (Table 3).

Ratio of Productivity

According to AHM's summary of the literature and interviews, the estimates for the productivity of newly hired workforce relative to that of experienced personnel vary from 0.33 to 0.64. We pick the interval of [0.4 0.6] for the quantitative extension.

Assimilation Delay

The range of proposed assimilation delay is quite large in the literature. It was set at 80 days by AHM [5], but 20 days by Madachy [6]. Although some attributes of their projects are different, the team size and project duration are comparable. We use a prototype project from AHM as our example project, so we employ a moderate range, [60 80] days, for this parameter.

The value ranges of *Project Size* and *Workforce Levels* highly depend on the particular project and organization. They are specified in Section 4.1.

3.3.2 Envelope Functions

As Fig. 2 indicates, there are two monotonic functions in the qualitative staffing model. Thus, we need to specify two numerical envelope functions for Q2 inference.

(M+ WF$_{NW}$ WF$_{ET}$).

When more new employees join in the project, more experienced people have to be assigned to train them. A linear relationship was reported in the literature. AHM summarized the ratio ranges from 15% to 25%, and set it to 20% [5]. Madachy set the value to 0.25[6]. We use the range of [0.15 0.25] in our example.

(M+ WF$_{TL}$ L$_{CM}$).

Brooks suggests that *communication and motivation overhead* (R$_{CM}$) increases by a factor of $n(n-1)/2$, where n is the project team size [8]. This implies that increasing the project team size increases R$_{CM}$. AHM used the function $(0.06n^2)$ to formulate a nonlinear relation between *total workforce* (WF$_{TL}$) and the percentage of *communication and motivation loss* (L$_{CM}$), which is consistent with Brooks' assumption.

An exact function (i.e. upper equal to lower) is imported into the Q2 equations. These two envelope functions are shown as below.

```
(envelopes ((M+ WFnw WFet)(upper (lambda (x) (* x 0.25)))
      (u-inv (lambda (y) (* y 4)))
      (lower (lambda (x) (* x 0.15)))
      (l-inv (lambda (y) (/ y 0.15))))
   ((M+ WFtl Lcm)(exact (* 0.0006 (square (x))))
      (e-inv (sqrt (/ y 0.0006))))))
```

4   Illustrative Example

4.1   Prototype Project

To illustrate the semi-quantitative simulation, we select AHM's EXAMPLE project, a prototype project for experimentation. EXAMPLE is a medium-size project and the workforce level is calculated by COCOMO. Its main attributes are shown in Table 2.

AHM specified two scenarios to investigate an aggressive manpower acquisition policy which adds new personnel at day 260, when testing starts, and increase the

Table 2. Attributes of EXAMPLE Project

Attributes	Values
Project size	64 KDSI
Man-days	3,795 man-days
Duration	430 days
Initial team size	4 men
Maximum team size	8/18 men
Average ratio of Productivity	0.5
Ratio of experienced mentors to novices	0.2
Average productivity of experienced workforce	36 DSI/man-day

Table 3. Value Ranges of Q2 Extension

Parameters	Value Ranges
Initial experienced workforce	[4 5] men
Newly hired workforce	[3 4][1]/[11 12][2]/[7 8][3] men
Ratio of Productivity	[0.4 0.6]
Ratio of experienced mentors to novices	[0.15 0.25]
Assimilation delay	[60 80]days

total workforce either to 8 or 18 [5]. We replicate these two scenarios in semi-quantitative simulation, and add one medium scenario for comparison: adding [3 4] new staff at day 260 (*Scenario 1*), adding [11 12] new staff at day 260 (*Scenario 2*); and adding [7 8] new staff at day 260 (*Scenario 3*).

With reference to the quantitative extension and EXAMPLE project, the numeric ranges assigned to parameters of the semi-quantitative model are shown in Table 3.

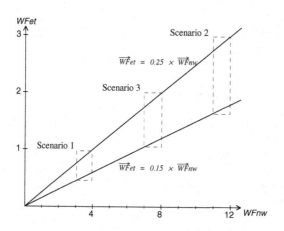

Fig. 3. Envelope Function of $(M+ WF_{TL} L_{CM})$

Accordingly, the monotonic envelope function $(M+ WF_{TL} L_{CM})$ has been updated with the value ranges of workforce as Fig. 3. The area of the broken line rectangle between two linear equations indicates the possible value range for each scenario.

4.2 Possible Behaviors

The QSIM staffing model generates 112 possible behaviors [9]. They can be classified into two categories:

Type 1: behaviors only passing the first transition point when the new staff are injected, i.e. the project finishes before the assimilation is complete;
Type 2: behaviors also passing the second transition point when the assimilation completes, and then being followed by project closure.

After the quantitative constraint propagation, Q2 outputs only 9 behaviors for Scenario 1 and 3 behaviors for Scenario 2 as final solutions. Comparing with the behaviors generated by QSIM, we found that all behaviors of Scenario 2 and 3 behaviors of Scenario 1 are Type 1, passing single transition, and other behaviors of Scenario 1 are Type 2, i.e. passing both transitions. (The behaviors of Scenario 3 are a mix of 2 of Type 1 plus 3 of Type 2.)

Fig. 4 shows the changes of main variables in Beh. 1 of Scenario 1. It is similar to the changes in most behaviors except the different numeric ranges of the landmarks.

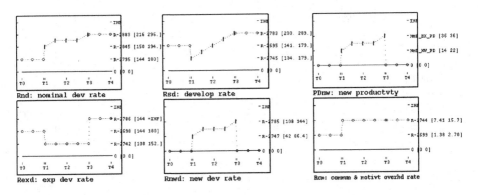

Fig. 4. Behavior 1 of Scenario 1

4.3 Software Development Rate

Because the project duration and development speed are directly determined by *software development rate* (R_{SD}), it can be regarded as the critical variable of our model. It also exhibits complex changes and important differences among the behaviors.

Fig. 5 shows three behavior patterns of R_{SD} in scenario 2, which are similar in scenario 1: when the new staff are injected, 1) R_{ND} ascends and R_{SD} falls immediately; 2) R_{ND} increases and R_{SD} starts to increase gradually; 3) both climb suddenly.

All behaviors indicate that the training overhead is less than the additional development rate of the new workforce. Pattern 1 implies the *communication and motivation overhead* (R_{CM}) is greater than the increase of R_{ND}. It results in the drop-off of R_{SD}. Whereas, R_{CM} is equal to and less than the extra R_{ND} in Pattern 2 and 3.

We note that Pattern 2 and 3 may be inconsistent with Brooks' Law, i.e. adding manpower imposes no negative impact on the overall software development productivity.

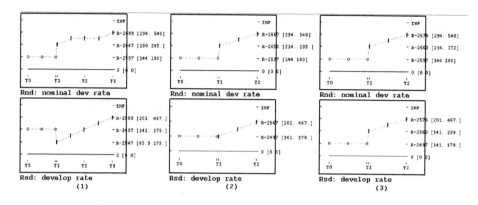

Fig. 5. Behavior Patterns of R_{ND} and R_{SD} in Scenario 2

4.4 Project Completion

The *remaining size* (S_R) and *completed size* (S_C) change in opposite directions during the project, at the *Software Development Rate* (R_{SD}). By investigating its behaviors in Fig. 5, the positive impact of new staff injection can be easily identified (Pattern 2 and 3), and it must lead to reduction in completion time.

Table 4. Simulated Project Completion Times

Scenario	Completion	Comment
S1	[339 423]days	add [3 4] @ day 260
S2	[309 386]days	add [11 12] @ day 260
S3	[320 396]days	add [7 8] @ day 260

Table 4 illustrates the simulated value ranges of project closure time for each scenario, instead of one numeric result generated from the quantitative model.

Fig. 6 shows the envelopes against the original completion time (430 days). Each rectangle indicates the injected new workforce and the corresponding possible project

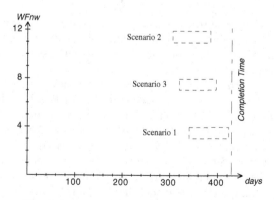

Fig. 6. Project Durations of Workforce Scenarios

duration. Given these three scenarios, it is guaranteed that the EXAMPLE project can finish earlier than initially planned.

5 Comparison and Discussion

Because a semi-quantitative simulation model may generate more than one possible behavior of a system, it cannot be fully evaluated by particular sets of quantitative data. In this section, we conduct the comparison with the previous related models.

5.1 Comparison with AHM's Model

AHM's model provides detailed insights into what happens under several assumptions as to how much manpower is added and when. According to their simulation, the completion times are less than but close to 400 days [5]. This outcome is included in the value ranges generated by the semi-quantitative model (Table 4). AHM also identified that new personnel always have an immediate negative impact on *software development rate*, and concluded that "Adding more people to a late project always makes it more costly, but it does not always cause it to be completed later".

Based on the outputs through the semi-quantitative simulation (Section 4),

1. adding new personnel might bring the immediate negative or positive impact on software development rate, but it does not always make a project completed later;
2. adding a large number of new staff in a late phase (e.g. testing) obviously makes the project costly, and might contribute more slightly to the schedule (Fig. 6).

These findings are supported by the results of AHM's and Madachy's models.

5.2 Discussion

For the specified scenarios, the semi-quantitative simulation indicates that the EXAMPLE project is mostly completed earlier than the original completion time. Thus, it is inconsistent with Brooks' Law. Other researchers also found Brooks' Law questionable. They suggested the causes as being the number of new manpower hired and when. In our model, we can identify other factors that may cause this result. These factors are located among the variables associated with the value ranges and the constrained monotonic functions, i.e. $M+$ or $M-$.

Assimilation delay. Different researchers reports very different assimilation delay values. The actual delay is affected by many factors. Our model uses a quantitative value range instead of a specific value allowing all consequent possible behaviors and their corresponding impacts to be examined.

New employees' productivity. The low productivity of new manpower is believed to be the vital factor that leads to the immediate decline of R_{SD}. Its value is different in different quantitative models. In contrast, the semi-quantitative model assumes the low productivity of new employees is [0.4 0.6] of experienced personnel's.

Ratio of experienced mentors relative to novices. Most researchers agree that the ratio should be set between 0.15 to 0.25 rather than a specific number. Adding more people results in an increase in trainers, which may increase the impact in the purely quantitative model. The semi-quantitative model simulates all possible states consistent with the specified range.

Thus, the practical meaning of Brooks' Law is to warn project managers against blindly making a simplistic response to a late project. However, by applying appropriate hiring, training and task assignment strategies, it is possible to assimilate novices without the consequent schedule problems.

6 Conclusion and Future Work

This paper reports a study of the applicability of semi-quantitative simulation to the software staffing process modeling with a set of qualitative assumptions and quantitative bounds. Semi-quantitative modeling and simulation are presented as powerful techniques for developing and running models if there is incomplete knowledge and uncertain scenarios. They allow qualitative models to be progressively refined while maintaining the integrity of final solutions. By contrast, a purely quantitative simulation is a one-point sample of the possible solutions [3]. Even if sensitivity analysis is applied, it only focuses on the finite impact of one factor with the risk of missing important behaviors and states of the process.

Semi-quantitative techniques can be extended to encompass other aspects of software process. Our future research plans include:

1. Investigating the use of semi-quantitative modeling in other areas of software engineering, e.g. modeling the relationships among the software risk factors.
2. Developing a procedure for evaluating non-quantitative (i.e. qualitative and semi-quantitative) simulation models of software process.

References

1. Abdel-Hamid, T., *The Dynamics of Software Project Staffing: A System Dynamics Based Simulation Approach.* IEEE Transactions on Software Engineering, 1989. 15(2): p. 109-119.
2. Ramil, J.F., Smith, N., *Qualitative Simulation of Models of Software Evolution.* Software process: Improvement and Practice, 2002. 7: p. 95-112.
3. Kuipers, B.J., *Qualitative Reasoning: Modeling and Simulation with Incomplete Knowledge.* . 1994, Cambridge, Massachusetts: MIT Press.
4. Kuipers, B., *Qualitative Simulation*, in *Encyclopedia of Physical Science and Technology*, R.A. Meyers, Editor. 2001, NY: Academic Press. p. 287-300.
5. Abdel-Hamid, T.K., Madnick., S.E., *Software Project Dynamics: An Integrated Approach.* 1991, Englewood Cliffs, NJ: Prentice-Hall.
6. Madachy, R., Tarbet D., *Case Studies in Software Process Modeling with System Dynamics.* Software process: Improvement and Practice, 2000. 5: p. 133-146.
7. Stutzke, R.D., *A Mathematical Expression of Brooks's Law*, in *Ninth International Forum on COCOMO and Cost Modeling.* 1994: Los Angeles.
8. Brooks, F.P., *The Mythical Man-Month: Essays on Software Engineering* 1975: Addison-Wesley.
9. Zhang, H., Huo, M., Kitchenham, B., Jeffery, R., *Qualitative Simulation Model for Software Engineering Process,* in *Australian Software Engineering Conference.* 2006: Sydney

Analysis of Software-Intensive System Acquisition Using Hybrid Software Process Simulation*

KeungSik Choi and Doo-Hwan Bae

Department of EECS, Korea Advanced Institute of Science and Technology (KAIST),
Daejon 305-701, Korea
{kschoi, bae}@se.kaist.ac.kr

Abstract. Many sources have reported that the technical and managerial maturity of the acquirer is the essential key to success of Software-Intensive System Acquisition (SISA) and recommended to adopt the best practices. However, DoD is inactive to implement the SISA practices because DoD doesn't fully understand how and why the SISA practices affect the performance of software-intensive system development.

In this research, we analyze the effects of SISA practices on acquirer and developer using hybrid software process simulation modeling. Our approach represents the dynamic characteristics (e.g., the interactions of acquisition organization and development organization and the effects of several SISA practices) and discrete characteristics (e.g., specific characteristics of discrete phase, etc.) of SISA programs. This research will contribute to reveal how the acquirer's activities influence the performance of the developer's process.

1 Introduction

The software is becoming a more dominant portion in defense systems such as weapon systems and C4I systems (Command, Control, Communications, Computers and Intelligence). Based on the report of the Defense Science Board (DSB) in 2000, the percentage of functionality requiring software of F-16 combat aircraft is 45% and that of F-22 is 80% [1]. Moreover, the annual cost to acquire, develop, and maintain defense software is approaching 20 Billion dollars [1].

The software-intensive characteristic of a defense system increases the complexity and uncertainty in Software-Intensive System Acquisition (SISA). A number of reports from the Inspector General (IG) and General Accounting Office (GAO) have raised issues with the way the U.S. DoD acquires software-intensive systems, and have identified numerous acquisition programs to be late, over-budget, and low quality [2][3].

The DSB concluded that the software acquisition problems came not from technical difficulties, but from poor management and recommended to adopt

---

* This work was supported by the Ministry of Information & Communication, Korea, under the Information Technology Research Center (ITRC) Support Program.

Q. Wang et al. (Eds.): SPW/ProSim 2006, LNCS 3966, pp. 254–261, 2006.

best practices for SISA [1] such as DoD-5000.2-R [4], 16 Critical Practices from Software Program Managers Network (SPMN) [5], Software Acquisition Capability Maturity Model (SA-CMM) [6], etc. A Best practice is a documented practice aimed at lowering an identified risk in system acquisition [7]. The practices are identified to improve the performance of the acquisition organization whose roles are illustrated in Fig. 1.

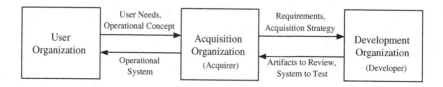

Fig. 1. Roles of acquisition organization in SISA

However, DoD was inactive in response to recommendations to implement best practices. Turner reported that the actual implementation is average 25% in 2002 [7]. Lisa Pracchia, a member of the Naval Air Systems Command's Software Resource Center, stated that subsequent DoD's inaction in response to GAO's recommendations played a pivotal role in Congress legislating software acquisition process improvement [8].

This phenomena indicate that there are some barriers to implement the acquisition practices in defense acquisition organizations. Some of the barriers reported were lack of management understanding, management commitment, and credible evidence [7]. This implies the acquisition managers don't fully understand how and why the acquisition best practices affect the performance of software intensive system development and don't believe the importance and effectiveness of the acquisition management practices.

In this research, we analyze the relationships between acquirer and developer and the effects of acquisition practices using hybrid software process simulation modeling (SPSM) method. This will help acquisition managers understand the importance of and evaluate the effects of the acquisition practices on software development organizations. We study the characteristics of SISA, analyze the potential effects of acquisition practices qualitatively, derive the quantitative information, and implement the simulation model.

We plan to apply the DEVS-based hybrid SPSM [9] method to realistically model the SISA. The military project usually takes long time, develops a large size product, and constrains the development process to follow various military standards (e.g., DoD 5000 series), which strictly distinguishes the milestones. The staffing profile can change discontinuously during the development because of the long development time and unexpected subcontract change. Moreover, large military software projects devote more effort to producing paper documents and to removing bugs or defects than to producing source code [10]. Therefore, we need a hybrid simulation modeling method which can analyze the specific characteristics of each phase with continuously changing dynamic properties.

The structure of this paper is as follows. In Section 2, we introduce previous SPSM approaches for acquisition. In Section 3, we qualitatively analyze the effects of SISA practices on acquisition programs and describe the hybrid simulation modeling approach. Section 4 describes the expected results and contributions.

2   Related Work

Häberlein [11] developed a system dynamics model for software acquisition projects. He captured causal structures common to all models of acquisition projects and designed a system dynamics framework focuses on the supplier monitoring and controlling activity. He analyzed that the acquisition projects are more complex because of the subjective variables such as perceived state of the project and reported state of the project. However, Häberlein's model does not clearly define the interactions between acquirer's and supplier's activities.

McCray and Clark [12] developed a system dynamics model for outsourcing decision support. The questions they ask and the problems they model are different from our research goal. They ask "Given a certain market or organizational situation, is it advisable to outsource software development and maintenance in the long run?".

D. Houston [13] identified significant software development risk factors and developed a dynamic simulation model to study the effects of risk factors. He developed the base model from published system dynamics models such as Abdel-Hamid & Madnick [14] and Tvedt [15], then incorporated the effects of risk factors in the base model. The simulation model is used to support risk analysis and risk management in software development organization. This approach gave us some insight into how to model the effects of acquisition practices on software development organization.

3   Develop Simulation Model for SISA

3.1   Qualitative Analysis of the Effects of Acquisition Practices

Fig. 2 qualitatively analyzes the relationships between acquirer and developer and describes the potential effects of acquisition practices on SISA. This figure does not include all the aspects of SISA, but tries to represent the most influential factors of general SISA environment. We derive the developer's external risk factors caused by the lack of acquirer's technical and managerial maturity, which affect the performance of the developer. The acquirer's technical and managerial maturity represents the overall performance of the acquirer, which is caused by many factors as shown in Fig. 2. The acquisition practices improve the technical and managerial maturity of the acquirer and mitigate or eliminate the external risk factors of developers.

We derive the developer's external risk factors by literature review [10][16][17], experts interview, and our experience: "Creeping requirements", "Excessive paperwork", "Long review/approval cycles", and "Variability in development process".

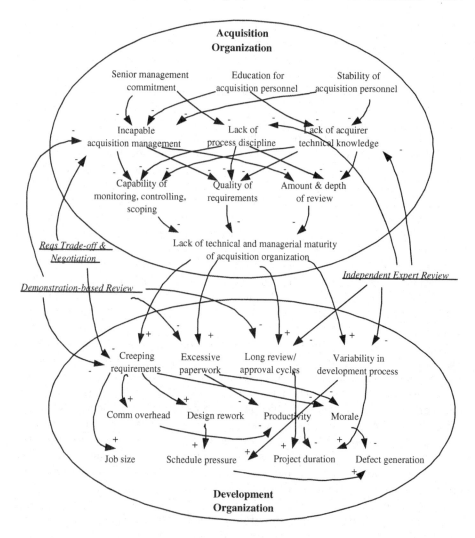

Fig. 2. Qualitative analysis of SISA

"Creeping requirements" are the requirements emerging slowly after basic requirements have been agreed, which cause the job size, communication overhead,
and design rework to be increased and the morale to be decreased. "Excessive
paperwork" can be caused by bureaucratic acquisition organization which ad-
heres to overly detailed development process or caused by acquisition staff inex-
perience, etc. "Excessive paperwork" makes the productivity and morale to be
lowered. "Long review/approval cycles" are due to the lack of acquirer's technical
knowledge on the project or lack of process discipline, which cause the project
duration increased. "Variability in development process" is caused by acquirer's
lack of process discipline, which causes the schedule pressure to be high and the
project duration to be increased.

We also define the acquirer's risk factors which affect the performance of the acquirer. We use negative names for risk factors rather than neutral names to represent the acquisition practices to mitigate the risk factors. In contrast to the developer, the acquirer does not produce the software system directly but monitors and controls the development process. Based on these characteristics of acquirer, we define the performance of an acquirer as follows: "Capability of monitoring, controlling, scoping", "Quality of requirements", and "Amount & depth of review". If the "Capability of monitoring, controlling, scoping" is low, the developer is put at risk of "Creeping requirements" and "Excessive paperwork". If the "Quality of requirements" are low, the developer can suffer the "Creeping requirements" risk. If the "Amount & depth of review" is small & not intensive, the developer can be in trouble of "Long review/approval cycles".

We analyze some of the acquisition practices discussed in Turner [7] for our research. Fig. 2 explains that the acquisition practices can mitigate the risk factors of SISA if an acquisition program adopts the practices. The *Requirements Trade-off and Negotiation* practice requires Program Managers to explicitly trade required functionality for schedule, time, project/product stability, and risk without compromising the overall system objectives [1]. This practice can mitigate the risks of "Incapable acquisition management" and "Creeping requirements".

The *Demonstration-based Review* recommends using executable demonstrations of relevant scenarios as an integral part of project reviews to stimulate earlier convergence on integration, support tangible understanding of design trade-offs, and eliminate architectural defects as early as possible [7]. This practice can mitigate the risks of "Incapable acquisition management", "Creeping requirements", "Excessive paperwork", and "Long review/approval cycles".

The *Independent Expert Review* intends to help the acquirer ensure that: the disciplined processes and methodologies are in place, the program's resources are adequately allocated, the technical baseline is understood and solid with attendant risks and opportunities identified and managed, and the adequate progress is being achieved [1]. The review team should consist of government, academic, and industry experts who have program and software management skills, technical skills appropriate to the program, and requisite domain knowledge. This practice can mitigate the risks of "Lack of process discipline", "Lack of acquirer's technical knowledge", "Long review/approval cycles", and "Variability in development process".

3.2   Hybrid SPSM for SISA

The software process simulation model should represent the dynamic interactions between acquirer and developer as well as discrete characteristics of SISA. The SISA program usually takes long time and distinguishes the milestones strictly, which makes the development phase to have specific characteristics (e.g., different production rate in each phase and discretely changing quality of staff).

Fig. 3 illustrates the high level view of software process simulation model for SISA. The process model of a developer should have an explicit interaction points to integrate with the acquirer's practice modules. Some of the practices can only be applied to a specific phase of a developer. The practice modules are plugged in to evaluate the effects on the development organization's process.

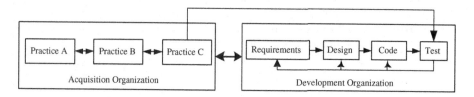

Fig. 3. High level view of hybrid SPSM for SISA

We apply the DEVS-based Hybrid SPSM approach which fully incorporates the feedback mechanism of the system dynamics, explicitly represents the discrete process phase, and analyzes the performance of it [9]. This approach also provides the explicit extension points to easily integrate the process models. For more detailed description, please read K.S. Choi et al. [9].

The simulation model implementation is still in progress at this point. We are implementing the base model of the development organization which shows the characteristics of the large size military software project by analyzing the previous models such as Tvedt [15] and Houston [13]. We are implementing the simulation model of the acquisition organization and deriving the parameters and equations for the model from the literatures and surveys.

Table 1 shows an excerpt of the SISA best practice profile reported in Turner's dissertation [7]. He surveyed various software-intensive system working groups[1] including renowned researchers such as Dr. Victor Basili, Dr. Barry Boehm, and Dr. Lawrence Putnam. Turner analyzed the responding data and developed a best practice profile which provides a reference for a practice that would include descriptive, qualitative, and quantitative information as shown in Table 1.

Table 1 provides high-level data for relationships between SISA practices and the performance of the project, so we will use the information as a reference behavior mode and to validate our simulation model. We also plan to apply the V&V guidelines by Richardson [18]. This will make our model useful to SISA managers.

4 Expected Results and Contributions

We defined the interactions between acquisition organization and development organization in SISA. The performance of the acquisition organization such as "Capability of monitoring, controlling, and scoping", "Quality of requirements",

---

[1] the Defense Software Collaborators, the Software Engineering Science and Technology Summit, the National Defense Industrial Association, the Tri-service Assessment Initiative assessor cadre, etc.

Table 1. Excerpt of the SISA practices profile [7]

Software-intensive System Acquisition Best Practice Profile	
Name	**Requirements trade-off and negotiation**
Description	Within a funding constrained environment, engaging in the explicit trade-off between required functionality, schedule, time, and risk without compromising overall system objectives

Characteristics	Overall Result
Ease of Implementation	Moderate (4-6%)
Cost to Apply	Moderate (4-6%)
Cost to Achieve Readiness	Moderate (4-6%)
Benefit to Cost (Effort)	High (15-30%)
Benefit to Schedule	Very High (> 30%)
Benefit to Quality (Defects)	High (15-30%)

and "Amount & depth of review" affects the external risk factors of the development organization. The external risk factors of the development organization affect the performance of the SISA program. The SISA practices are effective because they mitigate or eliminate the risks of acquisition organization and development organization. We analyzed the effects of the acquisition practices on the SISA programs qualitatively and showed the high level view of the DEVS-based hybrid software process simulation model.

We expect to develop a simulation model which can show the effects of SISA practices quantitatively. The results will contribute to persuade the decision makers and managers of SISA to fully understand and believe the importance of acquisition practices to make a success of SISA. Particularly, this research will reveal how the activities of the acquisition organization influence the performance of the development organization's process and provide integrative view on the SISA program. Furthermore, we can use this simulation model as a decision support system by analyzing the effects of new acquisition practices before actually implementing the practices.

However, this research is still in progress and has difficulties to derive the parameter values and equations for the simulation model. The most difficult problem is validating our model to give confidence on our results because we have very limited historical project data on SISA.

References

1. Defense Science Board (2000), Report of the Defense Science Board Task Force on Defense Software, Washington, DC, Department of Defense, (2000)
2. Summary of Audits of Acquisition of Information Technology, Washington, DC, Office of the Inspector General, Department of Defense, (2000)
3. Defense Software: Review of Defense Report on Software Development Best Practices, Washington, DC, General Accounting Office, (2000)

4. DoD Regulation 5000.2-R, Mandatory Procedures for Major Defense Acquisition Programs (MDAPS) and Major Automated Information System (MAIS) Acquisition Programs, Washington, DC, Department of Defense, (2002)
5. 16 Critical Software Practices For Performance-Based Management, Version 5.2, Inegratred Computer Engineering
6. J. Cooper and M. Fisher: Software Acquisition Capability Maturity Model (SA-CMM), Version 1.03, Pittsburgh, PA, Carnegie Mellon University: Software Engineering Institute, (2002)
7. R. Turner: Implementation of Best Practices in US Department of Defense Software-Intensive System Acquisition, Ph.D Dissertation, The School of Engineering and Applied Science, George Washington University, (2002)
8. Lisa Pracchia: Improving the DoD Software Acquisition Processes, CrossTalk: The Journal of Defense Software Engineering, April, (2004)
9. KeungSik Choi, Doo-Hwan Bae, and TagGon Kim: An Approach to a Hybrid Software Process Simulation using DEVS Formalism, Software Process Improvement and Practice, John Wiley & Sons, NJ (2006), will be published in Special Issue of ProSim'05
10. Capers Jones: Software Cost Estimation Methods for Large Projects, CrossTalk: The Journal of Defense Software Engineering, April, (2005)
11. T. Häberlein: Common Structures in System Dynamics Models of Software Acquisition Projects, Software Process Improvement and Practice, John Wiley & Sons, NJ **9** (2004) 67-80
12. McCray G.E. and Clark T.D.: Using system dynamics to anticipate the organizational impacts of outsourcing, System Dynamics Review **15**(4) (1999) 345-373
13. D. Houston: A Software Project Simulation Model for Risk Management, Ph.D Dissertation, Department of Computer Science & Engineering, Arizona State University, Tempe, AZ (2000)
14. T. Abdel-Hamid and S. Madnick: Software Project Dynamics: An Integrated Approach, Prentice-Hall, Englewood Cliffs, NJ, (1991)
15. J. Tvedt: An extensible model for evaluating the impact of process improvement on software development cycle time, Ph.D Dissertation, Department of Computer Science & Engineering, Arizona State University, Tempe, AZ (1996)
16. Capers Jones: Applied Software Measurement, Second Edition, McGraw-Hill, NY, (1996)
17. The Thomsett Company: Managing Large Projects, (2000) http://www.thomsett.com.au/main/articles/largeprojects/ managing_large_projects.pdf,
18. G.P. Richardson and A.L. Pugh: Introduction to System Dynamics Modeling with DYNAMO, The M.I.T. Press, Cambridge, MA, (1981)

Simulation-Based Stability Analysis for Software Release Plans

Dietmar Pfahl[1], Ahmed Al-Emran[1,2], and Günther Ruhe[1,2]

[1] University of Calgary, Schulich School of Engineering, Calgary, Canada
[2] University of Calgary, Software Engineering Decision Support Laboratory, Calgary, Canada
{dpfahl, aalemran, ruhe}@ucalgary.ca

Abstract. Release planning for incremental software development assigns features to releases such that most important technical, resource, risk and budget constraints are met. The research presented in this paper is based on a three staged procedure. In addition to an existing method for (i) strategic release planning that maps requirements to subsequent releases and (ii) a more fine-grained planning that defines resource allocations for each individual release, we propose a third step, i.e., (iii) stability analysis, which analyzes proposed release plans with regards to their sensitivity to unforeseen changes. Unforeseen changes can relate to alterations in expected personnel availability and productivity, feature-specific task size (measured in terms of effort), and degree of task dependency (measured in terms of work load that can only be processed if corresponding work in predecessor tasks has been completed). The focus of this paper is on stability analysis of proposed release plans. We present the simulation model REPSIM (Release Plan Simulator) and illustrate its usefulness for stability analysis with the help of a case example.

1 Introduction

Software release planning addresses the assignment of requirements to a sequence of releases. This process is a central planning task in incremental software development. The task is of extreme importance because without a good release plan, critical features are not provided at the right time. This might result in unsatisfied customers, time and budget overruns, and in decreased competitiveness. However, the question is how to determine 'good' release plans, e.g., plans that are efficient in terms of the resources to be used and effective in terms of the stated objective(s).

Both the formulation and solution of the planning problem is inherently difficult. Many factors of uncertainty are impacting the actual release decisions. The requirements to be assigned are not necessarily well understood. They are evolving over time. The effort estimates the planning is based upon are uncertain as well. The overall development process is human driven, and this again imposes uncertainties on the availability and productivity of the involved resources.

Decision support is considered an unstructured or semi-structured problem where you support the actual human user in the process to make decisions. Support might refer to different stages of the problem solving process to

Q. Wang et al. (Eds.): SPW/ProSim 2006, LNCS 3966, pp. 262–273, 2006.

(i)   facilitate understanding and structuring of the problem under investigations,

(ii)   understand the information needs for making good decisions,

(iii)   provide access to information that would otherwise be unavailable or difficult to obtain;

(iv)   generate and evaluate solution alternatives,

(v)   prioritize alternatives by using explicit models that provides structure for particular decisions, and

(vi)   explain solution alternatives.

In this paper, we consider decision support for software release planning with emphasis on evaluating solution alternatives in terms of their robustness to changes of problem parameters. For real-world decision-making it is important to know if and to what extend a proposed release plan remains feasible in the case of changes to the underlying developing process, changes in the availability of resources, or changes in the effort consumed to realize the proposed requirements. The purpose of our research is to proactively evaluate the impact of potential changes and initiate adaptive actions. Simulation is a fundamental and well-proven technique to address these issues.

The approach is applicable for a solution received from any of the existing release planning methods. However, the results are the more meaningful, the more qualified the proposed solution is. For our purposes, we consider a three staged solution procedure: (i) Planning of releases on a strategic level (which requirements are expected to be in which release?), (ii) Planning on a more fine-grained level for the next release (which resources are allocated to which tasks?) and (iii) Analyzing stability (for a proposed plan: how robust is the plan against changes?). In the remainder of the paper, we exclusively focus on stage (iii). Detailed information on existing methods supporting stages (i) and (ii) can be found in [9].

The paper is structured into five sections. Section 2 gives an overview of existing related work. Section 3 introduces and describes the simulation model REPSIM. Section 4 illustrates the applicability and usefulness of REPSIM with the help of a case example. Finally, Section 5 provides conclusions and makes suggestions for future extensions of REPSIM.

2   Related Work

A comparative analysis of both formal and informal release planning approaches was done in [11]:

- Estimation-Based Management Framework for Enhancive Maintenance [8]
- Incremental Funding Method [2],
- Cost-Value Approach for Prioritizing Requirements [6],
- Optimizing Value and Cost in Requirements Analysis [5],
- The Next Release Problem [1],
- Planning Software Evolution with Risk Management [3], and
- Hybrid Intelligence (EVOLVE*) [10].

Tasks, Features, and Developers serve as index variables. In addition, a level variable S (size) represents the amount of effort that – according to expert estimates – has to be spent on a specific task (per feature). The size level S is controlled by the rate variables S-inflow and S-outflow:

ReleasePlanner® (www.releaseplanner.com) is a tool suite that provides a flexible and web-based support for release planning. The tool was developed in the Laboratory for Software Engineering Decision Support (http://www.seng-decisionsupport.ucalgary.ca), University of Calgary, Canada. The overall architecture of this approach called EVOLVE* [10] is designed as an iterative and evolutionary procedure mediating between the real world problem of software release planning, the available tools of computational intelligence for handling explicit knowledge and crisp data, and the involvement of human intelligence for tackling tacit knowledge and fuzzy data. The existing approach provides a two-staged optimization method for solving both issues -- feature placement in subsequent releases and optimal resource allocation. Stage (i) applies integer programming to a relaxed version of the full problem. Stage (ii) uses genetic programming to generate operational plans for the involved human and non-human resources.

The simulation model REPSIM (Release Plan Simulator) studied in this paper is a continuation of the effort to combine computationally efficient methods for generating and analyzing solutions with human expertise. In our case, the expert is supposed to get early indication of potential risks and bottlenecks. Based on simulation results from REPSIM, re-planning of individual releases can be initiated.

To our knowledge, there exists only one simulation model that directly addresses the release planning problem [4]. This model helps analyzing release planning management processes by investigating potential bottlenecks within individual releases induced by requirements prioritization and resulting requirements distributions over subsequent releases. All analyses, however, are conducted on a coarse-grain level and do not take under consideration feature-specific assignment of individual resources (developers) to tasks (e.g., design, implementation, test). Hence, this model mainly relates to strategic release planning (stage (i) of our solution procedure), while REPSIM evaluates individual releases by systematically varying crucial parameters of a proposed release plan on a detailed level.

3   The REPSIM Model

REPSIM is a process simulation model that makes extensive use of subscripting in order to allow for individual representation of multiple features, tasks, and resources (developers). It was developed using the VENSIM® (http://www.vensim.com), a System Dynamics modeling and simulation tool.

3.1   Model Variables and Parameters

The current version of REPSIM defines the following variables:

- Tasks: T = {T[1], …, T[3]}, with
  T[1] represents "Design",
  T[2] represents "Implementation",
  T[3] represents "Test".
  The set of tasks T can easily be extended if needed.

- Features: F = {F[1], …, F[8]}.
- Developers: D = {D[1], …, D[6]}.

Tasks, Features, and Developers serve as index variables. In addition, a level variable S (size) represents the amount of effort that – according to expert estimates – has to be spent on a specific task (per feature). The size level S is controlled by the rate variables S-inflow and S-outflow:

- Effort to be spent to complete a task (per feature):
  S[j,k], with j = Feature index, k = Task index.
- Inflow rate to define the size of S (in terms of effort) based on the estimated effort of specific (feature, task)-combinations:
  S-inflow, with j = Feature index, k = Task index.
- Outflow rate to reduce the size of S (in terms of effort) by the amount of work spent on a specific (feature, task)-combination:
  S-outflow, with j = Feature index, k = Task index.

The REPSIM model offers the following input parameters (constants):

- Estimated Effort per Feature and Task:
  Eff-F-S[j, k], with j = Feature index, k = Task index.
- Estimated Productivity per Developer and Task:
  Prod-D-S[i, k], with i = Developer index, k = Task index.
- Planned assignment of Developers to (Feature, Task) combinations:
  Lookup-Availability-D-F-S[i, j, k], with i = Developer index, j = Feature index, k = Task index.
- Work load (effort) dependency between subsequent tasks:
  S1-S2-Dependency: percentage of feature-specific implementation work that can only be started if the related design work has been completed.
  S2-S3-Dependency: percentage of feature-specific test work that can only be started if the related implementation work has been completed.
  For both parameters, the default value equals 0, implying that there is no dependency of a task on completion of work in a predecessor task. The other extreme of the range, i.e., a dependency of 100%, implies that a predecessor task must fully be completed before work on a subsequent task can start.

In order to make intermediate calculations explicit, REPSIM defines the following auxiliary variables:

- Work load (effort) transformation factor between subsequent tasks (per feature):
  S1-S2-Transformation[j]: effort relationship between tasks Design and Implementation, with j = Feature index.
  S2-S3-Transformation[j]: effort relationship between tasks Implementation and Test, with j = Feature index.
- Actual productivity of the workforce per (Feature, Task) combinations:
  actual-Prod-D-F-S[i, j, k] , with i = Developer index, j = Feature index, k = Task index.

To support aggregated output presentation, REPSIM defines the following auxiliary variables:

- Aggregated size per task: Sum-S[k], with k = Task index.
- Aggregated size inflow rate per task: Sum-S-inflow[k], with k = Task index.

- Aggregated size outflow rate per task: Sum-S-outflow[k], with k = Task index.
- Aggregated workforce availability per developer: Sum-Availability-D[i], with i = Developer index.

The complete set of model equations can be found in Appendix A.

3.2   Model Structure

Figure 1 shows the structure of the REPSIM model in terms of its flow-graph. The structure is very simple. The subscripted level variable S is in the centre of the model. It represents the size of a (feature, task)-combination represented in terms of effort to be processed. The size level is determined by rate variables S-inflow and S-outflow, using the following integral equation:

$$S[j,k](t) = \int_0^t (S\_inflow[j,k](u) - S\_outflow[j,k](u))du$$

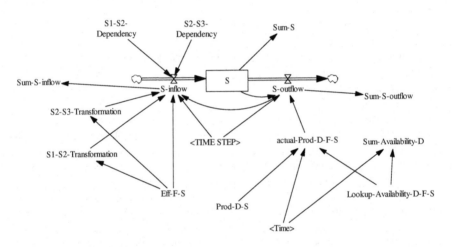

Fig. 1. Flow-graph of REPSIM

3.3   Model Calibration

The calibration of the REPSIM model is straightforward. All parameters are initially set to 0. As soon as effort estimates for (feature, task)-combinations, task-specific developer productivities, workforce allocations to (feature, task)-combinations and the degree of task dependency are known, the parameters Eff-F-S[j, k], Prod-D-S[i, k], Lookup-Availability-D-F-S[i, j, k], S1-S2-Overlap, and S2-S3-Overlap are defined accordingly.

4   Release Planning Simulation Application

In this section, we present a case example using several scenarios to demonstrate the applicability and usefulness of the simulation model REPSIM for analyzing the stability of a proposed release plan. For all scenarios of the case example, the following situation is given:

- Planned duration for realizing the proposed release plan: 12 weeks
- Features included in the release: F1, ..., F8
- Tasks to be conducted per release: T1, ..., T3
- Developers available: D1, ..., D6

The assumed productivity (in person-weeks per week) of developers per task type is shown in Table 1.

Table 1. Productivity of developers per task type

Developer	Task Type		
	T1: Design	T2: Implementation	T3: Test
D1	1.4	2	1.2
D2	1	0	2
D3	2	0	1
D4	1	2	1
D5	1	1.5	2
D6	2	1	2

Table 2. Estimated effort per feature and task, and allocation of developers to tasks

Feat.	Task	Effort	1	2	3	4	5	6	7	8	9	10	11	12
F1	T1	1	D4											
	T2	6		D4	D4	D4								
	T3	6	D5	D5		D5								
F2	T1	8	D6	D6	D6	D6								
	T2	4					D1	D1						
	T3	2						D2						
F3	T1	1				D5								
	T2	10					D4	D4	D4	D4	D4			
	T3	8					D5	D5	D5		D5			
F4	T1	2				D3								
	T2	4							D1	D1				
	T3	6					D6	D6		D6				
F5	T1	6					D3	D3	D3					
	T2	4									D1	D1		
	T3	4						D2			D2			
F6	T1	8								D3	D3	D3	D3	
	T2	6										D4	D4	D4
	T3	1												D1
F7	T1	10							D6		D6	D6	D6	D6
	T2	6								D5		D5	D5	D5
	T3	6								D2	D2			D2
F8	T1	6	D3	D3	D3									
	T2	8	D1	D1	D1	D1								
	T3	10	D2	D2	D2	D2	D2							

The starting point for the stability analyses conducted with the help of REPSIM is a release plan generated by the optimization algorithm described in [7]. The generated release plan is shown in Table 2. For a given set of features and tasks, the release plan allocates developers to (feature, task)-combinations. This allocation is optimal with regards to a defined objective function. The allocation is calculated using information about estimated effort per feature and task, and assumed productivity of developers per task type as defined in Table 1.

4.1 Scenario 1: Baseline

The Baseline scenario reproduces the situation summarized in Table 2. The REPSIM model is calibrated using the data provided in Tables 1 and 2. Moreover, to adequately reflect an underlying assumption of the release planning algorithm, i.e., that per feature all tasks can potentially be conducted in parallel, task dependency is set to 0 (i.e., no task dependency).

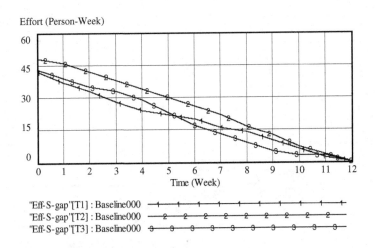

Fig. 2. Work load reduction per task type with S1-S2-Dependency = S2-S3-Dependency = 0

The simulation output for the baseline scenario is shown in Figure 2. It shows per task type, at any point in time during release development, how much work (in terms of estimated effort) still has to be processed. For each task type, the effort is cumulated over all features. As expected, at the end of week 12, all tasks are completed, i.e., the estimated effort has fully been spent.

From the simulation modeling point of view, the baseline scenario can be interpreted as a reference mode of REPSIM. The following scenarios 2 and 3 demonstrate how REPSIM can be used to analyze the stability of the reference mode by altering some of its underlying assumptions or starting conditions.

4.2 Scenario 2: Increasing Task Dependency

One assumption of the optimization algorithm that generated the release plan in Table 2 requires that for each feature a task cannot be finished before the completion of the predecessor task. This is a relatively weak assumption about task dependency. With the help of parameters S1-S2-Dependency and S2-S3-Dependency stronger dependencies between subsequent tasks can be defined. For example, setting both parameters to 1 implies that 100% of the work on a task can only be *started* when the work on the predecessor task (related to the same feature) has been completed.

Figure 3 shows the simulation output for this extreme condition. It can be seen that for the release plan defined in Table 2, there is no relevant effect on work related to Tasks 1 and 2 (Design and Implementation). There is, however, a considerable negative impact on work related to Task 3 (Test). A work backlog of about 12 person-weeks, i.e., 28% of the 43 person-weeks planned in total for Task 3, cannot be processed with the task schedule and developer allocation proposed in Table 2.

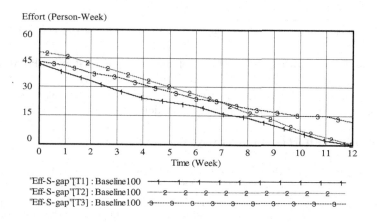

Fig. 3. Work load reduction per task type with S1-S2-Dependency = S2-S3-Dependency = 1

Figure 4 shows for each task type the resulting potential work backlog, if the model variables S1-S2-Dependency and S2-S3-Dependency vary over the full value range [0, 1]. Of particular interest are the values related to Task 3. It can be seen that the proposed feature test plan is stable until a task dependency of 30% is reached. Then, there is a moderate increase of test work backlog until a task dependency of 50% is reached. Beyond 50% task dependency, there is a constant increase of test work backlog up to 12 person-weeks (in the case of 100% task dependency).

The simulation results can be used by a decision maker in several ways. Firstly, the dependencies between implementation and test tasks can be further analyzed. If the test methods and techniques can be applied in its majority without the need to wait for a complete implementation of a feature, the risk of a delayed release is small. Secondly, if the dependency analysis shows tight coupling between test and implementation, the decision maker can try to modify the release plan, e.g., by adding developers

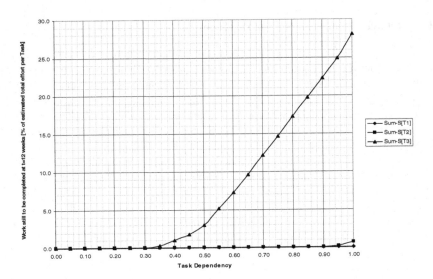

Fig. 4. Task-specific work backlog (cumulated over features) for varying task dependency

and/or revising the task schedules. This re-planning is supported by REPSIM by providing detailed work backlog data for each feature individually (not shown here due to space limitations). Thirdly, the modified release plan can be evaluated by running a new simulation with a re-calibrated REPSIM model.

4.3   Scenario 3: Effort (or Productivity) Variation

The release plan presented in Table 2 is based on feature-specific effort estimates and developer-specific productivities for each task type. REPSIM can be used to analyze the sensitivity of the proposed release plan to variations of these parameters. Since increase in actual effort consumption is comparable to decrease in developer productivity, we will exclusively focus on an effort variation scenario (cf. Figure 5).

As in Section 4.2 (Scenario 2) we express sensitivity to variation in feature-specific task effort in terms of generated work backlog (measured in person-weeks). Figure 5 shows three different simulation outcomes for task dependency set to 0 (Figure 5a), 0.5 (Figure 5b), and 1 (Figure 5c). In all cases, feature specific task effort varies in the interval [0.8, 1.2], representing a factor that is multiplied with the nominal effort estimates of the reference mode (Baseline – Scenario 1).

As is to be expected, in Figure 5a no work backlog is generated if feature-specific task effort is smaller than 100% of the estimated effort (for each feature), while a proportional work backlog is generated if it is above 100%. Figure 5b shows that even if the actual effort needed is 20% below the expert estimate, for Task 3 (Test) there is still work backlog generated, though of relatively marginal size (about 1% of the total estimated effort for testing). Figure 5c shows the most extreme situation (i.e., task dependency = 100%). Even if the actual feature-specific task effort is 20% below the expert estimate, there is still a work backlog of almost 15% for test tasks if no re-planning of the task schedule and developer allocation is performed. Again, as in Scenario 2, REPSIM can be used to evaluate the effectiveness of modified release plans.

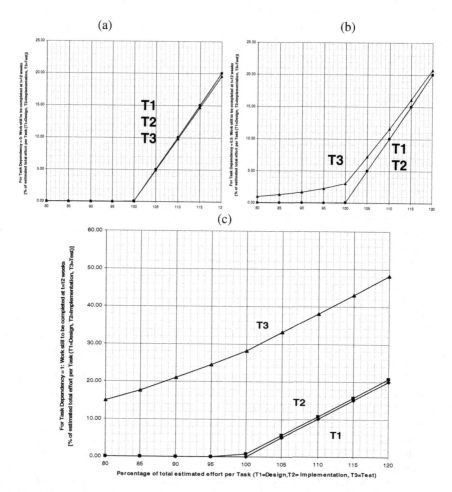

Fig. 5. Task-specific work-backlog (cumulated over features) for varying effort estimates. (a): with task dependency = 0% (b): with task dependency = 50% (c) with task dependency = 100%.

5 Summary and Future Work

In this paper, we presented the idea of a simulation-based approach to stability analysis of proposed release plans. We presented the simulation model REPSIM (Release Plan Simulator) and illustrate its usefulness with the help of a case example, demonstrating the feasibility of the proposed approach.

It should be pointed out, however, that the presented material is just the starting point of a work in progress. Future work will focus on validation of the proposed approach in an industrial environment, improvement of model usability (data input via GUI, connection to data base, etc.), and – most importantly – enhancement of the REPSIM model. Enhancement of REPSIM will in particular aim at adding a heuristic that allows for automatic allocation of unused manpower and for generating proposals for adding additional manpower if needed. Another enhancement aims at capturing feature dependencies within a release and their impact on the order in which features will be tested.

References

1. Bagnall, A.J., Rayward-Smith, V.J., and Whittley, I.M.: The Next Release Problem. Information and Software Technology, Vol. 43, No. 14 (2001) 883-890
2. Denne, M. and Cleland-Huang, J.: The Incremental Funding Method: Data Driven Software Development. IEEE Software, Vol. 21, No. 3 (2004) 39-47
3. Greer, D.: Decision Support for Planning Software Evolution with Risk Management. In: Proceedings of 16th International Conference on Software Engineering and Knowledge Engineering (SEKE'04), Banff, Canada (2004) 503-508
4. Höst, M., Regnell, B., Dag, J., Nedstam, J., and Nyberg, C.: Exploring Bootlenecks in Market-Driven Requirements Management Processes with Discrete Event Simulation. Journal of Systems and Software, Vol. 59, No. 3 (2001) 323-332
5. Jung, H.-W.: Optimizing Value and Cost in Requirements Analysis. IEEE Software (1998) 74-78
6. Karlsson, J. and Ryan, K.: A Cost-Value Approach for Prioritizing Requirements. IEEE Software, Vol. 14, No. 5 (1997) 67-74
7. Ngo-The, A. and Ruhe, G.: Optimized Resource Allocation for Incremental Software Development. Technical Report of the Laboratory for Software Engineering Decision Support, Report No. 049/2006 (2006)
8. Penny, D.A.: An Estimation-Based Management Framework for Enhancive Maintenance in Commercial Software Products. In: Proceedings of International Conference on Software Maintenance (ICSM'02), Montreal, Canada (2002) 122-130
9. Ruhe, G.: Software Release Planning. In: Handbook of Software Engineering and Knowledge Engineering, Vol. 3. World Scientific Publishing (2005) 365-394
10. Ruhe, G. and Ngo-The, A.: Hybrid Intelligence in Software Release Planning. International Journal of Hybrid Intelligent Systems, Vol. 1, No. 2 (2004) 99-110
11. Saliu, O. and Ruhe, G.: Supporting Software Release Planning Decisions for Evolving Systems. In: Proceedings of 29th IEEE/NASA Software Engineering Workshop, Greenbelt, MD, USA, 6-7 April (2005)

Appendix A. Model Equations

"S-inflow"[Feature,T1]="Eff-F-S"[T1,Feature]*PULSE(0,TIME STEP)/TIME STEP
"S-inflow"[Feature,T2]=
      "Eff-F-S"[T2,Feature]*PULSE(0,TIME STEP)/TIME STEP*(1-"S1-S2-Dependency")+"S1-S2-Dependency"*"S-outflow"[Feature,T1]*"S1-S2-Transformation" [Feature]
"S-inflow"[Feature,T3]=
      "Eff-F-S"[T3,Feature]*PULSE(0,TIME STEP)/TIME STEP*(1-"S2-S3-Dependency")+"S2-S3-Dependency"*"S-outflow"[Feature,T2]*"S2-S3-Transformation" [Feature]
S[Feature,Task]= INTEG ("S-inflow"[Feature,Task]-"S-outflow"[Feature,Task],0)
"S-outflow"[Feature,Task]=

MIN(SUM("actual-Prod-D-F-S"[Feature,Task,Developer!])),S[Feature,Task]/
TIME STEP)
"Lookup-Availability-D-F-S"[F1,T1,D1](
    [(0,0)-(12,2)],(0,0),(1,0),(1,0),(2,0),(2,0),(3,0),(3,0),(4,0),(4,0),(5,0),(5,0),(6,
    0),(6,0),(7,0),(7,0),(8,0),(8,0),(9,0),(9,0),(10,0),(10,0),(11,0),(11,0),(12,0))
(…)
"Lookup-Availability-D-F-S"[F8,T3,D6](
    [(0,0)-(12,2)],(0,0),(1,0),(1,0),(2,0),(2,0),(3,0),(3,0),(4,0),(4,0),(5,0),(5,0),(6,
    0),(6,0),(7,0),(7,0),(8,0),(8,0),(9,0),(9,0),(10,0),(10,0),(11,0),(11,0),(12,0))
"Eff-F-S"[Task,Feature]=1,8,1,2,6,8,10,6;6,4,10,4,4,6,6,8;6,2,8,6,4,1,6,10;
"Prod-D-S"[Task,Developer]=1.4,1,2,1,1,2;2,0,0,2,1.5,1;1.2,2,1,1,2,2;
"S1-S2-Dependency"=0
"S2-S3-Dependency"=0
"S1-S2-Transformation"[Feature]="Eff-F-S"[T2,Feature]/"Eff-F-S"[T1,Feature]
"S2-S3-Transformation"[Feature]="Eff-F-S"[T3,Feature]/"Eff-F-S"[T2,Feature]
"actual-Prod-D-F-S"[Feature,Task,Developer]=
    "Prod-D-S"[Task,Developer]*"Lookup-Availability-D-F-S"[Feature,Task,
    Developer](Time)
"Sum-S-inflow"[Task]=SUM("S-inflow"[Feature!,Task])
"Sum-S"[Task]=SUM(S[Feature!,Task])
"Sum-S-outflow"[Task]=SUM("S-outflow"[Feature!,Task])
"Sum-Availability-D"[Developer]=
    SUM("Lookup-Availability-D-F-S"[Feature!,Task!,Developer](Time))
Developer: D1,D2,D3,D4,D5,D6
Task: T1, T2, T3
Feature: F1,F2,F3,F4,F5,F6,F7,F8
FINAL TIME = 12   ~   Week / The final time for the simulation. |
INITIAL TIME = 0   ~   Week / The initial time for the simulation. |

Exploring the Impact of Task Allocation Strategies for Global Software Development Using Simulation

Siri-on Setamanit[1], Wayne Wakeland[2], and David Raffo[1]

[1] School of Business Administration, Portland State University, 631 SW Harrison St.,
Portland, OR, USA
{sirion, raffod}@pdx.edu
[2] Systems Science PhD, Portland State University, 1604 SW 10th Ave., Portland, OR, USA
wakeland@pdx.edu

Abstract. We describe a hybrid computer simulation model of the software development process that is specifically architected to study alternative ways to configure global software development projects, including phased-based, module-based, and follow-the-sun allocation strategies. The model is a hybrid system dynamics and discrete event model. In this paper, test cases have been developed for each allocation strategy, and project duration under each configuration is computed under a range of plausible assumptions for key parameters. The primary finding is that although under ideal assumptions, follow-the-sun is able to produce impressive reductions in time-to-market, under more realistic assumptions the reverse is true, thus corroborating findings by other researchers. Further analysis reveals the presence of some interaction between the assumptions, but the results remain robust.

1 Global Software Development

Since 1990, as communication media have become increasingly advanced, especially with the emergence of the Internet, there has been a growing trend towards the transition of software development from the traditional centralized, co-located form of development to a form in which software teams, working on the same project or system, collaborate across national boundaries or are dispersed geographically, hence the name "Global Software Development (GSD)". Currently, there are almost 100 nations participating in GSD [1]. There are several factors that drive companies to move toward GSD, including reduction in time-to-market, reduction in development costs, better use of scarce resources, and business advantages from proximity to customers [1-5]. The major reasons are reduction in development cost and the reduction in development time [1, 6].

Ideally, with the use of follow-the-sun or 24-hour development, it is expected that the cycle time can be reduced by 20% to 35% [2]. Unfortunately, follow-the sun development requires much more communication and coordination. Together with time-zone difference and cultural and language differences, few GSD projects have been able to realize the full (theoretical) benefits of follow-the-sun.

An IBM team described in Carmel's book [2] decided to abandon follow-the-sun strategy since the daily handoffs between sites were too difficult to coordinate. In

Q. Wang et al. (Eds.): SPW/ProSim 2006, LNCS 3966, pp. 274–285, 2006.

addition, based on an empirical studies, Herbsleb and Mockus found that for work of equal size and complexity, multi-site software development takes much longer than single-site development [7, 8]. The authors further recommend that the way to speed the development is to decouple the work so that each site can operate more independently.

This raises the question whether follow-the-sun development with daily handoffs is the best way to pursue if the goal of the GSD project is to reduce the cycle time. What factors contribute to the delay? Is there any better way to distribute work between sites?

The results from empirical study are often influenced by several factors. It is difficult to separate the factors and identify which factor actually influences the result and to what degree. For example, with empirical study and statistical modeling techniques, Herbsleb et al. [7, 8] found that communication, coordination, and social networks in multi-site development may differ from single-site development such that it requires more people to participate, and therefore introduces additional delays. The authors recognize that several factors such as "teamness" and cultural and language differences may also contribute to delay. Unfortunately, with their research design, it was not possible to assess the relative effect of each of these factors.

We believe that simulation models can be used to help expand and identify the factors that contribute to project delays. In Section 2, we explain how simulation modeling can help address this important issue. This model is a hybrid system dynamics and discrete event simulation model. We provide an overview of our GSD simulation model in Section 3. Experimental results are provided in Section 4, followed by discussion in Section 5.

2 A Simulation Model as an Experimentation Platform

In software engineering it is easy to propose hypotheses; however, it is very difficult to test them [9]. Controlled experiments are costly and time consuming [10], and are nearly impossible to conduct. In addition, the isolation of the effect and the evaluation of the impact of any given factor within a large, complex, and dynamic project environment (such as GSD) can be remarkably difficult [11].

With available empirical data software process simulation models can be constructed and calibrated so that they reflect real world behavior quite accurately. Such models can then be used as an experimental platform to investigate the situation/system and evaluate new hypotheses and theories. By varying individual parameters or combinations thereof, the magnitude and strength of the impact on variables of interest can be measured [12]. Simulation models enable controlled experimentation that allows the researcher to identify factors that profoundly impact the outcome. It is far less costly and less time-consuming to perform experimentation using simulation models.

The next section describes our hybrid simulation model of global software development.

3 A GSD Simulation Model

3.1 GSD Model Structure

As described previously [13], our proposed GSD model is a hybrid model combining system dynamics (SD) and discrete-event (DES) paradigms. A system dynamics sub-model is inspired by and adapted from the system dynamics model of software development created by Abdel-Hamid and Madnick [14]. The interface between SD and DES sub-models is inspired by the hybrid model of the software development process created by Martin [15].

In this paper we will give an overview of the complete GSD model at a high-level. Then, we will describe how the model works, focusing on the unique mechanisms and structures of the model that enable us to investigate alternative GSD configurations.

At a high level, the GSD model has three major components: DES sub-model, SD sub-model, and Interaction Effect (IE) sub-model. The DES sub-model includes a global DES sub-model and a site-specific DES sub-model for each development site. Each development site may have different process steps depending on how tasks are allocated and specific activities are performed. The site-specific DES allows us to represent these differences and to capture their impact. Different time zones are also be modeled. Artifacts or work products pass from one site to another at different times, depending upon the allocation strategy, in order to capture the effect of distribution overhead and distribution effort loss. The global DES sub-model aggregates the information from the site-specific DES sub-models to determine overall project progress.

The SD sub-model includes a global SD sub-model and a site-specific sub-model for each development site. The global SD sub-model captures the overall project environment, including the planning and controlling activities. The global SD sub-model has 3 modules: Human Resources (HR), Planning, and Control. The Human Resources module acts as an interface between HR module from each development site and the other modules in global SD sub-model. The control module receives information about the project progress (from global DES sub-model) and then evaluates whether adjustments to the schedule or the work rate are needed. The planning module monitors and identifies the workforce level required to meet the overall project schedule.

Each development site has its own site-specific SD sub-model. The site-specific SD sub-model represents aspects that may be different between development sites, including human resources (HR), productivity (PD), manpower allocation (MP), and defect generation and detection rates (QA). The HR module deals with human resource management, which includes hiring, training, assimilation, and transferring human resources in a particular site. The PD module models the rate at which developers at a particular site can develop software (productivity rate). The MP module assigns workforce to different activities. The QA module models defect generation, detection, and correction rates.

The IE sub-model comes into play when staff from different sites need to collaborate or work closely together; for example, during follow-the-sun development. When developers work with their colleagues from the same site, information such as productivity and defect rates will be sent from within the site-specific SD sub-models.

However, when developers have to collaborate with their colleagues from other sites, their productivity will be different. The IE sub-model takes those effects into account. More information about the GSD model logic is explained in section 3.2. Section 3.3 provides additional detail about the IE sub-model. Figure 1 shows the overall GSD model structure with two development sites.

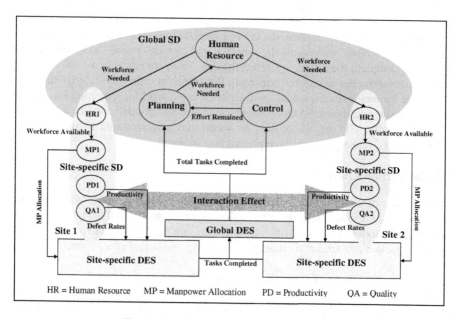

Fig. 1. Overview of the GSD model structure

3.2 GSD Model Logic

The GSD model is designed to be flexible and expandable. At the simplest level, the GSD model can be used to represent a single-site software development project. To add additional development sites, one site-specific SD and one site-specific DES sub-model are added to represent the characteristics of each new development site.

Assume that there are two development sites involved in a project (as shown in Figure 1). The following discussion illustrates how the GSD model works. The site-specific HR modules (HR1 and HR2) will send information about the workforce available to the site-specific MP module. The MP module will allocate the workforce to different tasks such as development and quality assurance. The PD module determines the productivity of the staff (depending on the workforce mix and the schedule pressure). The productivity rate will be sent to the IE module. If the developers in a particular site work only with other developers from the same site, the IE module will pass along the productivity rate to the site-specific DES without any modification. On the other hand, if the developers have to work with their colleagues from other sites, the IE module will modify the productivity rate before sending it to the DES sub-model.

The productivity rate and the manpower will be sent to site-specific DES sub-model. This information drives the software development activity in a particular site. Each site then sends information about tasks completed to the global DES sub-model.

The global DES sub-model aggregates information from all sites to determine the total task completion. The global DES sub-model sends information about total task completion to the control module. The control module reviews the project progress information and determines whether the schedule or work rate should be adjusted. If the schedule should be adjusted, the control module will signal the planning module. The planning module will adjust the schedule and also determine the number of staff needed to complete the remaining project tasks. The planning module will then send information about the workforce needed to the human resource module (in the global SD). The human resource module will determine the workforce needed for each development site and then send the information to site-specific HR module of each site. The site-specific HR module adjusts its workforce to correspond to the workforce needed. This cycle repeats until the project is completed.

3.3   Interaction Effect (IE) Sub-model

The structure of the interaction effect (IE) sub-model is based on literature regarding global software development, distributed development, and virtual teams. Factors and quantitative models relevant to the GSD model are reported in [13]. The IE sub-model impacts many factors including productivity and defect generation.

Interaction Effect on Productivity Rate. For knowledge-based work such as software development, tight coordination among various efforts is required for the project to be successful [16]. Problems of coordination leads to losses in productivity [17, 18]. Due to distance and time-zone differences, coordination within and across multi-site development teams is even more difficult, which further impacts productivity. The IE sub-model calculates the coordination efficiency of the distributed team (relative to the coordination efficiency of the single-site team), and then applies the coordination effect to the productivity before sending it to the DES sub-model. If the coordination efficiency of the distributed team is lower, the productivity will be lower. Figure 2 shows the interaction effects on productivity rate.

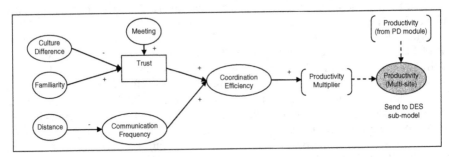

Fig. 2. The interaction effects on productivity rate

There are two primary factors that have a significant impact on coordination efficiency: Communication Frequency and Trust. More information about these two factors is provided in the next two sections.

Communication Frequency. Team members coordinate their work through communication (exchange of information). Several studies of software development projects [16, 19-21] found that informal, unplanned, and ad hoc communication is extremely important in supporting collaboration. Discussions with peers is the most used and valued coordination technique [16]. Thus, teams with frequent communications among their members tend to coordinate better. However, the distance between team members negatively affects the amount of communication [22]. This agrees with the finding by Kraut et al. [23] that physical proximity increases the likelihood of collaboration among scientists. In our GSD model, the IE sub-model will determine the relative frequency of communication when team members are at different sites compared to when they are at the same site. The relative communication frequency will positively impact the coordination efficiency.

Trust. Trust is a basic feature of social situations that requires cooperation and interdependence [24]. Without trust, it is unlikely that a team will work together effectively since the team members are unwilling to communicate openly across sites. Teams with higher trust tend to coordinate better, thus achieve better performance [25].

In the GSD model, trust will be modeled as a dynamic variable. The initial level of trust is determined by culture (individualist or collectivist, as defined by Hofstede [26]) and team member familiarity [27]. People from the same culture develop trust more quickly than people from different cultures. In addition, individuals from an individualistic culture tend to be more ready to trust others than individuals from a collectivist culture [28, 29]. Trust will be higher when team members become more familiar with each other.

Unfortunately, without face-to-face communication, trust tends to decrease overtime [30]. However, the GSD model includes a mechanism that triggers meetings between team members to re-establish trust whenever the trust level falls below a predetermined threshold.

Interaction Effect on Defect Injection Rate. When teams are separated by time and/or distance, communication effectiveness is hampered both in quality and timeliness [31]. Rich communication media (such as face-to-face interaction) tend to be more effective than leaner media (such as telephone or email). The leaner the communication media, the higher the likelihood of miscommunication, which can introduce defects [31]. In addition, different cultures (high-context and low-context [32]) also lead to miscommunication.

In our GSD model, communication media affects the defect generation multiplier. For example, email will lead to higher defect generation multiplier than telephone. The defect generation multiplier is applied to the defect generation rate from the QA module. The value of the defect generation multiplier is based on information from the coordination cost model developed by Espinosa and Carmel [33].

There are 3 factors that determine the choice of communication media: time-zone differences, message urgency, and native language. When there is no overlap working time, the choice of communication media is limited to asynchronous media.

The urgency of communication increases the use of synchronous communication. It has been reported that developers prefer to use telephone over email when the urgency category is within 10 minutes [34]. Regarding language, nonnative English-speaking people prefer asynchronous communication such as email over synchronous since it allows them to read and write at their own pace [35-37]. Therefore, if the developers speak different languages, they will prefer to use email instead of synchronous communication, except when the urgency is within 10 minutes.

Currently, there are three communication media options represented in our model: telephone, instant messaging (chat), and email.

4 Model Results

To illustrate the functionality and the usefulness of the GSD model, we created a simple example project. The example project has 2 development sites (site A and B), and has 5 phases including Requirements (REQ), Design (DES), Coding (CODE), Testing (TEST), and Rework (RWK). We created four model configurations. Each configuration represents a different task allocation strategy as defined by Carmel [2]: single-site, module-based, phase-based, and follow-the-sun, as shown in Figure 3.

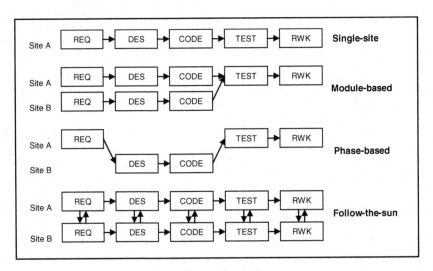

Fig. 3. Four configurations of the GSD model

4.1 Ideal Situation

It has been expected that global software development can reduce the development cycle time, especially the follow-the-sun strategy. In this scenario, we assume that everything is perfect. Developers can coordinate with colleagues from other sites just as efficiently as when they coordinate with their colleagues from the same site. There are no problems regarding cultural or language differences. In other words, the full benefit of GSD can be achieved. To represent this situation, we configure the GSD model to exclude all the effects from GSD factors mentioned in Section 3.3. Figure 4 shows project progress against time for the four configurations.

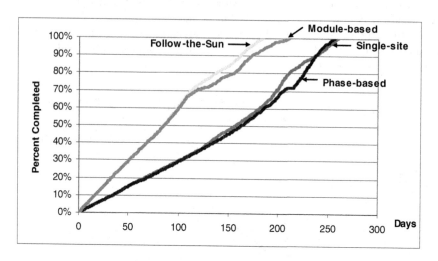

Fig. 4. Project progress comparison (Ideal Situation)

As expected by GSD enthusiasts, when everything works perfectly, follow-the-sun development has the shortest development cycle time. The development cycle time using follow-the-sun strategy is about 70% of the time it takes using single site. Module-based took a little longer than the follow-the-sun strategy since there is only one site working at the end of the development cycle. Phase-based took about the same time as single site since we assumed that the staff in both sites has approximately the same productivity rate.

4.2 Real World Situation

As mentioned before, there are several factors that may affect the efficiency and the effectiveness of the development in distributed environment. In this scenario, we include all the GSD factors described in section 3.3 such as coordination costs due to distance, language differences, time zone differences, culturally differences and so forth. Figure 5 shows the project progress against time for the four configurations.

When GSD factors are taken into account, the follow-the-sun strategy is no longer is the shortest. Communication and coordination problems coupled with cultural and language differences make it difficult to coordinate, which reduces the development productivity. Follow-the-sun took about 37% longer than single-site development. This agrees with the finding that multi-site development can take longer than single-site development [8].

The module-based approach has the shortest cycle time. This agrees with Herbsleb et al.'s [7, 8, 21] suggestion that the best strategy is to decouple the work so that each site can operate more independently.

One can imagine that it may be possible to speed up the module-based strategy by reducing the time to integrate work products from different sites (note the almost flat line at time 120 to 170). This is the same for phase-based development. There are two hand-off points. If the hand-offs can be made smoother and faster, then cycle times can be reduced. For the follow-the-sun strategy, coordination difficulties affect productivity, which leads to long cycle times. If coordination can be made more efficient, then cycle times could be reduced.

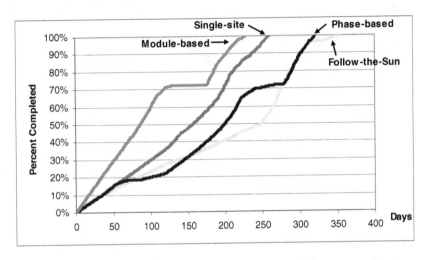

Fig. 5. Project progress comparison (Real World Situation)

4.3 Further Experimentation

Using realistic assumptions, we ran 30 replications of each configuration. The results indicated that the duration from single site and module-based configurations cannot be distinguished from each other. Follow-the-sun consistently takes the longest, with phase-based in the middle.

We then created a factorial design, varying the values for Distance, Culture, Language, Trust, and Time zone. Each had a plausible "high" value and "low" value. We applied this design to each configuration.

For the follow-the-sun configuration, the primary effects showed Distance and Trust to be the most influential, with a 30% impact on project duration. The further the distance between sites, the longer the duration of the project is. This is because the distance negatively affects the coordination efficiency, which reduces the productivity of the developers. On the other hand, trust among team members increases productivity, which in turn reduces the project duration. Time zone had a 5% impact by comparison. The impact of Culture and Language were negligible.

For the phased-based configuration, Distance and Time zone had the largest impacts, 15% and 10% respectively. The productivity of the developers is lower when they are far apart because of the difficulty in coordination, which leads to longer cycle time. Regarding the time zone, the cycle time tends to be shorter when there is less overlap working time between development sites (lower distribution effort loss). The other parameters had negligible impact.

For the module-based configuration, the impacts were negligible--less than 2% in all cases. The module-based strategy allows each site to work independently most of the times so the effects of the GSD factors are rather weak.

4.4 Discussion

The results provided above are just hypothetical results to illustrate the functionality and the usefulness of the GSD model. The model was calibrated with information from literature and the industry standard data collected by Capers Jones [38].

Despite the fact that our results are based on simplified models that were drawn from the literature, it is quite clear that the success of global software development depends on many factors. It is interesting to see how different factors affected the performance of different allocation strategies in unique ways. Hence, a specific approach might reduce development time by 20% under certain conditions while actually increasing development time under other conditions.

5 Conclusion

In this paper, we used the GSD model to evaluate the choice of task allocation strategy and its impact on project duration. By using the GSD simulation model, we were able to capture and assess the impact of a number of real world factors that have been presented in the literature. These included the factors of distance, culture, language, trust, and time zone. The results obtained, were consistent with those found in the literature [2, 7, 8, 21]. The results provided insight into how different factors dominate different task allocation strategies indicating that different strategies are appropriate for different types of development. This matches with real world experience and provides some initial validation for the model. In the future, we will collect the real world data and work with experts in the field to further calibrate and validate the GSD model.

We believe that a well implemented hybrid simulation model, constructed using an architecture similar to that shown here, could be used by managers to help determine which type of GSD configuration is likely to work the best for their particular situation. In addition, the GSD model also shows promise for exploring other globally distributed development issues such as:

General GSD project:
- Should work be distributed across multiple sites or should it be centralized at single site?
- Under what circumstances do dispersed teams perform better than co-located teams? When should a global software development approach be chosen?
- What are the critical success factors in GSD projects?
- What characteristics make a project suitable for GSD?
- What practices and tools are effective and worthwhile to apply to GSD projects?

Specific GSD project:

- Which development sites should be included in the project?
- How should work be divided up across sites? What task allocation strategy should be used for a particular project?
- What is the forecasted project performance in terms of cost, quality, and schedule?
- What is the impact of process changes in a GSD context? Should we add process A? Can we minimize or skip a portion of process B?

References

1. Carmel, E., Tija, P.: Offshoring Information Technology: Sourcing and Outsourcing to a Global Workforce. Cambridge University Press, Cambridge, UK (2005)
2. Carmel, E.: Global Software Teams. Prentice Hall PTR, Upper Saddle River, NJ (1999)
3. Gorton, I., Motwani, S.: Issues in Co-operative Software Engineering Using Globally Distributed Teams. Information and SoftwareTechnology **38** (1996) 647-655
4. Herbsleb, J.D., Moitra, D.: Global Software Development. IEEE Software (2001) 16-20
5. Norbjerg, J., Havn, E.C., Bansler, J.P.: Global Production: The Case of Offshore Programming. In: Krallmann, H. (ed.): Wirtschaftsinformatik '97, Physica-Verlag, Berlin (1997)
6. King, J.: IT's Global Itinerary: Offshore Outsourcing Is Inevitable. Computerworld (2003)
7. Herbsleb, J.D., Grinter, R.E., Finholt, T.A.: An Empirical Study of Global Software Development: Distance and Speed. ICSE 2001, Toronto, Canada (2001) 81-90
8. Herbsleb, J.D., Mockus, A.: An Empirical Study of Speed and Communication in Globally Distributed Software Development. IEEE Transactions on Software Engineering **29** (2003) 481-494
9. Abdel-Hamid, T.: The Economics of Software Quality Assurance: A Simulation-Based Case Study. MIS Quarterly (1988) 394-411
10. Myers, G.J.: Software Reliability: Principle and Practices. John Wiley & Sons, Inc., New York (1976)
11. Glass, R.L.: Modern Programming Practices: A Report from Industry. Prentice-Hall, Inc., Englewood Cliffs, NJ (1982)
12. Rus, I., Biffl, S., Halling, M.: Systematically Combining Process Simulation and Empirical Data in Support of Decision Analysis in Software Development. The fourteenth International Conference on Software Engineering and Knowledge Engineering (SEKE'02). ACM, Ischia, Italy (2002)
13. Raffo, D., Setamanit, S.: A Simulation Model for Global Software Development Project. The International Workshop on Software Process Simulation and Modeling, St. Louis, MO (2005)
14. Abdel-Hamid, T., Madnick, S.: Software Project Dynamics: An Integrated Approach. Prentice-Hall (1991)
15. Martin, R.: A Hybrid Model of the Software Development Process. Systems Science Ph.D. Program. Portland State University, Portland, OR (2002)
16. Kraut, R.E., Streeter, L.A.: Coordination in Software Development. Communications of the ACM **38** (1995) 69-81
17. Steiner, I.D.: Models for Inferring Relationships Between Group Size and Potential Group Productivity. Journal of Behavioral Science **5** (1966) 273-283
18. Brooks, F.P.: The Mythical Man-Month. Addison-Wesley, Reading, MA (1975)

19. Curtis, B., Krasner, H., Iscoe, N.: A Field Study of the Software Design Process for Large Systems. Communications of the ACM **31** (1988) 1268-1287
20. Perry, D.E., Staudenmayer, N.A., and Votta, L.G.: People, Organizations, and Process Improvement. IEEE Software **11** (1994) 36-45
21. Herbsleb, J.D., Grinter, R.E.: Splitting the Organization and Integrating the Code: Conway's Law Revisited. International Conference on Software Engineering (ICSE'99). ACM Press, Los Angeles, CA (1999) 85-95
22. Allen, T.J.: Managing the Flow of Technology. MIT press, Cambridge, MA (1977)
23. Kraut, R.E., Egido, C., Galegher, J.: Patterns of Contact and Communication in Scientific Research Collaborations. In: Galegher, J., Kraut, R.E., and Egido, C. (ed.): Intellectual Teamwork: Social Foundations of Cooperative Work. Lawrence Erlbaum Associates, New Jersey (1990) 149-172
24. Jennings, E.E.: Routes to the Executive Suite. McGraw-Hill, New York (1971)
25. Jarvenpaa, S.L.: Communication and Trust in Global Virtual Teams. Journal of Computer Mediated Communication **3** (1998)
26. Hofstede, G.: Culture's Consequences: Comparing values, behaviors, institutions, and organizations across nations. Sage Oublications, Inc., Thousand Oaks, CA (2001)
27. Consortium, S.P.: Measurement for Distributed Teams. Software Productivity Consortium, Herndon, Virginia (2002) 68
28. Pearce, W.B.: Trust in interpersonal communication. Speech Monographs **41** (1974) 236-244
29. Gudykunst, W.B., Matsumoto, Y., Ting-Toomey, S., Nishida, T., Linda, K.W., Heyman, S.: The influence of cultural individualism-collectivism, self construals, and individual values on communication style across cultures. Human Communication Research **22** (1996) 510-543
30. Meyer, D.: A. Tech talk: how managers are stimulating global R&D communication. Sloan Management Review (1991)
31. Espinosa, J.A., Carmel, E.: The Impact of Time Separation on Coordination in Global Software Teams: A Conceptual Foundation. Software Process Improvement and Practice **8** (2003) 249-266
32. Hall, E.T.: Beyond Culture. Doubleday Books, New York, NY (1976)
33. Espinosa, J.A., Carmel, E.: Modeling the Effect of Time Separation on Coordination Costs in Global Software Teams. The 37th Hawaii International Conference on System Sciences, Hawaii, USA (2003)
34. Wijayanayake, J., Higa, K.: Communication media choice by workers in distributed environment. Information and Management **36** (1999) 329-338
35. Ishii, H.: Cross-Cultural Communication and CSCW. In: Harasim, L.M. (ed.): Global Networks: Computers and International Communication. MIT Press, Cambridge, MA (1993) 143-151
36. Carmel, E., Agarwal, R.: Tactical Approached for Alleviating Distance in Global Software Development. IEEE Software (2001) 22-29
37. Keil, L., Eng., P.: Experiences in Distributed Development: A Case Study. The International Workshop on Global Software Development, Portland, OR USA (2003) 44-47
38. Jones, C.: Applied Software Measurement: Assuring Productivity and Quality. McGraw-Hill, New York (1977)

Users and Developers: An Agent-Based Simulation of Open Source Software Evolution

Neil Smith[1], Andrea Capiluppi[2], and Juan Fernández-Ramil[1]

[1] Centre for Research in Computing, The Open University,
Milton Keynes, MK7 6AA, UK
{N.Smith, J.F.Ramil}@open.ac.uk
http://mcs.open.ac.uk/{ns938/,jfr46/}
[2] University of Lincoln, Brayford Pool, Lincoln, LN6 7TS, UK
acapiluppi@lincoln.ac.uk
http://hemswell.lincoln.ac.uk/~acapiluppi/

Abstract. We present an agent-based simulation model of open source software (OSS). To our knowledge, this is the first model of OSS evolution that includes four significant factors: productivity limited by the complexity of software modules, the software's fitness for purpose, the motivation of developers, and the role of users in defining requirements. The model was evaluated by comparing the simulated results against four measures of software evolution (system size, proportion of highly complex modules, level of complexity control work, and distribution of changes) for four large OSS systems. The simulated results resembled all the observed data, including alternating periods of growth and stagnation. The fidelity of the model suggests that the factors included here have significant effects on the evolution of OSS systems.

Keywords: simulation models, software process, open source software, software evolution.

1 Introduction

Computing is a rapidly evolving discipline and there is a need to understand the evolutionary processes that prevail in new forms of software development, such as open source software (OSS) systems. Evolution in proprietary systems is becoming understood [1], but many OSS systems do not evolve in the same way [2,3]. This suggests that existing theories of software evolution are partial accounts of OSS evolution. Extending these theories can have a practical output by informing good practice, leading to the more efficient prodution of better software. This paper reports our attempts to use theories of software evolution to replicate and explain empirical observations of a set of OSS systems.

OSS evolution involves a community of individuals providing their work mainly on a voluntary basis and without a strong centralised leadership [4,5]. This invalidates one of the assumptions of many simulation models: the existence of a centralised management which reacts to the state of the software system by altering

Q. Wang et al. (Eds.): SPW/ProSim 2006, LNCS 3966, pp. 286–293, 2006.

the pattern of work performed [6]. This emphasis on individuals suggests that an agent-based model of the OSS evolution process is appropriate [7, 8].

We propose that each module within an OSS system is monolithic and will behave as such [1, 9]. However, the modular architecture will restrict the impact of growth stagnation to small parts of the system, where it will not have a significant global effect. To investigate this hypothesis, we have developed an agent-based model of OSS development. To our knowledge, the model presented here is the first model of open source evolution that includes four significant factors: the complexity of the software modules as a limiting factor in productivity; the fitness of the software to the requirements; the motivation of developers; and the role of users in defining requirements. We believe, based on our experiments, that these are important factors that need to be included in OSS evolution theories.

2   Agent-Based Simulation Model

Our motivation for developing this model lies in our understanding of the actions of individual OSS developers [10, 4]. OSS development is decentralised and non-coercive: generally, developers choose to become involved in an OSS project and choose which aspects of the project to work on. This focus on individual developers and specific software components suggests that such objects should be the primitive elements of our model, with the evolution of the OSS system being an emergent property of the interactions of those primitive elements.

We used the NetLogo [11] multi-agent simulation tool. In this tool, agents move around a virtual world (a grid of "patches"), interacting with it and with other agents. Each agent and patch has its own state and procedures. Simulation proceeds by each agent and patch performing its behaviour independently, often by following stochastic functions influenced by the agent's state and local environment. Agents perform their own actions asynchronously; there is no centralised co-ordination of the agents' actions.

In our model, patches represent *modules* of software source code and different types of agents represent *developers*, unfulfilled *requirements*, and *users*.

A *module* is a single modular part of a software system. Modules that are near each other are functionally related. Each module records both its fitness for purpose and its complexity. The complexity of a module acts as an inhibitor to future changes to that module. To model the changes in external requirements that drive software evolution, patches have a stochastic process for decreasing their fitness over time. Finally, modules have a chance to capture the attention of a developer passing through cyberspace and so create a new developer agent in the model; this only happens if the module is interesting (i.e. its fitness is below the developer's 'boredom threshold'; see below).

Users are responsible for adding new requirements to the system. Users walk randomly around the system space and, when they meet a code patch or an existing requirement, they create a new *requirement* that extends the functionality in this area. Newly created requirements attract new users, which reflects the tendency of users to suggest modifications to existing requirements.

Fig. 1. An example of simulated OSS development. The squares are code patches. The black circles are unfulfilled requirements. Note how the vertical "stem" in the top left is loosely connected to the rest of the system.

Developers walk randomly around the software system, changing code as they go. Agents have four behaviours, depending on their location. If a developer is on an unfulfilled requirement, it creates a *new module* that fulfils that requirement, with a certain (low) fitness and complexity. If a developer is on a module with high complexity and high fitness, it may attempt to *refactor* that module. Refactoring leaves the module's fitness unchanged, but reduces its complexity by a random amount. If the developer chooses not to refactor a module, it will attempt to *develop* the module: this increases the module's fitness and complexity by a random amount. However, if the module is complex, the agent may not be able to improve the module, in which case the module is left unchanged. Finally, developers have a *boredom threshold*. If the fitness of the module they are on is above this threshold, there is a chance that the developer will find the project boring and leave. Developers may also leave if they wander onto a patch and have no module or requirement to work on.

Simulation starts with a single module and a single user. These spawn new requirements and attract the attention of developers. The developers create modules to fulfil the requirements. As the project grows, more developers and users are attracted and more requirements are identified. The model's source code is available from `http://mcs.open.ac.uk/ns938/simulation/`.

3   Empirical Data

To validate the model, we compared the simulated output to empirically observed behaviour. The empirical data was derived from data in OSS repositories. Previous research has shown that data such as change-log records, program headers and configuration management offer a suitable source of data for the study of software evolution [12, 13, 14]. For this study, we selected four OSS systems which we have examined in previous studies [13, 14]. Table 1 indicates the data sources

Table 1. Data sources used

Software System Studied (URL of Code Repository)	Change Log?	CVS?	Number of Releases Considered
Arla (www.stacken.kth.se/projekt/arla)	Yes	Yes	70
Gaim (http://gaim.sourceforge.net)	N/A	Partial	100
MPlayer (www.mplayerhq.hu)	N/A	Partial	81
Wine (www.winehq.com)	Yes	Partial	90

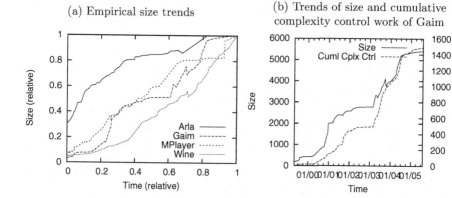

(a) Empirical size trends

(b) Trends of size and cumulative complexity control work of Gaim

Fig. 2. Empirical trends

we used to extract the empirical data used in this research. We extracted several attributes for each software system, taking measurements over releases.

Size was evaluated using number of source functions (as a surrogate for the systems' growth). Figure 2(a) shows the size trends for all the systems, using relative sizes and times. Only Wine has a smoothly increasing trend; the other systems had at least one period of reduced growth (i.e. stagnation).

Complexity was measured at the level of functions. We used the McCabe cyclomatic number [15] as a measure of complexity and the accepted threshold value of 15 to distinguish highly complex functions [16]. In all the analysed systems, the highly complex functions never make up more than 10% of the overall system.

We measured *complexity control work* by comparing every function between two consecutive releases and counting how many of them reduced in complexity. There is a high correlation between the trend of the size growth and the cumulative amount of complexity control work: figure 2(b) shows this for Gaim.

A function is *touched* when it is added, deleted, or modified. A small subset of elements is touched a large number of times by developers, whilst most of the elements receive few touches. The skewness of these distributions ranges from 2.73 in Wine to 4.55 in Arla.

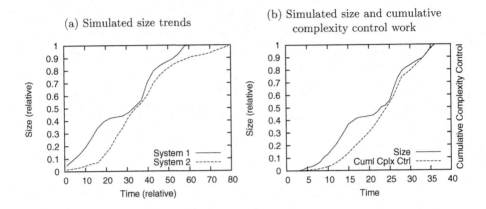

Fig. 3. Simulated trends

4   Results and Validation

We used the empirical data described above to calibrate and evaluate our model. We did this by exploring the parameter space of the models, looking at the generated output, and comparing it to the empirical evidence from the four OSS systems. Throughout most of the parameter space, the model generated results that were very similar to the empirical results.

The model was most sensitive to the value of the boredom threshold parameter, which controls when new developers join and leave the project. If the boredom threshold of developers was high, high-fitness modules attracted developers rather than forcing them to leave. The number of developers grew rapidly and soon swamped the development environment. In contrast, if the boredom threshold was low, the evolution of the first few modules resulted in a system that attracted no new developers; the original developers soon left and the project became moribund.

The behaviour of the users was important to produce both discontinuous and smooth growth patterns (figure 3(a)). Without the users clustering around new requirements, the requirements were spread evenly around the system and only smooth growth patterns were produced [17]. Even with the clustering, some simulations produced smooth growth.

In the simulations, the proportion of complex functions remained at a constant and low level as long as new modules have an initial complexity below the reporting threshold, similar to the empirical results. This behaviour was not seen if refactoring was ineffectual or not attempted. Moving to complexity control work, figure 3(b) shows that the simulation reproduces the empirical pattern of increasing complexity control work that eventually follows the growth trend.

Finally the simulation is able to partially reproduce the long-tailed distribution of touches, though the skew value is typically only 0.8–0.9.

The closeness of the simulated results to the empirical data indicate that our model reflects many of the processes that occur in OSS evolution.

5   Related Work

The OSS domain was originally studied using quantitative metric data extracted from OSS systems [10, 13, 14]. Godfrey & Tu [2] highlighted differences between the evolution of Linux and previously studied systems, particularly its apparently super-linear growth. Our model provides a possible explanation for such a super-linear growth: access to an effectively unlimited pool of developers and complexity which constrains productivity to the module level only.

Antoniades et al.'s [18] simulation of OSS processes has reproduced empirically observed patterns of growth and developer numbers. Robles et al. [19] propose a biologically-inspired simulation, where developers learn from other developers only through observing changes in the source code. Their research shares our focus on product characteristics (e.g. size and complexity) and on evolution. However, to our knowledge, the model presented here is the first model of open source evolution that includes the complexity of the software modules as a limiting factor in productivity, the fitness of the software to the requirements, and the motivation of developers.

6   Further Work

Our further work will initially focus on two areas. First is the surprising need to include the behaviour of the users in creating new requirements. As far as we know, the role of users in the evolution of OSS systems has not been deeply explored. We will examine the empirical data to try to identify how and when users generate new requirements and how they are dealt with by developers. Second is inability of the model to produce touch distributions that were as skewed as the empirical data. This may be due to the undiscriminating behaviour of the developer agents in modifying existing code patches and the initial values of a module's fitness and complexity: it appears that many modules in real systems are rarely touched because their initial implementation is adequate and not subject to change.

The other aspect of developer behaviour that we will soon add to the model is to take account of developers' experience in controlling and approving changes made to the system. In many OSS systems, there is a core of highly experienced super-developers that have a great influence on the evolution of the system [20]. We anticipate that including such super-developers in the model will have a significant effect on the simulation.

7   Conclusions

This paper presented an agent-based simulation model of OSS evolution. Our model, while simple, incorporates many of the features that may explain some of the differences between OSS and proprietary development [2, 3]. We found that the model was able to replicate the observed patterns in all four of the areas examined (size, complexity, complexity control, distribution of changes) in the four systems studied. The model presented here appears to provide an explanation for the unbounded growth trends observed in some OSS software [2,3]. This is an important contribution. We included four novel factors in our model: the complexity of software modules as a limiting factor in productivity, the fitness of the software to its requirements, the motivation of developers, and the role of users in incrementally defining requirements. As discussed in section 4, all four of these factors are required for the model to produce plausible results.

In conclusion, we have shown that an agent-based model of OSS evolution can faithfully produce the empirical behaviour of OSS systems, but only by including a number of factors that are not immediately obvious. This suggests that studies into the factors driving software evolution need to look beyond just the behaviour of developers.

Acknowledgements

Andrea Capiluppi acknowledges the Faculty of Maths and Computing, The Open University, and in particular to Drs Bashar Nuseibeh and Uwe Grimm, for financial support that made this work possible. Juan Fernández-Ramil gratefully acknowledges the UK EPSRC for funding under grant GR/590782/01 (2004–5).

References

1. Lehman, M.M., Fernández-Ramil, J.: Software Evolution. In: Software Evaluation and Feedback — Theory and Practice. Wiley (2006)
2. Godfrey, M., Tu, Q.: Growth, evolution and structural change in open source software. In: Proceedings of the 4th International Workshop on the Principles of Software Evolution, Vienna, Austria (2001)
3. Herraiz, I., Robles, G., Gonzalez-Barahona, J.M., Capiluppi, A., Fernández-Ramil, J.: Comparison between SLOCs and number of files as size metrics for software evolution analysis. In: Proceedings, 10th European Conference on Software Maintenance and Reengineering. (2006)
4. Raymond, E.S.: The Cathedral and the Bazaar. O'Reilly Media, Inc. (2001)
5. Scacchi, W.: Understanding Open Source Software Evolution. In: Software Evolution and Feedback, Theory and Practice. Wiley, NY (2006)
6. Smith, N., Capiluppi, A., Fernández-Ramil, J.: A study of open source software evolution data using qualitative simulation. Software Process Improvement and Practice **10** (2005) 287–300
7. Madey, G., Freeh, V.W., Tynan, R.O.: Agent-based modeling of open source using SWARM. In: Proceedings of the Americas Conference on Information Systems (AMCIS 2002), Dallas, USA (2002)
8. Dalle, J.M., David, P.A.: imCode: Agent-based simulation modelling of open-source software development. Technical report, MIT (2004)
9. Brooks, F.: The Mythical Man-Month: Essays on Software Engineering. 20th anniversary edn. Addison-Wesley (1995)
10. Mockus, A., Fielding, R.T., Herbsleb, J.: Two case studies of open source software development: Apache and mozilla. ACM Transactions Software Engineering and Methodology **11** (2002) 309–346

11. NetLogo: http://ccl.northwestern.edu/netlogo/ (2005)
12. Capiluppi, A.: Models for the evolution of OS projects. In: Proceedings, ICSM 2003, Amsterdam (2003) 65–74
13. Capiluppi, A., Morisio, M., Fernández-Ramil, J.: The evolution of source folder structure in actively evolved open source systems. In: Proceedings of the 10th International Symposium on Software Metrics, Chicago, USA (2004) 2–13
14. Capiluppi, A., Morisio, M., Fernández-Ramil, J.: Structural evolution of an open source system: A case study. In: Proceedings of the 12th International Workshop on Program Comprehension (IWPC), Bari, Italy (2004) 172–182
15. McCabe, T.: A complexity measure. IEEE Transactions on Software Engineering **2** (1976) 308–320
16. McCabe, T.J., Butler, C.W.: Design complexity measurement and testing. Communications of the ACM **32** (1989) 1415–1425
17. Smith, N., Capiluppi, A., Fernández-Ramil, J.: Agent-based simulation of open source evolution. Software Process Improvement and Practice (to appear)
18. Antoniades, P., Samoladas, I., Stamelos, I., Bleris, G.L.: Dynamical simulation models of the Open Source Development process. In: Free/Open Source Software Development. Idea Group, Inc. (2005)
19. Robles, G., Merelo, J.J., Gonzalez-Barahona, J.M.: Self-organized development in libre software: a model based on the stigmergy concept. In: ProSim 2005, St. Louis, USA (2005)
20. Mockus, A., Fielding, R.T., Herbsleb, J.: A case study of open source software development: the apache server. In: Proc. ICSE 22, Limerick, Ireland (2000) pp. 263 – 272

Simulating the Structural Evolution of Software

Benjamin Stopford[1] and Steve Counsell[2]

[1] School of Computer Science and Information Systems,
Birkbeck, University of London
[2] School of Information Systems, Computing and Mathematics,
Brunel University, London

Abstract. As functionality is added to an ageing piece of software, its original design and structure tends to erode. The underlying forces which cause such degradation have been the subject of much research. However, progress in this field is slow due to the difficultly faced in generating empirical data [6] as well as attributing observed effects to the various points in the causal chain [7]. This paper tackles these problems by providing a framework for simulating the structural evolution of software. A complete model is built by incrementally adding modules to the framework, each of which contribute an individual evolutionary effect. These effects are then combined to form a multi-faceted simulation that evolves a fictitious code base approximating real world behavior. Validation of a simple set of evolutionary parameters is provided, demonstrating agreement with current empirical observations.

1 Introduction

Software evolution is a complex phenomenon and deriving formulations for the interactions that make up its whole is a significant challenge. In fact, no theoretical framework exists to describe the evolution of software. There are nevertheless, a variety of behavioral observations and heuristics that describe the evolution of software. Examples vary from laws of software evolution, such as those proposed by Lehman [8], to more specific underlying behaviors such as the coupling types of Briand et al. [1]. Simulating rules individually is within the bounds of a software model and combining such effects would provide an interesting basis for experimentation.

This paper presents a method for exploring software evolution from the inside out. Individual laws can be proposed and added to a simulation framework. The effects of these laws can then be measured in isolation, under different environmental conditions and against other proposed laws.

The majority of research in software engineering simulation is concerned with the simulation of software process. Prominent examples of this include the modeling of project planning [4], defect levels and staffing profiles [9] as well as system size and effort trends [10]. The aims of process simulations are to investigate the processes by which people, technology and practices are organized to transform information, materials and energy into a piece of software. Conversely, this paper focuses on the effect that evolution has on the structure of software at a source code level and how this

Q. Wang et al. (Eds.): SPW/ProSim 2006, LNCS 3966, pp. 294–301, 2006.

structure varies over the evolution of a project. It is thus the code structure that is under analysis rather than the process through which it is generated.

2   The Simulation Model

The framework is based around a fictitious code base which defines the basic rules of software development such as the existence of classes and methods as well as their means of interaction. Agents (simulated developers) then evolve this code base through the addition and processing of requirements. The specifics of evolving and measuring the system are left to customizable plug-ins which can be tailored to fit individual experimental aims. The framework thus presents a controlled environment that enforces the evolution of the code base in a realistic manner - the direction that this evolution takes rests in the hands of the experimenter. The proposed model follows a simple feedback network. Its four basic elements are requirements, evolution, code metrics and the code base. The latter three are connected in a feedback circuit as shown in Figure 1:

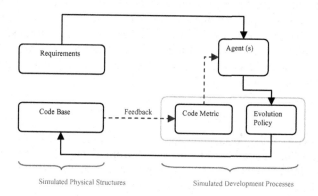

Fig. 1. An overview of the basic elements of the simulation framework and the data flows between them. The feedback loop from the Code Base back to the Agent via the Code Metric is also shown.

1. Requirements: Requirements are generated through a stochastic, configurable process and can be reused across experiments or created afresh. Requirements control the conceptual content of the simulation to later be turned into code constructs.
2. Evolution: The Agent and Evolution Policy evolve the code base using the requirements specified. Evolution is concerned with turning the hierarchy of requirements of different types into a structure of code constructs.
3. Measurement: Code metrics provide a means for the Agent to evaluate the code base prior to changing it. This supplies the closing section of the feedback loop in which agents can respond differently depending on their observation of the code base.
4. Code Base: The evolution of the relationships between physical code constructs is modeled inside the Code Base. The simulation considers only entities greater than, or at method level.

A run of the simulation starts with the generation of a set of requirements. These are then passed to an Agent to implement. The Agent implements the requirements through the use of an evolution policy specified for the particular experiment. The evolution policy defines a set of rules dictating how to structure code as it is added. The evolution policy can also take into account information on the current state of the code base fed back to it from the code metrics.

The evolution of the code base is measured using a cost function. The cost function is an arbitrary measure that can be used to compare the relative costs of different runs of the simulation. The costing model is split into two separate sections covering the implementation and metric costs. The implementation cost is that associated with the physical creation and alteration of code and is proportional to the number and size of the structures created. The metric cost is that associated with comprehension of code. In the default implementation the metric represents a basic complexity measure taking into account the local topology of the code.

The code metrics allow experimenters to model the cost of comprehending different structures as well as a means for agents to observe the code base. The act of observing the code base through metrics causes information to be fed back from the code base into the evolution policy so that the code base structure can influence how it is evolved. This is important since it allows the state of the code base to alter the evolutionary decisions made by agents. Such feedback loops, formed from simple concepts, are responsible for many of the processes observed in complex systems [3]. As such, the simulation can create responses that are likely to differ significantly from those formed by static analysis.

2.1 Requirements

Requirements control the conceptual content of the simulation to later be turned into code constructs; the separation of requirements from evolution is important. Running with different requirements allows the simulation to model different development environments (for example green field developments vs. mature products). Experiments can then either hold the requirements constant or deliberately vary them to explore how they effect the simulation. Requirements are generated though a stochastic process and can be serialized and reused across different experimental runs.

2.2 The Code Base

The code base acts as a repository for different code constructs created and linked together by Agents. These constructs can then refer to one another via the various calls made open to them by the simulation framework such as "Reference" or "Create Function". The code base encapsulates all creational calls and references so that responsibility for enforcing integrity within the resulting code is retained.

The code constructs used by the simulation are based on the work suggested by Kelsen [5]. They include Classes, Functions, Events, Properties and References. Classes and Functions represent standard classes and functions that might be encountered in a real code base. Events denote an interaction with an event outside of the system. Properties represent the internal storage of state through variables of a specified type. References link code constructs in a directional manor. References also specify a Coupling Type, determined by the evolution policy. Coupling types define the effect that a reference has on the code construct it operates upon, for example describing whether data is retrieved or changed through the coupling.

The execution path of the simulation starts at one of the system events. The code base in the simulation is constructed in such a way that this execution path is always enforced.

2.3 The Agent and Evolution Policy

The Agent is a system concept that embodies the role of a developer in a real software project. Agents are stateful with the ability to 'learn' about the system as they modify and add to it; the agent's primary concern is to facilitate the conversion of requirements into code using an "Evolution Policy". The Evolution Policy is the plug-in responsible for turning requirements into code. The agent is responsible for facilitating this (for example, by locating the class to change).

Each agent has a memory of the code constructs that they were responsible for implementing. This memory dissipates as time elapses in the simulation. An agent's memory can be accessed from the evolution policy or complexity metric to improve the depth of the simulation, particularly when considering multiple agents acting on the code base. When multiple agents are configured, each new requirement is implemented by an agent selected randomly from the pool.

The Evolution Policy is the plug-in that bears responsibility for evolving the code base and is thus a focal point for defining experiments. The experimenter must implement three functions in the Evolution Policy in response to the major categories of requirement type: New, Change and Augment. In addition, the evolution policy also provides a set of utilities that allow the experimenter to customize their implementation. These include:

☐ Code Metric: The evolution policy uses a code metric to retrieve feedback from the code base before making a change. The code metric also records a cost used as a measure of the experiment (see section 2.4).

☐ Memory: The memory of the agent is accessible from the evolution policy. This provides feedback on the agent's recall of the various code constructs that they created.

☐ Coupling Type: A specific coupling type is associated with References as they are created detailing the nature of interactions made through references.

As an example, consider the evolution policy that processes requirements that augment existing business functionality. In the default implementation this policy will cycle through all existing classes that are associated with the task being augmented. New functions will be added along with the addition of couplings to existing functions and properties.

2.4 Measurement

The simulation is measured via a cost function that provides a measure for comparing different runs. The total cost is split into two different sections that indicate the separation between the cost of creating and the cost of understanding code.

☐ Metric Cost is calculated by the code metric plug-in. This provides the means for customizing experiments by allowing an experimenter to specify how the evolutionary factors modeled in the experiment should be measured.
☐ Implementation Cost is that incurred through the physical creation of code. This is calculated automatically and is proportional to the number and type of code constructs created.

2.5 Complexity Injection

Complexity Injection is a feature of the framework that allows a random distribution of extra features (references, properties etc) to be added to a code construct when it is created. This allows the complexity of the simulation to be controlled without altering the logic in the evolution policy.

The Complexity Injector and the Evolution Policy have similar, but fundamentally different, roles. The Complexity Injector is responsible for the monotonous detail added to all code constructs when they are created (classes need functions and references, etc). The Evolution Policy is responsible for shaping how the structure between classes and functions evolve.

2.6 Default Plug-In Implementations

A default set of plug-ins are supplied and shipped with the simulation. They define a basic set of policies through which the code base can be evolved and are used in the validation experiments presented in this paper. It is anticipated that future experiments will improve on the basic assumptions they make, incorporating more realistic evolution policies and metrics. To this end, they are created in an extensible manner.

3 Using the Framework to Conduct Experiments

The Framework includes a GUI designed to ease the comprehension of the code base structure during a simulation run. The GUI has three views: one for the requirements and two for the code base. The code base views include a graphical representation of the class hierarchy and can be drilled into by the user. A second view represents the set of execution paths. More structured analysis can be performed using data provided through an output data file. The method for conducting an experiment is:

1. Identify the problem to be investigated and develop a dynamic hypothesis that describes its cause.
2. Create an evolution policy plug-in that changes the code base according to the dynamic hypothesis.
3. Amend the code metrics plug-in to ensure that it is sensitive to the evolutionary changes expected.
4. Test the evolution policy and metric in isolation to ensure that provide the expected behavior.
5. Add the implemented policy to the full simulation model so that it can be investigated in conjunction with other existing simulated factors.

4   Validation of the Simulation Framework

The simulation framework is validated through a suite of tests that analyze performance over different experimental conditions. The aim of each test is to validate a basic behavior of the system against an intuitive understanding or empirical observation.

4.1   Validation (1): Linear Evolution of Code Base Size

Empirical observations of the increase in size of an evolving code base, as measured by Capiluppi et al [2], show a linear increase in size over time. The simulation framework was used to reproduce this behavior using the default plug-ins. Both the original and simulated results show a linear increase corroborating this basic behavior.

Capiluppi et al. also provide a study of the distribution of average lines of code per file over various releases stating that the average number of lines per file should increase slightly as the system evolves. A comparable result was generated with the simulation framework.

In this paper Capiluppi's linear results were preferred as they provide a sound empirical and widely recognized basis from which the model could be validated. However research by other prominent authors has demonstrated examples of system growth that are inverse-square [11] and super-linear [12]. The validation of these behaviors through different evolution policies is left as a matter for future work.

4.2   Validation (2): The Effect of Requirement Type

An important function of the simulation is its ability to respond to different types of requirement in a distinct manner. This aspect is validated by measuring how Requirement Types affect evolution of the code base and ensuring that this agrees with expected behavior. The proposition is that developments simulated from requirements that include a high degree of re-visitation will cost more to develop. This assumption is made from the real world observation that existing code is harder to change (as it must be understood). The results in Figure 2(a) corroborate this hypothesis with the cost being significantly higher for simulations that have to revisit code.

4.3   Validation (3): Response to Different Numbers of Agents

The simulation provides a facility for specifying the number of agents that contribute to evolution. Each agent "remembers" the code they created and this memory is taken into account by the default code metric. The effect of this is to drop the associated metric cost incurred by an Agent that is changing code they were responsible for creating (and that they therefore remember). This effect was validated via the experiment results displayed in Figure 2(b). These show that development with two agents is most efficient and the one with thirty agents is least efficient. Where there are fewer developers, the cost is lower as each developer is responsible for the original construction of a higher proportion of the code base (and thus has less to learn). This validates the simulation through observation of an expected behavior.

The results presented in this section provide a level of confidence that the simulation performs in a manner approximating real world behavior. This conclusion is corroborated by both intuitive expectations and empirical results.

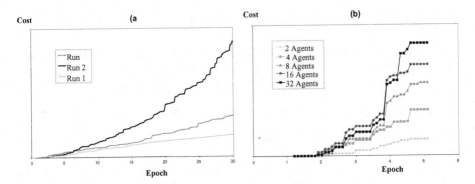

Fig. 2. (a) Metric Cost for Simulations with varying requirement types. Run (3) is the control, Run (2) represents requirements that incorporate a large proportion of changes and Run (1) is predominantly new requirements. **(b)** Evolution with different numbers of agents. The different profiles result from the effect of agent memory.

5 Conclusions

The evolution of software, in particular its structural erosion over successive generations is a primary concern of software engineering today. This paper presents a novel approach for investigating this problem. From a theoretical standpoint, the simulation framework can be used to build a causal model of software evolution from individual behaviors. These behaviors can be investigated in isolation as well as part of a collective model. Such a bottom-up approach cannot easily be replicated by any other method.

From an empirical standpoint, such a causal model can be calibrated with a relatively small amount of empirical data (Simple calibrations are presented here as space limitations preclude more detailed validation through methods such as sensitivity analysis; we thus consider this an aspect for future work). Once calibrated, the scope can be broadened to include different environments with little or no effort. This reduces the need for long and expensive empirical investigations.

Much as in other disciplines, simulation may provide a valuable window into a world otherwise inaccessible to current research, expediting the crystallization of laws as well as opening the doors to new insights. Full source code for the simulation framework can be found at: http://www.benstopford.com/devsim/devsim.shtml

References

[1] "A Unified Framework for Coupling Measurement in Object-Oriented Systems": L.C. Briand, J.W. Daly, J.K. Wust: IEEE Transactions on Software Engineering, Vol 25, No 1, Jan/Feb 1999
[2] "Studying the Evolution of Open Source Systems at Different Levels of Granularity": Capiluppi, Morisio and Ramil: Proceedings of the 12th International Workshop on Program Comprehension
[3] "Urban Dynamics" Forrester, J. W. Cambridge MA: Productivity Press. 1969.

[4] "Software Process Modeling Support for Management Planning and Control". Kellner, M. Proceedings of the first international conference on the software process 1991.

[5] "A Simple Static Model for Understanding the Dynamic Behavior of Programs." Kelsen: International Workshop on Program Comprehension 2004

[6] "Need for more Longitudinal Studies of Software Maintenance": C.F. Kemerer, S. Slaughter, Proc. Int'l Workshop Empirical Studies Software Maintenance, Monterey Calif., 1996

[7] "An Empirical Approach to Studying Software Evolution": C.F. Kemerer, S. Slaughter, IEEE Transactions on Software Engineering, Vol. 25, No. 4 July/August 1999

[8] "Program, Life Cycle and the Law of Program Evolution", M. Lehman, Proceedings of the IEEE, 68, 1060-1078, 1980

[9] "Modeling Software Processes Quantitatively and Assessing the Impact of Potential Process Changes on Process Performance" Raffo, D. – PhD Dissertation. Carnegie Mellon University 1996

[10] "Software Process White Box Modeling for FEAST/1", Wernick and Lehman: Journal of Software Systems 1999

[11] "Implications of Evolution Metrics on Software Maintenance", Lehman, Perry and Ramil: Proc of the 1998 Intl. Conf. of Software Maintenance (ICSM98)

[12] "Evolution in Open Source Software: A Case Study", Godfrey and Tu: Proceedings of the International Conference on Software Maintenance (ICSM00)

An Empirical Study on SW Metrics for Embedded System

Taehee Gwak and Yoonjung Jang

SE Group, SE Team, Software Laboratories, Samsung Electronics Co., Ltd.,
416, Maetan-3Dong, Yeongtong-gu, Suwon-City, Gyeonggi-Do 443-742, Korea
{th.gwak, yun.jang}@samsung.com

Abstract. One of the most important reasons to measure software projects is to increase visibility of the development process. High visibility enables the development team to estimate their project more accurately and to establish a reasonable project plan. It also provides a rationale for improving the software development process. We propose standard metrics needed for our organization to develop embedded systems and present the results of related data collection and measurement. To define software metrics, the GQM (Goal Question Metric) approach was used. This empirical study should benefit people on the SEPG (Software Engineering Process Group) of each software development division who drive to improve their software development process.

1 Introduction

As we face increasingly demanding software portions in embedded systems, it is needed to understand more precisely about what is happening during a software-intensive project and how to improve effectiveness of software development. To solve these problems related to visibility and effectiveness in software development, an evaluation of a software project and process should be preceded and measurement is a way to achieve this. Measurement enables us to understand how our current process works and see the potential areas of improvement. Besides, measurement provides the data needed to track our work and cope with difficulties timely and these data can also be used to make an estimate or a plan for the following projects.

Software projects and process can be measured in numerous ways. Therefore, a measurement program must include metrics that help us analyze various characteristics or attributes[7] of software projects, process or products. In establishing an organizational measurement program, it is helpful to start by considering what metrics we can use as standard throughout all the divisions of our organization. Currently, different process is applied to software development by divisions or by product types and measurements are conducted occasionally. Although measurement programs are operated systematically, there are many difficulties in data gathering and analysis due to conflictions of metrics between divisions. Our proposal for defining the standard metrics involves extracting common metrics from the diverse metrics in use through a survey of current measurement programs. These common metrics become candidates for the standard metrics. We'll also show that proposed standard metrics are applicable and useful to our organization by the results of actual measurements.

Q. Wang et al. (Eds.): SPW/ProSim 2006, LNCS 3966, pp. 302–313, 2006.

The remainder of this paper is organized as follows: In section 2, we introduce software metrics and the GQM Method used to define metrics for our organization. In section 3, we examine the current status of measurement programs in our organization and propose standard software metrics for embedded system. In section 4, we analyze the results of measurement and experiment conducted. Finally, describing the worth of proposed metrics and operational issues of measurement program, we conclude in section 5.

2   Related Studies

2.1 Software Metrics

Software metric define a way of measuring some characteristics of the software development process, product, and project. Software metrics can be classified into three categories: product metrics, process metrics, and project metrics[4]. Product metrics describe the characteristics of the product such as size, complexity, design features, performance, and quality level. Process metrics include defect removal effectiveness, testing defect arrival pattern, and response time of the fix process and they can be used for improving the software process. Finally, project metrics deal with the project characteristics and execution such as cost, schedule, and productivity. These metrics can be primitive or computed[3]. Primitive metrics such as the lines of code or the number of defects are directly countable. Computed metrics are combinations of two or more primitive metrics. Defect density or size estimation error range are some examples of computed metrics. In this study, proposed standard metrics deal with computed metrics on the assumption that primitive metrics regarding size, time, and defect are measured.

2.2 The Goal Question Metric

In order to be effective measurement, metrics must be based on the environmental characteristics and goals of the organization. The GQM methodology is a top-down approach for defining useful metrics from measurable goals. The GQM approach is based upon the assumption that for an organization to measure in a purposeful way it must first specify the goals for itself and its projects, then it must trace those goals to the data that are intended to define those goals operationally, and finally provide a framework for interpreting the data with respect to the stated goals[5]. The result of GQM approach is a measurement model that has three levels as described below.

- GOAL: A goal is defined for an object derived from industrial interests. Objects of measurement are products, processes, and resources.
- QUESTION: A set of questions for each goal is defined to determine whether or not the goals have been achieved.
- METRIC: Each question is refined into relevant metrics in order to answer the questions in a quantitative way.

3 Standard Software Metrics for Embedded System

There is no generally applicable collection of metrics that will satisfy the needs and characteristics of all organizations[1]. Our study aims to define a set of metrics for Samsung Electronics which is appropriate to measure some characteristics of embedded system. We first examined measurement programs that were operated in all software development divisions of our organization and extracted metrics used in common, so that the raw data can be easy to collect. Then we identified several metrics to be used as standard with consideration of the needs and environmental characteristics of our organization.

Standard metrics for our organization were defined by four steps as shown in Figure 1. We describe details in section 3.1 to 3.4.

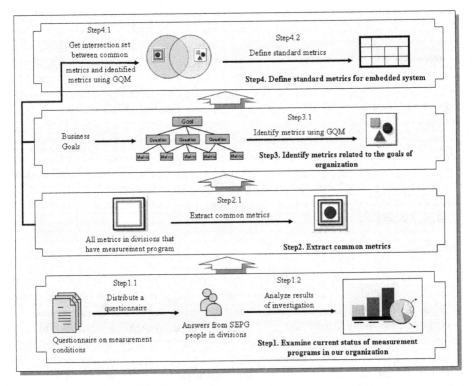

Fig. 1. Procedures for defining standard metrics

3.1 Examine Current Status of Measurement Programs in Organization

An examination started with making and distributing a questionnaire on measurement conditions. The targets of investigation were eleven divisions that had attained a certificate of software process capability. All possible metrics that could be measured in our organization were enumerated on the questionnaire and people on SEPG(Software Engineering Process Group) of each division were expected to answer the questions of what metrics were defined, how they were measured, who measured them, and how well they were used. The metrics included in the questionnaire consist of sixteen base metrics related to time, size, and defect and twenty-nine derived metrics with respect to productivity, schedule, quality, and risk.

The results of investigation showed that for base metrics, 45% of divisions measured them periodically, whereas derived metrics were used in only 17% of divisions.

3.2 Extract Common Metrics

The key area to investigate is to ascertain what metrics are applicable to all divisions. Therefore, it is important to extract common metrics from all the metrics listed in Table 1. Common metrics are a set of metrics which are used in common at all divisions that have measurement program as shown in Figure 2. However, because common metrics were not designed to support all the needs of our organization, we regarded them merely as candidates for standard metrics. Table 1 lists the extracted common metrics. If there are special needs or goals in only a few divisions, these should be dealt with in only metric set of those divisions and not common metrics.

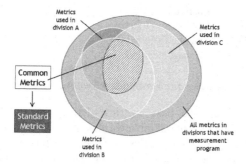

Fig. 2. Common Metrics

Table 1. Common Metrics

Measure	Metric
Time	Development time, Time in phase
Size	The number of pages of document, Lines of source code, The number of test cases
Defect	Total defects, Defects removed by phase, Post development defects(Problems)
Productivity	Development productivity, Productivity by phase
Quality	Audit score by phase, Average defect fix time, Defect density by phase
Schedule	Cost Performance Index(CPI), CPI by phase, Size estimate error

3.3 Identify Metrics with Respect to the Goals of Organization

There are many things we can measure about the software project or process. Therefore, for measurement activities to be cost effective, we should have definite goals of measurement devised to support the goals of organization. In order to establish the goals for our organization and extract metrics with respect to each goal, the GQM approach was used in this study.

The primary focus of our organization is to produce high-quality software on schedule and improve software development process. For each goal, questions in order to determine whether the specific goal is achieved or not and the metrics to answer these questions were identified as follows:

- Goal 1 To produce software on schedule by periodical monitoring
  - Question 1.1 What was checked periodically to develop software within scheduled time?
    - Metric 1.1.1 Cost Performance Index [6]
  - Question 1.2 Which elements have impact on development schedule?
    - Metric 1.2.1 Development Productivity[6]
- Goal 2 To detect defect early by quantitative quality management
  - Question 2.1 Which elements have impact on software quality management?
    - Metric 2.1.1 Defect Density[4]
  - Question 2.2 What was checked for early defect detection?
    - Metric 2.2.1 Defect Removal Effectiveness[4]
- Goal 3 To improve software process based on data collected from project to which software process are applied
  - Question 3.1 Which data is needed to understand and to improve current process?
    - Metric 3.1.1 Size Estimation Error[6]
    - Metric 3.1.2 Inspection (Review) Rate[6]
    - Metric 3.1.3 Defect Removal Efficiency[4]
    - Metric 3.1.4 Backlog Management Index[4]

3.4 Define Standard Metrics for Embedded System

Unlike the directly countable base metrics, derived metrics are for measuring characteristics or attributes of measurable entities indirectly. Standard metrics should be indicators that illustrate characteristics of project or process, so they must be a set of derived metrics. Because derived metrics consist of two or more base metrics and both planned data and actual data are need to measure the accuracy of estimating in project planning, defining standard metrics is based on two assumptions; 1) measure of base metrics with regard to time, size, and defect is mandatory, and 2) when base metrics are measured, both planned data and actual data should be collected.

To be standard metrics, they should support the goals of organization and be applicable to all divisions. Therefore, we defined an intersection set between a set of common metrics described in Section 3.2 and the set of metrics with respect to the goals of organization as described in Section 3.3 as standard metrics. This intersection included Metric 1.1.1, Metric 1.2.1, Metric 2.1.1, and Metric 3.1.1 in Section 3.3. Although Metric 2.2.1, the defect removal effectiveness was not included in the intersection, it was included in standard metrics because it is measurable at the current status and needed to check early defect detection. The development productivity and the cost performance index are related to the first goal and the defect density and the defect removal effectiveness are related to the second goal. For the third goal, the size estimation error was selected. Table 2 illustrates definition and measurement formula of five metrics selected as standard metrics.

Table 2. Standard Metrics

Metric Name	Description	
Development Productivity	Definition	This metric refers how many outputs can be produced per unit time. (The rate of output to investment)
	Measurement	Size / Time (LOC/Hr, LOD/Hr)
Defect Density	Definition	This metric is the number of defects found per unit size of product.
	Measurement	Defects / Size (Defects/KLOC, Defects/KLOD)
Defect Removal Effectiveness	Definition	This metric is the percentage of defects removed during that phase. Originally, this metric refers to the ability of the phase to remove defects that were present at that time. However, defect removal effectiveness as discussed here was calculated as just the formula below because our organization doesn't collect information on defect origin
	Measurement	Defects removed in that phase / Total defects *100 (%)
Cost Performance Index	Definition	This metric indicates the degree to which actual time spent is meeting time commitments.
	Measurement	Planned total development time / Actual total development time
Size Estimation Error	Definition	This metric indicates the degree to which the estimate matches the actual size.
	Measurement	(Actual size − Planned size) / Planned size * 100 (%)

4 An Empirical Study

In this section, we analyze the measurement results of standard metrics defined in Section 3.4. These five metrics were empirically studied to ascertain their usefulness.

We developed a data collection form for measuring standard metrics and distributed it to people on SEPG in each division. The input of measurement consisted of raw data related to time, size, and defect and project information such as project type, the number of developers, programming language, and precedentedness[2](the degree of domain experience of the development organization). Project information facilitates analyzing the result of measurement by project characteristics. Targets were eight divisions that developed various embedded systems such as printer, TV, multimedia system and network device. The data from fifteen projects, one or more projects per each division, were gathered. Although this study was based on the data from just fifteen projects, if there had been more number of projects, the analysis would have been more reliable.

4.1 Analyze Measurement Results of Standard Metrics

In analyzing the results, the primary criterion was project type. Project type is divided into two categories, in-house development and commercial development. Generally, final deliverable of in-house development projects is software system and end users are other developers compared to the end user of commercial development being customers. Unlike most projects in commercial development which handle the same line of products, in-house development are mainly for performance optimization or application of new technology and the development team has little previous experience. Cases that don't meet the assumption mentioned in Section 3.4 were excluded from the analysis because the result was not valid; 1) when size data is recorded without time data, 2) when only defect data in a specific phase was collected, and 3) when plan data doesn't exist. The measurement result of each metric is as follows.

• Development Productivity
Figure 3 illustrates document and code productivity by project types. Document productivity was calculated as lines of document per hour and one page was assumed to be 30 lines. In measuring code productivity, only lines of code newly added or modified in the current version were included. For every project except for project O, the code productivity of commercial development projects in which the team had abundant previous experience was higher than that of in-house development projects as shown in Figure 3. In addition, the data of projects of the same type agreed that the more experienced the team, the higher the productivity. L, P, and N on Figure 3 indicates the level of precendentedness and stands for Largely, Partially, and Not, respectively.

These measurement results can be referred when project planning. That is, the team can investigate the development productivity of previous similar projects and use it as benchmark for effort estimation or project scheduling.

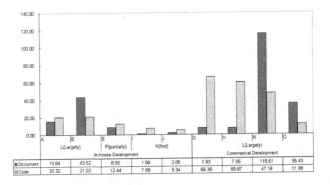

Fig. 3. Development Productivity by Project Types

• Defect Density
The defect density is an indicator which shows the quality level of product and is calculated as the number of defects per kilo lines of document or source code. For requirement and design phase, the number of defects removed by inspection is the numerator while for implementation and test phase, the number of defects removed by review, inspection, and test is the numerator. As shown in Figure 4, defect density of in-house development projects is on the decrease after design phase, whereas, in commercial development projects, defect density of test phase is much larger than that of implementation phase. Consequently, we can conclude that many defects escaped from previous phases are being found in test phase in commercial development projects considering the defect injection of test phase is usually a small number.

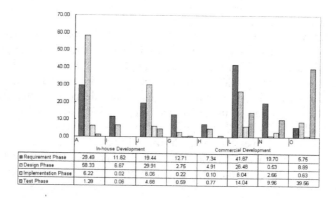

	In-house Development			Commercial Development			
	A		J	G	H	L	N	O
■ Requirement Phase	29.49	11.62	19.44	12.71	7.34	41.67	19.70	5.75
▣ Design Phase	58.33	6.67	29.91	2.75	4.91	26.48	0.53	8.89
▣ Implementation Phase	6.22	0.02	6.06	0.22	0.10	6.04	2.66	0.63
▣ Test Phase	1.28	0.06	4.68	0.59	0.77	14.04	9.96	39.56

Fig. 4. Defect Density

The results of this metric can be used for quality management during the development. For example, the team can compare the defect density of the current project with that of the previous project and decide if additional activities for defect removal are needed.

- Defect Removal Effectiveness

The defect removal effectiveness is the proportion in percentage of the number of defect removed at a particular phase out of the total number of defects. Testing is a very expensive way to find and fix defects compared to review or inspection [6]. It is thus desirable to remove as many defects as possible before test phase. Figure 5 shows the defect removal effectiveness by phase. For in-house development projects, the rate of defects removed before test phase is over 60% but for commercial development projects, it is not. This is due to the properties of commercial development that there is less uncertainty of requirements or design and testing is strengthened for product release.

This metric is used to evaluate defect removal effectiveness by development phase and find the phase that should be improved and also can be a benchmark for quality planning.

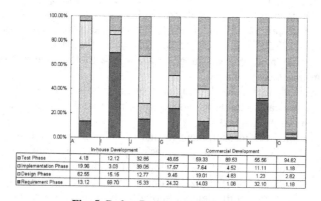

	In-house Development			Commercial Development			
	A		J	G	H	L	N	O
▣ Test Phase	4.18	12.12	32.85	48.65	59.33	89.53	55.56	94.82
▣ Implementation Phase	19.96	3.03	39.05	17.57	7.64	4.52	11.11	1.18
▣ Design Phase	62.55	15.15	12.77	9.46	19.01	4.83	1.23	2.82
■ Requirement Phase	13.12	69.70	15.33	24.32	14.03	1.08	32.10	1.18

Fig. 5. Defect Removal Effectiveness

• Cost Performance Index

The cost performance index shows the ratio of actual development time to the planned time. That is, a CPI of 1 means that total development time is equal to planned total development time and a CPI of greater than 1 implies that the work will finish within the planned time. A CPI of less than 1 implies that it will take more time than estimated. Therefore, it is possible to determine schedule performance based on the CPI. While 40% of projects in commercial development had finished within the planned time, all projects in in-house development had a CPI of less than 1, signifying that it took more time than estimated as shown in Figure 6.

With this metric, the team can calculate schedule growth due to effort estimation, predict when the project is completed and temper its concerns timely during the development.

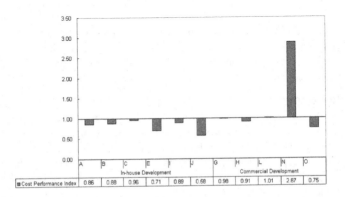

Fig. 6. Cost Performance Index

• Size Estimation Accuracy

The size estimation error divides the difference between actual size and estimate size by estimates and then converts it into a percentage. This is for measuring the degree of accuracy in the size estimation. A value of less than zero indicates an overestimate and a value of greater than 1 an underestimate. Zero value implies that the estimate size exactly corresponds to the actual size. In Figure 7, we can see that most projects in in-house development are under-estimated and the estimation error runs in the range between –27.31% and 266.65%. However, the size estimation error of commercial development projects range from –6.32% to 15.81and it is closer to zero than that of in-house development.

When project planning, the development effort estimates is usually based on the estimated size. We can examine the adequacy of the above approach and improve the estimating errors using this metric.

We have outlined the measurement results in Table 3. In conclusion, commercial development projects based on previous experience are superior to in-house development projects in terms of the development productivity, the defect density, the cost performance index, and the size estimate error, whereas in-house development projects are excellent in just the defect removal effectiveness before test phase.

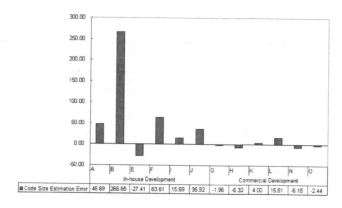

Fig. 7. Code Size Estimation Error

Table 3. The Measurement Result Summary by Project Types

	In-house Development	Commercial Development
Average Development Productivity	Doc: 14.2 LOD/hr Code: 13.3 LOC/hr	Doc: 41.6 LOD/hr Code: 46.4 LOC/hr
Average Defect Density	14.5 Defs/Klines	10.3 Defs/Klines
Average Defect Removal Effectiveness before test phase	83.6%	30.4%
Average Cost Performance Index	0.81	1.31
Average ISize Estimation Errorl	101.1%	11.0%

4.2 Analyze Relationship Between Metrics

Additionally, several regression analyses were conducted in order to understand the relationship between metrics. Should the value of one metric influence the value or interpretation of other metrics, examining their relationship is helpful to find out process areas to improve and to avoid misinterpretation of the metrics. Table 4 reports the results of a linear regression between metrics. The R-squared value denotes how well a regression line approximates real data points and varies from 0 to 1. If the value of R-squared is greater than 0.5, two sets of data are considered to be correlated. The value in parenthesis is the significance of correlation. It is for measuring the probability that the relationship could have occurred by chance. A significance of less than 0.05 is considered as strong evidence that there is a relationship between them.

As can be seen in Table 4, regardless of project type, the development time is proportional to the program size. In in-house development projects, the percentage of time in test phase decreases in proportion to the percentage of time in requirement and design phase and the size estimate error influences the time estimate error. In commercial development projects, the defect removal effectiveness and code productivity are considered to be correlated.

Therefore, for in-house development projects, the more the accurate size estimation, the better the time estimation. It is also necessary to strengthen requirement analysis and design activities in order to reduce time in test phase. For commercial development projects, it is important to remove defect as early as possible to increase code productivity.

Table 4. The Relationship between Metrics

Independent Value (X)	Dependent Value(Y)	In-house Development	Commercial Development
Size	Development Time	Y = - 807 + 0.145 X R^2=0.9158 (0.011)	Y = - 265 + 0.0165 X R^2=0.9434 (0.029)
% Time in Requirement and Design	% Time in Test	Y = 81.6 - 1.34 X R^2=0.6768 (0.023)	Y = 55.2 - 0.850 X R^2=0.3028 (0.158)
Size Estimate Error	(Implementation Phase + Test Phase) Time Estimate Error	Y = 0.406 + 0.00344 X R^2=0.8304 (0.030)	Y = 0.649 - 0.044 X R^2=0.0692 (0.743)
(Requirement Phase +Design Phase +Implementation Phase) Defect Removal Effectiveness	Code Productivity	Y = - 16.1 + 0.363 X R^2=0.3527 (0.291)	Y = 6.51 + 1.13 X R^2=0.9155 (0.043)

5   Conclusions

We can see where we are through the measurement of process or project and metrics is the vehicle of achieving such means. In this study, we defined standard metrics for our organization whose domain of development is the embedded system and analyzed the result of measurement. In addition, we described the relationship between metrics and ways to improve effectiveness in software development through an empirical study.

Metrics proposed in this paper have the following three contributions. First, because the selection of standard metrics was based on survey of current measurement program of our organization, it is applicable without the induction of a new measurement system or changing the current process. Second, the standard metrics were devised with relation to the goals of organization, so measuring them will be helpful to understand and solve the problems in software development of our organization. Third, the measurement results of each metric vary according to project types, languages, or the levels of previous experience. This point facilitates understanding of focus areas to improve by divisions or by project types.

In addition, many pending issues of organization can be settled as follows:

	Before	After
The number and type of metrics	Too many	About right
Useless metrics	Exist	Not exist
The concept and criteria of metrics	Different	Identical
Standardization of managerial regulations	Not Possible	Possible

Because size, time, and defect data are being collected by separate tools, there exists a limit that the data were gathered manually. However, if a tool to automate data gathering and measuring, and guidelines for measuring and analyzing are developed, the proposed standard metrics will be more useful. Finally, the basis for analyzing ROI (Return Of Investment) in view of cost will be provided through connection with cost estimate technique based on size.

References

1. Bassman, M.J.; McGarry, F. & Pajerski, R. Software Measurement Guidebook Revision 1 (Software Engineering Laboratory Series SEL-94-102). Greenbelt, MD: NASA Goddard Space Flight Center, June 1995
2. COCOMO II Model Definition Manual, Available at URL: http://sunset.usc.edu/research/COCOMOII
3. Robert B. Grady and Deborah L. Caswell, Software Metrics: establishing a company-wide program, Prentice-Hall, Englewood Cliffs, NJ, 1987
4. Stephen H. Kan, Metrics and Models in Software Quality Engineering, Addison Wesley, Reading, MA, 1995
5. Victor R. Basili, Gianluigi Caldiera, and H. Dieter Rombach, The Goal Question Metric Approach, Encyclopedia of Software Engineering, Volume 1, pp. 528-532, edited by John J. Marciniak, John Wiley & Sons, 1994
6. Watts S. Humphrey, A Discipline for Software Engineering, Addison Wesley, Reading, MA, 1995
7. William A. Florac, Robert E. Park, and Anita D. Carleton, "Practical Software Measurement: Measuring for Process Management and Improvement", CMU/SEI-97-HB-003, 1997

Process-Family-Points

Sebastian Kiebusch[1], Bogdan Franczyk[1], and Andreas Speck[2]

[1] University of Leipzig, Faculty of Economics and Management,
Information Systems Institute, Germany
kiebusch@wifa.uni-leipzig.de,
franczyk@wifa.uni-leipzig.de
[2] University of Jena, Faculty of Economics and Business Administration,
Commercial Inf. Systems, Germany
andreas.speck@uni-jena.de

Abstract. Software system families are characterized through a structured reuse of components and a high degree of automation based on a common infrastructure. It is possible to increase the efficiency of software system families by an explicit consideration of process flows in application domains which are driven by processes. Based on that fact this article briefly describes the approach of process family engineering. Afterwards the metrics of Process-Family-Points are explained in detail. These are the only framework to measure the size and estimate the effort of process families. Subsequently this paper shows the first results from a validation of the Process-Family-Points in the application domains of eBusiness and Automotive. After an evaluation of these empirical data this paper concludes with an outlook on future activities.

1 Introduction

Software systems families obtain a reduction of development time and costs as well as an improvement of quality in comparison to the traditional software engineering [cf. 10]. The consideration of software internal process flows realizes an additional optimization of the approach of software system families in domains which are driven by processes. These process families (PF) allow an inexpensive software engineering based on a optimized reuse and automation. PF require an adoption of the requirements from the focused domain due to the high complexity of software internal process flows. This work has been done so far for the domains of eBusiness and Automotive [cf. 9]. Figure 1 illustrates the actual version of the domain specific approach of process family engineering.

The size of the implementation and the effort of developing software products are dependant on the particular approach of software engineering. New paradigms in software engineering such as PF are characterized by reuse, automation and an explicit consideration of process flows. Therefore we need appropriate metrics to measure the size and estimate the effort for PF.

Due to the novelty of process family engineering there are no methods for quantifying the economic advantages of this new software engineering approach. However the existence of software metric is a main attribute for the acceptance of PF

Q. Wang et al. (Eds.): SPW/ProSim 2006, LNCS 3966, pp. 314–321, 2006.

in the future. Only a reliable measurement of economic advantages enables the practical use of process family engineering. The extensive utilization of PF will be restricted as long as there are no methods available to manage the cost, time and quality of development for PF.

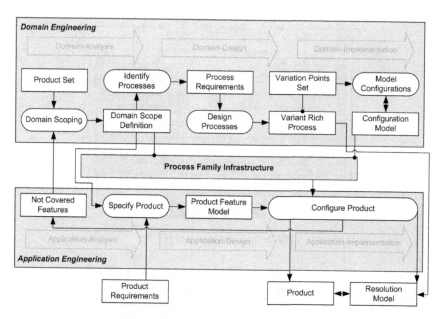

Fig. 1. Process family engineering [cf. 1]

The following essays were analyzed in detail as related work to our approach [cf. 5]:

- Böckle, G., et al.: A Cost Model for Software Product Lines [2];
- Lamine, S.: A Software Cost Estimation Model for Product Line Engineering [7];
- Poulin, J.: The Economics of Software Product Lines [8];
- Withey, J.: Investment Analysis of Software Assets for Product Lines [10].

The software metrics described in these articles measure the characteristics of software system families only from a certain and restricted viewpoint. Moreover they disregard the explicit process focus of PF and lose sight of quality influences or effort estimation. Because of these reasons the so called metrics of Process-Family-Points (PFP) were developed to realize a size measurement and effort estimation for PF. All PFP metrics are derived by goal-oriented actions according to the approved technique of the Goal Question Metric (GQM) paradigm.

2 Size Measurement

The functional specification of the requirements from a new PF-product are the informational foundation of the PFP approach in compliance with figure 2. Additional

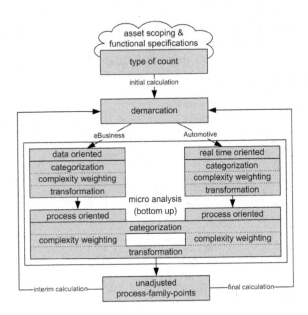

Fig. 2. Size measurement [cf. 5]

information about the specific reuse of common and variable PF-assets are necessary as well. These data are the main results of the asset scoping which is an central activity within the domain scoping of a PF according to figure 1.

The determination of the "type of count" is the first step for a size measurement by the PFP analysis corresponding to figure 2. The "type of count" defines if the PF is developed from scratch or built by a modification of an existing infrastructure. A third counting type is offered to measure a single software product which is derived from the PF. The determination of these counting types is similar to the Function Point Analysis (FPA) and affects the calculation of the implementation size from a PF. Based on these "types of count" the results of the PFP approach and the measures of the FPA are comparable. Therefore the general acceptance of the PFP metrics will be supported by this compatibility.

The following stage of the PFP analysis is called "demarcation" and identifies the counting scope as well as the system borders of the PF. At this point the dynamic boundaries are outlined between the common and variable assets. Hence it is possible to identify single variants of software products from the PF. The main goal of this stage is the meaningful differentiation of the assets which are to measure in the focused PF. An iterative execution of the demarcation (initial, interim and final calculation) enables the consideration of the evolution in the infrastructure of a PF as shown in figure 1. Consequently this step accesses the evolution which triggers the exchange between the common and variable assets in a PF. Furthermore the creeping scope phenomenon is considered during the development of a PF.

The micro analysis in figure 2 is characterized as an accumulation of software metrics to calculate an unadjusted size measure for PF. These metrics are partitioned in two sections as a result of the domain specific PF-usage:

- <u>eBusiness:</u> The actions to measure a PF in the domain of eBusiness comprise a data oriented and a process focused perspective. Both viewpoints realize a classification of the properties from PF in categories which differ in relation to their implementation size. Subsequently to this categorization a complexity weighting of every data and process function compose the foundation for the calculation of unadjusted PFP.
- <u>Automotive:</u> The metrics to measure PF in the automotive domain comprehend the characteristics of a real time and a process viewpoint with an important influence of the implementation size. The process to calculate the size measure of unadjusted PFP is also organized into the sections of categorization, complexity weighting and transformation.

Subsequently all calculated size measures were accumulated based on the preassigned "type of count" and attached to a project or a product. This sum of unadjusted PFP can be used as an early indicator to estimate future efforts. Furthermore this size measure is companionable to unadjusted FP and the COSMIC functional size unit (Cfsu). Consequently it is possible to compare PF with classical development approaches in the area of software engineering.

3   Effort Estimation

The PFP metrics which forecast efforts in developing or modifying a PF constitute a high flexible system to evaluate external influences in software engineering. Hence these metrics quantify environmental influences in a dynamic way and can be considered as an all-purpose concept. In addition to adjusting the PFP measures the macro analysis also enables a substitution of the out-of-time weighting procedures

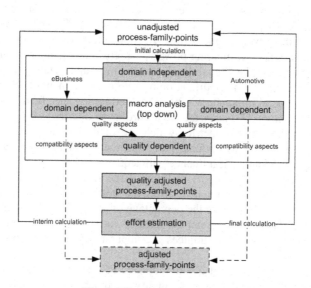

Fig. 3. Effort estimation [cf. 5]

from the FPA or Mark II analysis. With the flexible process model of figure 3 it is possible to take account of relevant effort influences which are up-to-date.

The domain independent software metrics from figure 3 consider four common conditions of PF, each subclassified in five exemplary influences. Environmental factors like "documentation", "infrastructure", "transition process" and "knowledge transfer" are evaluated as exemplary parameters of the flexible architecture from the PFP macro analysis. This general part of the PFP macro analysis calculates a numerical degree of influence which is connected to the evaluated factors and quantifies their impact on the effort to develop or modify a PF. The numeral influence of every domain independent influencing factor is calculated like in table 1.

Table 1. Documentation influences

ID	documentation	value	effect on effort
A 01	Is it necessary to create technical and/or functional specifications?	yes	increase
		no	decrease
A 02	Is it a must to documentate the usage of software metrics?	yes	increase
		no	decrease
A 03	Is it planned to documentate the code?	yes	increase
		no	decrease
A 04	Is it a must to develop a user guide?	yes	increase
		no	decrease
A 05	Is it planned to documentate defects and/or create a test paper?	yes	increase
		no	decrease
numeral influence		Σ increasing values	

After this evaluation of general influences the software metrics in figure 3 focus 30 exemplary characteristics which are domain dependent. Typical influences with a high impact on the development or modification effort for a PF in the automotive domain are for instance "computing power", "safety" and "memory volume". On the other hand influences like "flexibility", "marketing" and "legal position" have an effect on the development or modification of a PF in the domain of eBusiness. At this stage a second numeral influence will be calculated for the specific domain.

The consideration of 27 quality factors according to ISO/IEC 9126 is not obligatory in contrast with the preview metrics which are mandatory to execute [cf. 3]. The additional application of this optional part from the PFP macro analysis enables the computation of a third numeral influence with a quality focus.

According to the process model in figure 3 the size measure of adjusted PFP is calculated by the numeral influences from the domain dependent and the domain specific software metrics. Beside the percentage of adjustment, the number of general and domain specific influences can be selected in a flexible way. Furthermore the preassigned "type of count" guarantees a comparability between adjusted PFP and adjusted FP.

The optional size measure of quality adjusted PFP is a refinement of the adjusted PFP. An additional consideration of quality attributes realizes a high correlation between quality adjusted PFP and the effort for developing or modifying a PF. At the same time quality adjusted PFP are not compatible with alternative size measures because other metrics do not consider quality attributes on a satisfactory scale.

Normally the adjusted PFP are calculated to compare the productivity between PF and traditional approaches in software engineering. On the other hand quality adjusted PFP are preferred if alternative size measures are not available for a comparison and a high precision of the effort estimation is important.

The concluding estimation of effort for developing or modifying a PF is computed by usage of empirical equations. A number of functions to forecast efforts in man hours based on historical data are offered for the size measures of unadjusted, adjusted and quality adjusted PFP [figure 4, figure 5].

4 Validation

The correlation between the size measures of the PFP analysis and the effort to develop or modify a PF was investigated by scenarios of empirical validation. Within this framework it was possible to collect historical data for a derivation of domain specific equations to estimate the efforts in a PF project.

Every part of the PFP analysis with a focus on the domain of eBusiness was initially validated within a project at the *University of Leipzig*. Additionally to the development of a PF all efforts were estimated by a parallel usage of the PFP analysis and the traditional FPA. The size measures of the latter approach were characterized by a low correlation to the recorded efforts. On the other side the results of the PFP analysis have a significant higher coherence to the required efforts for developing a PF in the domain of eBusiness. Figure 4 illustrates the PFP size measure with the highest effort correlation. Furthermore an equation to estimate man hours in dependence on quality adjusted PFP ($y=3,4784x$) is calculated by a linear regression.

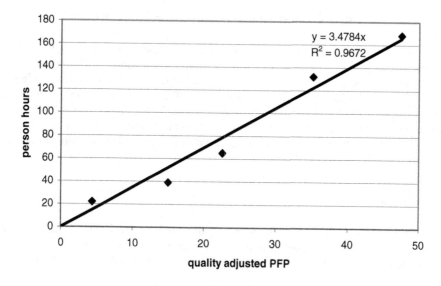

Fig. 4. Quality adjusted PFP and man hours (eBuiness)

A first validation of the PFP analysis to measure the size and estimate the effort for PF in the automotive domain was executed in cooperation with *DaimlerChrysler Research and Technology*. The potential effort to realize a theoretical PF was identified within the framework of a Delphi-Study as a multistage expert interview. Therefore it was possible to compare the identified person hours for developing a PF with the precalculated size measures of the PFP analysis and the COSMIC Cfsu. In contrast to the Cfsu all PFP size measures were characterized by a much higher correlation to the determined efforts. Figure 5 shows the coherence between quality adjusted PFP and the efforts for developing a PF in the domain of automotive by a empirical based equation (y=2,0534x).

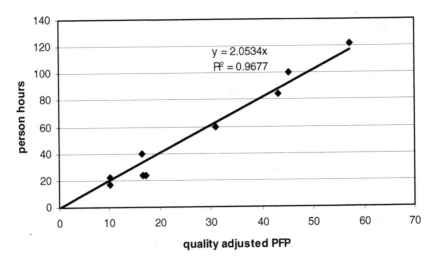

Fig. 5. Quality adjusted PFP and person hours (automotive)

The described validation is to be characterized as an laboratory study with an restricted scope. Nevertheless the PFP analysis is the only valid framework of software metrics to measure the size and forecast the effort in developing or modifying a PF. Moreover it is planned to collect additional data by usage of prototypical, domain specific implementations of the PFP software metrics.[1] Based on these measurement tools the actual equations to estimate the efforts will be calibrated and optimized during the research project *Process Family Engineering in Service-Oriented Applications* (PESOA).

5   Conclusion

The PFP analysis which was described in this article allows the identification of different influences to a project and supports an efficient problem management in software engineering for a PF. Furthermore, the discussed metrics enable a precise

---

project planning and a tracking of the development progression. Based on the delivery of size measures and the estimation of future effort the PFP software metrics calculate valuable information for the economical management of PF.

Despite the fact that these software metrics are the only approach to measure a PF they are first of all a scientific starting point which can be extended in different perspectives. For instance it is imaginable to match the PFP analysis with the rules of a functional size measurement according to ISO/IEC 14143 [cf. 4].

At the end it is to mention that the PFP macro analysis describes a high flexible system to access the impact of external influences which can be used also with traditional metrics like the FPA. These PFP metrics offer a model to optimize the accuracy of alternative approaches for effort estimation in the area of software engineering.

References

1. Bayer, J., Buhl, W., Giese, C., Lehner, T., Ocampo, A., Puhlmann, F., Richter, E., Schnieders, A., Weiland, J.: Process Family Engineering: Modeling variant-rich processes. PESOA Report No. 18/2005, 2005.
2. Böckle, G., Clements, P., McGregor, J. D., Muthig, D., Schmid, K. A Cost Model for Software Product Lines. In: van der Linden, F. (Ed.) Software Product-Family Engineering: 5th International Workshop, PFE 2003. Springer LNCS 3014, Berlin u. a. 2004, S. 310-316.
3. International Organization For Standardization/International Electrotechnical Commission (Ed.): Software engineering – Product quality – Part 1: Quality model. ISO/IEC 9126:2001, Geneva 2001.
4. International Organization For Standardization/International Electrotechnical Commission (Ed.): Information technology – Software measurement – Functional Size Measurement – Part 1: Definition of concepts. ISO/IEC 14143-1:1998, Geneva 1998.
5. Kiebusch, S. Metriken für prozessorientierte Software-System-Familien: Umfangskalkulation sowie Aufwandsprognose im Electronic Business und Automobilbereich. Dissertation, University of Leipzig, Leipzig 2006.
6. Kiebusch, S., Franczyk, B., Speck, A.: Measurement of Embedded Software System Families. In: Proceedings of the 6th International Workshop on Software Process Simulation and Modeling, St.-Louis 2005, pp. 48-56.
7. Lamine, S. Modèle d'estimation de coûts pour le développement logiciel basé sur la réutilisation: Cas de l'approche PLE. Master-Thesis, National School of Computer Science, Tunis 2004.
8. Poulin, J.: The Economics of Software Product Lines. In: International Journal of Applied Software Technology, 3 (1997) 1, pp. 20-34.
9. Process Family Engineering in Service-Oriented Applications (Ed.): PESOA Publikationen. http://www.pesoa.org/pages/Publications.html, 2005-12-23.
10. Withey, J.: Investment Analysis of Software Assets for Product Lines. CMU/SEI-96-TR-010, Carnegie Mellon University, 1996.

Automated Recognition of Low-Level Process: A Pilot Validation Study of Zorro for Test-Driven Development

Hongbing Kou and Philip M. Johnson

Collaborative Software Development Laboratory,
Department of Information and Computer Sciences,
University of Hawai'i,
1680 East-West Rd. POST307,
Honolulu, HI 96822, USA
{hongbing, johnson}@hawaii.edu
http://csdl.ics.hawaii.edu

Abstract. Zorro is a system designed to automatically determine whether a developer is complying with the Test-Driven Development (TDD) process. Automated recognition of TDD could benefit the software engineering community in a variety of ways, from pedagogical aids to support the learning of test-driven design, to support for more rigorous empirical studies on the effectiveness of TDD in practice. This paper presents the Zorro system and the results of a pilot validation study, which shows that Zorro was able to recognize test-driven design episodes correctly 89% of the time. The results also indicate ways to improve Zorro's classification accuracy further, and provide evidence for the effectiveness of this approach to low-level software process recognition.

1 Introduction

While software process research has historically focused on high-level, long-duration phases in software development, increasing attention is now being paid to low-level, short-duration activities as well. While a high-level activity such as "requirements specification" might take from weeks to months to complete, a low-level activity such as "refactor class Foo to extract interface IFoo" might take only seconds to complete in a modern interactive development environment.

The frequency and rapidity with which low-level process activities occur creates new barriers to answering classic software process questions, such as: what process is actually occurring (as opposed to what process is supposed to be occurring), what is the impact of a given process on important outcomes such as productivity and quality, and how could a given process be improved and/or tailored to a new domain?

Fortunately, the increasing sophistication of tool support for software development creates new ways to investigate low-level process. By capturing the behavior of developers as represented in their interactions with software development

Q. Wang et al. (Eds.): SPW/ProSim 2006, LNCS 3966, pp. 322–333, 2006.

tools, it may be possible to gain new insight into what low-level processes are occurring during development and their impact on productivity and quality.

This paper presents recent results from our ongoing research into automated support for recognition and analysis of low-level software processes. Our approach leverages the Hackystat framework for automated software engineering process and product data collection and analysis [1], which provides infrastructure for gathering a broad variety of developer behaviors. On top of Hackystat, we developed a generic, rule-based recognizer system for sensor data called "Software Development Stream Analysis" (SDSA). On top of SDSA, we developed a set of rules and other specializations designed to recognize a specific low-level process called Test-Driven Development (TDD) [2]. The system resulting from this combination of Hackystat, SDSA, and TDD-specific extensions is called "Zorro".

Test-driven development is an interesting low-level process to study because substantial claims have been made for its effectiveness. For example, TDD has been claimed to naturally generate 100% coverage, improve refactoring, provide useful executable documentation, produce higher code quality, and reduce defect rates [2, 3, 4]. It would be a significant contribution to the software engineering community to rigorously test these claims in controlled and/or professional settings to better understand the conditions under which they hold, and to further the evolution of the method itself.

Zorro can automatically monitor developer behavior and produce analyses describing certain sequences of behaviors as test-driven development and other sequences of behaviors as non-test-driven development. If Zorro recognizes TDD correctly, then we would have a powerful mechanism for exploring how test-driven development is used in practice and its effects on quality and productivity. The ease with which Hackystat sensors can be installed and the non-intrusive nature of data collection and analysis would make possible both classroom and industrial case studies into TDD compliance, the potential discovery of alternative processes, and the investigation of the impact of TDD on productivity and quality. Finally, Zorro could be used to teach TDD by providing real-time feedback to the developer on whether they are carrying out TDD or not.

Before we can apply Zorro to these TDD research questions, however, we must answer two general validation questions: (1) Does the system collect the behaviors necessary to determine TDD, and (2) Does the recognizer infer the TDD process correctly from the collected behaviors?

In this paper, we present the design of Zorro and the results from a pilot validation study. To do the validation, we needed an independent source of information about low-level developer behavior to compare to Zorro's. For this purpose, we designed and implemented an open source system called "Eclipse Screen Recorder" (ESR), [5]. ESR is a plug-in to the Eclipse IDE that captures a screen image approximately once per second and produces a quicktime movie of the developer's behaviors with respect to the Eclipse window.

Our validation analysis compared the representation of developer behavior captured by ESR to the representation of developer behavior inferred by Zorro, and classified the frequency and types of differences between these two independent representations. We discovered that Zorro classifies developer behavior correctly 89% of the time, and also discovered ways we can enhance the system in future to improve its classification accuracy further.

The contributions of this research include initial evidence that Zorro can be an effective tool for automatic recognition of the TDD low-level process. Zorro also provides evidence that SDSA is a useful framework for software process recognition. Finally, our results reveal the importance of validation using independent data sources as a component of the process modelling research process, and the usefulness of mechanisms like ESR for this purpose.

2   Related Work

Osterweil has developed a view of software process research that recognizes two complementary levels: macroprocess and microprocess [6]. Macroprocess research is focused on the outward manifestations of process—the time taken, costs incurred, defects generated, and so forth. Macroprocess research traditionally correlates such outcome measures to other project characteristics, which can suggest the impact of process changes to these outcomes, but which suffers from the lack of any underlying causal theory. Bridging this gap is the province of microprocess research, according to Osterweil, in which languages and formal notations are used to specify process details at a sufficient level of rigor and precision that they can be used to support causal explanation of the outcome measures observed at the macroprocess level. Our research most readily fits into the "microprocess" level, except that instead of producing a top-down language, our approach involves bottom-up recognition.

The Balboa research project, like Zorro, was concerned with inference of process from low-level event streams [7]. In Balboa, the event streams were taken from the commit records of a configuration management system, and finite state machines were created that could model the commit stream data observed in practice. Unlike Balboa, Zorro uses instrumentation attached to the developer's IDE, which enables access to much lower-level events than those available through the commit records of a configuration management system. Also, the Balboa research project was retrospective in nature, with the researchers limited to historical project records. Zorro's focus on active development makes additional research possible, such as the validation studies presented in this paper.

Our research also compares in interesting ways to recent work on understanding processes associated with open source software development processes [8]. In this research, "web information spaces" are mined with the goal of discovering software process workflows via analysis of their content, structure, update, and usage patterns. Our approach in Zorro has both strengths and weaknesses relative to this research. A strength of the Zorro approach is that by attaching instrumentation to the IDE, we can capture more detailed information concerning developer behavior than is possible from inspection of web information spaces.

However, this can also be viewed as a weakness, in that this instrumentation creates an adoption barrier not present when mining already publically available information.

Another strand of related research occurs in the areas of knowledge discovery and data mining, in which time ordered input streams are processed to discover and classify naturally recurring patterns. For example, the Episode Discovery (ED) algorithm supports natural forms of periodicity in human-generated timestamp data [9]. While such approaches are an interesting future research area for SDSA, our current episode discovery algorithm uses rules to decide upon episode boundaries regardless of their frequency of occurrence.

Finally, our research relates to prior research on evaluating test-driven design practices and their impact on productivity and quality [10, 11, 12, 13, 14, 15]. In these studies, researchers had limited ability to verify that the programmers who were supposed to be using test-driven development were, in fact, using that methodology. Zorro, if validated, would be an important contribution to this research community by providing a tool to ensure compliance with the process under the experimental conditions.

3   The Design of Zorro

The design of Zorro is highly modular and consists of three basic layers: Hackystat, an extension to Hackystat called Software Development Stream Analysis, and a set of rules and enhancements to SDSA to support recognition of the TDD process.

3.1   Hackystat

Hackystat is an open source framework for automated collection and analysis of software engineering process and product data that we have been developing since 2001. Hackystat supports unobtrusive data collection via specialized "sensors" that are attached to development environment tools and that send structured "sensor data type" instances via SOAP to a web server for analysis via server-side Hackystat "applications". Over two dozen sensors are currently available, including sensors for IDEs (Emacs, Eclipse, Vim, VisualStudio), configuration management (CVS, Subversion), bug tracking (Jira), testing and coverage (JUnit, CppUnit, Emma, JBlanket), system builds and packaging (Ant), static analysis (Checkstyle, PMD, FindBugs, LOCC, SCLC), and so forth. Applications of the Hackystat Framework in addition to our work on SDSA and Zorro include in-process project management [16], high performance computing [17], and software engineering education [18].

3.2   SDSA

Software Development Stream Analysis (SDSA) is a Hackystat application that provides a framework for organizing the various kinds of data received by Hackystat into a form amenable for time-series analysis. Figure 1 illustrates the start

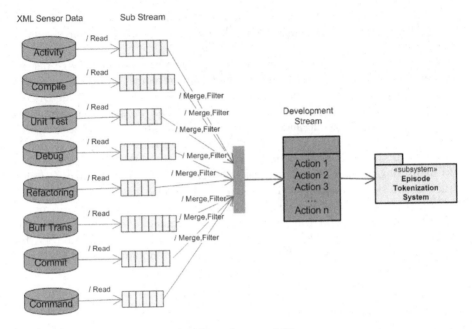

Constructing Development Stream

Fig. 1. Development Streams

of this process in which the various kinds of process and product data collected by Hackystat sensors are filtered and merged into an abstraction called a Development Stream.

The next stage of SDSA processing, called Tokenizing, involves partitioning the development stream into a sequence of "episodes" which should constitute the atomic building blocks of whatever process is being recognized. We have developed four kinds of tokenizers for identifying episode boundaries: the commit tokenizer uses configuration management checkins, the command tokenizer uses a distinguished commands or command sequences, the test pass tokenizer uses passing test invocations, and the buffer transition tokenizer uses sequences of buffer transitions. Figure 2 illustrates the process of splitting up the development stream into discrete episodes via tokenizers.

The final step in SDSA is to classify each episode according to the process model of interest. In SDSA, this classification is performed using the JESS rule based system augmented with rules to specify a particular process. Figure 3 illustrates this process.

3.3   SDSA Specializations for TDD

Zorro extends SDSA with rules and analyses oriented to the recognition and classification of TDD behaviors. Figure 4 illustrates the four kinds of behavioral

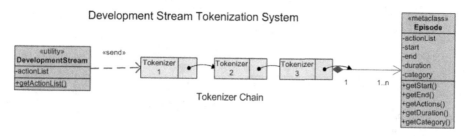

Fig. 2. Tokenizing into episodes

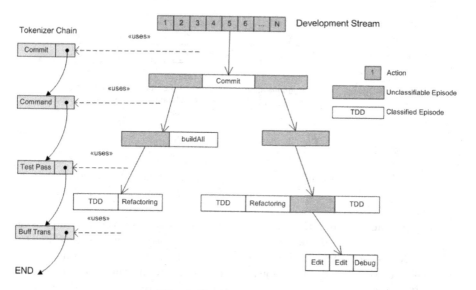

Fig. 3. Episode classification

sequences associated with test-driven development. Zorro includes JESS rules to recognize each of these four kinds of test-driven development behaviors.

Refactoring, in which the developer alters the programs internal structure without affecting its external behavior, is also a valid behavior during test-driven development. Figure 5 illustrates the four kinds of refactoring recognized by the Zorro rule base.

Finally, Zorro includes a user interface in the Hackystat server web application for display of the episodes, their classification, and their internal structure. Figure 6 illustrates the Zorro interface.

4   The Pilot Validation Study

As noted above, in order to feel confident in Zorro as an appropriate tool to investigate TDD, we must answer two basic validation questions: (1) Does Zorro collect the behaviors necessary to determine when TDD is occurring, and (2) Does Zorro recognize test-driven development when it is occurring? To answer

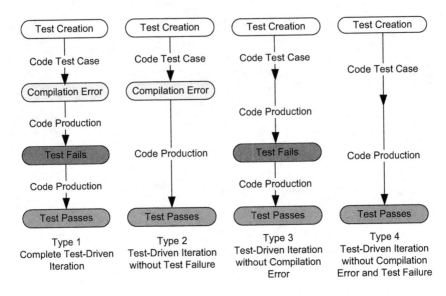

Fig. 4. TDD episode description

these questions, one must somehow gather an independent source of data regarding the developer's behaviors and compare that data to what was collected and analyzed by Zorro.

One approach to validating the system is to have an observer watching developers as they work, and take notes as to whether they are performing TDD or not. We considered this but discarded it as unworkable: the use of a human observer would be quite costly, and given the rapidity with which TDD cycles can occur, it would be quite hard for an observer to notate all of the TDD-related events that can occur literally within seconds of each other. We would end up having to validate our validation technique!

Instead, we developed a plugin to Eclipse that generates a Quicktime movie containing time-stamped screen shots of the Eclipse window at regular intervals. Figure 7 shows the Quicktime viewer with one screen image. The design of ESR allows adjustment of frame rate and resolution: the higher the frame rate and/or resolution, the larger the size of the resulting Quicktime file. We have found that a frame rate of 1 frame per second and a resolution of 960x640 pixels is sufficient for validation, while producing relatively compact Quicktime files (typically 7-8 MB per hour of screenshots). The Quicktime movie created by ESR provides a visual record of developer behavior that can be manually synchronized with the Zorro analysis using the timestamps and used to answer the two validation questions.

Our pilot validation study involved the following procedure. First, we obtained agreement from seven volunteer student subjects to participate in the pilot study. These subjects were experienced with both Java development and the Eclipse IDE, but not necessarily with test-driven development. Second, we provided them with a short description of test-driven design, and a sample problem to implement

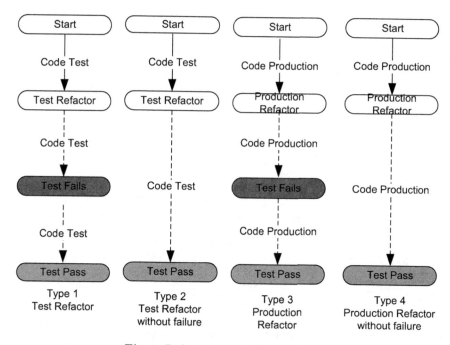

Fig. 5. Refactoring episode description

in a test-driven design style. The problem was to develop a Stack abstract data type using test-driven design, and we supplied them with an ordered list of tests to write and some sample test methods to get them started. Finally, they carried out the task using Eclipse with both ESR and Zorro data collection enabled.

To analyze the data, we created a spreadsheet in which we recorded the results of watching the Quicktime movie and manually encoding the developer activities that occurred. Then, we ran the Zorro analyses, added their results to the spreadsheet, and validated the Zorro classifications against the video record.

5   Results of the Pilot Study

Figure 8 summarizes the results of our analyses. Seven subjects participated, and spent between 28 and 66 minutes to complete the task. Zorro partitioned the overall development effort into 92 distinct episodes, out of which 86 were classified as either Test-Driven, Refactoring, or Test-Last; the remainder were "unclassified", which normally corresponded to startup or shutdown activities.

The most important result of this study is indicated by the "Wrongly Classified Episodes" column, which shows the results of comparing the ESR videos of the developer's Eclipse window to the classifications automatically made by the Zorro recognizer. Out of the 92 episodes under study, 82 were validated as correctly classified, for an accuracy rate of 89%.

The validation analysis also revealed several ways to increase the accuracy of Zorro. First, we discovered that our underlying Hackystat sensor sometimes

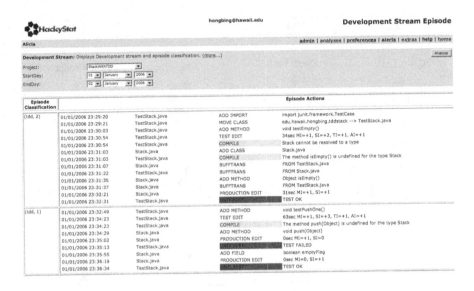

Fig. 6. Zorro interface

failed to record an edit to the program under development when the ESR video showed that the developer made a "quick change" lasting only a few seconds. Second, the sensor also failed to record a compilation error when a change to the production code created a compilation error in the non-active test code. Finally, the current Zorro rule set sometimes failed to partition the development stream along optimal episode boundaries, making it problematic for the classifier to recognize the developer's behaviors during this time period correctly. We intend to fix these issues in the next version of the system, which should raise the accuracy rate significantly.

It is also interesting to review the classification results apart from their accuracy, as they provide insight into the appropriate design of future studies. All four types of Test-Driven Development were recognized by Zorro, although only two of the four types of Refactoring were found. We believe that the simplicity of the software system under development in this study may have been a factor in the limited types of refactoring, and intend to scale up the problem complexity in future studies.

A provocative result of this study is that half the episodes (46) were classified as test-last, even though the subjects were instructed to do test-first development. To some extent, this may also be an artifact of the simplicity of the software under development. But it also reveals a hidden "secret" of test-first development: sometimes, while implementing the code to address one unit test, you can't help but implement additional features as well. At that point, the rational behavior is to implement the unit tests for those additional features, which effectively constitutes test-last design. The nature and frequency of embedded test-last within test-first development is an interesting topic for future research.

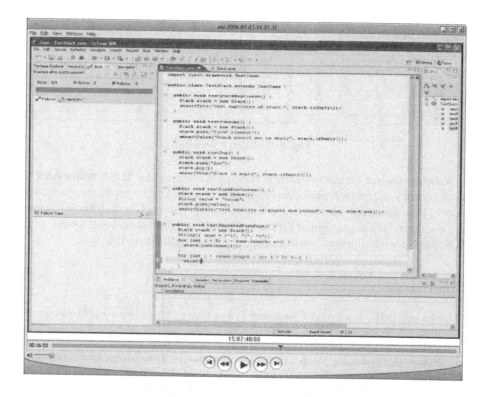

Fig. 7. An ESR Quicktime file

6   Conclusions and Future Directions

The pilot study has been successful in developing an effective validation methodology for the Zorro system, and in identifying several opportunities for improvement to the system that should result in higher classification accuracy in future.

After making these improvements, our next task will be to design and carry out a broad-scale validation study. We intend to expand the total number of subjects participating in the study, and solicit both student and professional developer participation. While we will provide a sample problem to implement in a test-driven design approach, we also hope to collect "in vivo" data from professionals who use test-driven design in their daily work. As before, we will collect both ESR and Zorro data from each subject and analyze it to assess the classification accuracy of Zorro, discover opportunities for improvement in the system, and perhaps discover new insights into the nature of test-driven design.

If the broad-scale validation study results demonstrate that Zorro has achieved high accuracy (95% or better) in recognizing TDD, then we will proceed to the next stage, which is the design of experiments to see how developers use (or don't use) TDD in practice, the factors influencing their decision, and the outcomes of their decisions on productivity and quality.

Subject Index	Duration	Num Episodes	Classified Episodes	Test-Driven Episode Breakdown				Refactoring Episode Breakdown				Test-Last Episodes	Wrongly Classified Episodes	Wrongly Classified Episodes (%)
				Type 1	Type 2	Type 3	Type 4	Type 1	Type 2	Type 3	Type 4			
1	44:53:00	15	15	2	3	1	0	0	1	0	0	8	2	13.3
2	28:17:00	13	13	0	5	0	0	0	0	0	0	8	3	23.1
3	48:00:00	14	14	0	6	3	0	0	0	0	0	5	1	7.1
4	66:32:00	14	14	0	4	0	1	0	0	0	1	8	1	7.1
5	43:14:00	16	11	2	1	0	0	0	1	0	0	7	1	6.3
6	45:57:00	11	11	1	0	1	2	0	0	0	0	7	1	9.1
7	32:40:00	9	8	1	2	1	0	0	0	0	1	3	1	11.1
Subtotal		92	86	6	21	6	3	0	2	0	2	46	10	10.9

Fig. 8. Summary Results

Another area of future research is the application of the SDSA framework to model other low-level software development processes. For example, there are a variety of best practices surrounding when a developer should commit their changes to a configuration management repository which we could model and assess using SDSA along with different sensors and different classification rule sets.

References

1. Johnson, P.M.: Hackystat Framework Home Page. (http://www.hackystat.org/)
2. Beck, K.: Test-Driven Development by Example. Addison Wesley, Massachusetts (2003)
3. George, B., Williams, L.: An Initial Investigation of Test-Driven Development in Industry. ACM Sympoium on Applied Computing **3**(1) (2003) 23
4. Maximilien, E.M., Williams, L.: Accessing Test-Driven Development at IBM. In: Proceedings of the 25th International Conference in Software Engineering, Washington, DC, USA, IEEE Computer Society (2003) 564
5. Kou, H.: Eclipse Screen Recorder Home Page. (http://csdl.ics.hawaii.edu/Tools/Esr/)
6. Osterweil, L.J.: Unifying microprocess and macroprocess research. In: Proceedings of the International Software Process Workshop. (2005) 68–74
7. Cook, J.E., Wolf, A.L.: Automating process discovery through event-data analysis. In: ICSE '95: Proceedings of the 17th international conference on Software engineering, New York, NY, USA, ACM Press (1995) 73–82
8. Jensen, C., Scacchi, W.: Experience in discovering, modeling, and reenacting open source software development processes. In: Proceedings of the International Software Process Workshop. (2005)
9. Heierman, E., Youngblood, G., Cook, D.: Mining temporal sequences to discover interesting patterns. In: Proceedings of the 2004 International Conference on Knowledge Discovery and Data Mining, Seattle, Washington (2004)
10. George, B., Williams, L.: A Structured Experiment of Test-Driven Development. Information & Software Technology **46**(5) (2004) 337–342
11. Muller, M.M., Hagner, O.: Experiment about Test-first Programming. In: Empirical Assesment in Software Engineering (EASE), IEEE Computer Society (2002)
12. Olan, M.: Unit testing: test early, test often. In: Journal of Computing Sciences in Colleges, The Consortium for Computing in Small Colleges (2003) 319
13. Edwards, S.H.: Using software testing to move students from trial-and-error to reflection-in-action. In: Proceedings of the 35th SIGCSE technical symposium on Computer science education, ACM Press (2004) 26–30

14. Geras, A., Smith, M., Miller, J.: A Prototype Empirical Evaluation of Test Driven Development. In: Software Metrics, 10th International Symposium on (METRICS'04), Chicago Illionis, USA, IEEE Computer Society (2004) 405
15. Pancur, M., Ciglaric, M.: Towards empirical evaluation of test-driven development in a university environment. In: Proceedings of EUROCON 2003, IEEE (2003)
16. Johnson, P.M., Kou, H., Paulding, M.G., Zhang, Q., Kagawa, A., Yamashita, T.: Improving software development management through software project telemetry. IEEE Software (2005)
17. Johnson, P.M., Paulding, M.G.: Understanding HPCS development through automated process and product measurement with Hackystat. In: Second Workshop on Productivity and Performance in High-End Computing (P-PHEC). (2005)
18. Johnson, P.M., Kou, H., Agustin, J.M., Zhang, Q., Kagawa, A., Yamashita, T.: Practical automated process and product metric collection and analysis in a classroom setting: Lessons learned from Hackystat-UH. In: Proceedings of the 2004 International Symposium on Empirical Software Engineering, Los Angeles, California (2004)

Process Evolution Supported by Rationale: An Empirical Investigation of Process Changes

Alexis Ocampo and Jürgen Münch

Fraunhofer Institute for Experimental Software Engineering,
Fraunhofer-Platz 1, 67663, Kaiserslautern, Germany
{ocampo, münch}@iese.fraunhofer.de

Abstract. Evolving a software process model without a retrospective and, in consequence, without an understanding of the process evolution, can lead to severe problems for the software development organization, e.g., inefficient performance as a consequence of the arbitrary introduction of changes or difficulty in demonstrating compliance to a given standard. Capturing information on the rationale behind changes can provide a means for better understanding process evolution. This article presents the results of an exploratory study with the goal of understanding the nature of process changes in a given context. It presents the most important issues that motivated process engineers changing important aerospace software process standards during an industrial project. The study is part of research work intended to incrementally define a systematic mechanism for process evolution supported by rationale information.

1 Introduction

Software process models are used as a means for supporting software engineers in systematically performing the engineering processes needed to develop software products. As these processes are performed, suggestions for adjustment or refinement can arise, which in turn demand evolving the models. Usually, certain events such as the introduction of a new software development technology in a development team (e.g., new testing support tools and techniques), a new/updated process engineering technology (e.g., a new process modeling technique), new/updated standards/guidelines for software development or process engineering, new/updated regulatory constraints, or new/updated best practices emerging from community experience generate issues that must be resolved by performing changes to the software process models.

In many cases, precipitous and arbitrary decisions are taken, and process models are evolved without storing or keeping track of the rationale behind such changes. One of the reasons is that this is an expensive activity that demands a dedicated role in the organization [1], especially because identifying the rationale of a change, or driving evolution activities in terms of rationale, is not an easy task. A mechanism (concept and tool) that can be used for collecting information about process changes and that could help in evolving the process in a systematic way is needed.

We believe that the first step towards such a systematic mechanism is to understand the nature of process changes. We assume that by having a predefined classification of

Q. Wang et al. (Eds.): SPW/ProSim 2006, LNCS 3966, pp. 334–341, 2006.

the most common reasons for process changes, the task of collecting the information related to such a rationale can be simplified and become more suitable for use in real process evolution projects. Additionally, this can be seen as an initial step for building a mechanism that supports systematic process evolution. Once this is understood, a structured conceptual model of rationale can be produced and tested in process evolution projects.

This article presents the results of an initial attempt to achieve such a predefined classification as follows: Section 2.1 briefly presents the basic concepts that we use for understanding the nature of changes to the software process and software process evolution. Section 2.2 provides short descriptions of related work where concepts for understanding process changes have been developed; Section 3 presents the context of the study performed for understanding the nature of changes to a process standard. Section 4 presents the issues derived from a repository of changes performed to a process standard, and an interpretation of the frequency with which such issues appeared during the project. Section 5 presents a discussion of the most relevant findings of the study together with research questions to be addressed in the future.

2 Background

2.1 Process Evolution Supported by Rationale

We believe that software process evolution should describe the relationships between an existing process model and its pre-existing version(s). Such relationships denote differences between versions due to distinguishable modifications.

One can distinguish the meaning of such modifications if one can understand the rationale behind them. Rationale is defined as the justification of decisions [1]. Historically, much research about rationale has focused on software/product design [9], [10], [11], and [12]. Rationale models represent the reasoning that leads to the system, including its functionality and its implementation [3]. In general, the capture, organization, and analysis of change rationale appears to be a research topic extensively addressed by software product designers but unknown to, or considered unimportant by, software process engineers. This conflicts with the obvious requirement that process engineers need to know the process evolution history in order to be able to effectively and efficiently tailor processes or update them. For example, tailoring a process model without considering what is or is not suitable for a given project can lead to undesired results. This was observed in the study presented in this paper. Process engineers found through interviews that a tailored process forced process practitioners to take part in system design activities that they felt they did not belong to, especially because this was not part of their work scope. Practitioners assured them that such activities were part of the tailored process although they did not know why, since a previous version of the tailored process did not have them. As a consequence, practitioners and process engineers were all confused and without information that could lead to a suitable solution. Tailoring can be successfully accomplished if a process engineer knows the issues, alternatives, arguments, and criteria that justify the definition of a process model. Equally, updating a process model without having knowledge of its history can lead to process models that do not reflect actual practices. Some other benefits of using the rationale as driver for software process model evolution are: supports reworking of software process standards; supports understanding the impact of changes due to specific issues; encourages making rational decisions instead of emotional ones; supports the analysis and identification of non-systematic and rushed decisions.

2.2 Related Work

There are not many studies that report on a classification or taxonomy of reasons for changing a process model. Nguyen and Conradi [2] present a framework for categorizing process evolution based on six dimensions (origin, cause, type, how, when, and by whom). A change categorized by this framework is called a change pattern. The change pattern, project characteristics, and product quality attributes are stored together so that they can be used for future projects. Data on the evolution of a software development project were collected in a case study performed in the software development department of a banking institution. With regard to the "where", i.e., the sources of process changes, 40% of the recorded changes were due to customer requests, and 60% were due to changes from senior or middle management. The most common observed reasons (why) were the following: a) misunderstanding originating from the customer; b) resources and competence was not always available; c) a new approach for solving the problem was adopted.

Madhavji [5] presents the Prism model of changes, which is an abstract description of a software environment specialized in the treatment of changes in a software development project. The Prism model serves as a classification scheme for structuring the decisions that change an item and as an information base suitable for analyzing the history changes that can help to make future decisions. Unfortunately, Madhavji [5] does not provide a deeper insight or data that show a classification of reasons.

Bandinelli et al. [4] identify three significant categories of changes caused by a variety of reasons and needs. They are: 1) incremental definition: Processes cannot be completely defined at the beginning of a project; therefore, changing them continuously can be viewed as a type of change that adds new parts to the process model; 2) environmental/organizational: Changes of this type are caused because, e.g., the company has acquired new tools to support the software development staff; 3) customization: Changes of this type allow process agents (humans who use the process) to select the parts of the process that suit them. There is no evidence of data or validation of such categories in the study.

Nejmeh and Riddle [6] present a Process Evolution Dynamics Framework that allows process change agents to describe, understand, learn from, plan, and manage process evolution efforts. They consider the organization's context as the determinant factor for defining and sequencing process evolution cycles and recommend exploring the context factors that influence process changes in order to better understand process evolution. Customer desires, market pressure, personnel availability, personnel capability, business goals, regulatory constraints, and available technologies are, among others, important business context factors.

Bhuta et al. [7], propose the development of process elements that can be built with reusable strategies, and be reused for creating different project plans. One strategy can be, e.g., to search for a process element, select a process element, understand the process element selected, and, if required, adapt the process element. This means that process elements must be accompanied by important information that can be easily understood by project managers. Examples of such information are: What the process element does, its value, how it could be executed, which resources are required to execute it, and its context information. Butha et al. [7] refer to Basili et al. [8] for the problems of capturing and storing context information in a project repository. Unfortunately, the case study presented by Butha et al. [7] neither provides evidence on context information, nor reasons for selecting certain process elements as part of a project plan.

3 Study Context

The study presented in this article was performed in the context of a project that aimed at the evolution of space standards.

The European Cooperation for Space Standardization (ECSS) [13] is an initiative established to develop a coherent, single set of easy-to-use standards for all European space activities, covering all areas of space activities, including engineering, quality assurance, and project management. Organizations or projects part of the European Space Agency (ESA) are supposed to develop and use their specific tailoring(s) of the ECSS standards. Tailoring can be done in a project-specific way (i.e., a separate tailoring for each project) or in an organization-specific way (i.e., one tailoring per organization, to be used for all their projects). The ESA Space Operations Center ESOC (i.e., the ESA organization where the project took place) chose the organization-specific tailoring approach. The applicable implementation of their ECSS tailoring was the Software Engineering and Management Guide (SEMG) [14], which was used for all their major projects.

After some years of experience with the ECSS standards, they were revised by ESA, and a new version was published. This also meant that the SEMG had to be revised, in order to be compliant to the revised ECSS standard. This compliance had to be proven by means of traceability of every ECSS requirement to its implementation, and by providing a tailoring justification for every tailored requirement. The process engineers' task was to tailor the relevant parts of the ECSS (comprising several hundred requirements) to ESOC's needs and to apply this tailoring in an update of their implementation of the standard, the SEMG.

Another important task assigned to process engineers was to improve the ease of use of the SEMG. For the purposes of this project, process engineers considered that the ease of use of a document is positively influenced by improving: (1) internal consistency, i.e., avoiding that one part of the document contradicts another, (2) external consistency, i.e., avoiding that the document at hand contradicts other documents and that links to external sources are correct, and (3) conciseness, i.e., indexed tables of contents allow people to find important things quickly, different concepts are explained and marked clearly, and the document is not larger than necessary.

Finally, process engineers had to maintain detailed change logs on a per-section basis, because of very different stakeholders who wanted to keep track of the changes performed to the SEMG and their justifications.

One initial analysis concerned compliance and showed that the SEMG was only partially compliant to the new ECSS software standard, and had to be updated accordingly. Another initial analysis concerned ease-of-use and was done by analyzing the SEMG documents and by means of structured interviews with SEMG users. Process engineers observed that the most predominant wish was for output simplification and clarification. Furthermore, the SEMG structure did not reflect actual process execution any more and had to be adjusted accordingly.

The SEMG was modified iteratively and incrementally as follows: Process engineers changed the SEMG and delivered a new version for review. Afterwards, reviewers discussed changes performed to the SEMG and accepted or rejected such changes. The reviewers documented their decisions and sent comments and suggestions to the process engineers. Process engineers reworked the SEMG based on the comments and suggestions. This iterative process allowed updating the SEMG in a controlled way and enabled a constant review of the accomplishment of the tasks.

4 Data Analysis

Process engineers documented the information related to the changes and their justifications and stored them in a database as they were evolving the SEMG. Two versions of the SEMG resulted from the editing-reviewing iterations. This was an initial attempt at collecting the rationale of process changes in order to understand the nature of changes and to understand how to capture rationale information adequately. The information collected about the changes was used as the basis for a detailed study of the most important and common issues that were resolved by each change. We accomplished this by querying the database that contains information on changes to the SEMG and by understanding each change's justification. While doing this, we derived a list of the most common issues that process engineers faced while doing the SEMG evolution. The following is the list and an explanation of the issues:

1. Improper sequence of processes: Process engineers found that the prescribed control flow of activities differed from the one followed in real projects.
2. Ambiguous activity description: Process engineers found activity descriptions capable of being understood in two or more possible senses or ways.
3. Improper placement of an output: Process engineers found that the prescribed product flow differed from the one present in real projects.
4. Non-compliant activity: Process engineers found cases where activities did not fulfill the requirements stated in the ECSS standards.
5. Ambiguous additional explanatory text: Process engineers found explanatory text that could be understood in two or more possible senses or ways.
6. Improper placement of additional explanatory text: Process engineers found examples of explanations that were incorrectly referenced.
7. Misleading name of an activity: Process engineers found names that did not reflect the meaning of the process for practitioners.
8. Activity description not concise: Process engineers found activity descriptions that contain superfluous or unnecessary statements.
9. Redundant activity description: Process engineers found duplicated descriptions of activities.

10. Additional explanatory text not concise: Process engineers found examples or explanations that contained superfluous or unnecessary statements.
11. Ambiguous output description: Process engineers found output descriptions capable of being understood in two or more possible senses or ways.

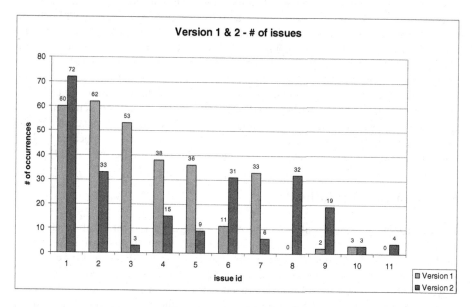

Fig. 1. # Occurrences per issue

Fig. 1 reflects the number of changes caused by the issues listed above when editing the process standards during the first and second iterations. It was found that during the first iteration, issues such as "improper sequence of processes", "ambiguous activity description", and "improper placement of an output", i.e., (1), (2), and (3) respectively, caused the largest number of changes to the process standards. This can be explained by the fact that in the first iteration, the process standards contents and its architecture were extensively modified in order to fulfill the objective of increasing the standard's ease of use.

The next most frequent issue is "non-compliant activity" (4), because one of the goals was to correct the standard's contents so that they were closer to the higher level standard. This leads to the suspicion that process standards were previously evolved without any historical perspective, producing as a consequence standards that totally deviated from the higher level standard.

Fig. 1 also reflects the relationship between the issues listed above and the number of changes they caused when editing the process standards during the second iteration. Compared to the first iteration, it can be seen how the number of changes due to "ambiguous activity description" (2) and "non-compliant activity" (4) were reduced more or less to half. Other issues such as "improper placements of an output" (3) and "ambiguous additional explanatory text" (5) were also drastically reduced. This suggests that after the first iteration, process engineers partially accomplished increasing ease of use and compliance to process standards. However, the number of occurrences for issues such as: "improper sequence of processes" (1), "redundant activity description" (9), and "improper placement of additional explanatory text" (6) increased. This can be attributed to the reviewers. Although reviewers were satisfied at the end of the first iteration with the reduced number of "non-compliant activity" issues (4) with respect to the ECSS and less "ambiguous activity descriptions" (2), they still believed that activity descriptions were not correctly grouped. In fact, there were several discussions about the interfaces (inputs and outputs) between system engineering and software engineering processes that demanded a better understanding of the actual practices and reflection in the standards. The reviewers were satisfied concerning the improvement of the process standards at the end of the first iteration and saw the opportunity of having high quality standards at the end of the second iteration. Therefore, they were stricter and demanded higher quality of the process standard contents for the second iteration. This is possibly the reason why new issues appeared such as: "activity description not concise" (8), and "ambiguous output description" (11).

5   Summary and Outlook

Processes may be more easily and rationally changed if the information about the process, its context, and the rationale of its evolution is captured. Existing approaches recognize the need for a mechanism (concept and tool) that can be used for collecting information about process changes that could help evolve the process in a systematic way. We observed that most of the approaches did not consider rationale information as an important part of their frameworks. This can be the reason for the small amount of evidence available on the rationale of process evolution. Having a predefined classification of the rationale for process changes, the task of collecting the information related to such rationale can be simplified and become more suitable for use in real process evolution projects. This may be seen as an initial step for building a mechanism that supports systematic process evolution. Therefore, more research effort should be invested into understanding how to introduce these rationale concepts for a systematic well-grounded evolution of software process models. The list of issues derived from analyzing the database with the information about the evolution of process standards provides an initial insight on the type of changes performed in the context of this type of projects. It can be said that the issues that generated the major number of occurrences such as "improper sequence of processes" (1), "ambiguous activity description" (2), and "improper placement of an output" (3), reflected the distance that existed between the process description and the actual understanding of stakeholders. It was observed that systematically documenting changes and discussing them in reviews provided a much more organized and well-grounded process standard evolution. However, a more structured mechanism for collecting the rationale of changes is needed for clearly identifying the observed alternatives and criteria, as well as the arguments and final resolution. More research has to be done for describing more precisely this initial list of issues, so that they are as orthogonal as possible. More empirical data is needed for that purpose. As part of our future work we will use the issues list as the basis for new process evolution projects.

Acknowledgements. We would like to thank Michael Jones and Mariella Spada from ESA Space Operations Center (ESOC) and Dr. William E. Riddle for their support and their valuable comments. Additionally, we would like to thank Sonnhild Namingha from Fraunhofer IESE for preparing the English editing of this paper. This work was supported in part by the German Federal Ministry of Education and Research (V-Bench Project, No.01I SE 11 A).

References

[1] Dutoit, H, A., Paech, B.: Rationale Management in Software Engineering. Stuttgart: Expected date of publication: Beginning of 2006.

[2] Nguyen, M, N., Conradi, R.: Towards a rigorous approach for managing process evolution. Software process technology: 5th European workshop, EWSPT '96, Nancy, France. 1996.

[3] Bruegge, B., Dutoit, A.H.: Object-Oriented Software Engineering. Using UML, Patterns, and Java. 2nd ed. Upper Saddle River: Pearson Education 2004.

[4] Bandinelli, S., Fugetta, A, Ghezzi, C.: Software Process Model Evolution in the SPADE environment. IEEE Transactions on Software Engineering 19:1128-1144. 1993

[5] Madhavji, N.: Environment evolution: The Prism model of changes. IEEE Transactions on Software Engineering, 18(5):380-392.

[6] Nejmeh, Brian A., Riddle, William E.: The PERFECT Approach to Experience-based Process Evolution. Advances in Computers, M. Zelkowitz (Ed.), Academic Press, 2006.

[7] Bhuta, J., Boehm, B., Meyers, S.: Process Elements: Components of Software Process Architectures. Software Process Workshop, China, (2005).

[8] Basili V., McGarry F.: The Experience Factory: How to Build and Run One. 19th International Conference on Software Engineering, Boston, Massachusetts, May (1997)

[9] Kunz, W., Rittel, H.: Issues as Elements of Information Systems. Working Paper No. 131, Institut für Grundlagen der Plannung, Universität Stuttgart, Germany, (1970).

[10] Lee, J.: A Qualitative Decision Management System. In P.H. Winston & S. Shellard (eds.) Artificial Intelligence at MIT: Expanding Frontiers, Vol.1, pp. 104-133, MIT Press, Cambridge, MA, 1990.

[11] MacLean, A., Young, R.M., Belloti, V., Moran, T.: Questions, Options, and Criteria: Elements of Design Space Analysis. Human-Computer Interaction, Vol. 6, pp. 201-250, 1991.

[12] Chung, L., Nixon, B.A., Yu, E., Mylopoulos, J.: Non-Functional Requirements in Software Engineering. Kluver Academic, Boston, 1999.

[13] European Cooperation for Space Standardization (ECSS) Standards available at http://www.ecss.nl. Last checked 2006-01-06.

[14] Ground Segment Tailoring of ECSS for ESOC (SETG), available at http://www.estec.esa.nl/wmwww/EME/Bssc/BSSCdocuments.htm, Last checked 2006-01-06

Implementing Process Change in a Software
Organization – An Experience Based Study

Shaowen Qin

School of Informatics and Engineering , Flinders University,
GPO Box 2100, Adelaide, South Australia 5001
Shaowen.qin@flinders.edu.au

Abstract. No matter how much better our software process becomes, it would
not bring us much benefit without being adopted by the targeted process users.
Based on the author's recent industrial working experience at Motorola Global
Software Group (GSG) as an organizational technology deployment champion,
with the implementation of Motorola's Enterprise Project Management System
in GSG during 2001 - 2003 as a background story, this paper presents a study
on the real world challenges in implementing process change in today's
software organizations. Upon reflection of the good practices and the do-
differentlies, the paper provides some strategic as well as practical recommend-
dations on dealing with the challenges, and points out the key success practices
for software process change management.

1 Introduction

Most of the relatively mature software development organizations today have realized
the importance of software process to their business, and therefore have committed to
implementing the best available processes at the start of the business. However,
software processes inevitably evolve as researchers and industrial practitioners try to
improve the reputation of the software industry, which calls for the change
deployment in the real world. Managing software process change is much more
difficult than implementing a new one for the simple reason that most people are
intrinsically resistant to change, especially when they don't see the immediate benefit
of such a change, or worse yet, when they perceive the change as inconvenient.
Further more, as software project teams – the process users - are always under the
pressure of balancing the schedule, budget and quality of a software delivery, it is
only natural that process improvement is given a much lower priority, even when the
process users agree that the change is necessary.

Based on more than 5 years of work experience at Motorola Global Software
Group(GSG) as an organizational technology deployment champion, this paper
attempts to provide some insights into the real-world challenges in software process
change implementation, together with some practical strategies for success. Section 2
will present the background story of this paper – implementing Motorola's Enterprise
Project Management System (EPMS) across GSG's many software centres worldwide. Section 3 will identify the challenges. Section 4 will reflect upon what worked

Q. Wang et al. (Eds.): SPW/ProSim 2006, LNCS 3966, pp. 342 – 347, 2006.

and the do-differentlies (a self-explanatory expression quite commonly used in Motorola and some other organizations for a learning best practice), and provide strategic as well as practical recommendations on how to deal with the challenges. Section 5 will present the concluding remarks on the key success practices in software process change management.

2   The Background Story – Implementing EPMS in GSG

EPMS is the common project management system selected by the Motorola System and Product Development Operation Council in 2001. It is a Motorola customized system that provides an integrated project management environment with tools (Primevera TeamPlay/TeamPlayer tool suite, Motorola project tracking/reporting tools) and methodologies (Motorola M-gate process, PMBOK, and organizational templates and best practices). The benefits of adopting EPMS include:

- Enterprise-wide Project Management data integration and rollup
- Improved resource coordination between organizations
- Visibility of resource utilization and project status
- Promote reuse and cycle-time reduction by adopting common processes and tools
- Improved customer satisfaction

However, only with 100% deployment we could reap substantial benefits from using EPMS.

GSG operates as Motorola's internal software service provider, with about a dozen software centers located world wide. GSG has a strong tradition on process improvement, and many of the GSG centers have been assessed as SEI CMM or CMMI level 5 organizations. GSG differs from the rest of Motorola in many aspects including mixture of project domain, short project duration and small to medium team size, workforce cultural and experience profile, and the strong process and commitment oriented work style, most of them are typical characteristics of a software organization. Of course, all centers already had their individual choices of project management processes and tools, which makes EPMS deployment a project management process/tool change implementation task.

GSG has been actively participating in the Motorola-wide implementation of EPMS since 2001. The project goal was to achieve 100% EPMS deployment throughout GSG by end of Q3 2003. In detail, the goal meant that

1. All projects shall use Teamplay as the sole project management tool, and
2. All projects shall use Teamplayer as the sole effort tracking and resource management tool. All billed engineers shall report both project and non-project activities using TeamPlayer.

We will skip the detailed activities involved in establishing the deployment program management plan, forming deployment team, assigning of roles and responsibilities, defining deployment requirement, providing training and setting up support model, etc.

at this point, and highlight the strategic decisions in dealing with specific challenges in Section 4.

A brief summary of the deployment status at key stages are as follows:

- Q2 2002: GSG-Australia achieved 100% deployment. A success story was published in Motorola EPMS News Letter.
- Q1 2003: Several other centers achieved 100% deployment.
- Q3 2003: The deployment goal was reportedly achieved as planned. However, it was understood that some projects use EPMS very proficiently, while some others only used the bare minimum functions to satisfy the deployment requirement.
- 2004: The journey continued with a focus on using GSG as a vehicle to achieve software production process commonality across GSG and integrating EPMS with other software engineering tools used in GSG.

3 Challenges

A close examination of the EPMS deployment story reveals the following challenges:

1. Software project teams are always busy, and they are concerned that making changes to the way they do things might make their lives more difficult.
2. It is a top-down initiative. A top-down initiative is unlikely to get support and commitment from people who were not involved in making the deployment decision. It makes the change deployment involuntary for most of the process users. Top-down deployment is the most often seen mode in the real world.
3. Accountability is lacking. Process change is managed by the Process and Quality Department (PQD) that is perceived as playing a supporting role. There is no direct negative impact on performance appraisal for putting a request from PQD on hold.
4. Deployment sponsor is not totally committed at all times. Since 2 is almost always true, the commitment and open communication of it from the General Manager of the organization becomes crucial to getting collaboration from stakeholders.
5. Diverse cultural backgrounds and experience profiles. One deployment plan does not fit all centers.
6. Unsynchronized training and application of the acquired knowledge and skills. Training is often offered at one go with a full coverage of relevant materials but for many users, a large portion of the learning is not applied until a later stage due to various reasons and is therefore forgotten.
7. Limited deployment resources. There is not enough face to face meeting and training opportunities offered to some sites due to budget constrains. This has become more common in recent years as companies become more cost conscious.
8. The Deployment Champion role and the associated roadblocks are often underappreciated by both the senior managers and the process users. In addition, the Deployment Champion almost always wields no real power and must rely on the goodwill of the often remotely located delegates who have their own functions and priorities to deal with.

4   Dealing with Challenges

The following paragraphs will reflect upon what worked and the do-differentlies for some situations, provide strategic recommendations for others as appropriate, and then link them to the numbered challenges listed in Section 3.

Staged Deployment: The deployment of EPMS through GSG was planned to be conducted in 2 stages:

- Stage 1: Local Pilot Stage: The Local Pilot will use the EMPS product at a local level to manage projects in a controlled manner. The pilots will feed requirements to both GSG and the Motorola EPMS steering committee. They will be the prime mechanism used by centres to gain skills in using the tool and to resolve local and GSG technical and managerial issues.
- Stage 2: Institutionalization across GSG: At this point it is expected that all new projects will start using this tool and that the tool will work for them. It is also expected that the GSG EPMS support infrastructure will be in place to enable this to happen.

The importance of local piloting can not be over emphasized. As with any change implementation, there will be small numbers of enthusiasts who are willing to be the early adopters [1, 2]. It is important to work with them at this stage. Feedback from different local pilots will help us tailor the deployment plan for each center (challenge 5). The early adopters usually become the so-called subject matter experts (SMEs) who can provide hands-on help to the new local users (challenges 6 & 7).

Stage 2 requires much more effort than stage 1, and often takes a much longer time to complete. At this stage, collaboration from all stakeholders is necessary yet difficult to obtain. It may take a long time before progress is seen. Sometimes one does need a lucky break from somewhere. The early success we had with GSG-Australia was largely due to the firm commitment made by a newly hired deputy managing director who used a similar project management system in her previous organization. This proves again the well known Chinese saying about the three factors for success: right time (Tian Shi), right place (Di Li), and right people (Ren He).

The success we had with GSG-Australia also proves the effectiveness of face to face communication and training – two of the key deployment drivers are based in Australia.

Getting Senior Manager's Commitment: By Q1 2003, we were more than half-way towards reaching our goal. However, deployment to the remaining sites required an extraordinary push. This was the time to work on getting a Senior Manager's Commitment renewal. With the effort of the deployment team and the help from the PQ department managers, an edict from GSG's General Manager was issued, which became the driving force for reaching the final goal (challenges 3 & 4).

Getting commitment from other stakeholders: Plan early. Build the change deployment into stakeholder's performance commitment list. Provide formal appreciation to supportive people and their supervisors through email, which could be used as a bonus at their annual performance appraisal (challenge 3).

Project Selection: Some times we have no choice but to implement a top-down initiative, although we could still try to tap into the "pulls" from the end users. If we have the opportunity to select a process improvement project, prioritization should be given to where "push" and "pull" meet. Consideration of return on investment is also important (challenge 2).

Communication: With a top-down initiative, the benefit should be thoroughly communicated at all levels to get buy-in from all stakeholders, especially the middle level managers who have to sponsor the change implementation and the process users who are directly impacted by the change (challenges1 & 2).

The change implementation program should be discussed and tracked at a monthly organizational review meeting. This provides the whole organization visibility of the importance of the initiative, and the progress being made. It also ensures systematic progress towards milestones, provides a forum for the organization to debate strategy, and provides inputs to initiative deployment decisions (challenges 3 & 4).

Creating Win-Win [3] Scenarios for All Stakeholders: Make the change easier for users to follow. Users are more likely to accept change when it helps to improve their work efficiency yet is an easy thing to do. For example, a win-win situation was created by making common Work Breakdown Structure/Activity list templates available in EPMS, which becomes an attractive feature to users. Deployment champions should always be thinking of ways to create win-win scenarios for all stakeholders (challenge 1).

Flexible Training Options: EPMS training was a two day course. We had delivered the training as it was during the early stages of the deployment. We later realized that a large portion of the learning does not get to be applied until a later stage, therefore is forgotten and needs repeating. We made the following changes to solve this problem (challenge 6):

- Have a 30 minute benefit overview training
- Break the 2 days training to 4 parts. Each can be delivered on demand.

Although face to face training is preferable, it is still possible to achieve a satisfactory level of effectiveness through training over the internet. In such cases, it is important to keep the group size small to increase effectiveness (challenge 7).

Don't take it personal when others are not supportive: Change deployment champions should be enthusiastic yet realistic about their job, and don't take it personal when others are not supportive. Setting realistic short term and long term goals would help in keeping them motivated and focused (challenge 8).

5 Concluding Remarks

Managing process change is one of the most difficult, yet inevitable tasks in today's software organization. The key success practices are thorough communication of the change benefit at all levels of the organization, and to create win-win scenarios for all involved. Although most process change projects are seemingly less successful than desired, more benefit will emerge in the long term.

References

1. Geoffrey A. Moore, Crossing the Chasm: Marketing and Selling Technology Products to Mainstream Customers. Harper Business (1991)
2. Rogers, E.: Diffusion of Innovations. 3rd edn. New York: The Free Press (1983)
3. Boeam, B., Egyed, A., Kwan, J., Port, D., Shah, A., and Madachy, R.: Using the Win-Win Spiral Model: A Case Study, IEEE Computer (July, 1998) 33-44
4. Qin, S.: GSG EPMS Deployment Program Management Notes (2001-2003)
5. Guinta L.R. and Praizler, N. C.: The QFD Book: The Team Approach to Solving Problems and Satisfying Customers through Quality Function Deployment. New York: AMACOM (1993)
6. Kotter, J.P.: Leading Change: Why Transformation Efforts Fail. Harvard Business Review (March-April, 1995) 59-67

Practical Experiences of Cost/Schedule Measure Through Earned Value Management and Statistical Process Control

Qing Wang[1], Nan Jiang[1,2], Lang Gou[1,2], Meiru Che[1,2], and Ronghui Zhang[1,2]

[1] Laboratory for Internet Software Technologies, Institute of Software,
The Chinese Academy of Sciences, Beijing 100080, China
[2] Graduate University of Chinese Academy of Sciences, Beijing 100039, China
{wq, jiangnan, goulang, chemeiru,
hangronghui}@itechs.iscas.ac.cn

Abstract. Cost and schedule measures are the most important support activities for the success of a project; it provides the basis for process improvement and project management. This paper reports practical experiences on using EVM (Earned Value Management) and SPC(Statistical Process Control) in cost/ schedule measure. The analysis of experience data indicates the distributions of CPI(Cost Performance Index) and SPI(Schedule Performance Index) index are generally following the normal distribution. And consequently, it is reasonable and effective to employ SPC in EVM.

1 Introduction

The ideal goal of software project is to produce high quality software within the limits of cost and schedule. However, a lot of cost and schedule of projects is out of control. The research based on practical project data shows that there are about 1/3 projects exceeding their estimations of cost and schedule by 25% [1]. Therefore, how to manage cost and schedule effectively is one of the most important problems concerned by most software organizations.

EVM[10][11] is a technology which is widely used to measure project cost and schedule performance. But there are some problems when applying EVM to software projects. The primary one is that it is too sensitive to detect abnormal signals. Each variance between earned value and planned value (or actual value) is considered as an abnormal signal. As we all know, software project is different from traditional engineering project by nature. Hence, variances between pairs of earned value and planned value are very common in software projects. Most of these variances are not influential to the success of the project, but they are still reported as abnormal signals by EVM, and the managers must spend a lot of unnecessary effort in processing these misreported abnormal signals. To solve this problem, we must set reasonable boundaries to determine those variances that affect the success measures.

SPC[6] is a method of quality control. There are a lot of studies in the last two decades discussing whether the SPC approach is suitable for software process [2][3][4][5], and a

Q. Wang et al. (Eds.): SPW/ProSim 2006, LNCS 3966, pp. 348–354, 2006.

lot of real-life examples of applying SPC in software process are reported[7]. The primary problem for using SPC in software process is that this technique is suitable for small piece or large batch repeatable process, however, software projects are often long term and do not completely follow any repeatable process. On the other hand, since cost and schedule data can be collected from every project, it is possible to construct a sufficiently large sample set. Therefore, it is reasonable to use SPC to control EVM indicators. Additionally, because SPC provides various control charts for different distributions, we must determine what distributions EVM indicators are in order to effectively apply SPC in controlling these indicators.

Lipke applied SPC techniques to two EVM indicators: CPI and SPI, to control the cost and schedule of software projects[8]. After further studies, he found that SPC did not provide reliable results when applied to CPI and SPI, it very seldom detects abnormal signals for CPI or SPI values less than 1.0[9]. His studies indicate distributions of CPI and SPI are not normal distribution and they are right-skewed. Lipke believed that the skew of the distribution was the likely culprit for the problem. So he suggested using SPC to the natural logarithm of CPI and SPI, instead of to CPI and SPI themselves.

In the practice of process improvement in ISCAS (Institute of Software, Chinese Academy of Sciences), we applied the method which integrates EVM and SPC, and collected a lot of real-life projects data. We applied the same indicators as Lipke did: CPI and SPI in EVM. However different results were concluded from our study. We believe that CPI and SPI are normally distributed, and in this case, applying SPC to CPI and SPI are more meaningful. In this paper, we report our experience using SPC to control EVM indicators, results we obtained from cost/schedule measure, and lessons learned from the experience.

2 Data Sample Construction

EVM contains three basic metrics: BCWS(Budgeted Cost of Work Scheduled), BCWP(Budgeted Cost of Work Performed), and ACWP(Actual Cost of Work Performed). There are many methods to get these three values. In our practice of project management, task is the basic unit of project. So, in this paper, we calculate BCWS, BCWP, and ACWP based on task plans and task reports. The method we used to calculate basic metrics of EVM contains labor effort only, other indirect cost must be converted to task efforts before they can be calculated. Since the labor is the most important factor of cost, it is reasonable for our study to only concentrate on labor. It is not reasonable to applied SPC to these three basic values directly. Because what we concerned are the variances between BCWP and BCWS (or ACWP), we use two derived indictors: CPI and SPI. Their definitions are: $CPI = BCWP / ACWP$ and $SPI = BCWP / BCWS$.

We have developed a tool called PM, which was integrated in SoftPM [12], based on our approach for cost/schedule measure, to help software organizations collect task reports and calculate CPI and SPI automatically.

In the last 3 years, we applied this Cost/Schedule measure in more than 15 projects, and collected lots of empirical data. The organization which we collected data from has high software process capability maturity level, which is CMMI level 4. Its applications cover different domains, such as Software process improvement, software quality assurance, software measurement. We select 6 projects in the organization. All these projects are web-based applications; use the same techniques and the same organization standard processes. The staffs are about 10 and stable, and the projects durations are 4-6 months, all the tasks are reported weekly. Table 1 shows SPI and CPI data from these projects.

Table 1. SPI and CPI data of projects in 2004-2005

NO.	SPI	CPI	NO	SPI	CPI	NO.	SPI	CPI	NO.	SPI	CPI	NO.	SPI	CPI
1	1.00	1.00	22	0.96	0.97	43	0.99	0.94	63	0.90	1.03	83	0.89	1.04
2	1.00	1.07	23	0.96	0.98	44	0.99	1.04	64	0.98	1.02	84	0.92	1.07
3	1.00	1.09	24	0.96	0.97	45	0.99	1.03	65	0.99	1.02	85	0.85	1.06
4	1.00	1.03	25	0.94	0.97	46	0.99	0.84	66	1.05	1.02	86	0.93	1.08
5	1.00	1.01	26	0.91	0.97	47	0.99	0.85	67	1.00	1.01	87	0.93	0.95
6	1.00	1.02	27	0.91	0.97	48	0.97	0.85	68	1.02	1.01	88	0.96	1.08
7	1.00	0.98	28	1.00	1.00	49	0.97	0.83	69	1.01	1.04	89	0.97	1.07
8	1.00	0.97	29	0.87	1.03	50	1.00	0.83	70	1.00	1.09	90	0.97	1.08
9	1.00	0.94	30	0.99	0.88	51	0.91	0.83	71	0.98	1.07	91	0.96	1.09
10	1.00	0.95	31	1.01	0.86	52	1.08	0.87	72	0.97	1.08	92	1.00	1.07
11	0.99	0.94	32	0.99	0.89	53	1.05	0.91	73	0.98	1.06	93	1.00	1.07
12	0.99	0.94	33	1.05	0.93	54	1.01	0.91	74	0.99	1.04	94	1.00	1.12
13	0.97	0.95	34	0.96	0.86	55	0.92	1.00	75	0.98	1.03	95	0.92	1.06
14	0.89	0.95	35	0.99	0.92	56	0.92	1.05	76	0.99	0.99	96	0.99	1.04
15	0.96	0.95	36	0.98	0.94	57	0.90	0.95	77	0.99	0.95	97	1.00	1.06
16	0.96	0.93	37	0.98	0.99	58	0.92	1.00	78	0.99	0.95	98	1.00	1.06
17	1.03	0.99	38	0.99	0.98	59	0.91	0.95	79	0.93	0.95	99	1.00	1.06
18	0.96	0.97	39	0.99	0.97	60	1.00	0.95	80	1.00	1.00	100	1.00	1.06
19	0.96	0.92	40	0.99	0.97	61	1.03	0.99	81	1.10	1.06	101	1.00	1.06
20	0.96	0.98	41	1.04	0.96	62	0.90	0.93	82	0.91	0.94	102	1.00	1.06
21	0.96	0.98	42	1.01	1.00									

Based on these data, we can construct a data sample of 102 task data points.

3   Analysis of Experience Results

3.1   Study on the Distribution of CPI and SPI

There are many SPC methods to make process control, which is appropriate depends on what statistical distribution of the data sample appears. Obviously, SPI and CPI is continuous distributed statistics. It is risky to use SPC to control continuous but non-normally distribution data sample. At first, we must test the normality of SPI and CPI. Lipke[8] found that SPI and CPI do not obey normally distribution, so they cannot be controlled by SPC directly. But in our empirical study, an interest and different phenomena appears. We use SPI data in table 1 as an example. First, we create frequency histogram of these data. The result is shown in table 2 and the frequency histogram is illustrated in Fig 1.

From the frequency histogram, SPI is approximately distributed normally. We use a statistical method for hypothesis testing the normality of data, which called skewness-kurtosis test. The null hypothesis is

H_0: Data sample is derived from normal population

Table 2. Frequency

Subgroup	Number	Frequency
0.845-0.875	2	0.0196
0.875-0.905	5	0.0490
0.905-0.935	13	0.1275
0.934-0.965	14	0.1373
0.965-0.995	31	0.3039
0.995-1.025	29	0.2843
1.025-1.055	6	0.0588
1.055-1.085	1	0.0098
1.085-1.115	1	0.0098

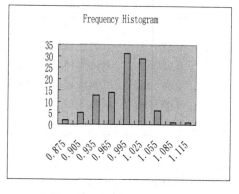

Fig. 1. Frequency Histogram

Assume $x_1, x_2 \ldots\ldots x_n$ is a sample of population x, the skewness of sample is $g_1 = \mu_3/\mu_2^{3/2}$, and the kurtosis of sample is $g_2 = \mu_4/\mu_2^2$, where $\mu_k = \frac{1}{n}\sum_{i=1}^{n}(x_i - \bar{x})^k$. We define $\sigma_1 = \sqrt{\frac{6(n-2)}{(n+1)(n+3)}}$, $\sigma_2 = \sqrt{\frac{24n(n-2)(n-3)}{(n+1)^2(n+3)(n+5)}}$ and $\mu = 3 - \frac{6}{n+1}$. From the knowledge of statistics, if the distribution of population is normal, when the volume of sample n is large enough, the statistic $U_1 = g_1/\sigma_1$ and $U_2 = (g_2 - \mu)/\sigma_2$ are approximately standard normal distribution. So if $|U_1|$ or $|U_2|$ is large enough, we can reject H_0. For data in table 1, at the significance level $\alpha = 0.05$, $|U_1| = 1.809 < u_{\alpha/4} = 2.24$, $|U_2| = 1.766 < u_{\alpha/4} = 2.24$, so we can accept H_0.

Similarly, we tested for CPI data in table 3. At the significance level $\alpha = 0.05$, $|U_1| = 1.843 < u_{\alpha/4} = 2.24$, $|U_2| = 0.785 < u_{\alpha/4} = 2.24$, so we can also accept H_0.

From these studies, we conclude SPI and CPI are normally distributed.

Similar tests are taken for other projects in the same organization and two other organizations. All the CPI and SPI data in these three organizations are likely distributed normally.

3.2 Statistical Control the SPI/CPI Indicator

Once we confirm the normality of the SPI and CPI distribution, we can use the method of parameter estimation to get the parameters of population distribution. For example, to the SPI data in table 3, we can get the average of population μ =0.98, and the standard deviation σ = 0.04. So the limits of SPI indicator fluctuating is $\mu \pm 3\sigma$. In other word, the upper control limit is 1.10, and the lower control limit is 0.86. Then we can use these limits to control new projects. Table 3 is SPI data of a new project, and Fig 2 is control chart for this project:

Table 3. SPI data of a project

NO.	SPI	NO.	SPI	NO.	SPI
1	1.00	7	0.92	13	0.91
2	0.85	8	0.92	14	1.01
3	0.91	9	0.90	15	0.99
4	1.08	10	0.84	16	1.13
5	1.05	11	0.92	17	1.00
6	1.01	12	0.87	18	1.01

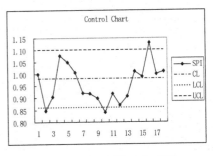

Fig. 2. Control Chart for SPI

In Fig.2, we can find the 2nd data is an abnormal signal (lower than LCL), which means the schedule delay at the 2nd data report period is out of control. We can identify all tasks which are behind schedule at this report period and classify them by cause, as shown in Table 4 and Fig.3.

In Fig 3 we can find there are 17 tasks delaying for the lack of communication, which is the primary cause of schedule variance. In fact this data comes from the

Table 4. Causes of schedule variance

Cause	Quantity of tasks	Freq	Cum Freq.
LoCo: Lack of communication	17	46%	46%
PoP: Poor quality of task performing	8	22%	68%
VoT: Variance of other task	4	11%	78%
IoE: Inaccuracy of Estimation	3	8%	86%
LoR: Lack of resource	2	5%	92%
PoI: Poor quality of input	2	5%	97%
LoCp: Lack of Capability	1	3%	100%
Total	37	100%	

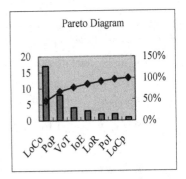

Fig. 3. Pareto Diagram

beginning of design phase in the project. Designers and requirement engineers didn't reach agreement and consistency with each other about the requirement, which led to a lot of reworks. For other abnormal signals in the control chart, the similar analysis could be applied. In traditional EVM, managers either analyze all the data not equal 1.0, or set glancing limits by experience(such as 1.0±0.2). Our approach applies SPC to EVM, and derives reasonable control limits from historical projects data[13], which can make cost and schedule alarm appropriately.

4 Conclusions

Our experience results show that the distributions of SPI/CPI are likely normal distributed. In this case, applying SPC to these two indicators of EVM is more reasonable. There are at least two benefits of this approach. First, it reduces the complexity of project state judgment. The SPC provides a set of rules to detect abnormal signals. We can simply use these rules to judge whether the cost and schedule are out of control. Second, it reduces the cost of measure and analysis; most false alarms (which SPI or CPI is not equal 1.0 exactly, but fall into the limits) are filtrated. The manager can concentrate on real problems of projects.

We have applied this approach more than 30 software organizations which use our SoftPM toolkit. Practical results show this approach is effective. The complexity and cost of measurement in these organizations are reduced, and most of warning points are identified effectively without the disturbing of false alarms.

Acknowledgements

This work is supported by the National Natural Science Foundation of China under Grant Nos. 60273026 and 60473060; the Hi-Tech Research and Development Program (863 Program) of China under Grant Nos. 2004AA1Z2100 and 2005AA113140.

References

1. L.H.Putnam and W.Myers. Industrial Strength Software-Effective Management Using Measure. IEEE Computer Society Press, 1997
2. Weller E F. Practical applications of statistical process control. IEEE Software, 2000, 17(3): 48-55
3. Florac W A. Statistical process control: Analyzing a space shuttle onboard software process. IEEE Software, 2000,17(4): 97-105
4. Stephen H.Kan Metrics And Models In Software Quality Engineering. Addison-Wesley Publishing Company, 2003
5. Layman, B., B. Curtis, J. Puffer, and C. Webet. Solving the Challenge of Quantitative Management, Section 4: Problems in the use of Control Charts. SEPG 2002 QM Tutorial, Phoenix, Arizon, Februay 18-21, 2002

6. Florac W A. Measuring software process- Statistical process control for software process improvement. Addson-Wesley, 1999
7. P. Jalote, CMM in Practice – Processes for executing software projects at Infosys, Addison-Wesley Longman,SEI Series on Software Engineering, 1999.
8. Lipke, W., Statistical Process Control of Project Performance, CrossTalk, The Journal of Defense Software Engineering, Vol 15, NO.3 March 2002, pp.15-18
9. Lipke, W., A Study of the Normality of Earned Value Management Indicators , The Measurable News, December 2002
10. Departments of the Air Force, the Army, the Navy, and the Defense Logistic Agency. Cost/Schedule Control Systems Criteria Joint Implementation Guide.1980
11. Department of the Air Force. Air Force Systems Command. Software Management Indicators. 1986
12. Wang, Q., Li, M.S., Software Process Management: Practices in China, In Proc. of the Software Process Workshop 2005 (SPW2005), Beijing, 2005.
13. Wang, Q., Jiang, N., BSR: A Statistic-based Approach for Establishing and Refining Software Process Performance Baseline, The 28th International Conference on Software Engineering (ICSE2006). Shanghai, May 20-28, 2006, accepted.

Author Index

Lecture Notes in Computer Science

For information about Vols. 1–3888

please contact your bookseller or Springer

Vol. 3936: M. Lalmas, A. MacFarlane, S. Rüger, A. Tombros, T. Tsikrika, A. Yavlinsky (Eds.), Advances in Information Retrieval. XIX, 584 pages. 2006.

Vol. 3935: D. Won, S. Kim (Eds.), Information Security and Cryptology - ICISC 2005. XIV, 458 pages. 2006.

Vol. 3934: J.A. Clark, R.F. Paige, F.A. C. Polack, P.J. Brooke (Eds.), Security in Pervasive Computing. X, 243 pages. 2006.

Vol. 3933: F. Bonchi, J.-F. Boulicaut (Eds.), Knowledge Discovery in Inductive Databases. VIII, 251 pages. 2006.

Vol. 3931: B. Apolloni, M. Marinaro, G. Nicosia, R. Tagliaferri (Eds.), Neural Nets. XIII, 370 pages. 2006.

Vol. 3930: D.S. Yeung, Z.-Q. Liu, X.-Z. Wang, H. Yan (Eds.), Advances in Machine Learning and Cybernetics. XXI, 1110 pages. 2006. (Sublibrary LNAI).

Vol. 3929: W. MacCaull, M. Winter, I. Düntsch (Eds.), Relational Methods in Computer Science. VIII, 263 pages. 2006.

Vol. 3928: J. Domingo-Ferrer, J. Posegga, D. Schreckling (Eds.), Smart Card Research and Advanced Applications. XI, 359 pages. 2006.

Vol. 3927: J. Hespanha, A. Tiwari (Eds.), Hybrid Systems: Computation and Control. XII, 584 pages. 2006.

Vol. 3925: A. Valmari (Ed.), Model Checking Software. X, 307 pages. 2006.

Vol. 3924: P. Sestoft (Ed.), Programming Languages and Systems. XII, 343 pages. 2006.

Vol. 3923: A. Mycroft, A. Zeller (Eds.), Compiler Construction. XIII, 277 pages. 2006.

Vol. 3922: L. Baresi, R. Heckel (Eds.), Fundamental Approaches to Software Engineering. XIII, 427 pages. 2006.

Vol. 3921: L. Aceto, A. Ingólfsdóttir (Eds.), Foundations of Software Science and Computation Structures. XV, 447 pages. 2006.

Vol. 3920: H. Hermanns, J. Palsberg (Eds.), Tools and Algorithms for the Construction and Analysis of Systems. XIV, 506 pages. 2006.

Vol. 3918: W.K. Ng, M. Kitsuregawa, J. Li, K. Chang (Eds.), Advances in Knowledge Discovery and Data Mining. XXIV, 879 pages. 2006. (Sublibrary LNAI).

Vol. 3917: H. Chen, F.Y. Wang, C.C. Yang, D. Zeng, M. Chau, K. Chang (Eds.), Intelligence and Security Informatics. XII, 186 pages. 2006.

Vol. 3916: J. Li, Q. Yang, A.-H. Tan (Eds.), Data Mining for Biomedical Applications. VIII, 155 pages. 2006. (Sublibrary LNBI).

Vol. 3915: R. Nayak, M.J. Zaki (Eds.), Knowledge Discovery from XML Documents. VIII, 105 pages. 2006.

Vol. 3914: A. Garcia, R. Choren, C. Lucena, P. Giorgini, T. Holvoet, A. Romanovsky (Eds.), Software Engineering for Multi-Agent Systems IV. XIV, 255 pages. 2006.

Vol. 3910: S.A. Brueckner, G.D.M. Serugendo, D. Hales, F. Zambonelli (Eds.), Engineering Self-Organising Systems. XII, 245 pages. 2006. (Sublibrary LNAI).

Vol. 3909: A. Apostolico, C. Guerra, S. Istrail, P. Pevzner, M. Waterman (Eds.), Research in Computational Molecular Biology. XVII, 612 pages. 2006. (Sublibrary LNBI).

Vol. 3908: A. Bui, M. Bui, T. Böhme, H. Unger (Eds.), Innovative Internet Community Systems. VIII, 207 pages. 2006.

Vol. 3907: F. Rothlauf, J. Branke, S. Cagnoni, E. Costa, C. Cotta, R. Drechsler, E. Lutton, P. Machado, J.H. Moore, J. Romero, G.D. Smith, G. Squillero, H. Takagi (Eds.), Applications of Evolutionary Computing. XXIV, 813 pages. 2006.

Vol. 3906: J. Gottlieb, G.R. Raidl (Eds.), Evolutionary Computation in Combinatorial Optimization. XI, 293 pages. 2006.

Vol. 3905: P. Collet, M. Tomassini, M. Ebner, S. Gustafson, A. Ekárt (Eds.), Genetic Programming. XI, 361 pages. 2006.

Vol. 3904: M. Baldoni, U. Endriss, A. Omicini, P. Torroni (Eds.), Declarative Agent Languages and Technologies III. XII, 245 pages. 2006. (Sublibrary LNAI).

Vol. 3903: K. Chen, R. Deng, X. Lai, J. Zhou (Eds.), Information Security Practice and Experience. XIV, 392 pages. 2006.

Vol. 3902: R. Kronland-Martinet, T. Voinier, S. Ystad (Eds.), Computer Music Modeling and Retrieval. XI, 275 pages. 2006.

Vol. 3901: P.M. Hill (Ed.), Logic Based Program Synthesis and Transformation. X, 179 pages. 2006.

Vol. 3900: F. Toni, P. Torroni (Eds.), Computational Logic in Multi-Agent Systems. XVII, 427 pages. 2006. (Sublibrary LNAI).

Vol. 3899: S. Frintrop, VOCUS: A Visual Attention System for Object Detection and Goal-Directed Search. XIV, 216 pages. 2006. (Sublibrary LNAI).

Vol. 3898: K. Tuyls, P.J. 't Hoen, K. Verbeeck, S. Sen (Eds.), Learning and Adaption in Multi-Agent Systems. X, 217 pages. 2006. (Sublibrary LNAI).

Vol. 3897: B. Preneel, S. Tavares (Eds.), Selected Areas in Cryptography. XI, 371 pages. 2006.

Vol. 3896: Y. Ioannidis, M.H. Scholl, J.W. Schmidt, F. Matthes, M. Hatzopoulos, K. Boehm, A. Kemper, T. Grust, C. Boehm (Eds.), Advances in Database Technology - EDBT 2006. XIV, 1208 pages. 2006.

Vol. 3895: O. Goldreich, A.L. Rosenberg, A.L. Selman (Eds.), Theoretical Computer Science. XII, 399 pages. 2006.

Vol. 3894: W. Grass, B. Sick, K. Waldschmidt (Eds.), Architecture of Computing Systems - ARCS 2006. XII, 496 pages. 2006.

Vol. 3893: L. Atzori, D.D. Giusto, R. Leonardi, F. Pereira (Eds.), Visual Content Processing and Representation. IX, 224 pages. 2006.

Vol. 3892: A. Carbone, N.A. Pierce (Eds.), DNA Computing. XI, 440 pages. 2006.

Vol. 3891: J.S. Sichman, L. Antunes (Eds.), Multi-Agent-Based Simulation VI. X, 191 pages. 2006. (Sublibrary LNAI).

Vol. 3890: S.G. Thompson, R. Ghanea-Hercock (Eds.), Defence Applications of Multi-Agent Systems. XII, 141 pages. 2006. (Sublibrary LNAI).

Vol. 3889: J. Rosca, D. Erdogmus, J.C. Príncipe, S. Haykin (Eds.), Independent Component Analysis and Blind Signal Separation. XXI, 980 pages. 2006.